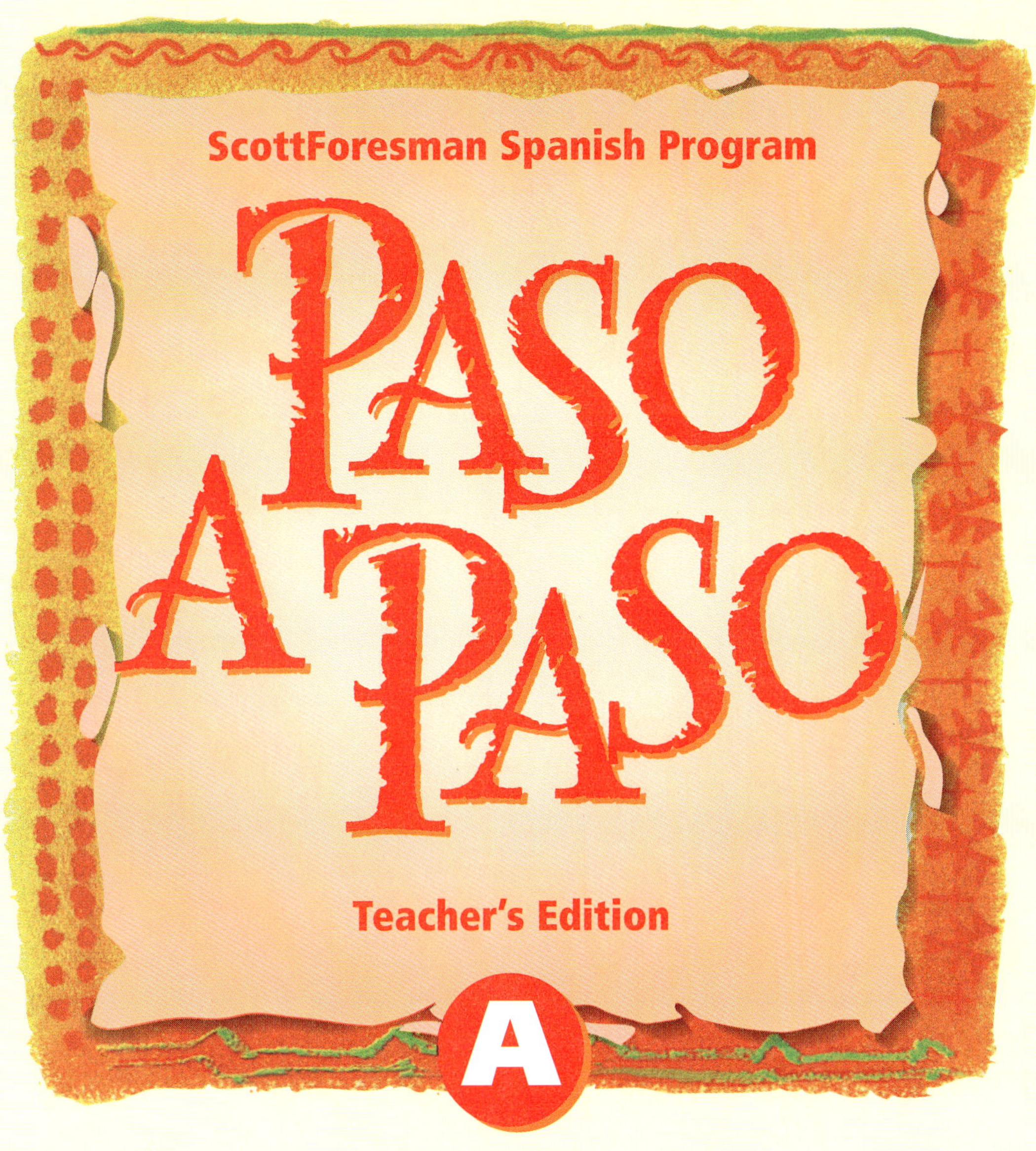

Myriam Met
Coordinator of Foreign Languages
Montgomery County Public Schools
Rockville, MD

Richard S. Sayers
Niwot High School
Longmont, CO

Carol Eubanks Wargin
Glen Crest Junior High School
Glen Ellyn, IL

Harriet Schottland Barnett
Manhattanville College
Purchase, NY
formerly of the Dobbs Ferry (NY)
Public Schools

ScottForesman

Editorial Offices: Glenview, Illinois
Regional Offices: San Jose, California • Atlanta, Georgia
Glenview, Illinois • Oakland, New Jersey • Dallas, Texas

Visit ScottForesman's Home Page at http://www.scottforesman.com

ADDITIONAL WRITERS AND CONTRIBUTORS

The following individuals contributed their expertise and creativity in developing the many notes and features in this Teacher's Edition.

Lynn Andersen
Chattahoochee High School
Alpharetta, GA

Mary Louise Carey
Natick (MA) High School

JoAnn DiGiandomenico
Natick (MA) High School

Susan Dobinsky
Niles North High School
Skokie, IL

Gail Glover
San Antonio, TX

Marjorie Hall Haley, Ph. D.
George Mason University
Fairfax, VA

Thomasina Pagán Hannum
Albuquerque, NM

Valerie Bryant Mantlo
Short Pump Middle School
Glen Allen, VA

Kaaran L. Martin
Beverly Hills Intermediate
Pasadena Independent School District
Houston, TX

Risima Micevic-Sayler
Dakota Hills Middle School
Eagan, MN

Lucía Nuñez
Stanford University
Stanford, CA

Bernadette M. Reynolds
Parker, CO

Luz Nuncio Schick
Naperville, IL

Judith B. Smith, Ed. D.
Baltimore City (MD) Public Schools

Christine S. Wells
Cheyenne Mountain Junior High School
Colorado Springs, CO

ISBN: 0-673-21714-0

Scott, Foresman and Company, Glenview, Illinois

1.800.554.4411

http://www.scottforesman.com

2345678910-DR-05040302010099989796

TABLE OF CONTENTS

PHILOSOPHY OF THE PROGRAM

Welcome to *PASO A PASO!*

This program is based on the belief that the purpose of learning Spanish is to communicate with the people who speak it and to understand their cultures. *PASO A PASO* is designed to help your students achieve that goal by getting them to communicate right from the start.

PASO A PASO reflects the most current thinking in the foreign language field. It reflects state-of-the-art research on how students learn languages and what teachers and materials need to do to help them become proficient language users, whether they are using their new language for oral or written communication.

Let's take a look at some basic premises about language and language learning, the components of *PASO A PASO,* and how each of these components contributes to developing language proficiency.

What is communication?

Communication is an authentic exchange of information for a real purpose between two or more people. By this we mean that people tell each other (through speech or writing) something the other person doesn't already know.

Communicating meaning has several aspects. Students need to learn to listen to and read Spanish in order to interpret intended meanings, to express meaning by conveying their own messages for a purpose and to a real audience, and to negotiate meaning through the natural give-and-take involved in understanding and in making oneself understood (Savignon, 1991). Research tells us that classroom activities must provide students practice in interpreting, expressing, and negotiating meaning through extensive and frequent peer interactions, preferably in pairs or small groups.

Communication is driven not only by meaning, but also by purpose. In real life, people communicate to get things done. They may communicate to transact business, to get to know someone else, or to find out something they really need to know. In authentic communication, people give and get new ideas or information. The information that one partner has and the other doesn't is often called an *information gap* or an *opinion gap.* How unlike the classrooms of old, where we typically asked students questions to which we (and everyone else) already knew the answer, questions such as, "Tom, what's your name?" and "Sally, are you a boy or a girl?" These questions are not heard in real life because they lack a communicative purpose: there is no information or opinion gap.

PASO A PASO is organized around the principle that just as meaning and purpose drive all language use, so too should they drive all language learning. Students are engaged in understanding messages, in sending their own messages, and thus in communicating on every page of every chapter. Because *PASO A PASO* structures almost all activities for pair or group interaction, students find themselves active participants in every lesson, every day. They communicate real ideas and real meanings for real purposes. Every component of *PASO A PASO* is designed with the goal of communication in mind.

Interpreting meaning

In the last decade we have learned more than ever before about how language is acquired. We know that students learn best when they have ample opportunities to internalize meanings before they have to produce them. That is, we know that comprehension precedes production. Many teachers will be familiar with the term "comprehensible input," first used by Stephen Krashen, who suggests that learners acquire language by understanding what they hear. Students need many opportunities to match what they hear with visual cues (pictures, video, or teacher pantomime) or experiences (physical actions) so that they can associate meanings with forms. This is as true for comprehending language structure and syntax as it is for vocabulary development.

In keeping with research on the importance of matching language with meaning, *PASO A PASO* gives students many opportunities to comprehend new language before producing it. The video allows students to hear native speakers using language in a contextualized format that makes the meanings of new words and structures clear. Students learn by matching what they hear with what they see. Numerous activities for providing comprehensible input are suggested in this Teacher's Edition and in the Pupil Edition prior to each new vocabulary section, activities that involve visuals (transparencies and pictures) and that physically engage students as they acquire new language. Whenever possible, in the pupil's text, vocabulary is visualized, so that both video and print materials provide examples of language in context.

What kind of practice promotes communication skills?

The first and most critical step in the language development process is getting meaning—learning to understand by matching what is heard with what is seen or experienced. But by itself, understanding is not enough. Students also need to use their new knowledge.

Research tells us that students need extensive practice in using their new language to create and convey their own messages. While there may be a legitimate role for simply drilling new structures or vocabulary, the most valuable practice comes from using them to send messages that have meaning for the learner and serve a legitimate communicative purpose. When teachers (or texts) structure activities so there is only one right answer, clearly students are sending messages that convey someone else's thoughts, not their own, and are serving someone else's communicative purpose. In these kinds of activities students are *practicing* language, but they are not really *using* language to communicate.

In contrast, when the answers are determined by the students themselves—and are therefore unpredictable, with no single correct response—students are involved in authentic communication. In these information- or opinion-gap activities, answers will vary. Research suggests that these types of activities are extremely important. After all, if the purpose of learning Spanish is to communicate, then students will need practice in doing just that! In contrast, if practice consists only (or mainly) of producing right answers determined by others, students will have difficulty spontaneously creating their own messages when needed. Thus language activities and tasks should not proceed from rote or de-contextualized to meaningful practice. All practice should be meaningful, with a predominance of activities that are truly communicative.

Research also tells us that pair and group language practice is far more effective than student-teacher practice alone. Cooperative learning and pair and group work both provide increased time for communicative language practice and promote the give-and-take necessary for negotiating meaning.

Working with a partner to make and share meaning lies at the heart of *PASO A PASO*. Everything students learn in each chapter is tied together in a meaningful way. The parts of language are taught and practiced (with a partner) within the context of the whole, with vocabulary and related grammar closely intertwined. Students use language in context to convey meaning and for a real purpose. All activities involve meaning, and most allow students to choose the meanings they want to convey. These are the kinds of information- and opinion-gap events that are characteristic of real-life communication. Even in structured activities designed to provide specific practice of forms and to elicit certain responses, teachers will find that students may still respond in ways that are personal and true for them. The activities are, however, focused, and you will often find "answers will vary, but look for correct use of . . ." in the answer keys.

To promote the development of communicative ability, *PASO A PASO* integrates vocabulary and grammar. They are then re-integrated continually, with gradually increasing complexity. In addition to the personalized and open-ended responses found in the vocabulary and grammar sections of the chapter, the *Todo junto* feature specifically focuses on weaving together newly learned material with material from previous chapters. It promotes the use of all the language that students have learned to that point, in oral tasks and through reading and writing.

Teaching for understanding: The whole is greater than the parts

In many academic disciplines today, instructional practices are based on constructivist theory, which suggests that learners are more likely to be successful when instruction focuses on making meaning, on students pursuing their natural inclination to try to make sense of what they are experiencing, and on ensuring that the parts are carefully integrated. In foreign languages, we traditionally taught the parts (grammar rules, vocabulary, pronunciation) hoping that eventually students would have the opportunity and ability to integrate them into the "whole" of communicating their own ideas. Today, integration of the parts of language takes place right from the start. It has been suggested that the relationship between learning the parts vs. integration with the whole is like learning to play a musical instrument. The focus is always on making music, and from the outset, learners need to have many experiences producing it. But they can't learn to play an instrument without knowing something about how to produce sounds (e.g., use the violin bow or play scales) or without practice. Just as students learn the specific skills they need to produce a piece of music in learning to play an instrument, in language-learning we proceed today by identifying the learner's communicative needs (that is, the "music" they want to be able to produce) and then identifying the vocabulary, structures, and cultural skills needed to accomplish their purpose. Vocabulary and grammar are thus taught in the context of the situations in which students will be communicating or the topics they will be communicating about. Everything ties together naturally.

All effective learning is rooted in a meaningful context. We know from research that information is most likely to be retained when it is connected to other information in a meaningful way. Thus, language learning is more successful and retention more likely when we present new language organized into topics or by situations. This also means that some things we have taught in the past may not get taught at the same point or in the same way. For example, students may need to learn the stem-changing verbs *jugar, perder,* and *querer* to describe leisure or sports activities. However, since *dormir, morir,* and *pedir* do not naturally fit with the theme of sports or leisure, they may not be introduced until another theme or situation arises that will logically involve the use of one or more of them.

PASO A PASO is organized into thematic chapters. All material—vocabulary, grammar, culture—is rooted in a context and used meaningfully. All the elements of a chapter tie together. Students learn the vocabulary related to the theme, the grammar they need to communicate about the theme, and the information that helps anchor language in its cultural context. The themes have been chosen to reflect what students want or need to talk about. And the end-of-chapter vocabulary list is organized to reflect how the new words are used to create and convey meaning.

Critical thinking: Understanding and making meaning

We know from research that language learners are active makers of meaning. They learn by creating their own understandings, not by memorizing ours. This means that students are more likely to remember vocabulary when they have acquired it by figuring out its meaning in a logical context (video situation, visual, teacher pantomime). Grammar is most likely to be understood and rules applied when students have been guided to discover underlying patterns or have formulated the rules for themselves. In contrast, retention and applicability are greatly reduced when students simply memorize lists or rules without real understanding.

In order for students to construct their own understandings and generate rules of language usage, they need to be guided through interaction with teacher and text. Strategic questioning (in the text or by the teacher) plays an important role in this process, a process that is not at all the same as groping blindly to make a random discovery. Rather, through well-chosen examples and appropriate, inductive questioning, students can be led to make significant discoveries on their own, leading to a deep understanding that is much more likely to stay with them and be reflected in their own language use.

Understanding grammar

Understanding and critical thinking are reflected throughout *PASO A PASO.* This text is unique in its approach to the development of grammar skills, emphasizing as it does the critical roles that comprehensible input and student construction of knowledge play in language learning. New structures are foreshadowed through lexical presentation in the vocabulary section, and by the use of the *yo / tú* verb forms in vocabulary practice prior to the grammar presentation. Vocabulary activities familiarize students with new grammar before it is formally presented, allowing them to construct their own understanding.

To further facilitate grammar learning, students observe patterns of use in the comprehensible input that introduces the grammar section. This is done through a visualized context and strategic inductive questions. Through interaction with the teacher and the text, observation and analysis lead students to understand grammar, not merely to memorize formulas to be applied in rote fashion.

Understanding culture

Guided discovery is also an effective means of helping students construct an understanding of culture. Not only do we want our students to know about the cultures of the people who speak Spanish, we also want them to understand the cultural framework that determines what people say or do. In other words, we want students to understand the *why* of culture that determines the *what.* Whenever and wherever students may encounter speakers of Spanish, they will likely confront cultural practices and behaviors that are new to them. Cultural understanding begins with developing sensitivity to the possibility that people vary in how they think, live, and behave. Students must learn to observe other cultures without judging and to use what they see to help them discover the meanings that underlie cultural practices or behaviors. Specific information provides knowledge that aids in understanding the system of attitudes, values, and beliefs that frames cultural practices or behaviors. Students also need to understand other cultures in relation to their own, so that they may gain a deeper understanding of why they think, live, and behave as they do.

Background knowledge can serve as an important tool for the construction of meaning. It may be contextual (What normally happens in a restaurant?), topical (What are some typical leisure activities?), linguistic (What words do I already know that look like this new word?), or cultural (I know that interpersonal relationships are very important in Hispanic cultures, so that may be why people put so much value on greeting one another). This can serve to help students interpret new cultural information or contrast that information with values and practices common to their own culture. Students should be encouraged to understand the close relationship between language and culture. The social / cultural meanings of words (What does "friendship" mean in Hispanic cultures?) should be taught along with their dictionary meanings.

PASO A PASO develops important cultural understandings through a unique guided-discovery approach. It provides students with a progression of activities that leads them from thoughtful observation to knowledge and understanding of Hispanic cultures and then to reflection on their own culture. A photo essay with strategic inductive questions leads them to reflect on what they are observing. An informative reading then provides cultural information or insights that expand upon the visual information and allows students to validate or reject the ideas they formulated at the beginning. They are then asked thought-provoking questions to lead to reflection upon their own culture and their own cultural perspectives.

Strategies for success

Effective learners not only construct their own understanding of new concepts, they also know how to help themselves be successful learners. One way they do this is by using specific problem-solving strategies. When confronted with unknown words in a reading passage, successful learners don't run for a dictionary or just give up. They know how to get around that obstacle.

PASO A PASO teaches students to use strategies to be effective listeners, readers, and writers. Each reading selection takes students through a multi-step process (Phillips, 1984). Before reading, they are encouraged to use their background knowledge to help them predict or anticipate information they are likely to encounter in the text. A first reading helps them focus on general ideas (gist) without getting mired in details or difficult expressions. Reading closely for specific information, with specific strategies for dealing with difficult aspects of a text, is a strategy frequently emphasized in the reading sections. Students are then encouraged to use what they have learned in the reading by applying it in a new way. Thus, from the start, students are empowered to deal with authentic print materials. Effective writing is promoted through a process approach in *PASO A PASO.* In the pre-writing stage, students think about the topic, generate needed language, and organize their ideas. They then write a first draft. Reviewing this draft with a peer yields insights into needed revisions or clarification and results in a revision that may be published or placed in a portfolio. This approach is consistent with the ways in which many students are learning to write in their English classes. It also provides them with a strategy or model for independent writing.

Authenticity in language learning

Language teaching today places great value on authenticity. The content that students are expected to learn and how they practice it (objectives and tasks) should be authentic to the learner's interests and to real-life uses. Tasks should require an authentic exchange of meaning (an information or opinion gap) and should have an authentic purpose. Students should be taught authentic, not "textbook," language. Most important, information and, to the extent possible, materials should be culturally authentic.

PASO A PASO opens authentic avenues to communication and culture. Students continually engage in authentic communicative tasks. Pair and group activities in which students fill information or opinion gaps constitute the great majority of exercises. These activities allow students to express their own views on topics and questions of interest to them. The language presented is culturally accurate. Videos show native speakers engaged in real-life situations and experiences. Videos, photos, realia, and readings provide authentic contacts with the cultures of Spanish speakers.

Meeting the needs of middle school learners

The middle school student is not a smaller, shorter version of a high school student, and materials for middle school students should not be a shorter version of high school materials. Rather, middle school materials should reflect the unique characteristics of early adolescent learners. These middle school texts are not simply the high school book cut in half. *PASO A PASO A* and *B* are designed to meet the needs of students in the middle grades while covering the same content as the first-level high school book. That is, the material covered in the middle and high school versions is the same, but the books are not.

Middle school materials should be appropriate to the age of the learner. There is extraordinary variety among middle school learners as they enter and progress through adolescence at different times and different rates. As such, middle school materials need to address the variety that characterizes the learners who use them.

PASO A PASO A and *B* acknowledge the diversity of learners in a number of ways. Activities are varied and challenging, and address different learning styles. The Teacher's Edition provides numerous alternatives for teaching subject matter. Because middle school learners are egocentric, it is important that students have extensive opportunities for personalized and meaningful self-expression. These are provided in *PASO A PASO.* Middle school learners are also social beings: they actively seek out interaction with peers. As a result, pair and group activities abound.

Because students this age need physical activity, each chapter provides for physical involvement of students as they encounter new vocabulary. Early adolescents also seek variety as they explore new identities, experiences, and challenges. In *PASO A PASO A* and *B* students will find variety in formats, activities, challenge levels, and artwork. Since pictures of older adolescents who are dating or driving cars do not allow early adolescents to see themselves reflected in their book, the middle school version of *PASO A PASO* has photographs and artwork specifically selected to reflect the age of the learner, artwork that is visually appealing, motivating, and colorful.

The middle school student is making the transition from a concrete to an abstract learner. At this age, students continue to benefit from concrete experiences, extensive use of visuals (such as pictured vocabulary and video presentation of new language), and contextualization of meaning. *PASO A PASO A* and *B* have extensive opportunities for students to engage in concrete learning experiences. All new vocabulary is presented thematically, and almost all new vocabulary is presented through visuals.

Many middle school learners also benefit from scaffolding of material. Like the scaffolding on buildings that allows workers to reach otherwise inaccessible heights, instructional scaffolding provides the support that allows learners to stretch beyond where they might succeed on their own. *PASO A PASO A* and *B* scaffold learning in many ways. Step-by-step introduction of new material and guided inductive tasks for new grammar points allow students to gain control over new language. Activities provide scaffolding that allows students to develop insights into the cultures of the Spanish-speaking world, and to relate these insights to their own culture.

In many middle schools, thematic interdisciplinary units characterize instruction across the curriculum. *PASO A PASO* suggests ways in which the themes of the text can be related to instruction in other subject areas. Numerous connections with mathematics, social studies, and science concepts are made in the *Conexiones.* These reinforce and extend age-appropriate learning drawn directly from curriculum goals for the middle grades.

Young teens need to experience a sense of accomplishment in reasonable and manageable time periods. *PASO A PASO A* and *B* divide the material into manageable chunks so that students can gain a feeling of accomplishment and closure as they move from section to section. At the same time, these chunks are set in meaningful contexts, so that learning is never reduced to isolated bits of material learned by rote. Assessment opportunities, writing activities, and reading selections have been adjusted to ensure that students experience success without in any way watering down material or lowering expectations.

PASO A PASO A and *B* represent a serious, deliberate attempt to address the needs of middle school learners. These books are not a "younger" version of the high school text. Rather, they meet learners on their own terms, and provide the foundation for successful articulation with second-year high school programs and beyond.

Bibliography

Adair-Hauck, Bonnie, Richard Donato and Philomena Cumo. 1994. "Using a Whole Language Approach to Teach Grammar," in Eileen Glisan and Judith Shrum, Eds. *Contextualized Language Instruction.* Boston: Heinle and Heinle Publishers, pp. 90–111.

Brooks, Jacqueline and Martin G. Brooks. 1993. *In Search of Understanding: The Case for Constructivist Classrooms.* Alexandria, VA: Association for Supervision and Curriculum Development.

Doughty, Catherine and Teresa Pica. 1986. "Information Gap Tasks: Do They Facilitate Second Language Acquisition?" *TESOL Quarterly.* 20:3, 305–325.

Ellis, Rod. 1993. "The Structural Syllabus and Second Language Acquisition." *TESOL Quarterly.* 27:1, 91–112.

Kagan, Spencer. 1992. *Cooperative Learning.* San Juan Capistrano, CA: Resource for Teachers Inc.

Krashen, Stephen. 1982. *Principles and Practice in Second Language Acquisition.* Oxford: Pergamon Press.

Nunan, D. 1991. "Communicative Tasks and the Language Curriculum." *TESOL Quarterly.* 25:2, 279–295.

Phillips, June K. "Practical Implication of Recent Research in Reading," *Foreign Language Annals.* 17:4 (September 1984), 285–299.

Resnick, Lauren B. 1989. *Knowing, Learning, and Instruction: Essays in Honor of Robert Glaser.* Hillsdale, New Jersey: Lawrence Erlbaum Associates, Publishers.

Savignon, S. J. 1991. "Communicative Language Teaching: State of the Art." *TESOL Quarterly.* 25:2, 261–277.

Swain, Merrill. 1985. "Communicative Competence: Some Roles of Comprehensible Input and Comprehensible Output in Its Development." In Susan Gass and Madden, C. (Eds.) *Input in Second Language Acquisition.* Rowley, Mass.: Newbury House.

COMPONENTS OF THE PROGRAM

PASO A PASO A/B is a complete, two-level series with a full range of ancillary components that allow you to tailor the materials to the needs of your students and to your teaching style. Students who finish *PASO A PASO A/B* in middle school would then go on to *PASO A PASO 2* at the high-school level.

Pupil's Edition

Presentation material begins with maps of Spanish-speaking countries and *El primer paso,* a preliminary unit focusing on basic, high-frequency communication objectives. This is followed by six thematic chapters and an appendix offering verb charts, a grammar index, and Spanish-English / English-Spanish vocabularies.

Teacher's Edition

This Teacher's Edition contains the student text in slightly reduced form, with answers, teaching suggestions, and cross references to ancillary materials. Each chapter presents an extensive array of Teacher Notes that includes:

- a scope and sequence chart with communicative, cultural, and grammar objectives
- an overview of components available for use in the chapter
- on-page cultural information for photos and realia
- on-page Learning Spanish Through Action notes (a modified version of Total Physical Response)
- on-page notes for Spanish-speaking students, students needing extra help, enrichment, cooperative learning, multicultural perspectives, cross-curricular activities, using the video, critical thinking, class starter reviews, reteach / review, and re-enter / recycle.

Ancillaries

Middle School Components

Overhead Transparencies: The transparencies for *PASO A PASO A/B* are combined into one package of 90 full-color overhead visuals that reproduce the vocabulary-teaching illustrations without labels or captions. Also included are maps, a pronoun chart, a clock, the realia from the *Gramática en contexto,* and additional teaching transparencies. Suggestions for use are provided in a separate booklet.

Audio Cassettes/CDs: A set of 10 audio tapes on cassette or CD containing listening activities for each chapter in *PASO A PASO A/B* and separate tapes for assessment, pronunciation and vocabulary, and songs. The primary focus is on developing listening comprehension, with secondary emphasis on supporting the beginning stages of speaking, including practice with pronunciation and some focused speaking opportunities.

Writing, Audio & Video Activities A and B: Writing Activities provide chapter-by-chapter practice that is at the same or a slightly higher level than that in the student text. Audio Activities offer the material necessary to focus attention on listening comprehension as students work with the audio tapes. Video Activities focus attention as students view the video. Follow-up activities verify and extend their understanding of what they have seen.

Teacher's Edition: Writing, Audio & Video Activities: Student material with overprinted answers and a complete tapescript of the audio tapes in one volume covering both student texts.

Assessment Program: Blackline master quizzes *(Pruebas)* for each vocabulary section and each grammar topic in *PASO A PASO A/B,* and two chapter proficiency tests *(Exámenes de habilidades)* for each chapter. Suggestions for administering and scoring proficiency tests are included.

Projects for Proficiency: Blackline Master Spanish Activities for Middle School Learners: A variety of templates and other materials on blackline masters. Included are blank menus, street maps, game boards, invitations, and other resources for projects and activities.

Teacher's Resource File: This convenient, desk-top organizer contains the Teacher's Edition of the Writing, Audio & Video Activities, the Assessment Program, and the Communicative Activities Blackline Masters.

Additional Resources from *PASO A PASO 1*

En vivo: A set of chapter-by-chapter videos taped on location in Miami, Guadalajara, and Madrid. Available on both tape and disc, the videos focus on culture, vocabulary, and real-life situational interactions. A Teacher's Guide is included with complete transcriptions, cultural information, teaching suggestions, and reduced reproductions of the Video Activities pages *(see previous page)* with overprinted answers.

***Pasos vivos* CD-ROM:** Chapter-by-chapter real-world activities based on *En vivo* offer creative, interactive practice opportunities for listening, speaking, reading, and writing, while extending students' knowledge of Hispanic cultures.

Test Generator: A multiple-choice test generator. Teachers can add their own questions to the question bank.

Practice Workbook: (with separate Teacher's Answer Key): Worksheets for basic, one-step writing practice for all vocabulary and grammar sections of the student text. Exercises include the support of learning strategies. Each chapter also has an Organizer that allows students to record and keep track of new vocabulary and structures.

Communicative Activities Blackline Masters (Pair and Small-Group Activities with Situation Cards): Oral activities for pair and group practice.

Un paso más: Actividades para ampliar tu español: A worktext for Spanish-speaking students designed to supplement the textbook activities.

Vocabulary Art Blackline Masters for Hands-On Learning: All teaching vocabulary art reproduced on blackline masters, ideal for making manipulatives or flashcards.

Classroom Crossword: A wall-size crossword puzzle to be completed over the course of Books A and B.

CHAPTER ORGANIZATION

Organization of the Text

PASO A PASO A contains a preliminary chapter *(El primer paso)* and six thematically organized chapters in which students learn to communicate about their own lives and how to interact with Hispanic cultures. The six themes are:

- **CAPÍTULO 1** Friendship
- **CAPÍTULO 2** School
- **CAPÍTULO 3** Sports and leisure activities
- **CAPÍTULO 4** Food
- **CAPÍTULO 5** Family
- **CAPÍTULO 6** Clothing

Using *El primer paso*

El primer paso is designed as a four- to five-week teaching unit to give students a successful start in Spanish. In this chapter students will:

1. gain insight into the importance of Spanish in the global community, in the United States, and in their own community
2. recognize the importance of Spanish in the workplace
3. begin to communicate with their peers
4. develop successful learning strategies
5. understand the book's chapter organization

Chapter organization

The six chapters follow a consistent organization that increases student confidence while allowing for easy classroom management. Chapters are organized according to the latest research on how students learn a second language and follow a clear pedagogical model:

1. Introduce/Preview
2. Present
3. Practice
4. Apply
5. Summarize/Assess

Each chapter follows this model:

Chapter Sections	Pedagogical Support
Objectives	Introduce
¡Piénsalo bien!	Preview
Sección 1:	
Vocabulario para conversar	
• *Visualized vocabulary*	Present
• También necesitas . . .	Present
• Empecemos a conversar	Practice
• Empecemos a leer y a escribir	Apply
Perspectiva cultural	Preview / Present
• La cultura desde tu perspectiva	Apply
Sección 2:	
Vocabulario para conversar	
• *Visualized vocabulary*	Present
• También necesitas . . .	Present
• Empecemos a conversar	Practice
• Empecemos a leer y a escribir	Apply
• Comuniquemos	Practice
• Ahora lo sabes	Practice / Assess
Conexiones	Apply
Sección 3:	
Gramática en contexto	Preview / Present / Practice
Perspectiva cultural	Preview / Present
• La cultura desde tu perspectiva	Apply
Sección 4:	
Gramática en contexto	Preview / Present / Practice
Todo junto	
• Actividades	Apply
• Ahora lo sabes	Practice / Assess
• ¡Vamos a leer!	Apply
• ¡Vamos a escribir!	Apply
Resumen del capítulo	Summarize

USING A CHAPTER

Chapter Opener *(Introduce)*

The chapter theme is introduced through a photograph and related communicative and cultural objectives.

Teaching ideas for the Chapter Opener

Wrap-around notes give many suggestions. Here are a few basic ideas for these two pages:

1. Prior to discussing the objectives, have students look at the photos and skim the chapter. Ask them to suggest objectives based upon what they have seen. Write these on the chalkboard and see if they compare with those listed in the text.
2. Show additional pictures, posters, or slides that preview the chapter theme.
3. You may wish to use the first video segment to provide a broad cultural overview of the chapter theme. (See the Video Guide for further suggestions.)

Objectives: Relate to real-life, purposeful communication and relevant cultural information. These will be referred to throughout the chapter so that students can monitor their own progress. Chapter assessment is based on the objectives.

¡Piénsalo bien! *(Preview)*

This section continues to preview the chapter theme. Students use their own experiences and background information to interact with the photographs.

Teaching ideas for *¡Piénsalo bien!*

1. Ask students to study the photographs and to suggest as many words, phrases, or short sentences as they can about them.
2. Use the inductive questions to elicit the similarities and differences. Focus on the similarities.
3. If you haven't yet done so, use the first video segment to preview the cultural theme.
4. At the end of the chapter, return to these photos. See how extensively students can describe the pictures. Choose a photo and have students bring it to life by acting out the situation.

Questions:
Students use critical thinking to answer inductive questions.

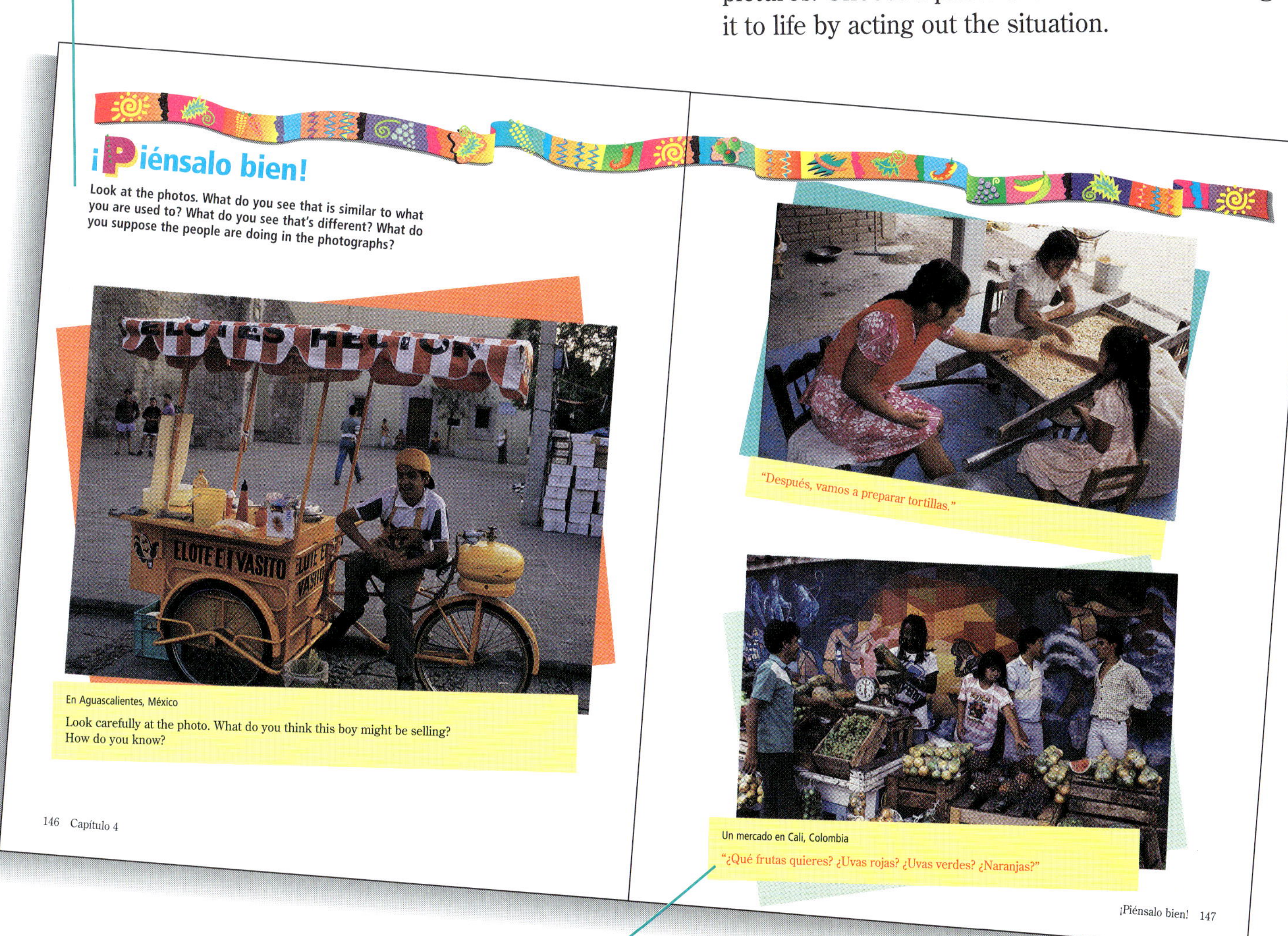

¡Piénsalo bien!

Look at the photos. What do you see that is similar to what you are used to? What do you see that's different? What do you suppose the people are doing in the photographs?

En Aguascalientes, México

Look carefully at the photo. What do you think this boy might be selling? How do you know?

146 Capítulo 4

"Después, vamos a preparar tortillas."

Un mercado en Cali, Colombia

"¿Qué frutas quieres? ¿Uvas rojas? ¿Uvas verdes? ¿Naranjas?"

¡Piénsalo bien! 147

Captions:
Easy-to-guess cognates and recycled vocabulary help build students' confidence. New vocabulary and structures are previewed.

Vocabulario para conversar *(Present, Practice & Apply)*

New vocabulary is presented in a visualized context in two short, manageable sections.

Teaching ideas

1 Use the Overhead Transparencies, the Vocabulary Audio Tape, the Vocabulary Art Blackline Masters, and / or the second video segment to introduce the new vocabulary.

2 Combine auditory, visual, and kinesthetic activities. Present the vocabulary using comprehensible input. Here are several suggestions:

A. Getting meaning from comprehensible input

The purpose of these activities is to allow students to match new language with its meaning.

- Using the Overhead Transparency, point to pictures as you simply and clearly name and talk about them in Spanish. Students should be able to understand new vocabulary from your body language and gestures. For example: *Es una manzana. La manzana es una fruta. Ésta es una manzana también. Tengo muchas manzanas.*
- You might also pantomime new vocabulary.
- As you progress through *PASO A PASO,* your descriptions will expand to include previously learned language.

Visualized vocabulary: Research indicates that we learn best in logical sets or categories and through immediately associating words with objects.

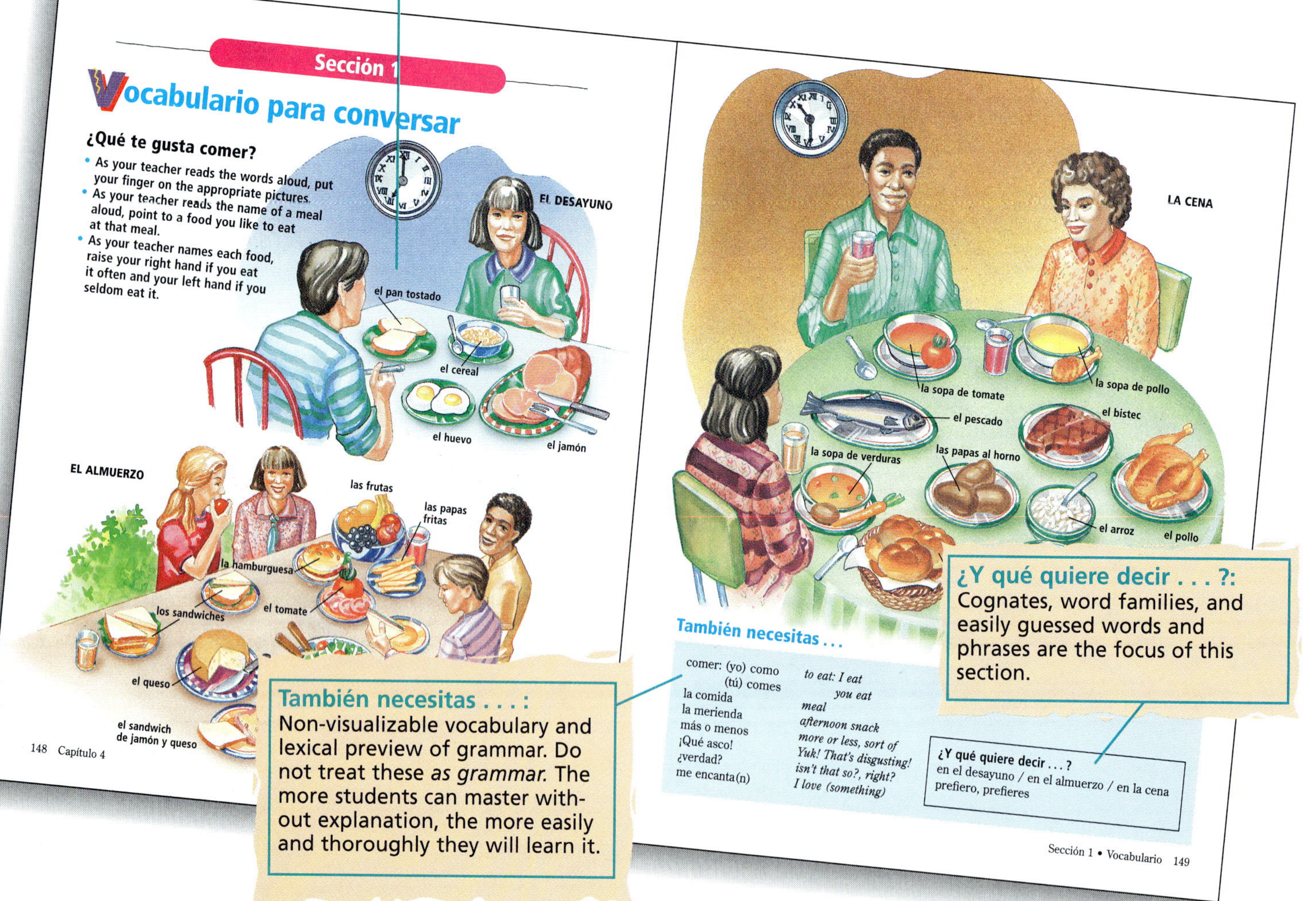

B. Demonstrating comprehension through physical response

The purpose of these activities is to allow students to demonstrate their comprehension non-verbally.

- After presenting two or three pictures of new vocabulary, review by asking yes / no questions, e.g., *¿Es un plátano? ¿Es una naranja? ¿Te gusta comer naranjas?* Students may respond as a group with thumbs up / down *(sí / no)*. Individuals may also be asked to respond in this way.
- As students become more proficient, vocabulary from previous chapters can be used in these questions, e.g., *¿Necesitas beber leche en la cena?*
- Continue alternating the steps in the first two paragraphs until all new vocabulary has been presented.
- Distribute Vocabulary Art BLMs. As you name each new item, point to it on the transparency. Have students point to the corresponding picture. Tell students: *Señalen el plátano. Señalen la naranja.* Repeat, but do not point to the picture on the transparency until students have pointed to it on their worksheet. Confirm student responses on the transparency.
- Have students point to pictures on the Overhead Transparency as you describe the picture, e.g., *A Miguel le gusta comer zanahorias* (student points to picture of carrots).
- Have students open their books and point to pictures you name or describe: *Señalen dos cosas que les gusta comer. Señalen dos cosas que no les gusta comer.*
- Have students pantomime vocabulary.
- Have students respond to commands: *Dale la hamburguesa a María. Muestra el sandwich a la clase.*
- Provide each student with a worksheet from the Vocabulary Art BLMs. Direct them to cut out each picture. Have students move the pictures as you direct: *Pongan los guisantes a la derecha de las papas. Pongan la lechuga entre las uvas y las cebollas. Pongan las comidas en dos columnas: Comidas que me gustan y comidas que no me gustan.* Or students may use them to make your sentence true by arranging pictures to match your oral description, e.g., *Hay uvas y manzanas en la mesa.*

Each chapter provides suggestions for Learning Spanish Through Action (TPR).

C. Limited verbal response

Once students have had an opportunity to internalize meaning and to demonstrate comprehension of new language physically, they may respond verbally.

- Ask yes / no or true / false questions, e.g., *¿Comes cereal en el desayuno? La lechuga es una fruta.*
- Ask questions that require comprehension of new vocabulary but do not require using it in the answer. Responses will use language from previous chapters, e.g., *¿Prefieres ver la tele o ir al cine los fines de semana?*
- Ask questions in which the correct answer is embedded: *¿Es una manzana o es una naranja? ¿Prefieres beber leche o té helado?*
- Have students repeat after you for pronunciation practice.

3 On subsequent days, add details by recycling previously learned vocabulary. Retell an earlier narration without visual support. Ask students to draw their own visual representation of what has been said.

4 Have students re-view the video segment. Turn the sound off and let students provide their own narration.

Empecemos a conversar *(Practice)*

Students practice the new vocabulary in paired activities that provide models for real-life language.

Teaching ideas for *Empecemos a conversar*

1. Place students in pairs. (There are many ways of doing this.) You may want to pair students of different abilities. Assign "study buddies" for each week or chapter. They are not only pair-practice partners, but they also keep track of each other's papers and assignments. (Be sure they exchange phone numbers.) You might award extra credit for partners who work well together and show improvement.
2. Always model the pair practice. Quickly review the vocabulary so that students can be more successful.
3. Set a time limit. Finish an activity when approximately three fourths of the class have finished. Walk around the class, listening for areas of difficulty such as pronunciation or grammar. Focus on these at a later time.
4. Ask pairs of students to do selected items for the whole class.
5. Have students work in pairs to answer the questions, then with another group to compare responses. Ask individuals to write this section as homework. Use the more open-ended questions as one-on-one questions with students or as topics for class discussion.
6. See the list of ancillaries for additional resources to help students work with the new vocabulary.

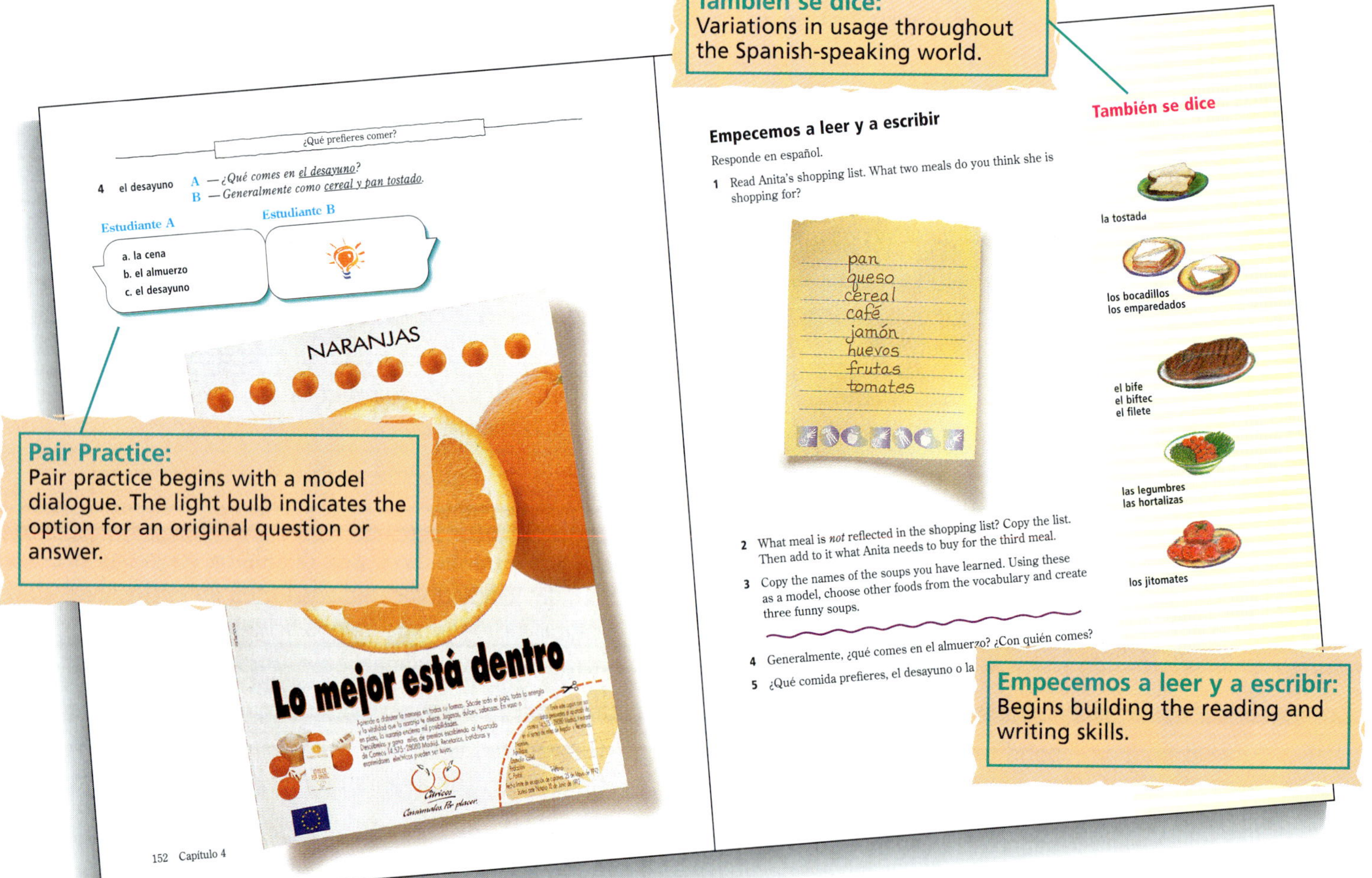

También se dice: Variations in usage throughout the Spanish-speaking world.

¿Qué prefieres comer?

4 el desayuno
A —*¿Qué comes en el desayuno?*
B —*Generalmente como cereal y pan tostado.*

Estudiante A
a. la cena
b. el almuerzo
c. el desayuno

Estudiante B

Pair Practice: Pair practice begins with a model dialogue. The light bulb indicates the option for an original question or answer.

152 Capítulo 4

Empecemos a leer y a escribir

Responde en español.

1 Read Anita's shopping list. What two meals do you think she is shopping for?

2 What meal is *not* reflected in the shopping list? Copy the list. Then add to it what Anita needs to buy for the third meal.

3 Copy the names of the soups you have learned. Using these as a model, choose other foods from the vocabulary and create three funny soups.

4 Generalmente, ¿qué comes en el almuerzo? ¿Con quién comes?

5 ¿Qué comida prefieres, el desayuno o la

También se dice

la tostada

los bocadillos
los emparedados

el bife
el biftec
el filete

las legumbres
las hortalizas

los jitomates

Empecemos a leer y a escribir: Begins building the reading and writing skills.

Perspectiva cultural *(Preview, Present & Apply)*

These two sections in each chapter offer a unique perspective into understanding the richness of Hispanic cultures. Using a combination of a photographic and narrative essay, they ask students to think about culture in such a way as to develop real cross-cultural understanding and sensitivity.

Teaching ideas for the *Perspectiva cultural*

1 Have students answer the inductive questions as a whole-class or small-group activity. Write their responses on the board. This will activate background information, prompt and recycle related vocabulary, and show that, even in their own class, they will find a variety of customs and traditions.

2 Use the photographs to encourage students to make observations about Hispanic cultures. Describe the photos in Spanish, adding more information.

3 Add personal information or anecdotes. If any students or their families have traveled to a Spanish-speaking country, let them share their experiences. Ask Spanish speakers to share family traditions.

4 In small groups or as a whole class, have students answer the questions in *La cultura desde tu perspectiva*. This is your best opportunity for helping students understand their own culture and the beliefs and attitudes they have formed.

5 You may want to ask how Spanish-speaking students coming to the U.S. might react to being in a culture with traditions such as those described by students when they answered the inductive questions.

Critical questioning: A series of inductive questions focusing on students' background knowledge and on the photos.

La cultura desde tu perspectiva: Students reflect upon and interact with new cultural information from the perspective of their own culture.

Mira las ilustraciones. ¿Para qué comidas son estos platos? ¿Son similares a o diferentes de platos que tú comes?

In Spanish-speaking countries, as in the United States, there are three main meals—*el desayuno, el almuerzo,* and *la cena.*

El desayuno

El desayuno generally takes place between 7 and 8:30 A.M. It is usually a light meal. It might consist of coffee or *café con leche,* which is half coffee and half hot milk, and bread or rolls with butter and jam. Children and teenagers sometimes drink hot chocolate or chocolate milk instead of coffee.

On weekends, when there is more time to prepare breakfast, people enjoy a variety of foods. The illustrations show two typical Sunday breakfasts in Spanish-speaking regions.

El almuerzo

El almuerzo (called *la comida* in Spain and Mexico) is the largest and most important meal of the day. It is eaten between 1 and 3 P.M. Many businesses and schools close so that families can enjoy *el almuerzo* together at home.

In some countries, for example, Spain, Chile, and Argentina, the midday meal may include several courses. There may be a soup, a meat course with vegetables or a salad, dessert, and coffee. In tropical areas, such as Puerto Rico, the Dominican Republic, and the Caribbean coast, it is usually just one main dish. It is often rice and beans served with a small portion of meat and a drink.

Although this lengthy midday break is still common, more and more businesses are adopting an uninterrupted schedule (*jornada continua*) similar to working hours in the United States. This does not leave time for employees to go home for lunch.

154

Cultural reading: Cultural information and insights that expand upon the information in the photos. Students validate or reject the ideas they formulated earlier.

La cultura desde tu perspectiva

1 Look at the photos. Are the people eating a breakfast or lunch that you might eat? What are the similarities? What are the differences?

2 Which meal would you like to try? Why?

3 What might be some of the advantages of a big midday meal in a tropical country? How do you think this custom might affect school and work schedules?

4 How would your day change if families in the United States went home to eat between 1 and 3 P.M.?

Un almuerzo familiar en Santiago, Chile

Perspectiva cultural 155

Photographs: Ask students to describe the pictures or write new captions. Have pairs create questions and ask them of another pair.

Comuniquemos (Practice)

This section follows the second vocabulary presentation and offers additional practice with the new vocabulary. The varied activities guide students to personalized communication.

Teaching ideas for *Comuniquemos*

Follow the guidelines for paired practice. At this point, students are familiar with the new vocabulary and the activities should go quickly, but choose from among them. Do not automatically attempt to do them all.

¿Qué prefieres comer?

COMUNIQUEMOS

Here's another opportunity for you and your partner to use the vocabulary you've just learned.

1 You and a friend are having dinner at a restaurant. Take turns asking each other about your food preferences. Discuss at least two preferences.

A —*¿Prefieres papas al horno o papas fritas?*
B —*Prefiero papas fritas, ¿y tú?*
A —*Yo prefiero papas fritas también.*
o: *Yo prefiero papas al horno.*
o: *A mí no me gustan ni las papas al horno ni las papas fritas.*

162 Capítulo 4

2 Imagine that you and your partner are checking out your refrigerator. Suggest a dish for a meal to your partner. Use the picture to help you decide what foods you already have and what you will need to buy.

A —*¿Quieres unos sandwiches para el almuerzo?*
B —*¿Hay jamón?*
A —*Sí, pero necesitamos pan y queso.*

unos sandwiches	el desayuno
una sopa	el almuerzo
una ensalada	la merienda
una ensalada de frutas	la cena

3 Do you remember all the ways you have learned to express your likes and dislikes? For example: *(A mí) me encanta* ___, *(A mí) no me gusta* ___, etc. Use these expressions in a conversation with your partner about food. Find two foods that you both like and two that you both dislike.

A —*Me encanta la sopa de pollo.*
B —*A mí también me gusta.*
o: *¡No me gusta nada la sopa de pollo!*

Ahora lo sabes

Using what you have learned so far, can you:

- tell what you like and don't like to eat and drink?
- say that you are hungry or thirsty?
- compare and contrast menus and mealtimes for breakfast and lunch in Spanish-speaking countries and in the United States?

Comuniquemos 163

Ahora lo sabes: Students begin to check their own progress toward achieving the chapter objectives.

Conexiones *(Apply)*

This section offers students the opportunity to apply the chapter content to other curriculum areas. These activities reinforce and broaden the applications of the new material by focusing on information and concepts from outside the Spanish classroom.

These are the cross-curricular connections that you will find in Book A:

Social Studies	Science
Chaps. 1, 2, 3 & 6	Chaps. 4 & 5
Mathematics	**Art**
Chaps. 1, 3, 5 & 6	Chap. 5
Geography	**Critical Thinking**
Chap. 4	Chaps. 2, 3, 4 & 6

Teaching ideas for *Conexiones*

1. Use these as whole-class or small-group activities. You might assign an activity or let the group choose which of them is of greatest interest.
2. Have the small groups share their results with the class.
3. Encourage students to make up their own *Conexiones* activity based on the chapter content. These can be given to another group to work with.
4. Expand the cross-curricular applications by working on a more extended project with the science, math, or social studies teacher, for example. You will find many opportunities to connect the content of *PASO A PASO* to what students are learning in other classes.

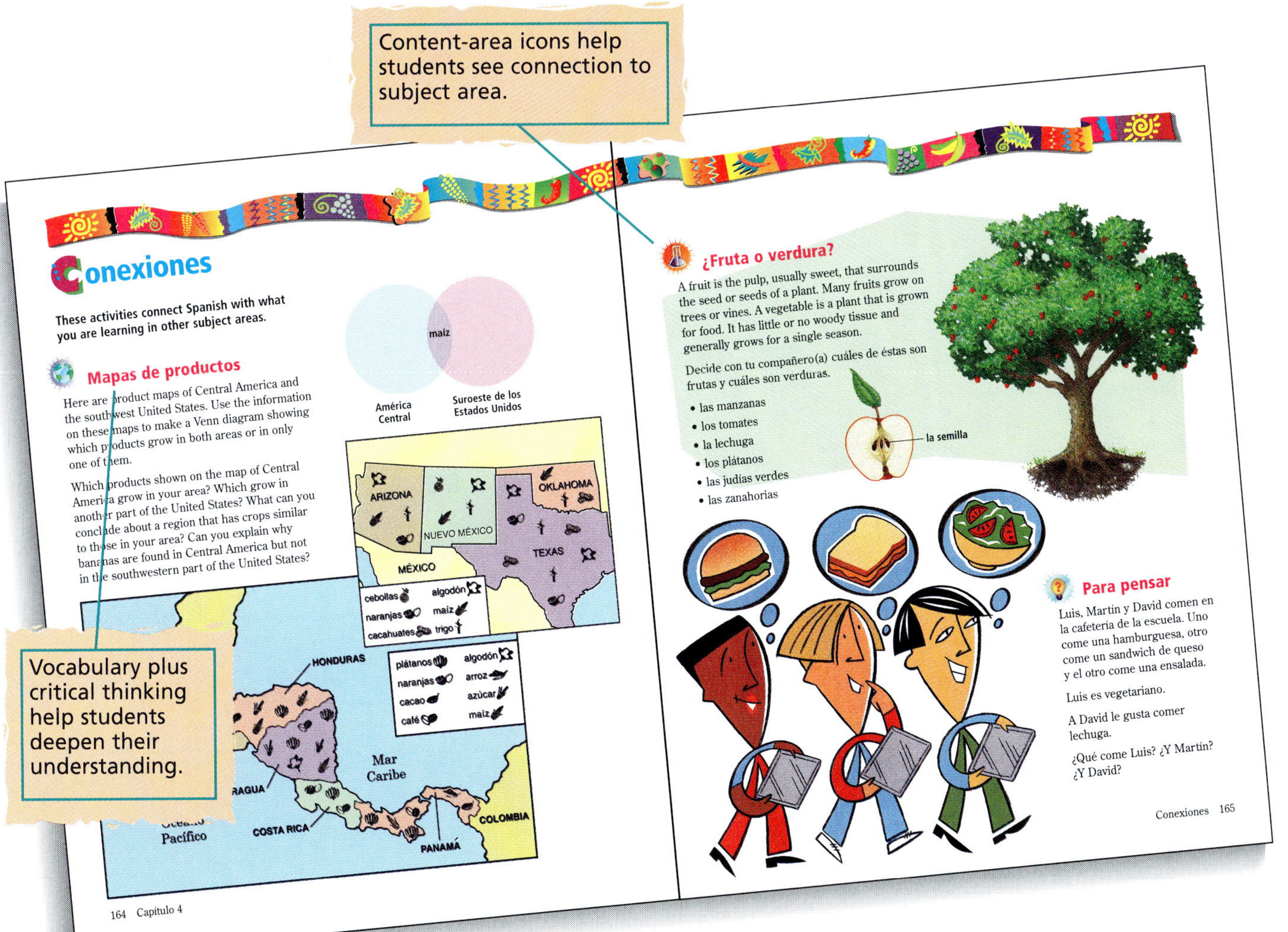

Conexiones

These activities connect Spanish with what you are learning in other subject areas.

Mapas de productos

Here are product maps of Central America and the southwest United States. Use the information on these maps to make a Venn diagram showing which products grow in both areas or in only one of them.

Which products shown on the map of Central America grow in your area? Which grow in another part of the United States? What can you conclude about a region that has crops similar to those in your area? Can you explain why bananas are found in Central America but not in the southwestern part of the United States?

164 Capítulo 4

¿Fruta o verdura?

A fruit is the pulp, usually sweet, that surrounds the seed or seeds of a plant. Many fruits grow on trees or vines. A vegetable is a plant that is grown for food. It has little or no woody tissue and generally grows for a single season.

Decide con tu compañero(a) cuáles de éstas son frutas y cuáles son verduras.

- las manzanas
- los tomates
- la lechuga
- los plátanos
- las judías verdes
- las zanahorias

Para pensar

Luis, Martín y David comen en la cafetería de la escuela. Uno come una hamburguesa, otro come un sandwich de queso y el otro come una ensalada.

Luis es vegetariano.

A David le gusta comer lechuga.

¿Qué come Luis? ¿Y Martín? ¿Y David?

Conexiones 165

Gramática en contexto *(Preview, Present & Practice)*

A realia-based reading provides comprehensible input for the new grammar in these sections. This gives students meaningful understanding of the structures by letting them intuit the rules. This inductive approach allows students to internalize and gain a deeper understanding of the grammar. Students were shown these structures in the vocabulary presentation and have practiced using them. They should not be uncomfortable with the structures themselves.

Teaching ideas for *Gramática en contexto*

1. Show the Overhead Transparency. Activate students' own experience by asking questions such as: How many students like cheese? What types of cheese? Ask what they might expect to find in an ad such as this. Have them skim the ad. Did they find what they expected?
2. Read the headline and ask what it means. Can students identify any of the flags? Read aloud the subhead. Can students tell you what it means? Have pairs of students read the ad and answer the questions. Let them verify their answers with another pair or as a whole-class activity.
3. As students generate an explanation, write it on the chalkboard along with examples from the reading.

Inductive questions: Students scan for information that leads them to produce their own explanation for the structures used.

Sección 3

Gramática en contexto

Look at this ad for imported cheeses. How many of these cheeses look familiar to you? Find the word *queso* and the word *quesos*. What do you think is the difference in their meanings?

A Work with a partner or a group.
- List all the words from the ad that describe cheese when it is written *quesos*.
- Find two words that describe cheese when it is written *queso*.
- Compare the two lists. What diff... you see?
- Make up a r... words when... item.

B Compare the questions *¿Te gustan los quesos importados?* and *¿Te gusta el queso americano?* Tell your partner if you would use *te gusta* or *te gustan* with *la leche* and with *las papas fritas*.

166 Capítulo 4

Realia-based reading: The reading combines cognates and previously learned vocabulary with the chapter's key grammar concepts.

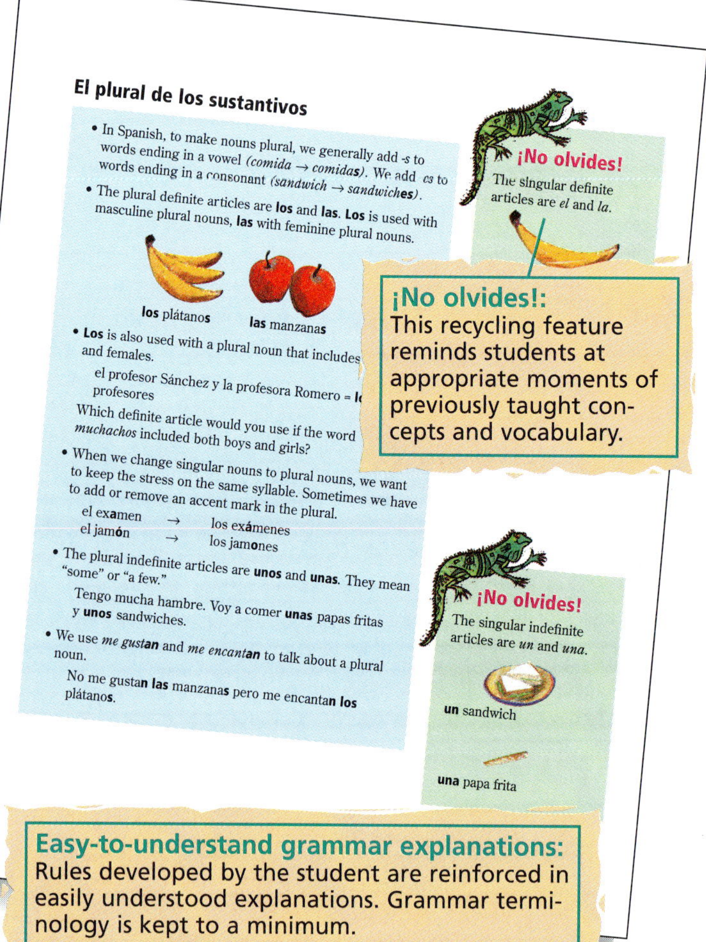

El plural de los sustantivos

- In Spanish, to make nouns plural, we generally add *-s* to words ending in a vowel *(comida → comidas)*. We add *-es* to words ending in a consonant *(sandwich → sandwiches)*.
- The plural definite articles are **los** and **las**. **Los** is used with masculine plural nouns, **las** with feminine plural nouns.

los plátanos las manzanas

- **Los** is also used with a plural noun that includes males and females.

el profesor Sánchez y la profesora Romero = lo... profesores

Which definite article would you use if the word *muchachos* included both boys and girls?

- When we change singular nouns to plural nouns, we want to keep the stress on the same syllable. Sometimes we have to add or remove an accent mark in the plural.

el examen → los exámenes
el jamón → los jamones

- The plural indefinite articles are **unos** and **unas**. They mean "some" or "a few."

Tengo mucha hambre. Voy a comer **unas** papas fritas y **unos** sandwiches.

- We use *me gustan* and *me encantan* to talk about a plural noun.

No me gustan **las** manzanas pero me encantan **los** plátanos.

¡No olvides! The singular definite articles are *el* and *la*.

¡No olvides! The singular indefinite articles are *un* and *una*.

un sandwich

una papa frita

¡No olvides!: This recycling feature reminds students at appropriate moments of previously taught concepts and vocabulary.

Easy-to-understand grammar explanations: Rules developed by the student are reinforced in easily understood explanations. Grammar terminology is kept to a minimum.

In this truly thematic approach, grammar is tied to the communicative objectives. What is not relevant is not presented. Here, for example, students work with three *-er* verbs appropriate to the theme: *deber, beber,* and *comer.* Additional *-er* verbs are, of course, taught, but in later chapters.

This thematic approach builds in regular review and recycling as students are reminded of the *-er* conjugation through the *¡No olvides!* feature. There are three to four grammar topics per chapter, each followed by a variety of activities.

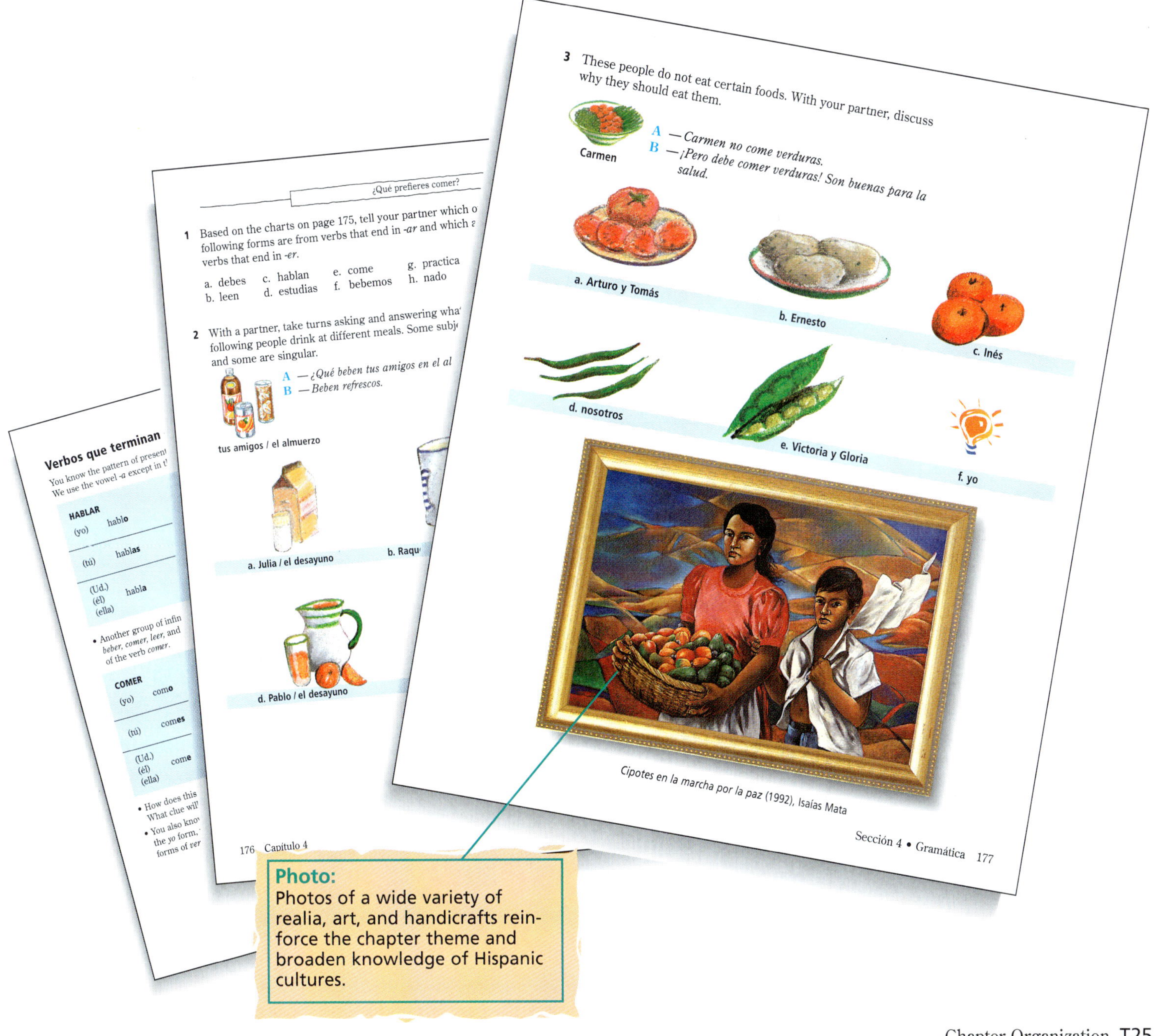

Photo:
Photos of a wide variety of realia, art, and handicrafts reinforce the chapter theme and broaden knowledge of Hispanic cultures.

Todo junto *(Apply)*

Todo junto is composed of three integrative sections: *Actividades, ¡Vamos a leer!,* and *¡Vamos a escribir!*

Teaching ideas for *Actividades*

1. To complement this section, use the third video segment in *En vivo.*
2. You may want to use different activities for different ability groupings. Better students might work together on Ex. 3 while others do either Ex. 1 or 2. Assess students on their effort, completion of the task, creativity, and ability to communicate rather than on accuracy.

Actividades: Pick and choose from among these activities.

Para decir más: These optional vocabulary suggestions enable students to personalize the activities.

Ahora lo sabes: Students re-assess their progress toward achieving the chapter objectives.

¿Qué prefieres comer?

Todo junto

Here's an opportunity for you to put together what you learned in this chapter with what you learned earlier.

1 ¿Qué comemos?

You and your partner are at the food court at the mall and are trying to decide what to eat for lunch.

- Ask your partner what foods he or she prefers to eat.
- Tell what you prefer to eat.
- Agree with your partner's suggestions.
  or
  Disagree and tell what *you* prefer to eat.

Keep your conversation going as long as you can. For example:

- Tell *why* you like or don't like to eat these foods.
- Tell *when* you like to eat them.

2 Menús especiales

Your class has been asked to plan some special menus in Spanish for the cafeteria. In groups, choose one of these menus, and plan a main dish, a beverage, and a dessert.

- menú vegetariano
- menú para deportistas
- menú para niños (*children*)

Then, with your group, make a sign announcing the menu. Draw or find pictures to illustrate it. Choose a member of your group to present the sign to the class.

¡Hoy menú especial!
Menú para deportistas
Para tener mucha energía
espaguetis
con salsa de tomate
con jamón y guisantes

180 Capítulo 4

3 Lotería de comida

With your teacher's help, first make a playing board. Then, take some paper squares and you're ready to play!

- When the caller names a food that he or she likes, cover that space with a paper square.
  STUDENT CALLER: *Me gusta el pescado.*
  Cover your picture of fish if you have one on your board.
- When the caller names a food that he or she does *not* like, you do nothing.
  STUDENT CALLER: *No me gusta el pescado.*
  Don't cover your picture of fish, even if you have one on your board.
- Call out "Lotería" when you have covered three spaces in a row horizontally, vertically, or diagonally. You'll be the winner. *¡Buena suerte!*
- The winner must correctly read back the names of the foods that the caller likes. For example:
  Te gusta el pescado. Te gustan las papas fritas. Te gustan las manzanas.

Para decir más

Here is some additional vocabulary that you might find useful for activities in this section.

la pizza *pizza*
el perro caliente *hot dog*
el tofu *tofu*
el yogur *yogurt*
el helado *ice cream*
la galleta *cookie*
el pastel *cake*

Ahora lo sabes

Using what you have learned so far, can you:

- tell what you and your family members eat and drink for dinner?
- tell what you like or don't like to eat and drink and why?
- describe two foods or drinks?
- compare and contrast times and menus for dinner and snacks in Spanish-speaking countries and in the United States?

Todo junto 181

¡Vamos a leer! *(Apply)*

Students learn how to become efficient readers through a four-step process. Real comprehension is achieved through strategies, questions, and activities in the *Infórmate* and *Aplicación.* Students encounter unknown vocabulary, but gain confidence by realizing they don't need to know every word to read successfully.

Teaching ideas

1. *Antes de leer:* Use the maps in the textbook or on the Overhead Transparencies to point out where the Mayas and Aztecs lived. Use a world map to show the routes the Spaniards followed to reach Mexico. Ask students if they like chocolate and if anyone knows its origin.
2. *Mira la lectura:* Have students work in groups and report back to the class. Write the names of the products students mention on the chalkboard to reinforce the concept of cognates.
3. *Infórmate:* This can best be done as an individual task or as pair work.
4. *Aplicación:* Students will complete this activity successfully because of the careful structuring of the early steps in the reading process. You might have students compare their lists in pairs or small groups.

• Step 1
Antes de leer: Activates students' background knowledge to help them predict or anticipate.

• Step 2
Mira la lectura: Initial reading section focusing on a specific reading strategy.

• Step 3
Infórmate: Students read for specific information or details, using strategies for dealing with difficult aspects of the text. Questions help focus on key information.

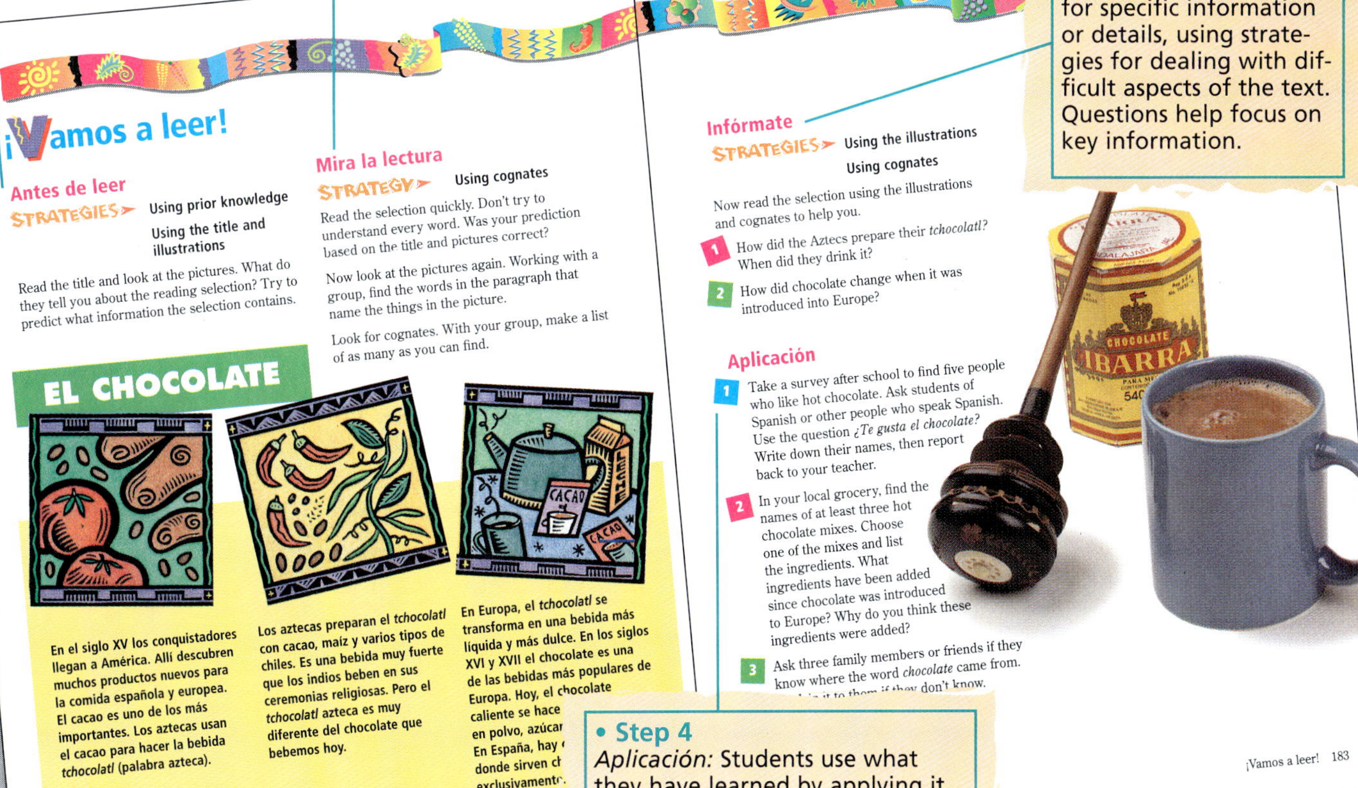

¡Vamos a leer!

Antes de leer

STRATEGIES ➤ Using prior knowledge
Using the title and illustrations

Read the title and look at the pictures. What do they tell you about the reading selection? Try to predict what information the selection contains.

Mira la lectura

STRATEGY ➤ Using cognates

Read the selection quickly. Don't try to understand every word. Was your prediction based on the title and pictures correct?

Now look at the pictures again. Working with a group, find the words in the paragraph that name the things in the picture.

Look for cognates. With your group, make a list of as many as you can find.

EL CHOCOLATE

En el siglo XV los conquistadores llegan a América. Allí descubren muchos productos nuevos para la comida española y europea. El cacao es uno de los más importantes. Los aztecas usan el cacao para hacer la bebida *tchocolatl* (palabra azteca).

Los aztecas preparan el *tchocolatl* con cacao, maíz y varios tipos de chiles. Es una bebida muy fuerte que los indios beben en sus ceremonias religiosas. Pero el *tchocolatl* azteca es muy diferente del chocolate que bebemos hoy.

En Europa, el *tchocolatl* se transforma en una bebida más líquida y más dulce. En los siglos XVI y XVII el chocolate es una de las bebidas más populares de Europa. Hoy, el chocolate caliente se hace en polvo, azúcar En España, hay donde sirven ch exclusivament

182 Capítulo 4

Infórmate

STRATEGIES ➤ Using the illustrations
Using cognates

Now read the selection using the illustrations and cognates to help you.

1. How did the Aztecs prepare their *tchocolatl?* When did they drink it?
2. How did chocolate change when it was introduced into Europe?

Aplicación

1. Take a survey after school to find five people who like hot chocolate. Ask students of Spanish or other people who speak Spanish. Use the question *¿Te gusta el chocolate?* Write down their names, then report back to your teacher.
2. In your local grocery, find the names of at least three hot chocolate mixes. Choose one of the mixes and list the ingredients. What ingredients have been added since chocolate was introduced to Europe? Why do you think these ingredients were added?
3. Ask three family members or friends if they know where the word *chocolate* came from.

¡Vamos a leer! 183

• Step 4
Aplicación: Students use what they have learned by applying it in a different way.

¡Vamos a escribir! *(Apply)*

As with reading, students develop effective writing through a process approach consistent with the way they are learning to write in their English classes. It also provides a strategy or model for writing independently. Each writing task provides a creative, personalized opportunity to expand the chapter theme.

Teaching ideas

1 This may be done in class or as homework. Students can work individually, in pairs, or in small groups to brainstorm the topic and needed vocabulary. They can jot down answers to the questions and share them with other students. They then use the questions and responses as a starting point for writing their first draft. You might have students skip lines on the first draft so that there is room for comments during the peer review.

2 Have students share their first draft with one or more partners. Peer reviewers should check for thoroughness and comprehensibility, as well as for errors in spelling, grammar, and punctuation. (You may want to make sure that each reviewer says at least one good thing about the writing sample.)

3 Students may want to include final drafts in their writing portfolios.

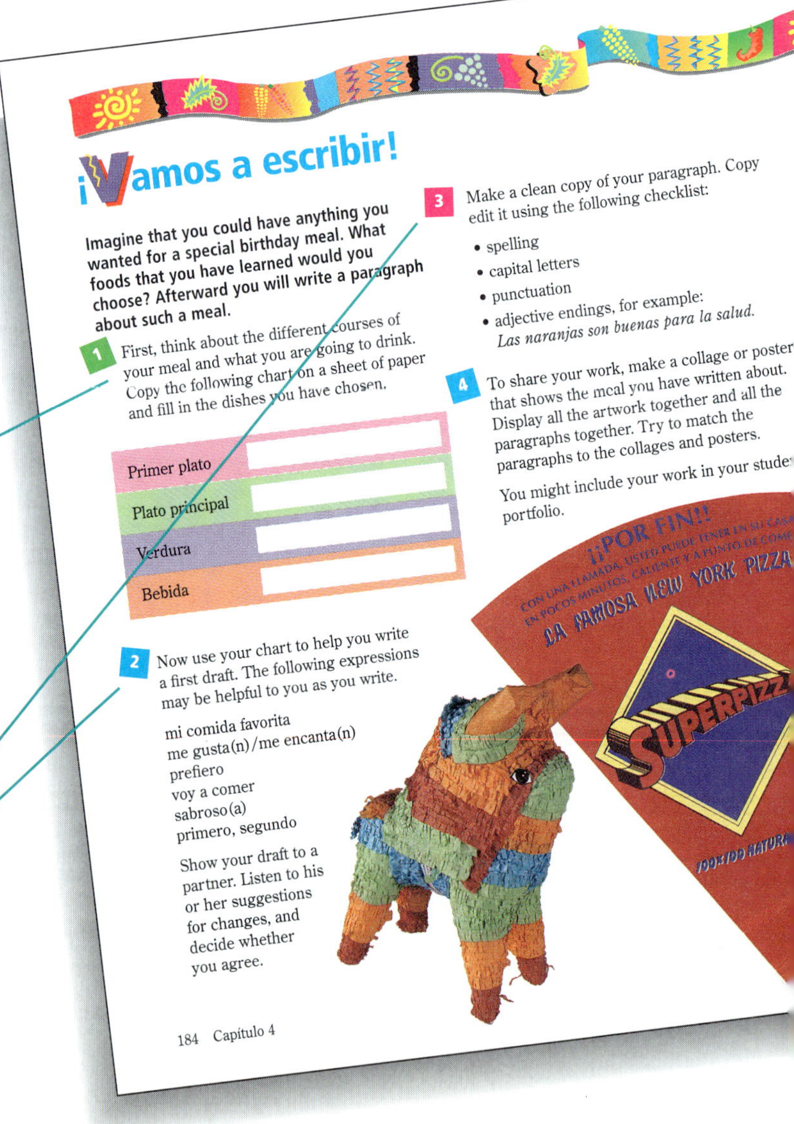

¡Vamos a escribir!

Imagine that you could have anything you wanted for a special birthday meal. What foods that you have learned would you choose? Afterward you will write a paragraph about such a meal.

1 First, think about the different courses of your meal and what you are going to drink. Copy the following chart on a sheet of paper and fill in the dishes you have chosen.

Primer plato	
Plato principal	
Verdura	
Bebida	

2 Now use your chart to help you write a first draft. The following expressions may be helpful to you as you write.

mi comida favorita
me gusta(n) / me encanta(n)
prefiero
voy a comer
sabroso(a)
primero, segundo

Show your draft to a partner. Listen to his or her suggestions for changes, and decide whether you agree.

3 Make a clean copy of your paragraph. Copy edit it using the following checklist:

- spelling
- capital letters
- punctuation
- adjective endings, for example: *Las naranjas son buenas para la salud.*

4 To share your work, make a collage or poster that shows the meal you have written about. Display all the artwork together and all the paragraphs together. Try to match the paragraphs to the collages and posters.

You might include your work in your student portfolio.

184 Capítulo 4

• Step 1
Pre-writing questions have students think about the topic, generate needed language, and organize their ideas. They then write the first draft.

• Steps 2 & 3
Through peer review students gain insights into needed revisions or clarifications for preparing the final draft.

esumen del capítulo *(Summarize)*

This section organizes the chapter vocabulary to reflect how it can be used to meet the communicative objectives. The objectives were stated in the chapter overview, and students have been given opportunities to assess their progress in the *Ahora lo sabes* sections.

esumen del capítulo 4

¡Eres un genio!

e vocabulary from this chapter to help you:
what you like and don't like to eat and drink
e reasons for your food and drink preferences
whether you are hungry or thirsty

dicate hunger or thirst
r hambre
er sed

describe meals
ber: (yo) bebo
(tú) bebes
mer: (yo) como
(tú) comes
almuerzo
cena
comida
el desayuno
la merienda
en el desayuno / en el almuerzo / en la cena

to talk about foods
el arroz
el bistec
el cereal
la ensalada
las frutas
la manzana
la naranja
el plátano
la uva
la hamburguesa
el huevo
el jamón
el pan
el pan tostado
la papa
las papas al horno
las papas fritas
el pescado
el pollo
el queso
el sandwich (de jamón y queso)
la sopa
la sopa de pollo
la sopa de tomate
la sopa de verduras
las verduras
la cebolla
los guisantes
las judías verdes
la lechuga
el tomate
la zanahoria

to talk about drinks
las bebidas
el agua *(f.)*
el café
el jugo de naranja
la leche
la limonada
el refresco
el té
el té helado

to describe foods
bueno, -a (para la salud)
horrible
malo, -a (para la salud)
sabroso, -a

to express likes or preferences
más o menos
me encanta(n)
preferir: (yo) prefiero
(tú) prefieres

to express an opinion
Creo que sí.
Creo que no.
¡Qué asco!

to elicit agreement
¿verdad?

to refer to obligation
deber: (yo) debo
(tú) debes

to indicate frequency
nunca
siempre

to refer to something you cannot name
algo

to request precise information
¿Cuál(es)?

other useful words
son
unos, unas

Resumen 185

Teaching ideas

1 Have pairs review the vocabulary. They might make up a sentence or dialogue in each category. For example, *Tengo hambre ahora* or:
—*¿Qué bebes cuando tienes sed?*
—*Bebo agua.*

2 If students have created flashcards, have them organize these according to the communicative categories.

3 Have students quiz each other using the list in the book or their flashcards. Ask them to indicate any words their partner had trouble with by writing them on a sheet of paper or placing a check on the flashcard. This will focus their test preparation on problem areas.

Assessment options

1 *Mi portafolio* is a section of the assessment program that provides an opportunity for students to summarize their learning and reflect on their progress and achievements.

2 There are two *Exámenes de habilidades* per chapter: one after *Sección 2;* the other at the end of *Sección 4.*

3 The Test Generator provides a test bank of multiple-choice questions to which you can add your own questions.

USING THE TEACHER'S EDITION

This Teacher's Edition provides all the support needed to work with the wide range of students in today's Spanish classes.

Each teacher chapter begins with a spread that provides organizational and cultural information for instructional planning.

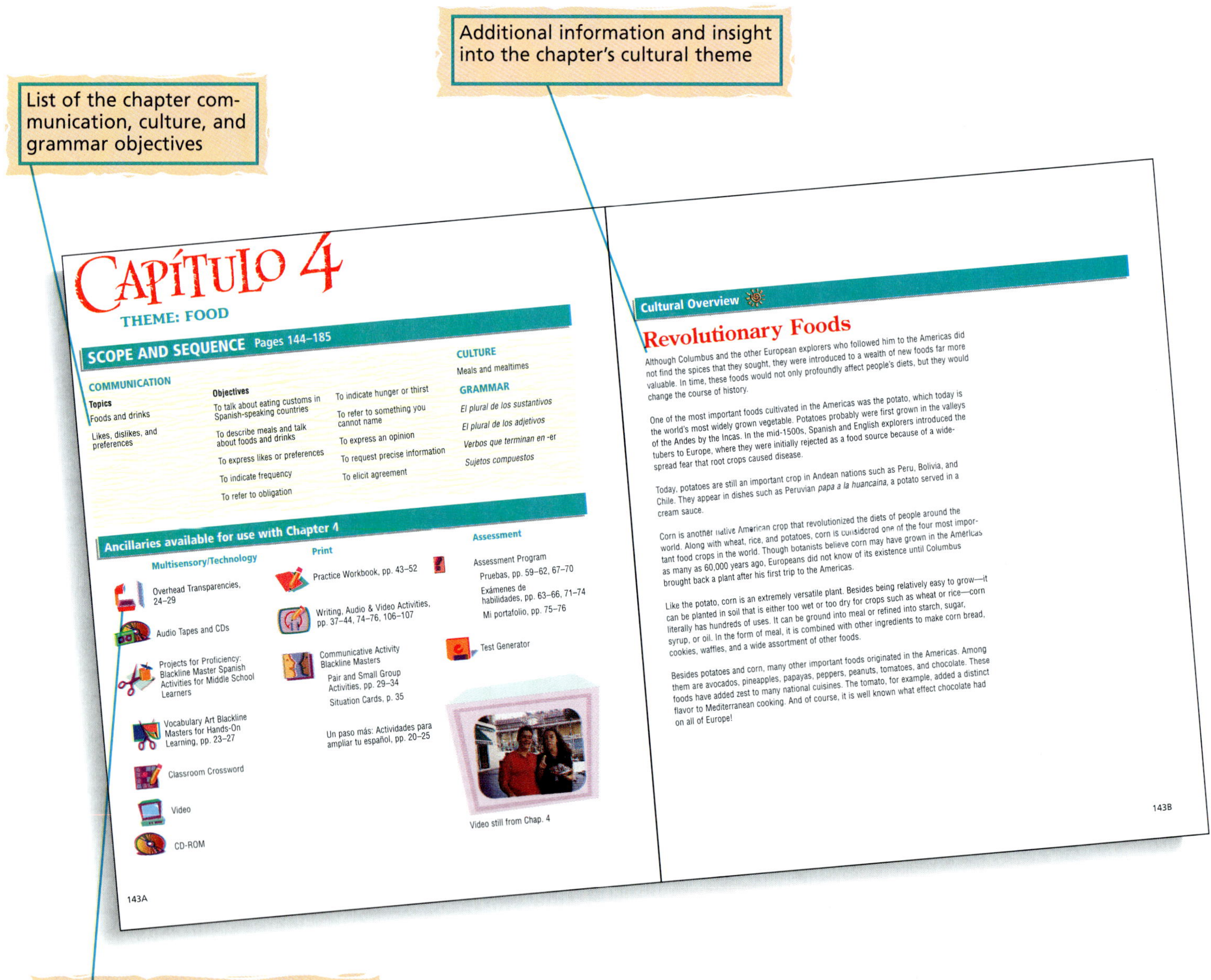

CAPÍTULO 4

THEME: FOOD

SCOPE AND SEQUENCE Pages 144–185

COMMUNICATION

Topics
Foods and drinks
Likes, dislikes, and preferences

Objectives
To talk about eating customs in Spanish-speaking countries
To describe meals and talk about foods and drinks
To express likes or preferences
To indicate frequency
To refer to obligation
To indicate hunger or thirst
To refer to something you cannot name
To express an opinion
To request precise information
To elicit agreement

CULTURE
Meals and mealtimes

GRAMMAR
El plural de los sustantivos
El plural de los adjetivos
Verbos que terminan en -er
Sujetos compuestos

Ancillaries available for use with Chapter 4

Multisensory/Technology
Overhead Transparencies, 24–29
Audio Tapes and CDs
Projects for Proficiency: Blackline Master Spanish Activities for Middle School Learners
Vocabulary Art Blackline Masters for Hands-On Learning, pp. 23–27
Classroom Crossword
Video
CD-ROM

Print
Practice Workbook, pp. 43–52
Writing, Audio & Video Activities, pp. 37–44, 74–76, 106–107
Communicative Activity Blackline Masters
Pair and Small Group Activities, pp. 29–34
Situation Cards, p. 35
Un paso más: Actividades para ampliar tu español, pp. 20–25

Assessment
Assessment Program
Pruebas, pp. 59–62, 67–70
Exámenes de habilidades, pp. 63–66, 71–74
Mi portafolio, pp. 75–76
Test Generator

Video still from Chap. 4

143A

Cultural Overview

Revolutionary Foods

Although Columbus and the other European explorers who followed him to the Americas did not find the spices that they sought, they were introduced to a wealth of new foods far more valuable. In time, these foods would not only profoundly affect people's diets, but they would change the course of history.

One of the most important foods cultivated in the Americas was the potato, which today is the world's most widely grown vegetable. Potatoes probably were first grown in the valleys of the Andes by the Incas. In the mid-1500s, Spanish and English explorers introduced the tubers to Europe, where they were initially rejected as a food source because of a widespread fear that root crops caused disease.

Today, potatoes are still an important crop in Andean nations such as Peru, Bolivia, and Chile. They appear in dishes such as Peruvian *papa a la huancaína*, a potato served in a cream sauce.

Corn is another native American crop that revolutionized the diets of people around the world. Along with wheat, rice, and potatoes, corn is considered one of the four most important food crops in the world. Though botanists believe corn may have grown in the Americas as many as 60,000 years ago, Europeans did not know of its existence until Columbus brought back a plant after his first trip to the Americas.

Like the potato, corn is an extremely versatile plant. Besides being relatively easy to grow—it can be planted in soil that is either too wet or too dry for crops such as wheat or rice—corn literally has hundreds of uses. It can be ground into meal or refined into starch, sugar, syrup, or oil. In the form of meal, it is combined with other ingredients to make corn bread, cookies, waffles, and a wide assortment of other foods.

Besides potatoes and corn, many other important foods originated in the Americas. Among them are avocados, pineapples, papayas, peppers, peanuts, tomatoes, and chocolate. These foods have added zest to many national cuisines. The tomato, for example, added a distinct flavor to Mediterranean cooking. And of course, it is well known what effect chocolate had on all of Europe!

143B

This Teacher's Edition is organized to provide for maximum ease of use. The student page is slightly reduced. Teacher notes appear regularly in the same place on the page.

Sidenotes are organized around the five-step pedagogical model used throughout *PASO A PASO:*

- **Introduce / Preview**
- **Present**
- **Practice**
- **Apply**
- **Summarize / Assess**

Notes provide answers, teaching suggestions, ancillary cross-references, recycling references, and other useful information.

Previously taught vocabulary sets that are re-entered in the chapter

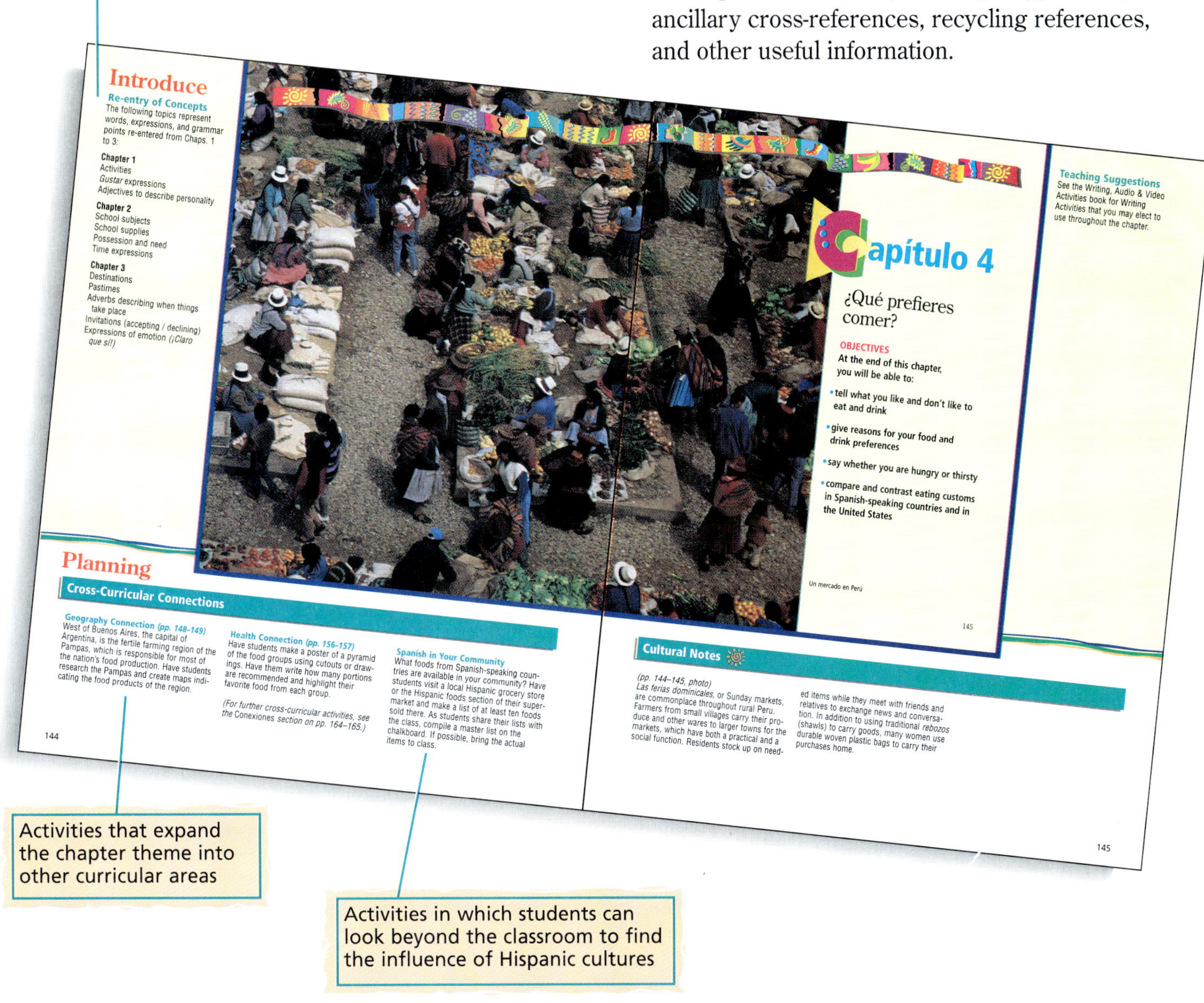

Introduce

Re-entry of Concepts
The following topics represent words, expressions, and grammar points re-entered from Chaps. 1 to 3:

Chapter 1
Activities
Gustar expressions
Adjectives to describe personality

Chapter 2
School subjects
School supplies
Possession and need
Time expressions

Chapter 3
Destinations
Pastimes
Adverbs describing when things take place
Invitations (accepting / declining)
Expressions of emotion (*¡Claro que sí!*)

Capítulo 4

¿Qué prefieres comer?

OBJECTIVES
At the end of this chapter, you will be able to:

- tell what you like and don't like to eat and drink
- give reasons for your food and drink preferences
- say whether you are hungry or thirsty
- compare and contrast eating customs in Spanish-speaking countries and in the United States

Un mercado en Perú

145

Teaching Suggestions
See the Writing, Audio & Video Activities book for Writing Activities that you may elect to use throughout the chapter.

Planning

Cross-Curricular Connections

Geography Connection *(pp. 148–149)*
West of Buenos Aires, the capital of Argentina, is the fertile farming region of the Pampas, which is responsible for most of the nation's food production. Have students research the Pampas and create maps indicating the food products of the region.

Health Connection *(pp. 156–157)*
Have students make a poster of a pyramid of the food groups using cutouts or drawings. Have them write how many portions are recommended and highlight their favorite food from each group.

(For further cross-curricular activities, see the Conexiones section on pp. 164–165.)

Spanish in Your Community
What foods from Spanish-speaking countries are available in your community? Have students visit a local Hispanic grocery store or the Hispanic foods section of their supermarket and make a list of at least ten foods sold there. As students share their lists with the class, compile a master list on the chalkboard. If possible, bring the actual items to class.

144

Cultural Notes

(pp. 144–145, photo)
Las ferias dominicales, or Sunday markets, are commonplace throughout rural Peru. Farmers from small villages carry their produce and other wares to larger towns for the markets, which have both a practical and a social function. Residents stock up on needed items while they meet with friends and relatives to exchange news and conversation. In addition to using traditional *rebozos* (shawls) to carry goods, many women use durable woven plastic bags to carry their purchases home.

145

Activities that expand the chapter theme into other curricular areas

Activities in which students can look beyond the classroom to find the influence of Hispanic cultures

Ideas for planning, strategies for reaching all students, and expansions on cultural themes

References to help with planning and instruction

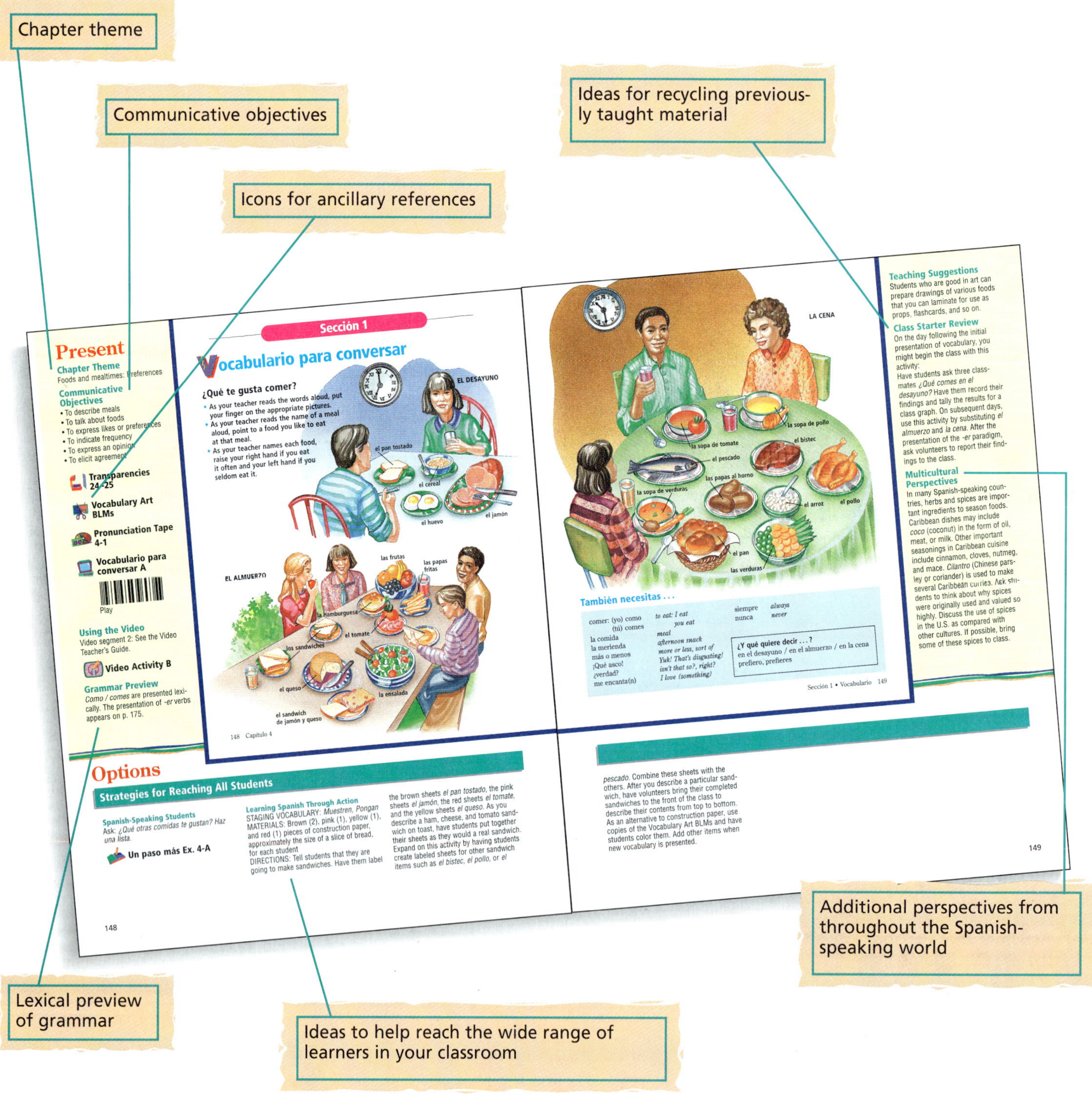

Present

Chapter Theme
Foods and mealtimes: Preferences

Communicative Objectives
- To describe meals
- To talk about foods
- To express likes or preferences
- To indicate frequency
- To express an opinion
- To elicit agreement

Transparencies 24–25

Vocabulary Art BLMs

Pronunciation Tape 4-1

Vocabulario para conversar A

Play

Using the Video
Video segment 2: See the Video Teacher's Guide.

Video Activity B

Grammar Preview
Como / comes are presented lexically. The presentation of *-er* verbs appears on p. 175.

Sección 1

Vocabulario para conversar

¿Qué te gusta comer?

- As your teacher reads the words aloud, put your finger on the appropriate pictures.
- As your teacher reads the name of a meal aloud, point to a food you like to eat at that meal.
- As your teacher names each food, raise your right hand if you eat it often and your left hand if you seldom eat it.

148 Capítulo 4

También necesitas . . .

comer: (yo) como	*to eat: I eat*	siempre	*always*
(tú) comes	*you eat*	nunca	*never*
la comida	*meal*		
la merienda	*afternoon snack*		
más o menos	*more or less, sort of*		
¡Qué asco!	*Yuk! That's disgusting!*		
¿verdad?	*isn't that so?, right?*		
me encanta(n)	*I love (something)*		

¿Y qué quiere decir . . . ?
en el desayuno / en el almuerzo / en la cena
prefiero, prefieres

Sección 1 • Vocabulario 149

Teaching Suggestions
Students who are good in art can prepare drawings of various foods that you can laminate for use as props, flashcards, and so on.

Class Starter Review
On the day following the initial presentation of vocabulary, you might begin the class with this activity:
Have students ask three classmates *¿Qué comes en el desayuno?* Have them record their findings and tally the results for a class graph. On subsequent days, use this activity by substituting *el almuerzo* and *la cena*. After the presentation of the *-er* paradigm, ask volunteers to report their findings to the class.

Multicultural Perspectives
In many Spanish-speaking countries, herbs and spices are important ingredients to season foods. Caribbean dishes may include *coco* (coconut) in the form of oil, meat, or milk. Other important seasonings in Caribbean cuisine include cinnamon, cloves, nutmeg, and mace. *Cilantro* (Chinese parsley or coriander) is used to make several Caribbean curries. Ask students to think about why spices were originally used and valued so highly. Discuss the use of spices in the U.S. as compared with other cultures. If possible, bring some of these spices to class.

Options

Strategies for Reaching All Students

Spanish-Speaking Students
Ask: *¿Qué otras comidas te gustan? Haz una lista.*

Un paso más Ex. 4-A

Learning Spanish Through Action
STAGING VOCABULARY: *Muestren, Pongan*
MATERIALS: Brown (2), pink (1), yellow (1), and red (1) pieces of construction paper, approximately the size of a slice of bread, for each student
DIRECTIONS: Tell students that they are going to make sandwiches. Have them label the brown sheets *el pan tostado*, the pink sheets *el jamón*, the red sheets *el tomate*, and the yellow sheets *el queso*. As you describe a ham, cheese, and tomato sandwich on toast, have students put together their sheets as they would a real sandwich. Expand on this activity by having students create labeled sheets for other sandwich items such as *el bistec*, *el pollo*, or *el pescado*. Combine these sheets with the others. After you describe a particular sandwich, have volunteers bring their completed sandwiches to the front of the class to describe their contents from top to bottom. As an alternative to construction paper, use copies of the Vocabulary Art BLMs and have students color them. Add other items when new vocabulary is presented.

148

149

MANAGEMENT AND PACING

Management and pacing will vary due to the number of teaching days, the number of hours of class time, the age of the students, and the amount of additional material that the teacher chooses to present.

Program Organization

PASO A PASO A has an introductory section *(El primer paso)* followed by six chapters, each divided into four sections. The first two sections focus on vocabulary development. The last two integrate the grammar with the vocabulary and include the *Todo junto* activities, strategic reading, and process writing.

PASO A PASO A and *B* have been developed expressly for middle school to be taught over two or three years. If a district begins Spanish instruction in Grade 7, Book A would be used in seventh grade and Book B in eighth. If, however, instruction begins in Grade 6, with classes meeting 30 minutes a day, two or three times a week, teachers might want to focus on *El primer paso* plus Chapter 1 (or possibly Chapters 1 and 2). Students would continue with *PASO A PASO A* in Grade 7 and then move into Book B in Grade 8.

In a more rigorous sixth-grade curriculum, students might complete Book A in one year and move into Book B the next.

The following chart shows the options for using *PASO A PASO A* and *B*. By no matter which route, after completing Books A and B, students are fully prepared for *PASO A PASO 2* or for any other second-year text.

Option	1	2	3
Grade 6	A	A	—
Grade 7	A	B	A
Grade 8	B	2	B
Grade 9	2	3	2

Bridging to *PASO A PASO B*

We strongly suggest that students complete *PASO A PASO A* before moving into *PASO A PASO B*. As they begin Book B, vocabulary and grammar from Book A are reviewed in the *Pasodoble* review section. Bear in mind, however, that though the material from Book A will be recycled throughout Book B, it is not formally retaught.

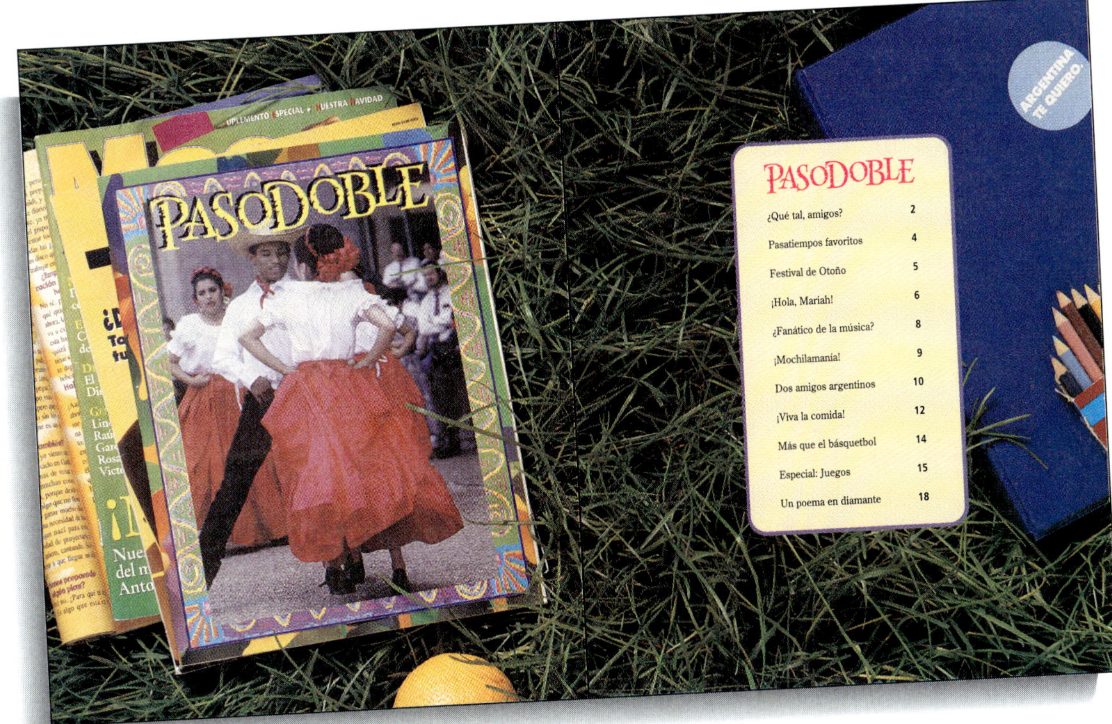

Pacing for *El primer paso*

The amount of time spent on *El primer paso* will depend upon how long and how often a class meets each week. If you are teaching *PASO A PASO A* and *B* over two years, plan on spending four to five weeks on this introductory unit. Students will gain a strong foundation of basic communication skills and cultural information and will begin learning good study habits that will benefit them as they continue their Spanish study. While students will need to know the vocabulary, they will not need spelling mastery at this point. All of the concepts presented will be recycled throughout the text.

Pacing for Chapters 1–6

Again, pacing will depend upon the particular teaching situation. Teachers should determine the amount of class time over the year and develop a schedule that will permit finishing the book. If Books A and B are being used over two years, a plan should be developed allowing approximately four to five weeks, including assessment, for each chapter.

As you begin teaching with *PASO A PASO A,* you will sense a rhythm, a flow that helps students move smoothly and successfully through the chapter. The thematic integration and spiraling, the extensive use of context and comprehensible input, the inductive questioning that leads to real understanding, and the recycling of previously taught material are all part of the carefully thought-out program design.

Block Scheduling

In recent years, some school districts have adopted block scheduling. While there are many variations in this type of scheduling, the most common change from the traditional 45- or 50-minute class period is to one of longer duration, typically from 70 to 90 minutes. In some schools, these classes meet daily and complete the year-long program in 4.5 to 6 months. In others, they meet every other day for the entire school year.

Some teachers have expressed concerns about the extended period of time that students are in a given session. How can one avoid their becoming bored? The answer lies in the variety of engaging activities offered during a given class period. Using *PASO A PASO,* teachers have at hand a wealth of varied activities that allow students to learn using paired and large- and small-group activities (open-ended and personalized), unusually engaging audiotape material, video-viewing activities, Total Physical Response, and inductive approaches both to culture and to grammar—all in addition to the unique ideas and approaches that each teacher brings to the classroom.

Another question raised by block scheduling is that of retention rate. In one approach, students have to remember a day's lesson from, say, Monday to Wednesday; in the other, they may have a six-month time lag between levels of language study. Research demonstrates that when material has been thoroughly acquired, the retention rate is significantly higher. Returning students are more quickly able to return to the level of language where they left off the year before. *PASO A PASO*'s in-depth thematic emphasis enables students to make this transition as smoothly as possible.

PASO A PASO is designed to offer the best possible instructional opportunities for either approach to scheduling.

ROLE OF THE VIDEO

Ever-increasing attention is being given to the important role that video can play in language learning. Today's teachers find video a highly effective tool in developing students' language proficiency and cultural understanding.

Video can provide access to new language and its meanings. In our native language we regularly acquire new vocabulary and grammar by hearing them used in meaningful contexts and surrounded by visual cues to meaning. That is, we figure out new meanings by our knowledge of the situation and what we observe people doing (think, for example, of how you learned what "to boot up" a computer means). Video provides the visual needed to match language with its meaning. It is a primary source of comprehensible input.

Video is also an important tool for preparing students for encounters with native speakers outside the classroom. Too often students lament that while they can ask questions they can't always understand the answers. That's because in classrooms there are limited opportunities to hear native speakers use the language in a natural way, without oversimplification of the content or a reduction of the rate of their speech. Video provides repeated opportunities for students to hear authentic language used in authentic situations by native speakers, thus gaining an increasing ability to understand the language in direct encounters outside the classroom.

Video can best be utilized when it is viewed several times, although each viewing may have a different purpose. A first viewing, perhaps with the sound off, allows students to understand the context, to draw on their background knowledge to anticipate what the segment will be about, and to anticipate what people might be saying. For example, a waiter holding a pad and pencil while talking to two people seated at a table will let students know that this is a restaurant. They may anticipate that he might be asking "What would you like to order?" A second viewing, with the sound on, might focus on getting the gist of what is happening and what people are saying. Repeated viewings might focus on specific meanings of words and then longer speech segments. With the picture off and the sound on, students may refine their ability to get meaning from spoken language because the visual supports are withdrawn. Conversely, with the picture on and the sound off, students can concentrate on the cultural information provided, whether it is of elements in the target culture environment (e.g., what one teenager's bedroom in Mexico looks like or what kinds of cars are most common in Spanish cities) or the body language used by native speakers when they interact.

En vivo is the video program that accompanies *PASO A PASO A/B,* as well as *PASO A PASO 1.* The program contains an integrated, three-segment video episode for each chapter in the text. The first segment is a mostly visual sequence that provides an overview of the chapter theme, allowing students to anticipate the situations they will see. This segment also provides a visual context for the language and cultural information they will be learning. In segment 2, students hear new language used by native speakers. The new language is presented in ways that help make the meanings clear (comprehensible input). In segment 3, which has been designed to be shown after all new chapter vocabulary and grammar have been presented and practiced, the new language is again used, but with fewer direct visual cues to meaning. This requires students to integrate and apply the newly learned material and to rely on the meanings they have acquired. An extensive Teacher's Guide accompanies *En vivo.* The Guide offers many suggestions for using the video program.

While it is certainly possible to teach *PASO A PASO A/B* without using the video, teachers will find it a powerful tool in promoting the acquisition of new language, in developing the listening comprehension skills students need to function outside the sheltered environment of the classroom, and in bringing the cultures of the Spanish-speaking world into the classroom in a vivid and interesting way.

STRATEGIES FOR REACHING ALL STUDENTS

PASO A PASO provides teachers the support and strategies needed to reach all students in the Spanish classroom. We offer an unprecedented commitment to providing materials that help meet the realities of today's classroom. This article focuses on strategies from *PASO A PASO* that will help you and all of your students enjoy a successful experience learning Spanish . . . step by step!

1 The middle school student

Middle school students are not miniature high school students, but are personalities in their own right with characteristics unique to that age group. At this stage, they are generally sensitive and uncomfortable with the physical, emotional, and social changes they are experiencing but often do not understand. Because of this, students tend to be focused on themselves and to feel awkward. They are driven by peer pressure and the strong desire to be accepted by the group. Academics are not as important as socializing and being liked by peers and teachers.

In order to succeed in a learning environment, teachers need to be patient, sensitive, flexible, and sympathetic to what the students are experiencing. It is important for students to interact with materials that fall within their personal and group interest. It is with this in mind that this special middle school edition of *PASO A PASO* was written by experienced middle school teachers. It includes elements of the typical middle school, such as interdisciplinary activities, group and pair activities, group projects, and inherent flexibility and opportunities for interaction. It capitalizes on the students' self-absorption and desire to talk through communicative activities relating to their lives and interests.

2 Material that builds upon students' experiences

Language students learn best by using what they know, by building new knowledge on old, and by experiencing and doing. As you use the text, you will see that *PASO A PASO* provides for an authentic, meaningful experience for the learner. The chapter themes were developed by asking, "What do students want to talk about?" The vocabulary taught is high-frequency language that students want to learn. The grammar supports communication and is practiced communicatively. The cultural content provides a means toward understanding and a global perspective that will be meaningful to all students. The activities ask students to interact, to become active participants in the learning process, and to express real ideas and real meanings with their peers for real purposes.

3 A multisensory approach to learning

Students enter the Spanish classroom with different learning styles and abilities. Some work best with an aural / oral approach; others need a strong visual approach. Many need to touch and be physically involved in learning. An approach that addresses the needs and strengths of each student lays the groundwork for reaching all.

PASO A PASO provides a strong multisensory approach to language learning. Students have varied opportunities for success by working with activities that acknowledge different learning styles and employ more than one modality. Each chapter provides suggestions for incorporating TPR, which we call Learning Spanish Through Action. The *Todo junto* offers activities that involve different learning skills and interests (creating a collage, preparing a skit, drawing a house).

The cornerstone of success in ScottForesman's foreign language programs has always been our strong visual approach. We have expanded this in *PASO A PASO*. Each chapter opens with culturally authentic photographs *(¡Piénsalo bien!)* that call upon students' background knowledge in discussing the chapter theme. Vocabulary presentation is facilitated by contextual visualization that is then recycled in the practice activities to reinforce learning. This approach is supported by the Overhead Transparencies and the Vocabulary

Art Blackline Masters. We have enhanced the visual approach through a photo essay in the *Perspectiva cultural.* A new, realia-based approach offers students an opportunity to study grammar in a real-life context. And reading and writing practice are made more accessible through the strong use of visual cues.

The multisensory approach is further expanded through use of the chapter-by-chapter audio tapes, video, and the interactive multimedia CD-ROM. The video program brings the culture to students while providing support to the chapter's content. Language use is presented in an authentic context. The CD-ROM, *Pasos vivos,* provides opportunities for students to work at their own pace while engaging all learning styles.

4 Learning strategies

PASO A PASO reinforces the strategies and skill-building techniques that students are using in their other classes. Some of these may be new to you but are easily implemented in the Spanish classroom. Strategies include building on background knowledge and experience, making lists or webs to organize their learning, inductive questioning, and consistent application of reading strategies and process writing.

5 Higher-order and inductive thinking

It sometimes seems that every day researchers are discovering new facts about the workings of the brain. We now know that information is stored in many areas of the brain and connected by a rich network of neurons. The goal of instruction should be to maximize the use of this network by helping students make connections and to learn information from a variety of perspectives and in a variety of ways. Activities aimed toward this goal are inherently interesting and motivating.

Students learn more successfully when they create their own understanding. Throughout *PASO A PASO* you will find activities that ask students to do just this. Inductive questions, for example, are the starting point of the following chapter features: *¡Piénsalo bien!, Perspectiva cultural, Gramática en contexto,* and *¡Vamos a leer!* Activities that engage students in higher-level thinking skills are the initial focus in each of these sections, as well as in the *¡Vamos a escribir!* We sequence these activities so that all students can be successful.

Another important learning strategy that middle school students enjoy, informed guessing, is embedded in the vocabulary section entitled *¿Y qué quiere decir . . . ?* and is focused on in the inductive questions about photographs, as well as in the process reading and writing sections of each chapter.

6 Multiple learning opportunities

We know that students will improve at different rates and will be stronger in some areas than in others. In addition, developing proficiency takes time for everyone, no matter how gifted. Therefore, instruction must provide multiple opportunities for learning and improvement.

PASO A PASO offers these opportunities. New vocabulary is presented, practiced, and recycled throughout a chapter and in subsequent chapters. Students are first exposed to grammar lexically, use it as they practice, and have some degree of understanding and control of it before it is presented and practiced as grammar. It is presented in easy-to-deal-with increments. Direct object pronouns, for example, are first explained in Chapter 6, with reminders and/or additional information being presented in *PASO A PASO B,* Chapters 10–13; similarly with the preterite, which is first presented lexically in Chapter 6, and later explained in *PASO A PASO B,* Chapters 10–12.

Throughout the text students will find reminder notes entitled *¡No olvides!* These focus on previously learned concepts that they will need in order to do a particular exercise or to understand better an extension of a given structure. These reminders are important tools for mastery.

Realizing the importance of projects and games for middle school students, a book of blackline masters, *Projects for Proficiency,* provides the tools and suggestions for multiple appropriate activities.

Additional opportunities for students who need them

A regular on-page feature of this Teacher's Edition entitled "Strategies for Reaching All Students" provides you support for working with:

- Spanish-speaking students
- students needing extra help
- the gifted

For working with Spanish speakers, there are suggestions throughout the text, as well as a specially written supplemental worktext, *Un paso más: Actividades para ampliar tu español.* Notes under the heading "Students Needing Extra Help" suggest adaptations of the textbook activities or grammar explanations for those with learning difficulties. Enrichment suggestions allow students who are capable of doing so to move beyond the textbook. You will also find notes for cooperative learning, an excellent strategy for reaching all students and for giving middle school students the margin of comfort that helps them succeed.

Varied assessment options

Students do better in assessment situations if they have a clear understanding of the objectives and of how they will be assessed, and if they are assessed in such a way as to focus on their strengths. *PASO A PASO* offers a variety of options. Besides the *Pruebas* and *Exámenes de habilidades* in the Assessment Program, the *Actividades* in the integrative *Comuniquemos* and *Todo junto* offer different types of opportunities for assessment, asking students to draw upon auditory, visual, and kinesthetic strengths. The many paired activities also offer natural oral / aural assessment possibilities.

Through the clearly stated objectives at the beginning of each chapter and the mini-assessments within the chapter *(Ahora lo sabes),* students are able to monitor and evaluate their own progress. The end-of-chapter *Mi portafolio* offers the opportunity for reflection, self-assessment, and the ability to showcase the student's best work.

PASO A PASO is committed to helping every teacher reach every student in the middle school Spanish class. By providing materials that are strategy-based, that are written with the problems, interests, and strengths of middle school students in mind, and that have built-in teacher support, we believe that we are enabling both you and your students to experience real enjoyment and unparalleled success.

ASSESSMENT

Assessment in a communicative middle school foreign language classroom should take many forms:

- informal daily assessments
- short quizzes that check knowledge of discrete points of vocabulary and grammar
- longer end-of-chapter assessments that verify what students can do in the target language
- student portfolios
- projects

Students should always understand what is expected of them. To be most effective, assessment should:

- have clear objectives that focus on meaningful and purposeful communication
- reflect what students have done in the classroom as they went through a chapter
- vary so as to reflect the strengths of each student

Informal assessment

Class performance and homework are key elements in assessment. Throughout, *PASO A PASO* offers a wide variety of daily assessment opportunities. Regular informal assessment builds self-confidence, particularly for students who do not perform well in more formal or traditional testing situations. Encouraging creativity in activities and homework assignments often evokes rewarding results for the individual, the class, and the teacher.

At all stages of *PASO A PASO,* students participate in meaningful, purposeful activities that are ideal for informal assessment. The abundant ancillaries that accompany the text also provide for flexible and varied assessment opportunities.

Using creative homework as assessment opportunities

The following are creative ideas for expanding on the various chapter sections.

Vocabulario para conversar

Students can:

- make collages of the vocabulary words and present them to the class
- make flashcards showing pictograms of the vocabulary
- create crossword puzzles, word searches, and scrambled word lists (including answer keys) with new vocabulary to share with a partner
- find and describe additional photographs related to the vocabulary theme and present these to the class
- photograph or videotape people and objects representative of the chapter vocabulary; write captions for the photographs or narrate the video
- write expanded captions for the photographs in the textbook and explain them to a partner
- use a computer to create word games using chapter vocabulary

Empecemos a conversar

Students can:

- practice conversations on the phone and then present them to a small group or to the class
- tape record a brief exchange in Spanish
- write new dialogues using pictures or talk bubbles and then present the dialogues in class
- audiotape conversations

Empecemos a leer y a escribir

Students can:

- summarize the main idea in a brief paragraph
- make up original questions and then interview a partner; write up the results of the interviews as summaries of what they learned from one another
- create new questions or dialogues, including illustrations, such as talk balloons or magazine cutouts; practice and then perform the dialogues in class

Perspectiva cultural

Students can:

- make original posters that illustrate the main idea
- create travel brochures with illustrations and captions
- interview someone who is knowledgeable about the topic; make videos or audio cassettes of the interview; write illustrated summaries
- make posters showing similarities and differences between cultures
- find photographs that illustrate the cultural theme and write a caption or description

Ahora lo sabes

Students can:

- illustrate the sentences or dialogues, including talk balloons that show what the characters are saying
- create collages representing the answers to the questions
- record the answers on an audio cassette
- create dialogues, practicing them with a partner on the telephone and then presenting them to a small group or to the class

Conexiones

Students can:

- make up their own cross-curricular activities to share with other students and with teachers of other disciplines

Gramática en contexto

Students can:

- write modified versions of the realia-based readings
- make charts illustrating one or more of the grammar rules presented, color-coding the essential points
- create mnemonic devices that will help them and others remember the grammar points
- compose simple lyrics or poems illustrating a grammar rule

Todo junto

These activities are designed for pair and group work and can provide rich opportunities for assessment.

- After groups have done one of the activities, reassign students to new groups to do a different activity. Assess each student in the group on individual performance.
- Assign partners a topic or question related to the chapter theme. Give them five minutes to plan their response. Allow them to write up to five key words on an index card as a memory aid, but do not allow them to write out verbatim what they will say. Have students perform before you alone or in front of the class.
- Use the Situation Cards in the *Communicative Activity Blackline Masters* or those found in the *Let's Talk Cards* (ScottForesman, 1989) to assess students' ability to integrate newer and previously learned material.
- Have students produce videotapes with props and then present them to the class.

There are several ways to evaluate student performance in informal assessment. You might want to evaluate some creative homework assignments and, at other times, let students evaluate each other's work or their own. There are several criteria you can use:

- completion of task
- quantity and/or variety of information
- appropriateness of response or information
- comprehensibility
- originality
- individual improvement
- accuracy
- ease in using the language

Formal assessment

Pruebas

The *PASO A PASO* quizzes assess student learning of discrete points. There are two quizzes for each vocabulary section and two for each grammar section. The first quiz focuses on *recognition;* students do not have to produce the new material, merely recognize and demonstrate understanding of it. The second quiz focuses on *production* of the new vocabulary or structures. Some students will not be able to go beyond the recognition quiz, others will not need it. However, for most students, we recommend that you give the recognition quiz first, then the production quiz.

Exámenes de habilidades

The *Exámenes de habilidades* are thematic, contextualized assessments of listening, reading comprehension, writing, cultural knowledge, and speaking. *PASO A PASO* provides two such examinations for each chapter. One is designed to be given after the second vocabulary section, the other to be given after the second grammar section.

Mi portafolio

This section of the assessment program provides an opportunity for students to summarize their learning and reflect on their progress and achievements over the course of the chapter. Present this option after the chapter is completed. It should not be graded, but should be viewed as an opportunity for both teacher and student to review accomplishments and focus on areas of needed improvement.

Test Generator

The test generator provides a bank of multiple-choice questions for each chapter. You can add your own questions to the test bank.

Portfolios in the second-language classroom

Student portfolios can have many functions. In some second-language classrooms, teachers use portfolios to supplement more traditional assessment methods, such as quizzes and tests, or as the primary means of assessing student progress. In others, students maintain portfolios to assess their own progress throughout the year. Among the advantages of portfolios are that students are encouraged:

- to edit and revise their work
- to be creative
- to take pride in their work and to strive for improvement
- to take responsibility for their own learning and progress

If you use portfolios for assessment purposes, the following might be used to evaluate the skills established in the chapters' objectives:

- quizzes, lists, charts, and other activities from the *Infórmate* and *Aplicación* sections in the *¡Vamos a leer!*
- audio and video activities from the Writing, Audio & Video Activities book

- cultural projects exhibiting understanding of or sensitivity to the target culture
- audio and/or video cassettes of student performance where learned material is used appropriately
- original creative writing, demonstrating acceptable command of grammar and vocabulary

You will probably be unable to allot a great deal of space to portfolio storage. Large, bulky items, such as projects, can be represented by a photograph or a written description; speaking tasks, by an audio or video tape. It is important that students have relatively easy access to their own portfolios. You may want to encourage them to decorate their folders with pictures, drawings, and Spanish words or expressions. This will give students an additional sense of pride and ownership.

Teachers who use portfolios to evaluate students often find it helpful to specify which kinds of student work are to be included in the portfolios (for example, three samples of good writing). It is also important for students to receive copies of the scoring rubrics in advance, so that they know the criteria by which their work will be evaluated.

The portfolio provides a structured opportunity for students to select their own best work. Above all, it encourages them to examine and reflect upon their progress. In some approaches to portfolio development, students may replace older examples with newer, better pieces. In contrast, students may not replace items, but add so as to have a cumulative record of their progress. Portfolio contents might include:

- written work, such as short paragraphs, compositions, or journals
- student-produced audio and/or video cassettes of student performance
- quizzes and tests
- evidence of reading comprehension
- evidence of listening comprehension
- individual projects
- pair or group projects
- art work
- cultural projects
- picture dictionaries
- story boards
- evidence that the language skills were practiced outside of the classroom
- evidence of contact with Hispanic cultures in the community
- original creative writing, such as poems, short stories, narratives, or explanations
- student-produced newspapers
- evidence of student reflection on his or her own writing or speaking

Informal assessment for Students Needing Extra Help

Because language production is a skill and involves considerable risk, it is important to encourage student participation and to use a variety of assessment options whenever possible. Students should be acknowledged with positive remarks and by receiving credit for:

- doing activities outside of the classroom
- actively participating in class activities
- trying to use Spanish rather than English
- completing assignments
- showing improvement

Acknowledgment of these efforts will help maintain students' enthusiasm.

Formal assessment for Students Needing Extra Help

Students with learning problems have a particularly difficult time taking quizzes and tests. Apprehension, insecurity, lack of preparedness and/or mastery all serve to put the student in a less-than-desirable position prior to test time. Help students perform optimally by following these suggestions:

- provide a pre-quiz or pre-test practice opportunity that is identical in format to the actual quiz or test; be sure directions are also the same
- provide students with test-preparation guides that focus on what will be tested; tell them what they need to know and exactly how you will grade them
- permit students to use the chapter's Practice Workbook Organizer during a test
- allow extra time
- explain all directions and give examples (in English if necessary)
- underline important words in directions and test items
- allow some students to take the test orally or to dictate answers to you
- if possible, tape record questions so that students can read and hear them simultaneously
- weight the scoring to reflect individual strengths; do not require all students to do the entire test (allow them to do every other item or even to skip certain sections)
- when appropriate, be lenient with spelling
- avoid unannounced quizzes and tests
- require a certain level of performance and retest if necessary
- be willing to accept projects or demonstrations as an alternative to a final test; give quizzes a cumulative grade
- use a grading system that rewards effort and participation
- allow students to write verb, pronoun, and other charts on their test papers so they don't have to rethink paradigms for each question
- before photocopying the quizzes and tests, add models and paste in pictures and icons; in question-and-answer sections, add pronouns

INDEX OF CULTURAL REFERENCES

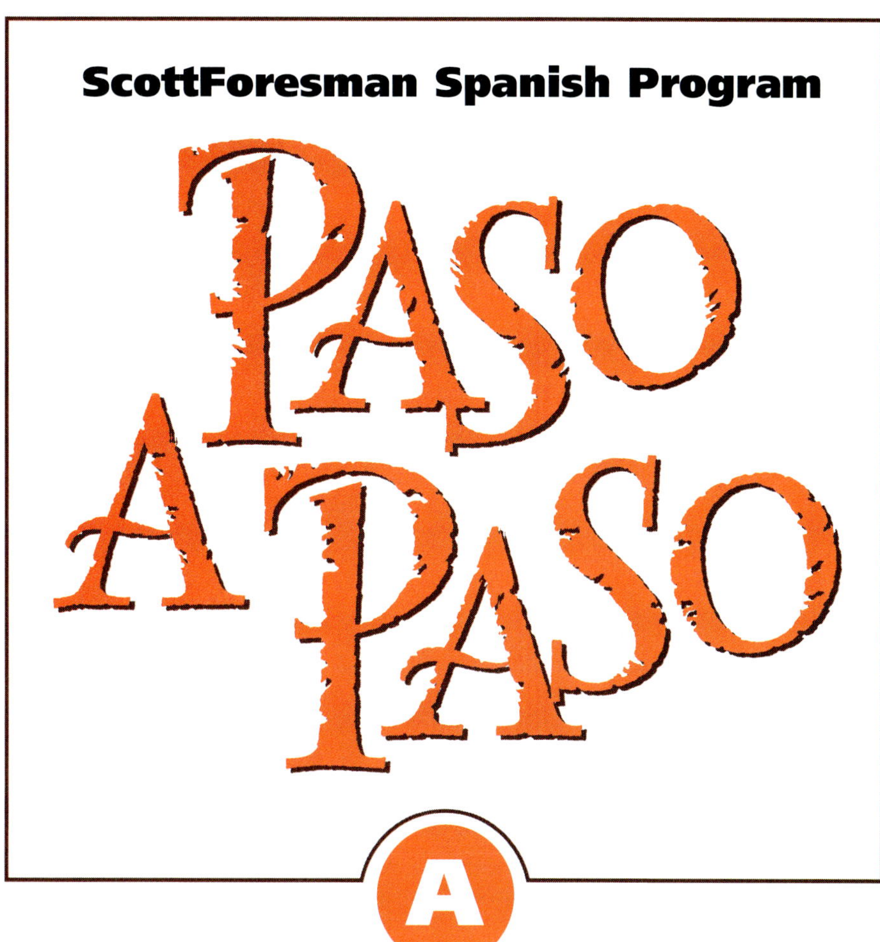
ScottForesman Spanish Program
PASO A PASO
A

Festival de barriletes gigantes del Día de los Muertos, Santiago, Guatemala

(p. II, front and back covers)
Santiago Sacatepéquez (pop. 14,000), is approximately 15 kilometers northwest of Guatemala City. On November 1, Santiago celebrates All Saints' Day with a giant kite festival, *el festival de los barriletes,* shown in the photo. The kites rising into the sky symbolize a connection between the living and the spirits of their ancestors.

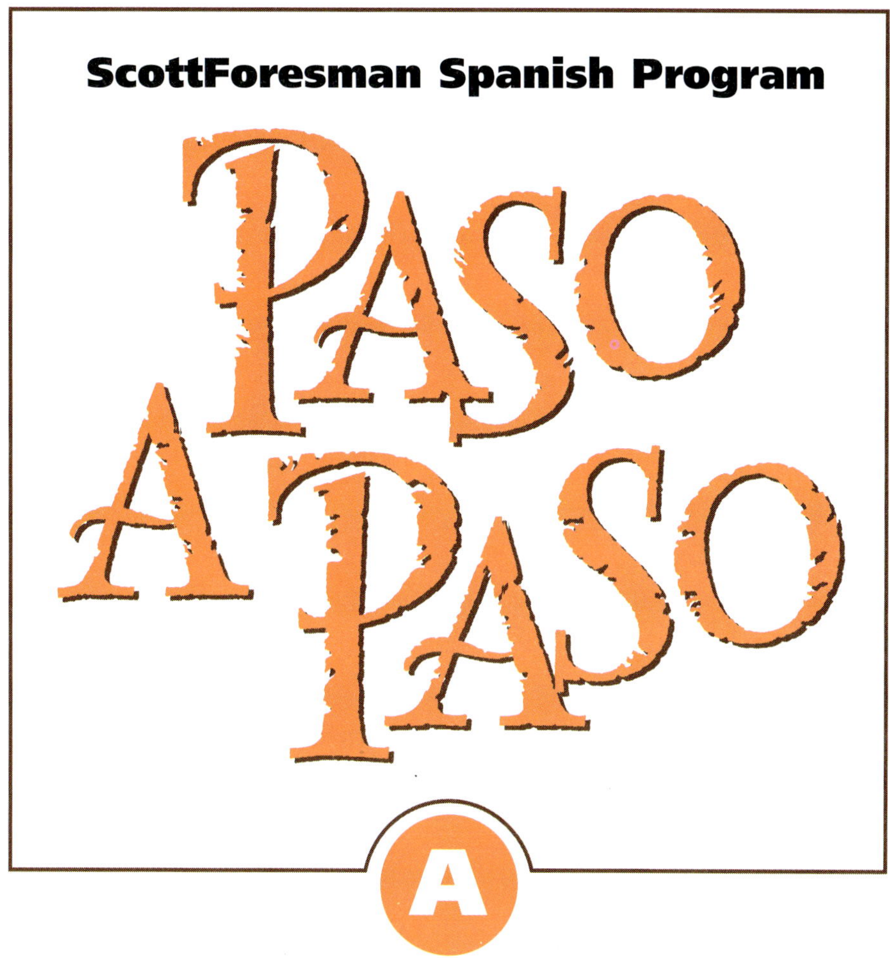

Myriam Met
Coordinator of Foreign Languages
Montgomery County Public Schools
Rockville, MD

Richard S. Sayers
Niwot High School
Longmont, CO

Harriet Schottland Barnett
Manhattanville College
Purchase, NY
formerly of the Dobbs Ferry (NY)
Public Schools

Carol Eubanks Wargin
Glen Crest Junior High School
Glen Ellyn, IL

ScottForesman

Editorial Offices: Glenview, Illinois
Regional Offices: San Jose, California • Atlanta, Georgia
Glenview, Illinois • Oakland, New Jersey • Dallas, Texas

Visit ScottForesman's Home Page at http://www.scottforesman.com

ISBN: 0-673-21712-4

For information regarding permission, write to:
Scott, Foresman and Company, 1900 East Lake Avenue, Glenview, Illinois 60025.

1.800.554.4411
http://www.scottforesman.com

2 3 4 5 6 7 8 9 10 DQ03020 100 99 98 97 96
Acknowledgments for illustrations appear on page 294.
The acknowledgments section should be considered an extension of the copyright page.

Contributing Writers

Gail Glover
San Antonio, TX

Mari Haas
Teachers College
Columbia University

Lori Langer de Ramírez
Poly Prep Country Day School
Brooklyn, NY

Albert T. Martino, Jr.
Chairperson, Foreign Languages
Norwich City School District
Norwich, NY

Zenaida Merced de Muslin
Upper School Spanish Teacher
Bank Street School for Children
New York, NY

Reader Consultants

The authors and editors would like to express their heartfelt thanks to the following team of reader consultants. Each of them read the manuscript, chapter by chapter, offering many suggestions and providing continual encouragement. Their contribution has been invaluable.

Sheree Altmann
Simpson Middle School
Marietta, GA

Isabel A. Bayon
Head, Foreign Languages
Bancroft School
Worcester, MA

Carolyn Bowman Carroll
Fairfax County Public Schools
Fairfax, VA

Lloyd Adolph Emshoff, M.A.
Teacher, Department Chair
El Toro High School
Lake Forest, CA

David B. Graham
Foreign Language Chairperson
Plainview–Old Bethpage Central School District
Plainview, NY

Kerri Holman
Eckert Intermediate
Aldine Independent School District
Houston, TX

Lewis C. Johnson
Hook Junior High School
Victorville, CA

Nancy A. Lee
Lincoln Junior High School
Mount Prospect, IL

Valerie Bryant Mantlo
Short Pump Middle School
Glen Allen, VA

Kaaran Martin
Beverly Hills Intermediate
Pasadena Independent School District
Houston, TX

Risima Micevic–Sayler
Dakota Hills Middle School
Eagan, MN

Gonzalo Moraga
Walter B. Hill School
Long Beach Unified School District
Long Beach, CA

Luci Platas
Team Leader
Taylor Road Middle School
Fulton Co., GA

Christine S. Wells
Cheyenne Mountain Junior High School
Colorado Springs, CO

Carmine R. Zinn
Pinellas County Schools
Largo, FL

Tabla de materias

El Primer Paso

VI

CAPÍTULO 1

Y tú, ¿cómo eres?

Capítulo 2

¿Qué clases tienes?

Capítulo 3

Los pasatiempos

Capítulo 4

¿Qué prefieres comer?

x

Capítulo 5

¿Cómo es tu familia?

CAPÍTULO 6

¿Qué desea Ud.?

XII

Sección de consulta

México, América Central y el Caribe
Límites internacionales
Otras ciudades
Capitales nacionales
Picos montañosos
0 300 600 kilómetros
0 300 600 millas
ESTADOS UNIDOS
MÉXICO
GOLFO DE MÉXICO
OCÉANO PACÍFICO
Golfo de California
Baja California
SIERRA MADRE OCCIDENTAL
SIERRA MADRE ORIENTAL
SIERRA MADRE DEL SUR
Golfo de Campeche
Golfo de Tehuantepec
Península de Yucatán
Río Grande
Río Bravo
Río Conchos
Río Pánuco
Río Grande de Santiago
Río Balsas
Río Usumacinta
Mexicali
Nogales
Ciudad Juárez
Hermosillo
Chihuahua
Nuevo Laredo
Monterrey
Durango
Mazatlán
Aguascalientes
San Luis Potosí
Tampico
León
Guanajuato
Guadalajara
Iztaccíhuatl (5286 m)
Popocatépetl (5452 m)
Citlaltépetl (5700 m)
México D. F.
Cuernavaca
Taxco
Puebla
Veracruz
Oaxaca
Acapulco
Mérida
Campeche
Trópico de Cáncer
La Habana
Isla de la Juventud
Belmopan
BELICE
GUATEMALA
Guatemala
HONDURAS
Tegucigalpa
San Salvador
EL SALVADOR
NICARAGUA
Lago de Managua
Lago de Nicaragua
Managua
San José
COSTA RICA
N
O
E
S

XIV

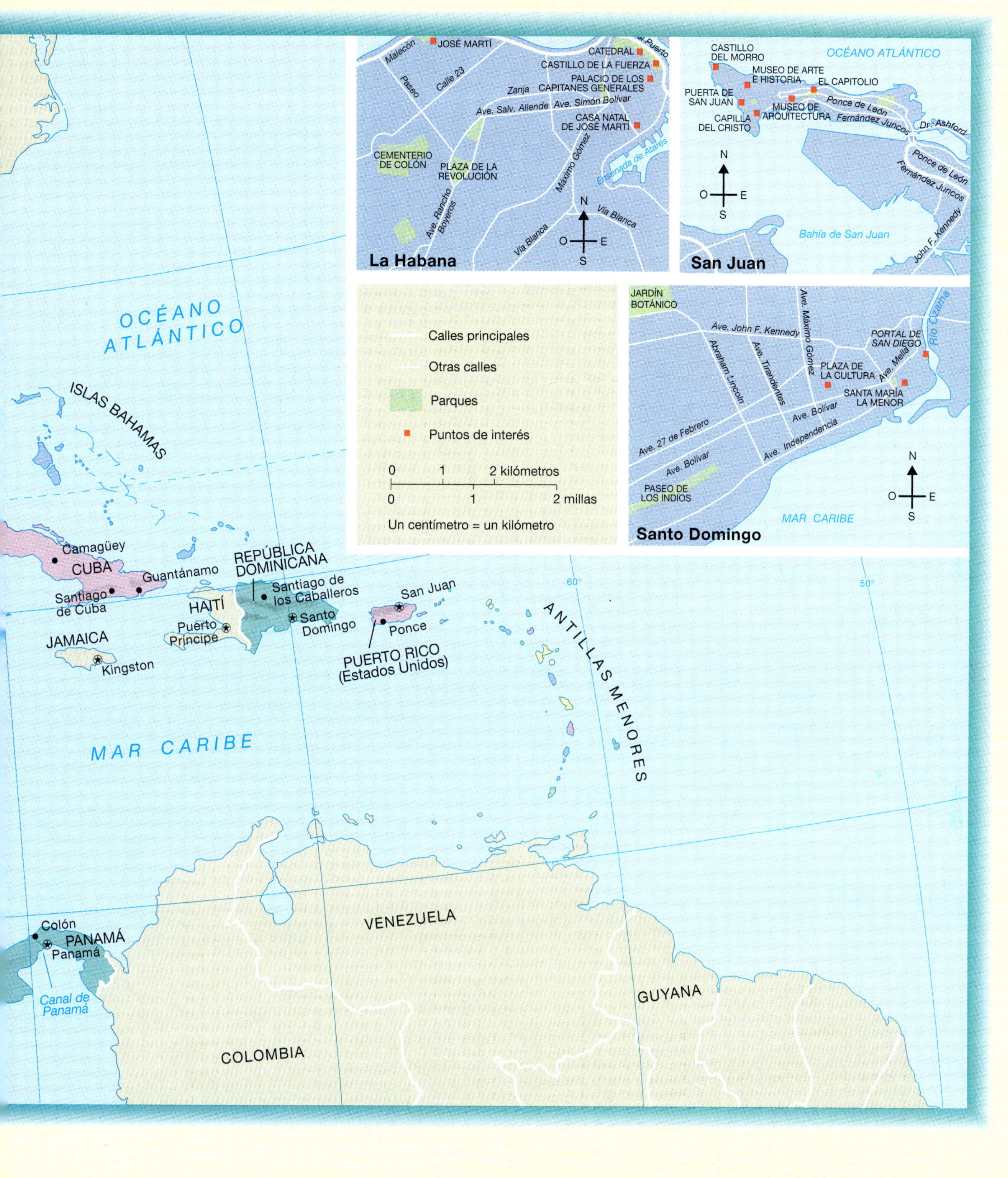
La Habana
JOSÉ MARTÍ
Malecón
Paseo
Calle 23
CATEDRAL
CASTILLO DE LA FUERZA
PALACIO DE LOS CAPITANES GENERALES
Zanja
Ave. Salv. Allende
Ave. Simón Bolívar
CASA NATAL DE JOSÉ MARTÍ
CEMENTERIO DE COLÓN
PLAZA DE LA REVOLUCIÓN
Máximo Gómez
Ensenada de Atarés
Ave. Rancho Boyeros
Vía Blanca
San Juan
CASTILLO DEL MORRO
OCÉANO ATLÁNTICO
MUSEO DE ARTE E HISTORIA
EL CAPITOLIO
PUERTA DE SAN JUAN
MUSEO DE ARQUITECTURA
CAPILLA DEL CRISTO
Ponce de León
Fernández Juncos
Dr. Ashford
Bahía de San Juan
John F. Kennedy
Calles principales
Otras calles
Parques
Puntos de interés
0 1 2 kilómetros
0 1 2 millas
Un centímetro = un kilómetro
Santo Domingo
JARDÍN BOTÁNICO
Ave. John F. Kennedy
Ave. Máximo Gómez
Abraham Lincoln
Ave. Tirandentes
PORTAL DE SAN DIEGO
Río Ozama
PLAZA DE LA CULTURA
Ave. Mella
SANTA MARÍA LA MENOR
Ave. Bolívar
Ave. 27 de Febrero
Ave. Independencia
PASEO DE LOS INDIOS
MAR CARIBE
N
S
E
O
OCÉANO ATLÁNTICO
ISLAS BAHAMAS
CUBA
Camagüey
Guantánamo
Santiago de Cuba
REPÚBLICA DOMINICANA
Santiago de los Caballeros
Santo Domingo
HAITÍ
Puerto Príncipe
JAMAICA
Kingston
San Juan
Ponce
PUERTO RICO (Estados Unidos)
ANTILLAS MENORES
60°
50°
MAR CARIBE
VENEZUELA
GUYANA
COLOMBIA
Colón
PANAMÁ
Panamá
Canal de Panamá

España
Límites internacionales
Capitales nacionales
Otras ciudades
Picos montañosos
MAR CANTÁBRICO
FRANCIA
Golfo de Vizcaya
La Coruña
Santiago de Compostela
Oviedo
Santander
San Sebastián
Bilbao
CORDILLERA CANTÁBRICA
PIRINEOS
Pamplona
León
Burgos
Río Ebro
Pico de Aneto (3404 m)
ANDORRA
Vigo
Valladolid
Río Duero
Zaragoza
Costa Brava
Barcelona
Tarragona
Salamanca
SIERRA DE GUADARRAMA
Ávila
PORTUGAL
Madrid
Río Tajo
MENORCA
Islas Baleares
Castellón de la Plana
Toledo
Valencia
Palma de Mallorca
MALLORCA
ESPAÑA
Río Guadiana
IBIZA
Badajoz
FORMENTERA
SIERRA MORENA
Río Guadalquivir
Costa Blanca
Alicante
Murcia
MAR MEDITERRÁNEO
Córdoba
Huelva
Sevilla
Cartagena
Granada
SIERRA NEVADA
Mulhacén (3478 m)
Golfo de Cádiz
Costa del Sol
Cádiz
Málaga
Almería
Estrecho de Gibraltar
Gibraltar (Reino Unido)
OCÉANO ATLÁNTICO
ARGELIA
MARRUECOS
N
O
E
S
0
100
200 kilómetros
0
100
200 millas
ESPAÑA
OCÉANO ATLÁNTICO
Islas Baleares
ÁFRICA
Islas Canarias
200 kilómetros
200 millas
ISLAS CANARIAS (España)
LANZAROTE
LA PALMA
Santa Cruz de Tenerife
FUERTEVENTURA
GOMERA
TENERIFE
GRAN CANARIA
Las Palmas de Gran Canaria
HIERRO
ÁFRICA
OCÉANO ATLÁNTICO
100 kilómetros
100 millas
© SF

XVI

América del Sur
Límites internacionales
Capitales nacionales
Otras ciudades
Picos montañosos
OCÉANO ATLÁNTICO
OCÉANO PACÍFICO
NICARAGUA
COSTA RICA
PANAMÁ
Barranquilla
Maracaibo
Lago de Maracaibo
Caracas
Puerto España
TRINIDAD Y TOBAGO
Río Orinoco
Medellín
Bogotá
VENEZUELA
GUYANA
Georgetown
Paramaribo
Cayena
SURINAM
GUAYANA FRANCESA (Fr.)
Cali
COLOMBIA
Quito
ECUADOR
0° Ecuador
Islas Galápagos (Ecuador)
Guayaquil
Iquitos
Manaus
Río Amazonas
Belém
Río Marañón
Río Madeira
Río Ucayali
Trujillo
BRASIL
Recife
Huascarán (6768 m)
PERÚ
Lima
Cuzco
CORDILLERA DE LOS ANDES
Lago Titicaca
Río Mamoré
Illampu (6550 m)
La Paz
BOLIVIA
Arequipa
Salvador
Brasilia
Río Paraguay
Sucre
Río Pilcomayo
PARAGUAY
Río Paraná
Belo Horizonte
N
O
E
S
20°
São Paulo
Río de Janeiro
Asunción
Santos
Trópico de Capricornio
San Miguel de Tucumán
CHILE
Porto Alegre
Córdoba
Río Salado
Aconcagua (6959 m)
Valparaíso
Santiago
Rosario
Buenos Aires
URUGUAY
Montevideo
Río de la Plata
Mar del Plata
Concepción
ARGENTINA
40°
Islas Malvinas (Reino Unido)
Estrecho de Magallanes
Tierra del Fuego
Cabo de Hornos
0 300 600 kilómetros
0 300 600 millas
© SF

EL PRIMER PASO

THEME: INTRODUCTION TO THE WORLD OF SPANISH

SCOPE AND SEQUENCE Pages 1–25

COMMUNICATION

Topics

Greetings and leave-takings

Names of countries

Professions

Classroom objects

Alphabet / Numbers 0–31

Classroom expressions

Objectives

To discuss the influence of Spanish language and culture

To greet people and say good-by

To tell how you feel

To ask someone's name and tell your name

To acknowledge introductions

To ask for and give information

To say when something takes place

To count or give dates

To say thank you

To talk about your classroom

CULTURE

Names and locations of Spanish-speaking countries

Spanish names

Ancillaries available for use with *El primer paso*

Multisensory/Technology

Overhead Transparencies, 1–5

Audio Tapes and CDs

Projects for Proficiency: Blackline Master Spanish Activities for Middle School Learners

Vocabulary Art Blackline Masters for Hands-On Learning, pp. 3–7

Classroom Crossword

Video

CD-ROM

Print

Practice Workbook, pp. 1–11

Writing, Audio & Video Activities, pp. 7–12, 63–64, 99

Communicative Activity Blackline Masters

Pair and Small Group Activities, pp. 1–6

Situation Cards, p. 7

Assessment

Assessment Program

Prueba, pp. 1–6

Test Generator

Video still from *El primer paso*

Cultural Overview

The Richly Diverse Hispanic Americans

According to the 1990 census, 22,354,000 people (about 9 percent of the total population in the U.S.) classified themselves as being of Spanish or Hispanic descent. Out of that number, 17,268,000 indicated that they were of either Mexican, Puerto Rican, or Cuban descent. The remaining 5,086,000 people checked "Other Spanish / Hispanic" on their census questionnaires. This broad category included people who came from or who had ancestral ties to other Spanish-speaking countries in the Caribbean, Central and South America, or Spain.

The nation's Hispanic population is growing at a tremendous rate. Between 1980 and 1990 it grew by an astounding 53 percent. In contrast, the nation as a whole expanded only 9.8 percent. The Census Bureau estimates that by 2080, people in the Spanish or Hispanic group will number almost 60 million and constitute more than 19 percent of the population. Collectively, the group would outnumber African Americans by that date.

The influence of the many diverse Hispanic cultures is everywhere. The Southwestern look, drawing on traditional Spanish architecture as well as contemporary influences, has emerged as an important design style. Ethnic groceries specializing in ingredients essential to many of the traditional dishes served in Hispanic cultures have sprung up across the country. The music of Celia Cruz, Gloria Estefan, Rubén Blades, and Los Lobos has introduced Spanish vocabulary into everyday English. Hispanic actors such as Raúl Julia and Rosie Pérez have earned great acclaim in recent years for their outstanding work. Motion pictures such as *La Bamba, Stand and Deliver,* and *Like Water for Chocolate* were hits at the box office.

Perhaps most important, Hispanic Americans have increased their political power in recent years. During the last several presidential administrations, Hispanics have been appointed to many major political posts. In 1988 President Reagan appointed Lauro F. Cavazos, a Mexican American, as Secretary of Education. He was the first Hispanic American appointed to the Cabinet. In 1990, Dr. Antonia Coello Novello, with roots in Puerto Rico, became the first woman and the first Hispanic American to become Surgeon General. Many other Hispanic Americans also achieved success in national, state, and local politics, and their numbers in the House of Representatives continue to increase.

Planning

Cross-Curricular Connections

Math Connection *(p. 4)*

Use the population figures to have students calculate the percentage of Spanish speakers from a certain city by comparing the information to all the cities or countries listed. For example, Buenos Aires represents 16.7 percent of Spanish speakers from all the listed cities, and 3.8 percent from all the countries. If necessary, ask students to bring calculators to class the day before this activity.

Geography Connection *(p. 4)*

In pairs, have one student call out the different countries shown on the graph as the other locates them on the maps in the front of their books (pp. XIV–XVII). Then have them reverse roles, in which one student says a country and the other says the capital. Have the names of countries and capitals on index cards for practice during the school year.

Art Connection *(p. 8)*

Get together with the art teacher to show slides of examples of Mayan weavings or have students create a Mayan-style weaving, painting, or paper *mola* (decorative, hand-sewn blouse inserts embroidered by reverse appliqué, a technique in which patterns are cut out and stitched over other fabrics). Check with the librarian for picture resources.

el Primer paso

You are about to start on a wonderful journey through the Spanish-speaking world. To help get you off to a good start, this chapter, *El primer paso*, contains:

- **P** Presentations of useful, everyday vocabulary so that you can start using Spanish right away
- **A** Activities to introduce you to the rich cultures of the Spanish-speaking world
- **S** Strategies to help you make sense of what you hear and read
- **O** Opportunities to make new friends and understand your own language and culture better

Celebrando una fiesta en Pasto, Colombia

1

Cultural Notes 

Language Arts Connection *(p. 10)*

Assign portions of the glossary in the back of the book to groups or pairs of students. Have them look for cognates and note the spelling differences between the Spanish and English. For example: *-ología* and *-ology; -dad* and *-ty; -mente* and *-ly.*

Spanish in Your Community

How has Hispanic culture influenced your community or a nearby one? Where does one need to know Spanish? Have small groups of students brainstorm ideas and then develop lists. If students have difficulty, you might suggest broad categories under which they can supply specific examples. Encourage students to check with parents or older siblings for information. Groups can then share their findings with the class.

(pp. XVIII–1, photo)
Pasto, founded in 1539, is a commercial center and is especially well known for woolen hats and textiles manufactured by the indigenous population. *Pastusos,* or residents of Pasto, Nariño department, put on an extravagant annual festival and parade including floats *(carrozas de procesiones)* like the one in this photo. Over 200,000 people live in this city located on a high plateau in southwestern Colombia, 76 miles from the Ecuadorian border.

Introduce

Teaching Suggestions

At the beginning of every chapter there is a set of student objectives, in addition to a list of communicative objectives on the first Teacher's page *(see p. 1A)*. You may wish to share these with your students as a checklist come assessment time.

See the Projects for Proficiency BLMs for activity ideas that you may elect to use throughout the chapter. You may also wish to give students a copy of the Textbook Inventory List. This will help them become familiarized with their own pupil books.

 **¡Piénsalo bien!**

Play

 **Video Activity A**

Estudiantes en Barcelona, España

Options

Strategies for Reaching All Students

Students Needing Extra Help

Students who have had learning problems are often intimidated by a foreign language. This opening section gives you an opportunity to calm their fears with non-threatening activities.

Cultural Notes 

(p. 2, photo)
High-school students in Barcelona, Spain. As recently as 1965, Spain had a centralized educational system that provided secondary schooling to only 38 percent of its youth. In 1985, after a series of educational reforms, this figure had risen dramatically to 89 percent. Women made the greatest gains as a result of these reforms, with their enrollment in secondary schools rising from 29 percent in 1965 to 91 percent in 1985.

el Primer paso

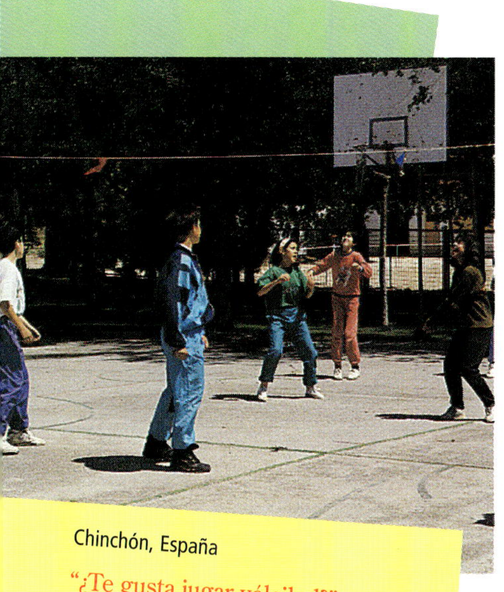

Chinchón, España

"¿Te gusta jugar vóleibol?"

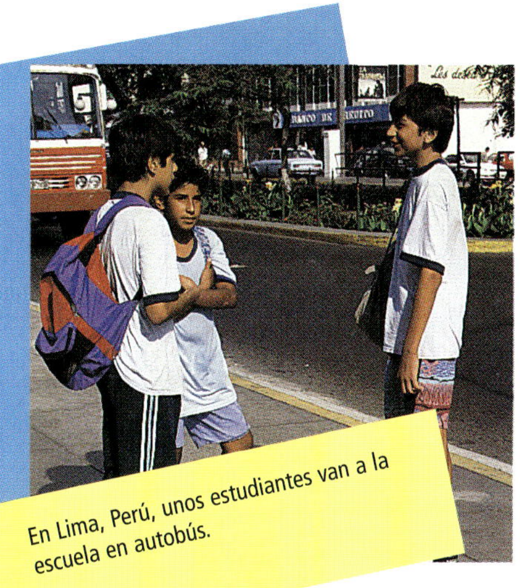

En Lima, Perú, unos estudiantes van a la escuela en autobús.

OBJECTIVES

At the end of this chapter, you will be able to:

- talk about the influence of the Spanish language and the cultures of the Spanish-speaking world
- greet people and introduce yourself
- ask how someone is feeling and tell how you are
- ask where someone is from and tell where you are from
- say good-by
- use the Spanish alphabet to spell
- use numbers to count and tell your age, phone number, and the date
- ask questions and respond to requests in the classroom
- use your textbook to help you learn Spanish

Using the Video

This chapter's video provides an overview of the video series and introduces the *En vivo* hosts: Alexander in Miami, Karina in Guadalajara, and Gracia and Jorge in Madrid. Alexander interviews Spanish-speaking patrons at Miami's Bayside Marketplace, asking them about their cultural backgrounds and interests.

Before students watch the video, ask them to predict what it will be about.

For future chapters, you may want to show the first segment of the video as an introduction to the chapter theme, the second segment as an introduction to chapter vocabulary, and the third segment as reinforcement. Encourage students to watch and understand. Remind them that the video will be shown various times and that they may not understand every word at first. Replay the video segments, each time asking students to listen to or watch for something different.

Video segment 1: For more teaching suggestions, see the Video Teacher's Guide.

(p. 3, top photo)
The quiet town of Chinchón (pop. 4,000) is a pleasant destination for people wishing to escape Madrid's big-city pace. Chinchón is an old town, with narrow streets radiating out from the Plaza Mayor. Its most famous church dates from the sixteenth and seventeenth centuries. A painting completed by the great Spanish artist Francisco de Goya hangs in the church. Tourists may stay in the Parador, a seventeenth-century convent that has been converted into a hotel.

(p. 3, bottom photo)
While these young men are standing on a street corner in Lima, Peru, their clothing style is international. Like young people everywhere, they enjoy wearing sports shoes, t-shirts, sweat pants, and shorts. Sports heroes play an important role in popular culture, and professional athletes influence the way we dress to the point that we may select familiar brand names based on who wears them. Athletic clothing has now become ubiquitous with young people.

Present & Apply

Cultural Objective

- To discuss the influence of Spanish language and culture

Vocabulario para conversar

Play

Step

Video Activity B

Using the Video

Video segment 2: See the Video Teacher's Guide.

Background Information

The names of countries, Spanish names, Spanish alphabet, and classroom expressions presented in this chapter are for recognition only.

Current usage dictates the use of the country's name without a definite article *(Perú* rather than *el Perú,* for example). In this book, names of countries will appear without the definite article, with the exceptions of *El Salvador, la República Dominicana,* and *los Estados Unidos.*

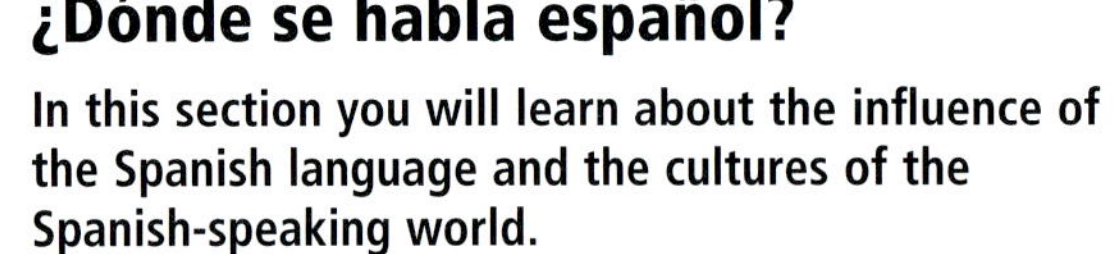

Vocabulario para conversar

¿Dónde se habla español?

In this section you will learn about the influence of the Spanish language and the cultures of the Spanish-speaking world.

Countries with the largest Spanish-speaking populations

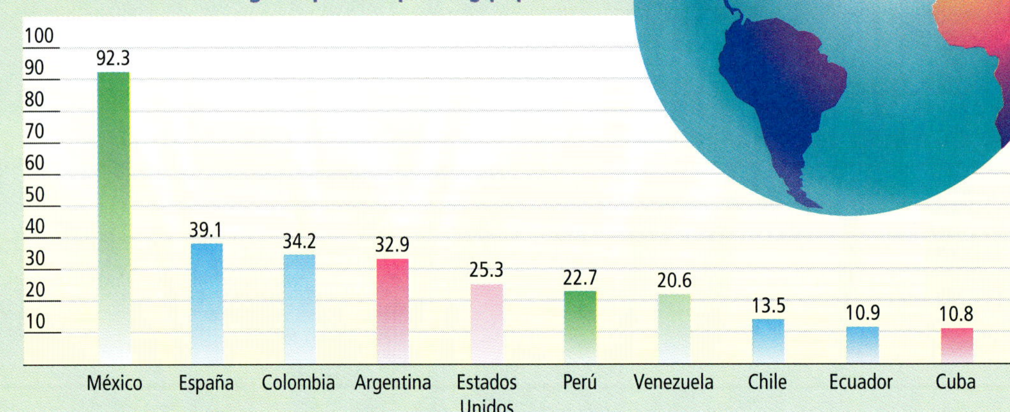

Numbers shown in millions

Cities with the largest Spanish-speaking populations

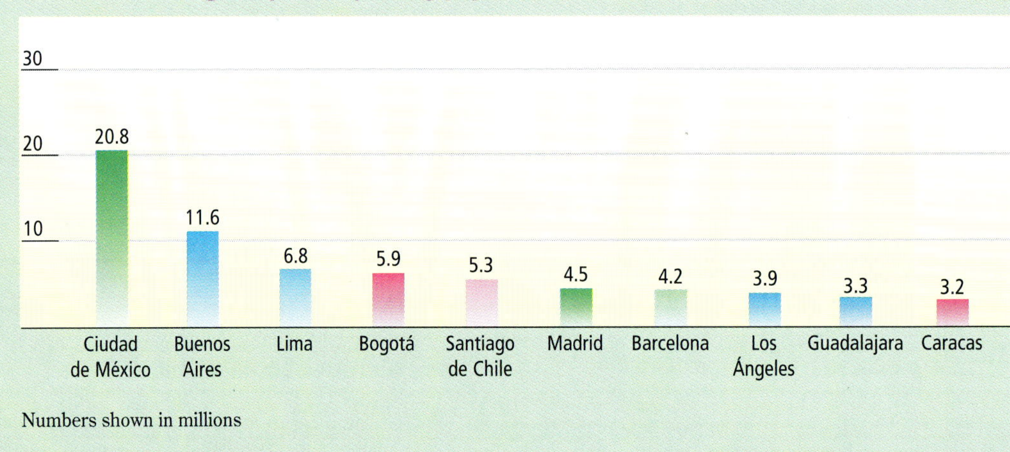

Numbers shown in millions

Options

Strategies for Reaching All Students

Students Needing Extra Help

Review basic graph-reading skills. Have students locate the countries listed in the top graph on p. 4 on the maps in the front of their books (pp. XIV–XVII) or on a wall map. In addition, review the location and what countries comprise North America, Central America, and South America.

Ex. C: Many students are so used to these words that they don't realize that they are borrowed from another language.

Ex. D: Emphasize the word *cognate.* Tell students that a cognate is a tool for helping them understand the meaning of words. Say the Spanish words aloud so students can hear the difference in pronunciation from English.

Explain that accent marks appear only over vowels. Tell students to omit the dot over the *i* when adding an accent mark. Have them practice writing inverted exclamation marks and question marks. For the question marks, tell them to start at the top and draw a dot, a vertical line, and then a *c: ¿.* Have them practice the direction of accent marks, from top to bottom.

A Work with a partner or in a group. Look at the graph of the countries with the largest Spanish-speaking populations. Where does the United States fall in rank order?

Now look at the graph of the cities. Can you find a U.S. city? Where does it fall in rank order?

B Which fact was most surprising to you or your partner or group? Which facts did you know before you saw these graphs?

C We use many words in English that come from Spanish. You probably already know some of these. Can you add more words to this list?

Animals: armadillo, pinto
Buildings: adobe, patio
Clothing: sombrero, chaps
Expressions: olé, adiós
Foods: salsa, tortilla
Western terms: rodeo, lariat
Geography: mesa, canyon
Weather: hurricane, tornado
Music/Dance: mariachi, tango
People: amigo, hombre
Place names: Amarillo, Los Ángeles, Colorado, Nevada

D We call Spanish a Romance language because it comes from Latin, the language of the Romans. Latin had a great influence on English too, so there are many words in Spanish that look and/or sound similar to English words. These are called *cognates*. Take advantage of this!

Can you figure out the meaning of these Spanish words?

- *aplicación*
- *béisbol*
- *clase*
- *conexión*
- *conversar*
- *delicioso*
- *estudiante*
- *fabuloso*
- *farmacia*
- *laboratorio*
- *septiembre*
- *vocabulario*

The word *ojo* means "eye" in Spanish. It is a reminder to pay attention. Whenever you see ¡OJO! you should look carefully because you will find important information.

Look again at the title of this section. What do you notice about the punctuation? In Spanish, both exclamations ¡. . . ! and questions ¿. . . ? have beginning and ending marks. The beginning marks let you know that what follows should be read as a question or an exclamation. You may also have noticed an accent mark on the o in *Dónde.* Your teacher will explain the use and importance of accents.

Teaching Suggestions

The Teaching Suggestions include hints to ensure success for *all* students, even in mixed-ability classes.

To enhance the discussion of Spanish-speaking populations in the U.S., bring in statistical information, such as population projections prepared by the Census Bureau, found in almanacs.

Point out the meanings of the place names: Amarillo (yellow); Los Ángeles (the angels); Colorado (red); Nevada (snow-covered)

Answers

A the U.S., fifth / Los Angeles, eighth

B Answers will vary, but students may be surprised to find that the U.S. ranks so high.

C Some possible answers: *animals:* llama, condor, puma, bronco; *buildings:* veranda, hacienda, ranch, cabana; *clothing:* brocade, serape; *expressions:* compadre, hombre, gusto; *foods:* enchilada, chocolate; *western terms:* corral; *geography:* sierra; *weather:* monsoon, tropical; *music / dance:* rumba, castanet; *people:* señorita, padre; *place names:* Montana, Florida

D Assist students as needed.

Cultural Notes

Enrichment

As a written assignment, have students research a city or town near them that has a significant Spanish-speaking population. Ask them to include such census data as the estimated size, countries of origin, and average age of that population. Your school or area library can assist with this information. On a map of your state, have students look for any Spanish place names. Check the dictionary to see if the name is or isn't of Spanish origin.

(p. 5, background photo)
Santiago Sacatepéquez, a small town near Guatemala City, hosts the *festival de barriletes,* or giant kite festival, every year on the first of November. Thousands of kites (detail shown here) fill the skies above this town as Guatemalans from all parts of the country show off their kite-building talents. *(See also p. II for more information.)*

Apply

Teaching Suggestions

To prepare for the discussion of professions, post pictures of people working at the jobs mentioned on this page. (One possible source for these images would be a primary-school coloring book on careers.) Label each picture in Spanish. Help students pronounce the names of the occupations, since some students may be tempted to pronounce cognates as they know them in English. You may also wish to include the professions of the parents of some of your students.

Answers

E List: actor, actress; architect; astronaut; banker; carpenter; chauffeur; scientist; dentist; photographer; engineer; mechanic; doctor; pilot; professor; secretary

Photo captions: *arqueólogo* (archaeologist); *policía* (police officer); *veterinario* (veterinarian); *política* (politician)

Answers will vary. / Answers may include: delivering newpapers, walking dogs, mowing lawns, babysitting, tutoring, volunteering at a hospital. If any of these jobs are in a Spanish-speaking community, knowing Spanish would be especially helpful, because communication with the "customer" or the person who hired you is essential.

E Look at these photos and read the captions.

Can you figure out what these professions are in English? Here is an additional list for you to practice with:

el actor / la actriz
el arquitecto / la arquitecta
el / la astronauta
el banquero / la banquera
el carpintero / la carpintera
el / la chofer
el científico / la científica
el / la dentista
el fotógrafo / la fotógrafa
el ingeniero / la ingeniera
el mecánico / la mecánica
el médico / la médica
el piloto / la pilota
el profesor / la profesora
el secretario / la secretaria

"Soy arqueólogo y soy de Honduras."

"Soy policía y soy de México."

"Soy veterinario y soy de Ecuador."

- With a partner, discuss why knowing Spanish would be valuable in at least five of these careers. Be prepared to explain your reasons to the class.
- With a partner, make a list of six popular jobs or volunteer positions that students might have. Are there summer jobs in which knowing Spanish would be especially helpful? Which ones? Why?

"Me llamo Lulu Flores. Soy de Texas y soy política."

You have made a great decision to study Spanish.
Let's take it *PASO A PASO*, step by step.
You'll be communicating in Spanish very soon.

Options

Strategies for Reaching All Students

Enrichment

Bring in photocopies of the classified ads page from a Spanish-language newspaper. Have students look for cognates.
For another activity, have students name adults they know who use Spanish at work. Perhaps some of your students know someone in the school who speaks Spanish.
Invite professionals from the community to speak about the importance of knowing Spanish in the workplace.

Sección 2

Vocabulario para conversar

¿Cómo te llamas?

Here are some words you will need to greet people, ask their names, introduce yourself, and say how you are. To help you understand the conversations, look at the pictures and think of what people usually say when they meet.

You will need to learn both the new words that are pictured and the words in *También necesitas . . .* Writing words down will help you remember them, but be sure to copy them carefully. You could make flashcards with the Spanish word on one side and a picture or the English word on the other. Practice these with a classmate. If you practice with family members, maybe they can learn some Spanish too! You will find that practicing words for just a few minutes every day is the best way to learn them. Don't wait until the day before a test.

También necesitas . . .

Mucho gusto.	*Pleased / Nice to meet you.*
Igualmente.	*Likewise.*
Muy bien.	*Very well.*
Así, así.	*So-so.*

También necesitas . . . means "you also need . . ." This section gives you additional words and phrases to help expand your conversations.

Present

Chapter Theme
Greetings

Communicative Objectives
- To greet people and say good-by
- To tell how you feel
- To ask someone's name and tell your name
- To acknowledge introductions

Transparency 1

Vocabulary Art BLMs

Pronunciation Tape P-1

Teaching Suggestions
Preparing students to speak: Use one or two options from each of the categories of Comprehensible Input, Physical Response, or Limited Verbal Response. For a complete explanation of these categories and some sample activities, see pp. T18–T19 of this Teacher's Edition.

Explain the use of punctuation marks at the beginning of questions and exclamations. Elicit how these provide a clue about the type of sentence that follows, including intonation and expression.

Cultural Notes 

(p. 6, top left photo)
Ornate stone carvings of deities and hieroglyphs appear on the structures at Copán, a Mayan ruin dating from the Classic period (A.D. 250–900). Copán, located in western Honduras, is one of Central America's most important Mayan sites. During recent years an international team of archaeologists has conducted extensive excavations there.

(p. 6, bottom photo)
In recent decades, increasing numbers of women have entered careers that traditionally were not available to them, including that of elected official. This photo shows Lulu Flores campaigning for state representative in Texas. In 1994, more than 1,600 Latinas held publicly elected positions in the U.S. These women included two members of Congress: Ileana Ros-Lehtinen (R-Florida) and Lucille Roybal-Allard (D-Calif.).

Present & Practice

Teaching Suggestions

Have students make cardboard name plates or tags to display on their desks. You may wish to use large envelopes to record their names, as these could be decorated by students. Punch holes in the envelopes and have students keep them in three-ring binders. Use their name plates for spelling practice later in the chapter.

Class Starter Review

On the day after students have chosen the Spanish name they might use in class, have them ask three classmates their names. On a subsequent day, have students ask three classmates how they are feeling. You or a volunteer may want to take attendance every day using students' Spanish names.

Teaching Suggestions

Every chapter in this book has an Organizer, found in the *Practice Workbook.* The purpose of the Organizer is to provide all students with access to vocabulary and grammar points. It can be used as a type of clipboard sheet of important information they will be filling in so that they can perform the exercises and activities in the chapter. Begin the vocabulary section of the Organizer.

Here is a list of common names in Spanish. You might want to choose one that is equivalent to yours, or another name that you prefer to use in class. If your name is not on the list, you might choose your middle name or a name that starts with the same sound as yours. In which list would you look for your name, *muchachos* or *muchachas*? Look at the names for a clue.

Nombres de muchachos

Adán
Agustín
Alejandro (Ale)
Andrés
Antonio (Toño)
Armando
Arturo
Benito
Benjamín
Bernardo
Carlos (Chacho, Cacho)
Claudio
Cristian
Cristóbal
Daniel (Dani)
David
Eduardo (Edu)
Emilio
Enrique (Quique)
Ernesto
Esteban
Federico
Felipe
Fernando
Francisco (Paco)
Gerardo (Gérar)
Gonzalo
Gregorio
Guillermo (Guille)
Ignacio (Nacho)
Jaime
Jesús
Jorge
Jorge Luis
José (Pepe)
José Eduardo
José Emilio
José Luis
Juan (Juancho)
Juan Carlos (Juanca, Juaca)
Julio
Julio César
Luis (Lucho)
Luis Miguel
Manuel (Manolo)
Marco Antonio
Marcos
Mario
Mateo
Miguel
Miguel Ángel
Nicolás (Nico)
Óscar
Pablo
Patricio
Pedro
Rafael (Rafa)
Ramón
Raúl
Ricardo
Roberto (Beto)
Rodrigo
Samuel
Santiago (Santi)
Sergio
Timoteo (Timo)
Tomás (Tomi)
Vicente
Víctor

Nombres de muchachas

Alejandra
Alicia
Ana
Ana Luisa
Ana María
Ángela
Bárbara
Carmen
Carolina (Caro)
Catalina (Cata)
Cecilia (Ceci)
Clara
Claudia
Cristina (Tina)
Daniela
Diana
Dolores (Lola)
Elena
Elisa
Emilia
Esperanza
Ester
Eva
Gloria
Guadalupe (Lupe)
Guillermina
Inés
Irene
Isabel (Chabela, Isa)
Josefina
Juana
Julia
Laura
Lorena
Lourdes
Lucía
Luisa
Luz
Magdalena
Margarita
María
María del Carmen
María Elena
María Eugenia
María José (Marijó)
María Luisa
María Soledad
María Teresa (Maite, Marité)
Mariana
Marisol
Marta
Mónica (Moni)
Olivia
Patricia (Pati)
Pilar
Raquel
Rebeca
Reina
Rocío
Rosa (Rosi)
Rosario
Sara (Saruca)
Soledad
Susana (Susa)
Teresa (Tere)
Verónica (Vero)
Victoria
Virginia

Options

Strategies for Reaching All Students

Spanish-Speaking Students

Have students add names to the list: *Haz una lista de otros nombres posibles. Empecemos a conversar:* Pair bilingual with non-bilingual students whenever possible for oral exercises. Bilingual students can model pronunciation.

Students Needing Extra Help

Encourage students to use their Organizers often. If necessary, explain why students will be using Spanish names. (For example: John might feel funny speaking Spanish, but Juan never does.)

Empecemos a conversar

In these exercises you will create conversations according to a model. With a partner, take turns being *Estudiante A* and *Estudiante B.* Use the words that are cued or given in the boxes to replace the underlined words in the example.  means you can make your own choices in your conversation. When it is your turn to be *Estudiante B,* try to answer truthfully.

¡Ojo! Empecemos means "Let's begin." What do you think Empecemos a conversar means?

1 Estudiante A —*¡Hola! Me llamo Ana. ¿Cómo te llamas?*
Estudiante B —*Me llamo Pablo.*
Estudiante A —*Mucho gusto, Pablo.*
Estudiante B —*Igualmente, Ana.*

Estudiante A | Estudiante B

Did you use your own name in the conversation? Now have the conversation again with five other classmates. Play both roles. Your teacher may ask you to tell your classmates' names, so you may want to write them down.

¡Ojo! You might want to look over the exercises first in order to get the idea of how to do them. If you need help, review the *Vocabulario para conversar* or *También necesitas . . .* sections.

2 A —*Buenos días. ¿Cómo estás, Inés?*
B —*Muy bien, gracias. ¿Y tú?*
A —*Así, así.*

Estudiante A | Estudiante B

Did you keep using the same answers for how you feel? Repeat this conversation with four other classmates. Show by your expression and your voice how a person might say *"muy bien"* and *"así, así."*

Ex. 1: Choose a student to help you model the dialogue. This will make it clear from the beginning that the dialogues in the *Empecemos a conversar* throughout the text are active, involving two contributing students as partners. Point out the use of dashes before each line in the model dialogue. Explain that these markers indicate a dialogue exchange. Remind students to reverse roles with their partner as they work through the exercises. Encourage them to give logical responses when appropriate. You may wish to set time limits for their partner practice. Establish a cue or signal for students to let them know when an activity is to end.

Multicultural Perspectives

Mexico is the world's largest Spanish-speaking country. Not all its citizens speak Spanish, however. Several million people speak indigenous languages, which may include Maya, Mixtec, Nahuatl, Otomí, Tarascan, or Zapotec. Ask students to share their knowledge of languages in other cultures.

Answers: Empecemos a conversar

1–2 Dialogues will vary.

 **Practice Wkbk. P-1**

 **Writing Activities**

 **Comm. Act. BLM P-1**

Cultural Notes

(p. 8, background photo)
Guatemalan fabrics, renowned for their intricate patterns and vibrant colors, are some of the most prized textiles in the world. Artisans employ a variety of techniques including backstrap weaving, embroidery, knitting or a tie-dye technique called *ikat* or *jaspé* to produce the textiles. Chichicastenango, in the province of El Quiché, is famous for its Thursday and Sunday markets where many fine textiles are sold. Professional buyers often visit "Chichi" to purchase items for export to North America and Europe.

Present & Practice

Chapter Theme
Greetings, leave-takings, and introductions

Communicative Objectives
- To greet people and say good-by
- To tell how you feel
- To ask for and give information
- To say thank you

 **Transparency 2**

 **Vocabulary Art BLMs**

 **Pronunciation Tape P-2**

Teaching Suggestions
Preparing students to speak: Use one or two options from each of the categories of Comprehensible Input, Physical Response, or Limited Verbal Response. For a complete explanation of these categories and some sample activities, see pp. T18–T19 of this Teacher's Edition.

To assess oral skills, walk around the class with your grade sheet (see the front section of the Assessment Program book) monitoring various pairs of students during paired practice activities. Have students work with the same

Sección 3

Vocabulario para conversar

¿De dónde eres?

Here are some more words and expressions you will need to greet people and tell where you are from.

¡Ojo!

Do you remember *¿Y tú?* and *¿Cómo estás?* There is another way to say "How are you?" in Spanish. We use *usted* to mean "you" to show respect when speaking to an older person. In writing, *usted* is often abbreviated *Ud.* And what do you think the abbreviations *Sr., Sra.,* and *Srta.* stand for?

También necesitas . . .

¿Qué tal?	*How's it going?*
¿Y usted?	*And you?*
Hasta luego.	*See you later.*
Buenas noches.*	*Good night.*

¿Y qué quiere decir . . . ?

sí	o	señor	señorita
no	Adiós	señora	

* We usually use *Buenas noches* in the evening to say good-by.

Options

Strategies for Reaching All Students

Spanish-Speaking Students
Ask: *¿A quién le hablas de "Ud."? ¿A quién le hablas de "tú"?*

Students Needing Extra Help
Introduce the idea of formality with titles and levels of speech by role playing with props, such as hats or other articles of clothing.
Ex. 1: If necessary, help students with the expressions *Soy de El Salvador, de Perú, de los Estados Unidos, de la República Dominicana.*

Enrichment
Explain that the important distinction between "you" formal *(usted)* and "you" familiar *(tú)* still exists in many languages. In English, "one" is still used in place of the indefinite pronoun "you" in formal situations. For example, instead of saying "It's a good book, if *you* like sports," formal usage dictates saying "It's a good book, if *one* likes sports."

Empecemos a conversar

For Exercise 1, refer to the map below.

1 A —*¡Hola! Me llamo Carlos. ¿Y tú?*
B —*Me llamo María. ¿De dónde eres?*
A —*Soy de Bolivia. ¿Y tú?*
B —*Soy de Guatemala.*

Estudiante A

Estudiante B

Did you use your own name and country? Now repeat this dialogue with three classmates. Pretend to be someone else, and use different Spanish names and countries.

2 Now repeat the conversation with five classmates, using a city name from page 4.

On page 10, look at the words in the section titled *¿Y qué quiere decir . . . ?* This title asks the question "And what does . . . mean?" Remember that some words that look or sound like English words are probably cognates. Other words are closely related to words you have already learned. The words in this section should be easy to learn. What do you think they mean?

11

partner *(compañero[a])* for at least part, if not the entire chapter.

¿Y qué quiere decir . . . ? This section will appear from time to time in the *También necesitas . . .* to facilitate language learning through the use of cognates and word families. Use comprehensible input to introduce this new vocabulary without giving students an English equivalent, unless necessary.

Point out the two ways of saying "How are you?" and the concept of respect or formality in the Spanish language. This is presented later in Chap. 2.

Have students choose an index card on which you have written the names of the Spanish speaking countries and say: *(Yo) soy de* ___. Encourage them to choose a country that hasn't already been chosen. (You may wish to set this activity in a context. For example, students could be representatives in a contest or convention.)

Answers: Empecemos a conversar

1–2 Answers will vary. You may wish to use Transparencies 86–89 for the maps of Spanish-speaking countries with the Spanish names from the list on p. 8. Students can then choose their name and their country of origin at the same time.

Learning Spanish Through Action

STAGING VOCABULARY: *Apunten, Señalen*
MATERIALS: transparency of a map of the Spanish-speaking world (Transparencies 86–89) or a wall map of the same areas
DIRECTIONS: Tell students to imagine that they are from the country you announce. Have them point to the country and ask: *¿De dónde eres?* They should respond orally. (As an alternative, cut out shapes of the countries from construction paper so that students can hold each one.)

Apply

Teaching Suggestions

The *Empecemos a leer y a escribir* sections serve as an opportunity to help develop students' reading and writing skills. You may wish to use them as homework assignments throughout the chapters. Emphasize to students the importance of keeping track of their progress. If these sections are done in class, have them work in groups to figure out the answers, but have individuals write their answers on a separate sheet.

Answers: Empecemos a leer y a escribir

1–3 Answers will vary.

4 Answers will vary, but may include: *buenos días, buenas tardes, buenas noches, ¿cómo está usted?, ¿cómo estás?, ¡hola!, ¿qué tal?*

5 adiós, hasta luego

6 Answers will vary, but look for the *usted* form: *Buenas tardes, señora. ¿Cómo está usted?*

7 a. *no;* b. *no;* c. *sí;* d. *no;* e. *no*

 **Practice Wkbk. P-2**

 **Audio Activity P.1**

 **Writing Activities**

Empecemos a leer y a escribir

Responde en español.

1 ¿Cómo te llamas?

2 ¿Cómo estás?

3 ¿De dónde eres?

¡Ojo! Do you remember what *Empecemos* means? *Empecemos a leer y a escribir* means "Let's begin to read and write."

4 List four ways to greet someone.

5 What are two ways to say good-by?

6 How do you greet an older person and ask how he or she is feeling?

7 Read the following conversation, then respond to each statement with *sí* or *no*.

Profesor: Buenas tardes. Soy el señor Soto. Y tú, ¿cómo te llamas?

Estudiante: Me llamo Miguel Ángel Portillo. Mucho gusto.

Profesor: Igualmente. ¿De dónde eres? ¿De los Estados Unidos?

Estudiante: No, soy de Guatemala. ¿Es Ud. de Argentina o de Chile?

Profesor: Yo soy de Uruguay. Adiós, Miguel Ángel. Hasta luego.

Estudiante: Adiós, profesor.

a. The people in the dialogue know each other.
b. The teacher is a woman.
c. We know the last names of both people.
d. The student is from the United States.
e. The conversation takes place in the morning.

In this section you will write your answers in Spanish. You can refer to *Vocabulario para conversar* and *También necesitas . . .* or to the *Resumen* at the end of the chapter to check your spelling.

You may want to read the passage twice, once to get the general meaning, and a second time to try to figure out any important words you don't know. Often you can guess the meaning of a word just by how it is used. YOU DON'T NEED TO UNDERSTAND EVERY WORD TO GET THE OVERALL MEANING.

***¡Felicitaciones!* You have now begun to read in Spanish.**

Options

Strategies for Reaching All Students

Spanish-Speaking Students

Empecemos a leer y a escribir: Ask students if they know other ways to say hello or good-by: *¿Sabes otras maneras de saludar a alguien o de despedirte? ¿Cuáles son?* Have students respond orally so others can hear and benefit from the exchange. Write the responses on the chalkboard and have students copy the information.

Students Needing Extra Help

Have students create a chart with four columns with headings: Greetings, Ways to Ask How Someone Is, Responses, and Ways to End a Conversation. Have students share them in class and create a class chart for everyone to use, or, photocopy the best student chart for all students to use. Display the chart until your students feel comfortable using the expressions. Encourage students to copy and / or use the posted charts.

Tell students to jot down items mentioned in the activities and then use this list when their turn comes. They should list the items in their notebooks for future reference. Check their Organizers or notebooks from time to time for completeness and accuracy.

Sección 4

Vocabulario para conversar

La sala de clases

También necesitas . . .

¿Cómo se dice ___ en español?	*How do you say ___ in Spanish?*
Se dice ___.	*It's said ___.*
¿Cómo se escribe ___?	*How do you spell ___?*
Se escribe ___.	*It's spelled ___.*

Present

Chapter Theme

The classroom

Communicative Objectives

- To ask for and give information
- To talk about your classroom

 **Transparency 3**

 **Vocabulary Art BLMs**

 **Pronunciation Tape P-3**

Teaching Suggestions

Preparing students to speak: Use one or two options from each of the categories of Comprehensible Input, Physical Response, or Limited Verbal Response. For a complete explanation of these categories and some sample activities, see pp. T16–T17 of this Teacher's Edition.

Vocabulario para conversar: You may want to informally introduce *el lápiz* as one of the classroom items. *Lápices* (and *marcadores)* are formally introduced in Chap. 2.

Point out the gender differences in the vocabulary words. One way to help students remember gender is to have them color-code flashcards. You may wish to laminate the cards for future use.

Present

Background Information

In April of 1994, the Association of Spanish Language Academies *(La Real Academia)* voted 17–1 to eliminate *ch* and *ll* as separate letters from the Spanish alphabet. The change was made primarily to simplify dictionaries and make the language more computer compatible. Spelling, pronunciation, and usage are not, of course, affected.

Some sources indicate that the *rr* is only a sound and not a distinct letter of the alphabet. We have opted to retain the *rr* as a letter.

Teaching Suggestions

Have students look in an older dictionary to find examples of words in the *ch* and *ll* sections and compare their placement in the *Vocabulario español-inglés* section at the back of their books.

Tell students to be prepared to spell their Spanish name using their name tags. The following day, use the Spanish alphabet to spell a student's Spanish name. Ask this student to stand if he or she doesn't recognize the name, and have another student say *Es* ___.

For the question on this page regarding the *ll* sound, students should be able to answer with *llama* and *me llamo* ___ *(¿cómo te llamas?).* Assist as needed.

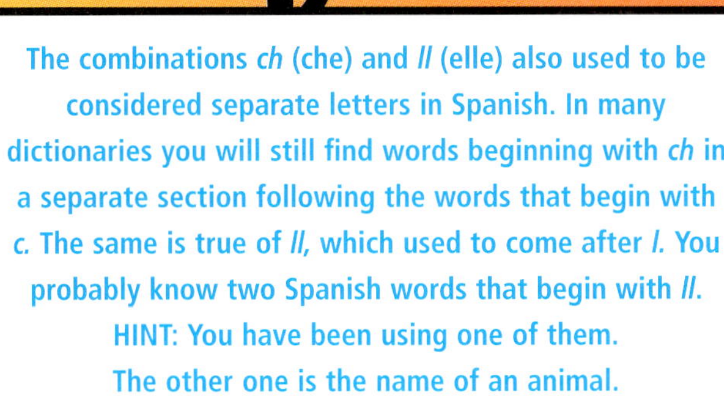

The combinations *ch* (che) and *ll* (elle) also used to be considered separate letters in Spanish. In many dictionaries you will still find words beginning with *ch* in a separate section following the words that begin with *c*. The same is true of *ll*, which used to come after *l*. You probably know two Spanish words that begin with *ll*. HINT: You have been using one of them. The other one is the name of an animal.

EL ALFABETO

a	(a)	o	(o)
b	(be)	p	(pe)
c	(ce)	q	(cu)
d	(de)	r	(ere)
e	(e)	rr	(erre)
f	(efe)	s	(ese)
g	(ge)	t	(te)
h	(hache)	u	(u)
i	(i)	v	(ve *or* uve)
j	(jota)	w	(doble ve *or* doble u)
k	(ka)	x	(equis)
l	(ele)	y	(i griega *or* ye)
m	(eme)	z	(zeta)
n	(ene)		
ñ	(eñe)		

¡Ojo!

The Spanish alphabet has two more letters than the English alphabet. Can you find them?

Options

Strategies for Reaching All Students

Enrichment

Tell students that when they are spelling aloud, they should say *acento* after a vowel that has an accent mark on it: *país se escribe pe-a-i acento-ese.* You might also have them say *mayúscula* after a capital letter: *Manolo se escribe eme mayúscula-a-ene-o-ele-o.* Give students a list of words that contain accent marks so that they can practice.

If students ask, tell them that all the letters of the Spanish alphabet are feminine.

Learning Spanish Through Action

STAGING VOCABULARY: *Digan, Levanten*

MATERIALS: sheets of paper labeled with the letters of the Spanish alphabet

DIRECTIONS: Pass a letter or letters to each student. As you recite the letters, have students raise their sheets, pronouncing the letters as they do so. As a variation, have students stand as you say or spell out a word.

Empecemos a conversar

1 A —*¿Cómo se dice "pen" en español?*
B —*Bolígrafo.*

Estudiante A — Estudiante B

2 A —*¿Cómo se escribe mesa?*
B —*Se escribe eme-e-ese-a.*

Estudiante A — Estudiante B

a. b. c. d.

Have the following conversation with four classmates. As they spell their names, you write them down from dictation.

3 A —*¿Cómo te llamas?*
B —*Me llamo Esteban Rodríguez.*
A —*¿Cómo se escribe tu nombre?*
B —*E-ese-te-e-be-a-ene. Ere-o-de-ere-i-acento-ge-u-e-zeta.*

Practice

Answers: Empecemos a conversar

1 ESTUDIANTE A
a. ¿Cómo se dice *table* en español?
b. . . . *chalkboard* . . .
c. . . . *book* . . .
d. . . . *teacher* . . .
e. . . . *paper* . . .
f. . . . *classmates (students)* . . .
g. . . . *student desk* . . .
h. . . . *student (classmate)* . . .

ESTUDIANTE B
a. Mesa.
b. Pizarra.
c. Libro.
d. Profesor.
e. Hoja de papel.
f. Compañeros (Estudiantes).
g. Pupitre.
h. Estudiante (Compañera).

2 ESTUDIANTE A
a. ¿Cómo se escribe *libro?*
b. . . . *pupitre?*
c. . . . *pizarra?*
d. Questions will vary.

ESTUDIANTE B
a. Se escribe *ele-i-be-ere-o.*
b. . . . *pe-u-pe-i-te-ere-e.*
c. . . . *pe-i-zeta-a-erre-a.*
d. Answers will vary.

3 Dialogues will vary.

 **Practice Wkbk. P-3**

 **Writing Activities**

Present

Chapter Theme

Calendar expressions and numbers 0–31

Communicative Objectives

- To ask for and give information
- To say when something takes place
- To count or give dates

 **Transparencies 4–5**

 **Vocabulary Art BLMs**

 **Pronunciation Tape P-4**

Teaching Suggestions

Preparing students to speak: Use one or two options from each of the categories of Comprehensible Input, Physical Response, or Limited Verbal Response. For a complete explanation of these categories and some sample activities, see pp. T18–T19 of this Teacher's Edition.

Have students write their names and birthdays in English on slips of paper; fold the slips in half. Collect the slips of paper in a basket, choose one, and read the date aloud in Spanish. When the student hears his or her birthdate, that individual should raise his or her hand and say *Es mi cumpleaños.* If the student doesn't

Sección 5

Vocabulario para conversar

Uno, dos, tres, . . .

MARZO

el mes · la semana · el día

LUNES	MARTES	MIÉRCOLES	JUEVES	VIERNES	SÁBADO	DOMINGO
						1 UNO
2 DOS	3 TRES	4 CUATRO	5 CINCO	6 SEIS	7 SIETE	8 OCHO
9 NUEVE	10 DIEZ	11 ONCE	12 DOCE	13 TRECE	14 CATORCE	15 QUINCE
16* DIECISÉIS	17 DIECISIETE	18 DIECIOCHO	19 DIECINUEVE	20 VEINTE	21 VEINTIUNO	22 VEINTIDÓS
23 VEINTITRÉS	24 VEINTICUATRO	25 VEINTICINCO	26 VEINTISÉIS	27 VEINTISIETE	28 VEINTIOCHO	29 VEINTINUEVE
30 TREINTA	31 TREINTA Y UNO					

¡Ojo! Spanish calendars begin the week with Monday (*lunes*) and end with Sunday (*domingo*).

¡Ojo! The days of the week and months of the year do not begin with capital letters in Spanish. On calendars, however, people sometimes do capitalize them.

¿Cuándo es tu cumpleaños?

Mi cumpleaños es el 3 de diciembre.

* You will also see the numbers 16–19 written *diez y seis, diez y siete, diez y ocho, diez y nueve.* The numbers 21–29 may also be written *veinte y uno, veinte y dos,* and so on.

Options

Strategies for Reaching All Students

Students Needing Extra Help

Demonstrate on the chalkboard how *diez y seis* becomes *dieciséis.*

También necesitas . . . : Have students put these phrases in an organizer / notebook so that they will have them throughout the year for easy reference.

Learning Spanish Through Action

STAGING VOCABULARY: *Escriban, Pasen a la pizarra*

MATERIALS: cards with numbers 0–31 written on them

DIRECTIONS: Direct four to eight students to go to the chalkboard to write numbers. Show the class the card as you say the number while students at the chalkboard write the numeral(s).

Enrichment

For students' birthdays, have the class sing *Las mañanitas,* available on the tape and CD of songs.

También necesitas . . .

¿Cuántos(as) ___ hay?*	*How many ___ are there?*
¿Cuántos años tienes?	*How old are you?*
Tengo ___ años.	*I'm ___ years old.*
el año	*year*
¿Cuál es tu número de teléfono?	*What's your phone number?*
¿Cuándo es ___?	*When is ___?*
¿Cuál es la fecha de hoy?	*What's the date today?*
Hoy es ___.	*Today is ___.*
Mañana es ___.	*Tomorrow is ___.*
¿Qué día es hoy?	*What day is today?*
mi / tu cumpleaños	*my / your birthday*
el 6 de febrero	*the 6th of February / February 6*
el primero de mayo	*the first of May / May 1*
hay	*there is, there are*
mi / tu	*my / your*
por favor	*please*

¡Ojo!

We form dates using *el* + number + *de* + month. We use *primero* for "first," but we use the regular numbers for the rest of the dates: *el 9 de junio* = June 9, but *el primero de agosto* = August 1.

¿Y qué quiere decir . . . ?
cero
en

* We say *cuántos libros,* but *cuántas mesas.* We use *cuántos* with masculine nouns like *libros,* and *cuántas* with feminine nouns like *mesas.* Most nouns that use *el* are masculine and those that use *la* are feminine. You will learn more about this in Chapter 2.

respond after you say the date three times, say the student's name and repeat the date: *Javier, el dos de julio es tu cumpleaños,* and put the slip of paper back in the basket.

Class Starter Review

On the day following vocabulary presentation, you might start the class with either of these activities:
1) Have students count to ten (and later to 20 and 31), forward and backward.
2) Have students share the date of their birthday with a partner. Partners should then be prepared to share the information with the class *(El cumpleaños de ___ es ___.).*

Multicultural Perspectives

Many Catholics in Latin America and Spain not only celebrate their birthday, but their *día santo* as well. Each day of the Catholic Church calendar is dedicated to one or more saints. Many people are named after their *día santo.* For example, a girl born on December 4 might be named Bárbara because this date is *el día de Santa Bárbara.* Ask students to find out if any of them share their names with a saint. Encourage them to find out how people in other cultures celebrate birthdays. If possible, visit a local Hispanic bookstore to obtain a Saints' Day calendar in Spanish.

Practice & Apply

Teaching Suggestions

For reinforcement of vocabulary, write the days of the week and months of the year on paper plates. Distribute among students and ask them to stand in the correct order of the days or months. Repeat the following day, but in reverse order.

Answers: Empecemos a conversar

1 ESTUDIANTE A

a. cinco, diez, quince . . .
b. uno, tres, cinco . . .
c. cero, tres, seis . . .

ESTUDIANTE B

a. veinte, veinticinco, treinta . . .
b. siete, nueve, once . . .
c. nueve, doce, quince . . .

2 ESTUDIANTE A

a. ¿Cuántos pupitres hay?
b. ¿Cuántos bolígrafos . . .
c. ¿Cuántos estudiantes . . .
d. ¿Cuántas hojas de papel . . .
e. ¿Cuántas pizarras . . .

ESTUDIANTE B

a. Hay dos pupitres.
b. . . . seis bolígrafos.
c. . . . cuatro estudiantes.
d. . . . cinco hojas de papel.
e. . . . tres pizarras.

 **Audio Activity P.2**

Empecemos a conversar

1 **0, 2, 4** A — *Cero, dos, cuatro*, . . .
B — *seis, ocho, diez*, . . .

Estudiante A **Estudiante B**

a. **5, 10, 15, . . .**
b. **1, 3, 5, . . .**
c. **0, 3, 6, . . .**

2  A — *¿Cuántos libros hay?*
B — *Hay seis libros.*

Estudiante A **Estudiante B**

Options

Strategies for Reaching All Students

Spanish-Speaking Students

Empecemos a conversar: Pair bilingual with non-bilingual students.
Empecemos a leer y a escribir: Ask: *¿Cuáles son otros días de fiesta hispanos que celebras con tu familia? ¿En qué fecha se celebran?*
Have students interview family members and then later follow up with a report to the class.

Empecemos a leer y a escribir

Responde en español.

1 Find out when these popular Hispanic holidays occur and write down the dates for each of them: *el Año Nuevo* (New Year's Day), *el Día de los Reyes* (Twelfth Night / Epiphany), *el Día de la Raza* (Columbus Day), *el Día de los Muertos* (Day of the Dead / All Souls' Day), *la Navidad* (Christmas).

2 Count the following things aloud and write the answers in Spanish. Compare your answers with those of a partner.

a. books on your desk
b. girls in the class
c. countries in Central America
d. people wearing jeans
e. letters in your teacher's last name

3 Read the following sentences and rewrite them, making the necessary corrections:

a. Mi cumpleaños es el 15 de diciembre.
b. El cumpleaños de Martin Luther King es en octubre.
c. El Día de San Patricio es el 14 de enero.
d. El Día de San Valentín es en junio.
e. Chanukah es en febrero.

4 ¿Cuál es la fecha de hoy? ¿Y de mañana?

5 ¿Qué día es hoy? ¿Y mañana?

6 ¿Cuál es tu número de teléfono? ¿Y el número de teléfono de tu compañero(a) de clase?

Celebrando el Cinco de Mayo, San Francisco

Teaching Suggestions

Ex. 6: If privacy is an issue, students can use 555 as a prefix or make up a phone number.

Answers: Empecemos a leer y a escribir

1 el Año Nuevo: el primero de enero; el Día de los Reyes: el seis de enero; el Día de la Raza: el 12 de octubre; el Día de los Muertos: el dos de noviembre; la Navidad: el veinticinco de diciembre

2 Answers will vary. For item c., the answer is *siete,* if you count *Belice* (Belize).

3 If necessary, provide students with a calendar with these holidays marked on it.
a. Answers will vary.
b. El cumpleaños de Martin Luther King es en enero.
c. El Día de San Patricio es el 17 de marzo.
d. El Día de San Valentín es en febrero.
e. Chanukah es en noviembre o diciembre.

4–6 Answers will vary.

 **Practice Wkbk. P-4, P-5, P-6**

 **Writing Activities**

 **Comm. Act. BLMs P-2, P-3**

Cultural Notes

(p. 19, photo)
Mexican folk dancing at a *Cinco de Mayo* celebration in San Francisco. On May 5, 1862, invading French troops reached the city of Puebla, expecting little resistance on their way to Mexico City. At Puebla, however, they were overwhelmed by Mexican forces and forced to withdraw from battle. Although the French eventually established an empire in Mexico (1863–1867), this victory is commemorated as a national holiday.

Practice

Teaching Suggestions

Create a birthday graph by having students write their names and birthdays on self-stick removable notes. Place these notes under the months that you have written on a board or large sheet of paper. Ask: *¿Hay más estudiantes con su cumpleaños en enero o febrero? ¿Febrero o junio? ¿Cuántos hay en ___?* etc.

Answers: Comuniquemos

1–3 Dialogues will vary.

 **Todo junto A**

Play

 **Todo junto B**

Play

 **Video Activity C**

Using the Video

Video segment 3: See the Video Teacher's Guide.

Audio Activities P.3, P.4

Comuniquemos

This is another opportunity for you to use the vocabulary you've just learned.

1 In groups of six, ask each other when your birthdays are. Then tally the results to find out which month has the most birthdays. Share your group's results with the class.

A —*¿Cuándo es tu cumpleaños?*
B —*Es el cinco de julio.*

2 Role-play a conversation with a partner in which you:

- greet each other
- find out each other's names
- ask and answer how you are
- say good-by

3 How many of your classmates' phone numbers can you collect in five minutes? Once your teacher sets the clock, you're ready to begin. Remember to ask and answer in Spanish!

In the *Comuniquemos* section, you can have fun using all the language you already know. Try to use different expressions for the same ideas. ARE YOU AWARE THAT YOU ARE NOW REALLY COMMUNICATING IN SPANISH?

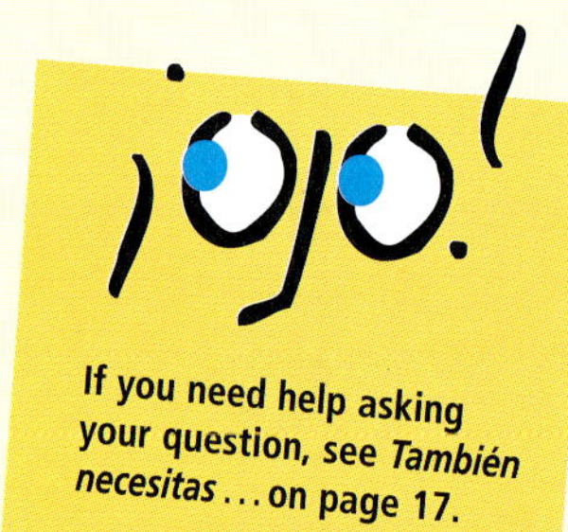

Options

Strategies for Reaching All Students

Spanish-Speaking Students

Ask students to mention any variations they know for the list of requests and instructions on pp. 21–23.

Enrichment

Play *Simón dice* with appropriate classroom commands. You may want to have a student become the caller after some practice. For another fast-paced activity, have students form a circle. The class decides on the actions for the commands. Give a command and point to a student who must then perform the action by the count of *tres.*

Cooperative Learning

Divide the class into groups of three. Provide students with an index card and tell them that they are going to assume the identity of a Hispanic American by completing some sentences. On the chalkboard, write *Me llamo* ____. Have students write out the sentence and tell them to fill in a name from the list on p. 8. After they write the sentence, have them pass their cards to

Expresiones para la clase

Por favor

Here is a list of requests and instructions. You will need to know what to do when your teacher says them, but you will **not** need to know how to say or write them.

Present

Teaching Suggestions

Present the classroom expressions from pp. 21–23 a few at a time, starting with four and adding one or two every day. (You may want to write these on strips of paper, have them laminated, and then display them around the classroom for reference.) Start with the most common commands. At your discretion, include a few more commands used in Learning Spanish Through Action: *dibuja, para, señala.* Review each time before presenting new ones. Act out each command so that students have a visual image.

Have students play *Simón dice* after you present all the expressions.

the left. On the chalkboard, write *Tengo ____ años.* Have them write out the sentence, fill in the blank with a number, and then pass their cards to the left. Finally, write *Soy de ____.* Have them write out the sentence and fill in the blank with the name of a Spanish-speaking country. Call on individual students to read their "autobiographies."

Present

Teaching Suggestions

Have pairs of students play the roles of student and teacher. The student asks permission to do something and the teacher responds appropriately.

Options

Strategies for Reaching All Students

Students Needing Extra Help

Make sure students understand each class expression by having individuals act out or mimic the expressions.

Enrichment

Have pairs of students make a set of index cards, with each card bearing one of the questions and responses on p. 23. Students can practice the material by pulling a card from the deck, reading it aloud, and having their partner give appropriate responses.

Learning Spanish Through Action

STAGING VOCABULARY: *Miren*
MATERIALS: pictures of an open window, a pencil with a broken tip, a locker, the nurse's office, the restroom door
DIRECTIONS: Hold up a picture and have students make an appropriate request and react according to your response.

Profesor(a), ¿puedo . . . ?

When you need to ask for permission to do something, you should ask in Spanish. Here are some questions that you may frequently ask in class, and some of the answers you might expect.

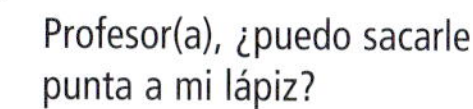

Your teacher may respond to your requests in any of the following ways:

Sí, ve (al baño, a tu armario, etc.).	*Yes, go ahead (to ___).*
Sí, ábrela / ciérrala.	*Yes, open it / close it.*
Claro.	*Of course.*
Ahora no.	*Not now.*
No, lo siento.	*No, I'm sorry.*

Multicultural Perspectives

In Spain, the federal government runs about two-thirds of all the primary and secondary schools. Approximately one out of every six students attends a school run by the Roman Catholic Church. (About 99 percent of Spain's population is Roman Catholic.) Spanish law requires that students attend school until they are 14. Ask students if they are familiar with the rules or regulations regarding school attendance in their area.

Practice Wkbk. P-7, P-8, P-9

Comm. Act. BLMs P-4, P-5

Summarize

 **Prueba**

 **Test Generator**

Viña del Mar, Chile

"¡Hola! ¿Qué tal?"

Estudiantes en Quito, Ecuador

En camino a la escuela, La Paz, Bolivia

Cultural Notes 

(p. 24, top photo)
Viña del Mar is a community with both a permanent, year-round population and a part-time population of vacationers who descend on the resort from about September 15 until March 15. Santiago residents frequently make the 85-mile trip to visit friends or family for the weekend or to rent accommodations and enjoy the beaches, restaurants, nightlife, and other amenities the area has to offer.

(p. 24, center photo)
Quito, the second-highest capital city in South America (after La Paz, Bolivia) is blessed with an agreeable climate and beautiful surroundings. Daytime temperatures range from the 60s to the lower 70s (Fahrenheit) all year long. Night temperatures cool off just enough to require a sweater. Quito lies between two Andean mountain ranges and offers a panorama of lovely scenery. Ecuador's capital has always been a market and cultural center because of its location between the coast, the *sierra,* and the rain forests.

Resumen: El primer paso

¡Fantástico! Eres el Número 1.

Use the vocabulary from this chapter to help you:

- **greet people and talk about how you and they are feeling**
- **talk about your classroom**
- **use the Spanish alphabet to spell**
- **give telephone numbers and dates**
- **tell where people come from**

to greet people and say good-by
Buenos días.
Buenas tardes.
Buenas noches.
¿Cómo está usted?
¿Cómo estás?
¡Hola!
¿Qué tal?
Adiós.
Hasta luego.

to ask someone's name and tell your name
¿Cómo te llamas?
(Yo) me llamo ___.

to acknowledge introductions
Mucho gusto.
Igualmente.
señor
señora
señorita

to ask for and give information
¿Cómo se dice ___ en español?
Se dice ___.
¿Cómo se escribe ___?
Se escribe ___.
¿Cuál es la fecha de hoy?
por favor
Hoy es ___. / Mañana es ___.
¿Cuál es tu número de teléfono?
mi / tu (cumpleaños)
¿Cuándo es ___?
el año
¿Cuántos años tienes?
Tengo ___ años.
¿Cuántos, -as ___ hay?
hay
¿De dónde eres?
(Yo) soy de ___.
¿Qué día es hoy?
es
¿Y tú? / ¿Y usted?
sí / no
o

to say when something takes place
el día / el mes / la semana
en
el + *number* + de + *month*

lunes
martes
miércoles
jueves
viernes
sábado
domingo

enero
febrero
marzo
abril
mayo
junio
julio
agosto
septiembre
octubre
noviembre
diciembre

to count or give dates
el primero de ___
cero, uno, dos, tres, cuatro, cinco, seis, siete, ocho, nueve, diez
once, doce, trece, catorce, quince, dieciséis, diecisiete, dieciocho, diecinueve, veinte
veintiuno, veintidós, veintitrés, veinticuatro, veinticinco, veintiséis, veintisiete, veintiocho, veintinueve, treinta, treinta y uno

to say thank you
gracias

to tell how you feel
Así, así.
(Muy) bien.

to talk about your classroom
el bolígrafo
el compañero, la compañera
el / la estudiante
la hoja de papel
el libro
la mesa
la pizarra
el profesor, la profesora
el pupitre
la sala de clases

(p. 24, bottom photo)
Visitors to La Paz, Bolivia, may not be able to stride down the street as briskly as these students. At 12,000 feet above sea level, the air in La Paz contains less oxygen than cities at lower elevations, and newcomers to the city may experience *soroche* (lightheadedness). The lack of oxygen has benefits, however. Fires burn out quickly in the low-oxygen air. Until recently, La Paz did not have a municipal fire department.

CAPÍTULO 1

THEME: FRIENDSHIP

SCOPE AND SEQUENCE Pages 26–63

COMMUNICATION

Topics

Friendship

Likes and dislikes

Personality characteristics

Sports and leisure activities

Objectives

To talk about the concept of friendship in Spanish-speaking countries

To talk about activities

To say what you like and do not like

To ask someone what he or she likes

To ask if a statement is accurate

To say what you are like or what someone else is like

To ask someone what he or she is like

To describe yourself or others

CULTURE

Concept of friendship

GRAMMAR

Los adjetivos

Sí / tampoco

Ni...ni

Ancillaries available for use with Chapter 1

Multisensory/Technology

Overhead Transparencies, 6–11

Audio Tapes and CDs

Projects for Proficiency: Blackline Master Spanish Activities for Middle School Learners

Vocabulary Art Blackline Masters for Hands-On Learning, pp. 8–12

Classroom Crossword

Video

CD-ROM

Print

Practice Workbook, pp. 13–22

Writing, Audio & Video Activities, pp. 13–20, 65–67, 100–101

Communicative Activity Blackline Masters

Pair and Small Group Activities, pp. 8–13

Situation Cards, p. 14

Un paso más: Actividades para ampliar tu español, pp. 1–6

Assessment

Assessment Program

Pruebas, pp. 7–10, 15–18

Exámenes de habilidades, pp. 11–14, 19–22

Mi portafolio, pp. 23–24

Test Generator

Video still from Chap. 1

Cultural Overview

The Foundations of Friendship

Friendship has many components which include individual personality traits and cultural values. For example, when people of different Latin American nationalities meet, they may form friendships partly based on shared interests and personality traits and partly on common cultural values they share as Latin Americans.

For many young Latin Americans, two very strong influences in their lives are family and a close-knit group of friends. They are part of a larger group of friends from diverse Hispanic nations, including Guatemala, Colombia, El Salvador, and so on. There may be several sets of brothers and sisters in the group and, as is common in Latin America, these siblings act as peers.

These friends spend free time and study time at each other's houses and all know each other's family members. Close friends, rather like extended family, are often included in family events and celebrations. Parties that young people attend commonly include several generations, from babies to grandparents.

Intimate friendship among Latin Americans is sometimes marked by *apodos,* or nicknames, denoting the special relationship. In Mexico, *primo(a), hermano(a),* or *cuate* (for males, meaning "pal" or, literally, "twin") are used. Other terms, more frequently employed by Spanish-speaking adults, are *compadre* or *comadre* (godfather or godmother with respect to each other's child and, literally, "co-father, co-mother"), *maestro(a)* (master or teacher), *cuñado(a)* (in-law), or, in Venezuela, *poeta* (poet).

While friendship is a universal phenomenon, each friendship is unique. As any camaraderie between two or more people illustrates, the expression of friendship is a singular blending of personal affinities and shared culture.

Introduce

Re-entry of Concepts

The following topic represents words and expressions re-entered from *El primer paso:*

Greetings

Planning

Cross-Curricular Connections

Civics Connection ***(pp. 38–39)***
Have pairs of students make illustrated posters for a person, real or imaginary, who is running for president of the U.S. Allow students creative latitude, but make sure posters include a list of the candidates' good characteristics.

Career Connection ***(pp. 38–39)***
Have students draw or bring in pictures of people in various occupations. Ask them to name a personality characteristic that might contribute to success in that occupation.

Geography Connection ***(pp. 60–61)***
Have students refer to a political map of Mexico to locate and count the different states. Then have them refer to a political map of the U.S. Invite students to make size and number comparisons between states in each country. List any similarities.

(For further cross-curricular activities, see the Conexiones *section on pp. 46–47.)*

Capítulo 1

Y tú, ¿cómo eres?

OBJECTIVES

At the end of this chapter, you will be able to:

- **describe yourself**
- **find out what other people are like**
- **talk about what you like and don't like to do**
- **compare your likes and dislikes with other people's**
- **explain what "friendship" means in Spanish-speaking countries**

Grupo de estudiantes en Chinchón, España

27

Teaching Suggestions

See the Writing, Audio & Video Activities book for Writing Activities that you may elect to use throughout the chapter.

Cultural Notes 

Spanish in Your Community
How many students in your school came from or have parents who came from a Spanish-speaking country? Conduct a survey in class to get a rough idea of how many students there might be and the countries from which they came. Record the countries on the chalkboard. As you do so, have volunteers point to or flag each country on a world map. If possible, highlight the area and leave on display throughout the year.

(pp. 26–27, photo)
The superior level or cycle of *Educación General Básica* or EGB in Spain roughly corresponds to middle school in the U.S. Students begin the initial cycle of EGB when they are six. At age nine they pass to the intermediate cycle for two years and then graduate at age 11 to the superior cycle, where they usually complete three years, graduating at age 14.

The Spanish school day consists of three hours of classes in the morning and two in the afternoon. Spain follows a national curriculum that divides the school week into 5 hours for languages, 3.25 for math, 2.5 each for social and natural sciences, and 3 hours for art, music, and physical education. Religious instruction is voluntary. Many students study three languages: Castilian Spanish, the language of a region in Spain (Basque, Catalan, or Galician) and a foreign language such as English.

Preview

Cultural Objective

- To talk about activities and the concept of friendship in Spanish-speaking countries

¡Piénsalo bien!

Play

Video Activity A

Teaching Suggestions

At the end of each chapter, return to the photos in the *¡Piénsalo bien!* See how extensively students can describe them.

Point out the use of quotation marks in the photo captions on pp. 28–29. Tell students that these indicate a statement from a person in the photo. Contrast this with the other captions that give an explanation of the photo content.

See the Projects for Proficiency BLMs for activity ideas that you may elect to use throughout the chapter.

See how many classmates students can name. (Remind them that they saw *¿Cómo te llamas?* and *Me llamo ___* in *El primer paso.)* The winner is the person who names all or most of his or her classmates.

¡Piénsalo bien!

Look at the people in the photos. Which ones might be casual friends? Which ones might be close friends? With a partner, discuss the reasons for your opinions.

Grupo de estudiantes en Montevideo, Uruguay

"A mí me gusta practicar deportes con mis amigos."

Tres estudiantes en Santiago, Chile

"Me gusta mucho estar con mis amigas."

Options

Strategies for Reaching All Students

Spanish-Speaking Students

Ask individual students: *¿Cómo saludas a tus buenos amigos? ¿Y a los conocidos?*

Un paso más Ex. 1-A

Students Needing Extra Help

Tell students to look at the pictures, read the captions, and think of the chapter theme for clues to help them answer the inductive questions. Point out the varying degrees of physical contact or proximity among the people in the photos.

Dos muchachas en Zacatecas, México

"¡Hola, María! ¿Qué tal?"

Dos muchachos en la Ciudad de México

"¿Cómo estás, Pablo?"
"Muy bien, gracias. ¿Y tú?"

Using the Video

This chapter's video focuses on friendship, what people are like, and what they like to do. Students will see our host in Miami interviewing several people and also talking about himself.

Show students segment one once through, then ask them to predict what this chapter's tape will be about. Then have students watch the segment again several times. Remind them not to worry if they don't understand at first. After the first time, you may wish to have them brainstorm possible vocabulary and expressions they will need to learn in order to talk about what they saw on the video. Ask students to identify things they saw that looked familiar but were somewhat different from what they might see in their own community.

Video segment 1: For more teaching suggestions, see the Video Teacher's Guide.

Answers: ¡Piénsalo bien!

Answers will vary, but students may say that the boys in the bottom photo on p. 29 might be casual friends because of the more formal structure of their greeting and the distance between them. In the other photos, people are closer together, implying an intimacy shared among close friends.

Cultural Notes 

(pp. 28–29, photos)
Latin Americans and Spaniards are often more demonstrative when greeting friends than Americans in the U.S. While customs differ among countries, friends in Spanish-speaking countries often brush cheeks lightly and "kiss the air" when meeting. Men often shake hands. After they know each other, they may embrace or pat one another on the back. Argentine women shake hands during introductions, a custom that is less common in Chile.

Seek out volunteers to demonstrate how people in Spanish-speaking countries greet each other. Explain the *abrazo* and the act of kissing each other's cheeks when meeting. As an activity, ask volunteers to greet another classmate, pretending to be people from a Spanish-speaking country. Encourage them to role play based on the photos and the cultural information presented here. You yourself might begin with a volunteer and have others join in the activity.

Present

Chapter Theme
Friendship: Things friends do together

Communicative Objectives
- To talk about activities
- To say what you like and do not like
- To ask someone what he or she likes
- To ask if a statement is accurate

 **Transparencies 6–7**

 **Vocabulary Art BLMs**

 **Pronunciation Tape 1-1**

 **Vocabulario para conversar A**

Using the Video
Video segment 2: See the Video Teacher's Guide.

 **Video Activity B**

Grammar Preview
Emphatic *sí* and *tampoco* are presented lexically. A brief explanation and practice appear on p. 55.

Sección 1

Vocabulario para conversar

¿Qué te gusta hacer?

- As your teacher reads each word, make a thumbs up gesture if you like the activity. Make a thumbs down gesture if you do *not* like it.
- With your partner, point to the activities that you like and say *"Me gusta."* Then point to activities that you don't like and say *"No me gusta."*
- Pantomime for your partner your favorite activities, and see if he or she can point to the new vocabulary word or expression you are acting out.

Options

Strategies for Reaching All Students

Enrichment
También necesitas. . . : To reinforce *me gusta (más / mucho)* and *no me gusta (mucho / nada),* have students rate fast-food restaurants, entertainers, movies, or TV programs. They may set up their assignment as a line continuum and check off accordingly from *me gusta más* down to *no me gusta nada.* Have students also conduct interviews in pairs and determine whether they like, dislike, or prefer any of the restaurants, entertainers, etc. Remind them to reverse roles.

Learning Spanish Through Action
STAGING VOCABULARY: *Señalen, Toquen*
MATERIALS: transparency of activities in the *Vocabulario para conversar* or pictures of similar activities from magazines
DIRECTIONS: Using the overhead or pictures placed along the chalkboard edge, ask students to touch or point to various activities you call out at random. OR: Have students come up, pick what they like or don't like, touch it, and say *me gusta* or *no me gusta.*

Use the *Overhead Transparencies or Vocabulary Art BLMs* for initial vocabulary presentation. Later, you may wish to use the Vocabulary Art to make your own copies for additional written / oral assessment or for manipulatives.

También necesitas . . .

¿Qué te gusta (hacer)?	*What do you like (to do)?*	A mí también.	*I do (like it) too.*
¿Te gusta ___?	*Do you like ___?*	(A mí) no me gusta ___.	*I don't like ___.*
estar con amigos	*to be with friends*	(A mí) no me gusta mucho___.	*I don't like ___ very much.*
(A mí) me gusta ___.	*I like ___.*	(A mí) no me gusta nada ___.	*I don't like ___ at all.*
(A mí) me gusta mucho ___.	*I like ___ a lot.*	A mí tampoco me gusta ___.	*I don't like ___ either.*
(A mí) me gusta más ___.	*I like ___ better. (I prefer.)*	¿De veras?	*Really?*
¿Y a ti?	*And you?*	Pues	*Well . . .*
(A mí) sí me gusta ___.	*I do like ___.*	y	*and*

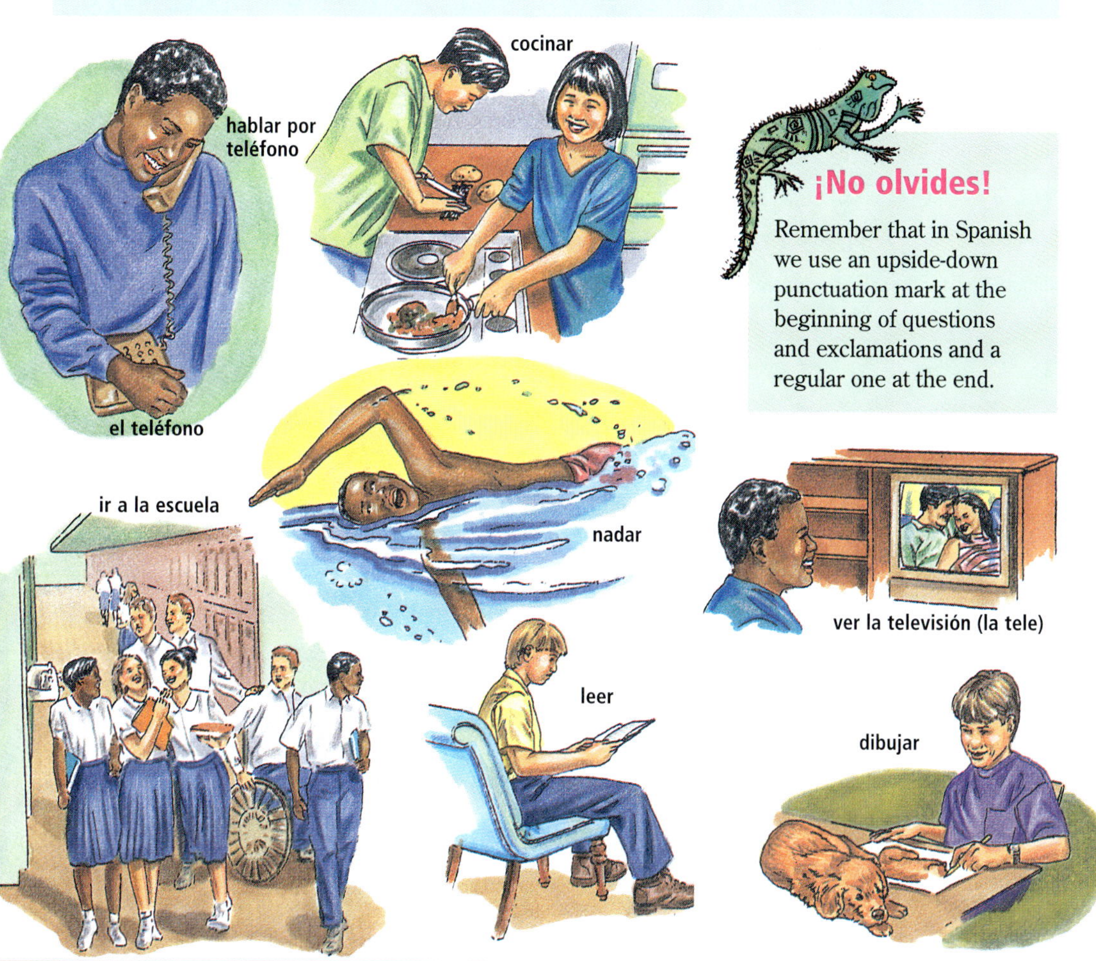

¡No olvides!

Remember that in Spanish we use an upside-down punctuation mark at the beginning of questions and exclamations and a regular one at the end.

Teaching Suggestions

Preparing students to speak: Use one or two options from each of the categories of Comprehensible Input, Physical Response, or Limited Verbal Response. For a complete explanation of these categories and some sample activities, see pp. T18–T19.

By introducing new vocabulary via overheads or video, students will begin to learn and acquire the language by matching what they see or read to what they hear. This is known as comprehensible input. Students can also deduce the meaning of new grammatical structures or endings by listening or reading in a context that makes their meaning apparent.

Point out the *¡No olvides!* on p. 31. These recycling features will appear from time to time to remind students of previously taught concepts and vocabulary.

Class Starter Review

On the day following initial presentation of vocabulary, you might begin the class with this activity:
Using visuals, state each of the vocabulary activities and have students signal *Me gusta* or *No me gusta.* They may call out or use index cards on which they have written those statements.

Practice

Teaching Suggestions

Set the stage and tone for practice exercises. Model examples so students understand what to do. Ask volunteers to model so others can hear and compare how they are doing in class.

For the first few times that students are in pairs, monitor their progress and keep them on task. You may wish to walk around the room and listen to individuals, offering assistance as needed.

Answers: Empecemos a conversar

1 ESTUDIANTE A

a. ¿Qué te gusta hacer? ¿Te gusta nadar?
b. . . . ¿Te gusta dibujar?
c. . . . ¿Te gusta escuchar música?
d. . . . ¿Te gusta estudiar?
e. . . . ¿Te gusta cocinar?
f. Questions will vary, but look for *¿te gusta* + inf.? in second question.

ESTUDIANTE B

a.–f. Answers will vary.

Empecemos a conversar

With a partner, take turns being *Estudiante A* and *Estudiante B*. Use the words that are cued or given in the boxes to replace the underlined words in the example. 💡 means you can make your own choices. When it is your turn to be *Estudiante B*, try to answer truthfully.

1 

A —*¿Qué te gusta hacer? ¿Te gusta <u>patinar</u>?*
B —*<u>Sí, me gusta</u>.*

Estudiante A

Estudiante B

Sí, me gusta.
No, no me gusta.
No, ¡no me gusta nada!

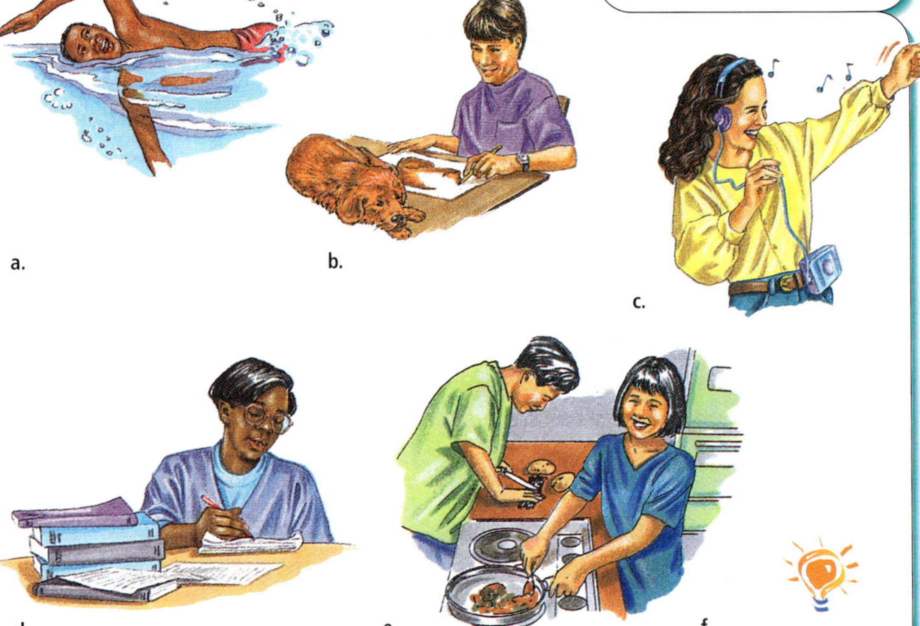

Options

Strategies for Reaching All Students

Spanish-Speaking Students

To model pronunciation, pair bilingual and non-bilingual students for Exs. 1–2. For more advanced practice, pair Spanish-speaking students with each other for Exs. 3–4.

 **Un paso más Exs. 1-B, 1-C**

Students Needing Extra Help

Have students fill in their Organizers (available in the *Practice Workbook)* before doing the exercises that require them to make choices. As students continue through the chapter, have them add to the Organizer whenever they are required to use newly presented vocabulary. Go over the Organizers in class so students can compare and correct them.

Ex. 1: Make sure students understand that *Estudiante B* has three choices for each response. Explain when to use each response. Do some examples aloud for those students who don't see the possible choices. Model at least one negative item.

Ex. 2: Review *pues*. Show what remains the same in the sentence when substitutions occur. Emphasize that *Estudiante B* creates his or her own answer when a situation is open ended.

Ex. 3: Model both possibilities for *Estudiante B*. Explain the use of the responses.

2  A — *¿Qué te gusta más, ir al cine o ver la televisión?*
B — *Pues, me gusta más ver la televisión.*

Estudiante A **Estudiante B**

a. b. c. d. e. f.

3 A — *No me gusta mucho hablar por teléfono.*
B — *A mí tampoco me gusta.*

Estudiante A **Estudiante B**

A mí tampoco me gusta.
¿De veras? A mí sí me gusta.

2 ESTUDIANTE A
a. ¿Qué te gusta más, escuchar música o tocar la guitarra?
b. . . . practicar deportes o hablar por teléfono?
c. . . . ir a la escuela o ayudar en casa?
d. . . . dibujar o leer?
e. . . . nadar o patinar?
f. Questions will vary, but look for *¿qué te gusta más?* + inf.

ESTUDIANTE B
a.–f. Answers will vary, but should include one of the infinitives suggested by *Estudiante A.*

3 Statements will vary. Encourage at least three exchanges. Have volunteers read some of their dialogues to the class.

Enrichment

Ex. 1: Encourage pairs of students to extend their dialogues by having *Estudiante B* ask *Estudiante A* what he or she likes: *¿Y a ti? ¿Qué te gusta hacer?*

Practice & Apply

Answers: Empecemos a conversar

4 Dialogues will vary, but look for *a mí me gusta* + inf.

Answers: Empecemos a leer y a escribir

Note that Exs. 5–7 are directed to students in Spanish for further comprehension practice in the target language.

1 a. Not used
b. Julia Martínez
c. Jaime Iglesias
d. Eddie Soto

2 Student posters will vary.

3 Answers will vary.
Entertainment includes: *dibujar, escuchar música, hablar por teléfono, ir al cine, leer, nadar, patinar, practicar deportes, tocar la guitarra, ver la tele(visión).*
Duties include: *ayudar en casa, cocinar, estudiar, ir a la escuela.*

4 Student lists will vary.

5–7 Answers will vary.

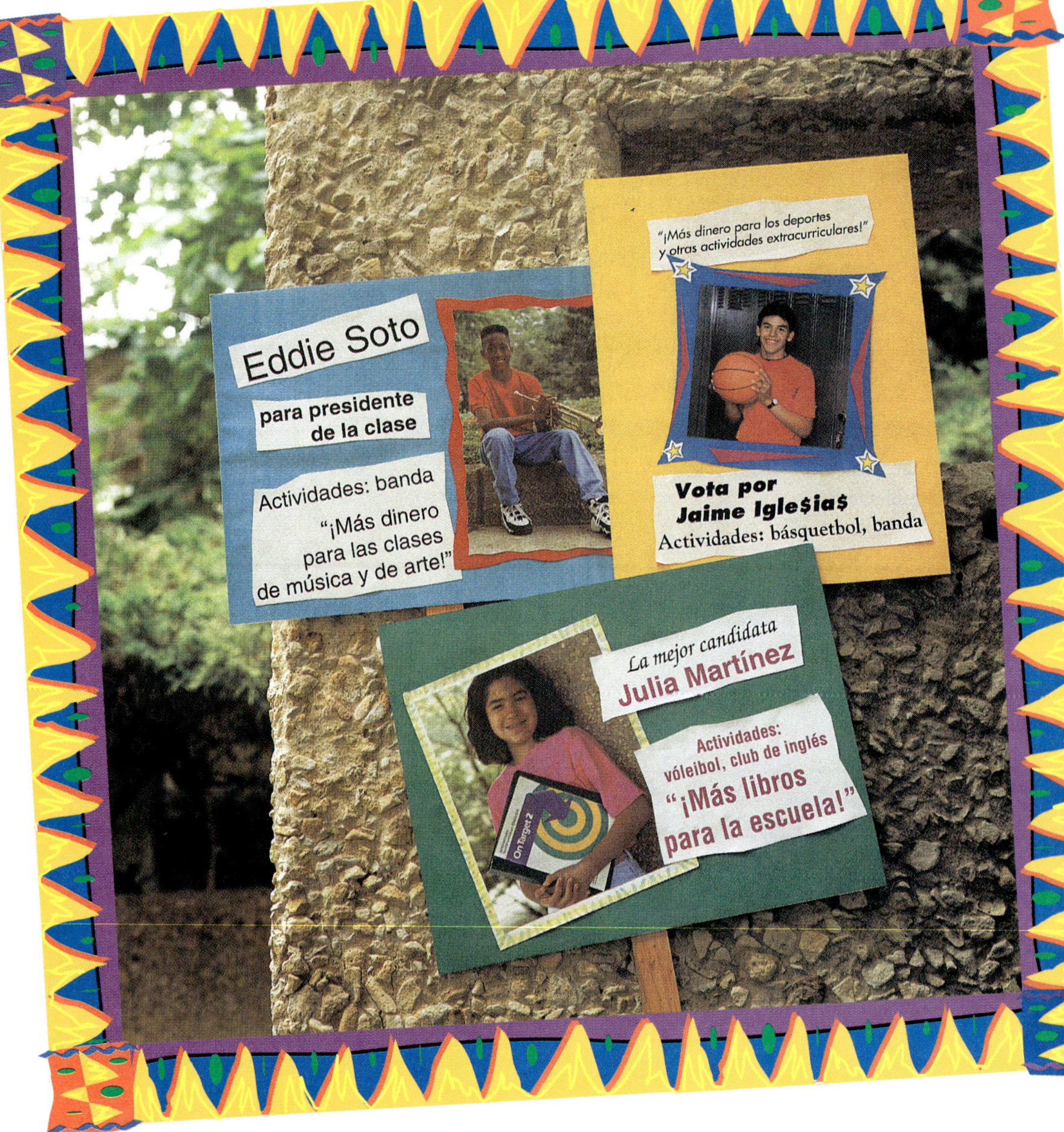

Options

Strategies for Reaching All Students

Students Needing Extra Help

Ex. 4 *(top of p. 35):* Point out that *o:* indicates a choice. Have students use the Organizer for possible answers.
Empecemos a leer y a escribir: Ex. 1: Show students the number of tools (cognates, patterns, etc.) they have to help them, and the number of times they have already seen these words.

Enrichment

Ex. 2: Display the posters in the classroom. Extend this activity by having a mock election based on the posters. Have students vote for the best one.

Cooperative Learning

Prepare four cards numbered 1–4, each listing one of the activities in Ex. 1. After placing a card in each corner of the room, ask students to write and then recite in Spanish the number and name of the activity that they least like among the four. After reciting, each student goes to the appropriate corner and gives one reason why his or her group disliked the particular activity they chose. A spokesperson for each group then summarizes the reasons given.

4 A —*A mí me gusta* <u>*practicar deportes*</u>*. ¿Y a ti?*
B —*Pues, a mí me gusta* <u>*escuchar música*</u>*.*
o: *Pues, a mí también.*

Estudiante A **Estudiante B**

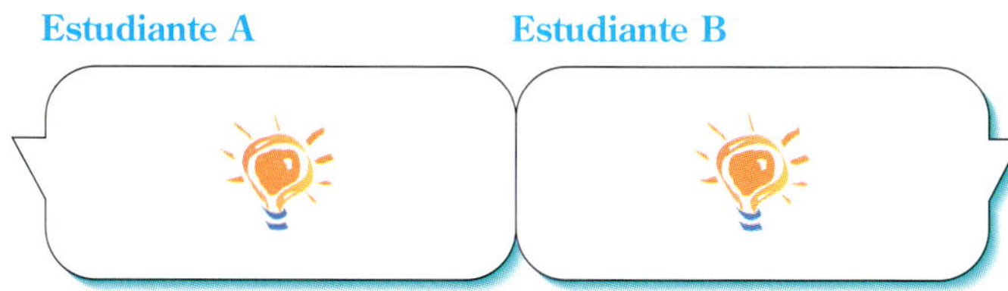

Empecemos a leer y a escribir

Responde en español.

1 The posters on page 34 are for candidates in a student election. Read them, then match the logical pastimes to the candidates. (One set of pastimes will be left over.)

Pasatiempos

a. jugar videojuegos, ir al cine
b. leer, hablar inglés
c. practicar deportes, escuchar música
d. tocar la guitarra, dibujar

2 Make a poster of yourself or of another student as a candidate for class president. Use the posters in Exercise 1 as models.

3 Look at the activities pictured on pages 30–31. Which ones are entertainment? Which ones are duties? Make two lists. Put a check next to any duties you enjoy.

4 Make a list of all the activities on pages 30–31 that you do on a normal school day.

5 ¿Qué te gusta más, leer o ver la tele?

6 ¿Qué te gusta hacer? Escribe una lista de cuatro actividades, por lo menos.

7 ¿Qué no te gusta hacer? Escribe una lista de dos actividades, por lo menos.

También se dice

People in different English-speaking countries often use different words to refer to the same thing. For example, what we call an "apartment" the English call a "flat." What we call a "truck," they call a "lorry." (Do you know any other examples?) We even use different words for the same thing in different parts of the United States. For example, in some regions we call a soft drink "soda"; in other regions we call it "pop." And do you say "stand *in* line" or "stand *on* line"? That, too, will depend on where you live. Similarly, in various Spanish-speaking countries, there are sometimes different words for the same thing.

mirar la televisión (la tele)

También se dice

This feature offers examples of how Spanish vocabulary differs from region to region and discourages viewing vocabulary choice as a matter of right or wrong. These sections are for enrichment only. They point out to students that they might hear variant forms depending on the speaker's native country or region. Allow Spanish-speaking students who may use other words or expressions to add to this section.

 **Practice Wkbk. 1-1, 1-2, 1-3**

 **Audio Activities 1.1, 1.2**

 **Writing Activities**

 **Pruebas 1-1, 1-2**

Present & Apply

Cultural Objective

- To talk about the concept of friendship in Spanish-speaking countries

Teaching Suggestions

In order to prepare students for a meaningful discussion about the similarities and differences between the concept of friendship in the U.S. and Spanish-speaking countries, you might wish to have them read the text the night before you present the lesson in class. Ask them to begin thinking about what friendship means to them.

Critical Thinking: Comparing and Contrasting

Although friendship is defined somewhat differently in the U.S. than it is in some Spanish-speaking countries, there are some aspects of friendship that would apply to both cultures. Ask students to suggest what some of these aspects might be and if some of them might be universally applicable. List the common ones on the chalkboard for the whole class to see.

¿Tienes muchos amigos? ¿Qué es un amigo para ti?

"Mike, this is my friend Luis." That is how my classmate introduced me to another boy in our class. It was my first day of school here. I was in the fifth grade. My family had come from El Salvador in July, so I had not met any English speakers my age. And here was someone introducing me as his friend when we had just met that morning! What a strange place I was in!

By the end of that year, I did have friends, friends in the Spanish sense. They are still my friends. I think that they will always be, because that is what we mean by *amigo,* a friend for life.

Where I came from, people don't move around a lot. You would probably grow up in one neighborhood or town and might even live there your whole life. Yes, you might miss out on a few things, but you would form deep friendships and keep them. You would know people well, and would usually see your friends every day. You'd also get to know each other's families well.

Of course, we are warm and welcoming to people we don't know very well, but we call them *conocidos* (acquaintances). We may get along quite well, but they are not friends for life (*amigos*). Perhaps some day they will be, but that takes a long time.

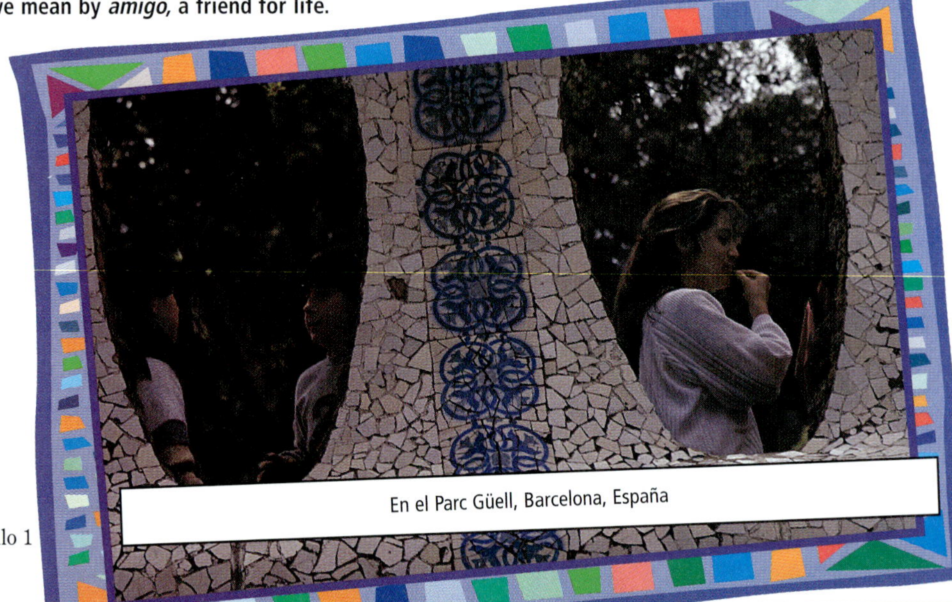

En el Parc Güell, Barcelona, España

36 Capítulo 1

Options

Strategies for Reaching All Students

Spanish-Speaking Students

After reading the text, ask: *¿Te gusta salir con tus amigos? ¿Cuándo salen ustedes juntos? ¿Adónde van? ¿Salen los fines de semana? ¿Qué hacen?*

Enrichment

Tell students that in Mexican Spanish, the word *cuate* is used to name a very special, trusted friend. Point out that another meaning of this word is "twin." Ask if they can think of any words in English that would be the equivalent for naming this kind of friend (buddy, pal, etc.). Be prepared for slang terms.

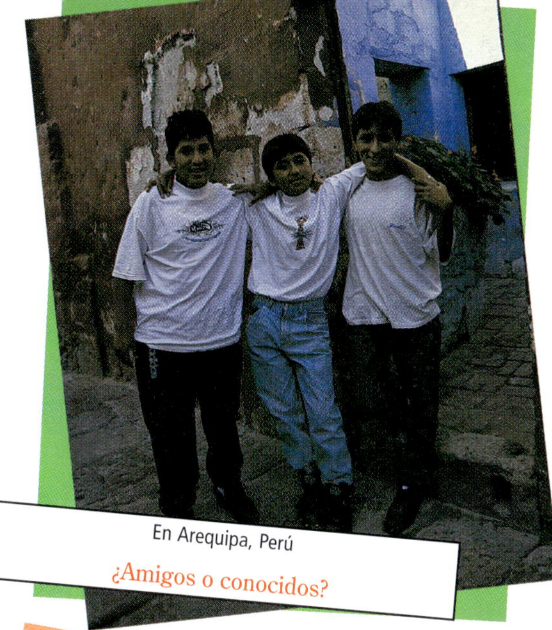

En Arequipa, Perú

¿Amigos o conocidos?

La cultura desde tu perspectiva

1 Whom do you consider to be a friend? Whom would a Spanish-speaking person consider to be a friend? Why do you think there is a difference?

2 What do you think would happen if we called only our close friends "friends" in the United States? How would you feel if someone you thought of as a friend described you as an acquaintance?

En una escuela en la Ciudad de México

"¿Estás preparada para el examen, Gloria?"

Answers

Answers will vary for inductive questions. Ask for their definition of a friend and see if it matches the description in the text. Have the class come to a final agreement on a definition.

Answers: La cultura desde tu perspectiva

1 Answers will vary, but students may mention that they consider someone a friend if they enjoy spending time with that person and have similar likes and dislikes, regardless of how long they have known each other. In a Spanish-speaking country, a friend is not usually someone whom you've just met. There may be a difference in the way the two cultures view friendship because people in the U.S. tend to relocate more often than people in a Spanish-speaking country. People in the U.S. rarely spend their entire lives in the town they were born in.

2 Answers will vary, but students may say they might feel isolated if the only people they could call friends were those they had known since childhood, and they would probably feel offended if someone they considered a friend described them as an acquaintance.

Cultural Notes 

(p. 36, photo)
An agreeable meeting place in many Spanish and Latin American cities is a park or *plaza* where friends can rest, talk, "people watch," sit in a *café,* or patronize vendors selling items such as food, drinks, gum, cassettes, books, and other treats. It is common for school friends to meet in a park for a study session which, of course, also includes some socializing.

(p. 37, photos)
In Latin America and Spain, physical contact is a part of daily life for friends. Boys in Arequipa, Peru, may greet each other with a pat on the back or by putting an arm around the shoulder. In Mexico and in other Spanish-speaking countries, personal space tends to be small. What we consider as perhaps an invasion of privacy is all but a natural and comfortable way of sitting or standing next to someone.

Present

Chapter Theme

Friendship: Describing friends

Communicative Objectives

- To say what you are like or what someone else is like
- To ask someone what he or she is like
- To describe yourself or others

 **Transparencies 8–9**

 **Vocabulary Art BLMs**

 **Pronunciation Tape 1-2**

 **Vocabulario para conversar B**

Play

Step

Using the Video

Video segment 2: See the Video Teacher's Guide.

 **Video Activity B**

Sección 2

Vocabulario para conversar

¿Cómo eres?

- **As your teacher reads the words aloud, put your finger on the pictures.**
- **As your teacher reads each word, point to yourself when you hear one that describes you. Shake your head if it does *not* describe you.**
- **Pantomime three of the qualities listed on these pages and see if your partner can point to the correct pictures.**

generoso generosa tacaño tacaña impaciente paciente

ordenado ordenada

desordenado desordenada

Options

Strategies for Reaching All Students

Students Needing Extra Help

Ask what an adjective is and how it functions in English. Explain that although the sets of adjectives are two words *(serio and seria,* for example), they mean the same thing. To emphasize this point, tell students to assume everyone in the class is serious. Then walk down the aisles pointing to boys, saying *es serio,* and to girls, *es seria.* You may wish to hold up color-coded index cards as you are doing so.

Enrichment

Although students are just beginning to learn adjectives, here are several cognates you can use to express approval or encouragement: *brillante, estupendo, excelente, excepcional, fabuloso, fantástico, magnífico, perfecto, super.* Vary your responses. You may wish to display these words for a while as a visual reminder.

Learning Spanish Through Action

STAGING VOCABULARY: *Señalen, Toquen*
MATERIALS: transparency of adjectives in the *Vocabulario para conversar* or magazine pictures of people in professions such as police officer, firefighter, judge, athlete, comedian, talk-show host, mime, stuntperson, artist, and chess player (If pictures are not available, use "symbols" cut out from construction paper: a badge to represent a police officer, a firefighter's helmet, and so on.)

trabajador trabajadora perezoso perezosa gracioso graciosa serio seria

atrevido atrevida prudente deportista artístico artística

También necesitas . . .

¿Cómo eres?	*What are you like?*	pero	*but*
(Yo) soy ___.	*I am (I'm) ___.*	a veces	*sometimes, at times*
(Tú) eres ___.	*You are (You're) ___.*		
es	*(he/she/it) is ___.*		
muy	*very*		
amable	*nice, kind*		
callado, -a	*quiet*		

¿Y qué quiere decir . . . ?
sociable

Grammar Preview

Allow students to use these adjectives *before* presenting rules of agreement. The visuals will help them intuit the rule, making the understanding of grammar a natural outgrowth of its use and facilitating learning.

Teaching Suggestions

Preparing students to speak: Use one or two options from each of the categories of Comprehensible Input, Physical Response, or Limited Verbal Response. For a complete explanation of these categories and some sample activities, see pp. T18–T19.

¿Y qué quiere decir...?: Remind students that the vocabulary in this section consists of cognates or previously seen words or expressions. See if they can identify other cognates from the visualized vocabulary on these two pages.

Class Starter Review

On the day following initial presentation of vocabulary, you might begin the class with this activity: Using the Overhead Transparencies, do a quick review of the adjectives that students just learned. Then have them turn to a partner and describe themselves, using three adjectives. On the next day, have students do this same activity in written form.

DIRECTIONS: Have students touch or point to the appropriate overhead image or magazine picture as you call out various adjectives. If you do this activity with magazine pictures after presenting the grammar, have students listen carefully to masculine and feminine forms.

Practice

Grammar Preview

The explanation of adjective agreement appears on p. 49. If students ask why it is *-o* in some cases and *-a* in others, encourage them to develop their own explanation. They will almost certainly decide on the right answer and teach themselves the grammar rule. You might have them write out this grammar rule and then post it, leaving it displayed until they have mastered the concept.

Teaching Suggestions

Ex. 1: Model this exercise carefully, alternating between male and female students. Ask students the reason for two different adjective endings. Ask what an adjective is and what it does.

As a visual aid for this and future exercises, you may wish to color code index cards to help students distuinguish between masculine and feminine (nouns, adjectives, pronouns, etc.).

Answers: Empecemos a conversar

1 ESTUDIANTE A

a. ¿Cómo eres, ordenado(a) o desordenado(a)?
b. . . . trabajador(a) o perezoso(a)?
c. . . . impaciente o paciente?
d. . . . generoso(a) o tacaño(a)?
e. . . . atrevido(a) o prudente?

ESTUDIANTE B

a.–e. Answers will vary, but look for adjective agreement.

Empecemos a conversar

1 

A —*¿Cómo eres, gracioso(a) o serio(a)?*
B —*Soy serio(a), pero a veces soy gracioso(a).*

Estudiante A **Estudiante B**

Options

Strategies for Reaching All Students

Enrichment

Ex. 1: For extra practice, begin by asking someone what he or she is like. That person should answer and then ask someone else the same question. Continue until everyone has participated. To save time, you may want to let each row or section do its own question-and-answer exercise. For example:

A —*Luis, ¿cómo eres?*
B —*Soy (muy) paciente y (muy) sociable también. Enrique, ¿cómo eres?*
C —*Pues, soy . . . .*

Ex. 3: Extend this exercise by encouraging students to give the opposite adjective when appropriate: *No, no soy ordenado(a). Soy desordenado(a).*

2  A —*¿Te gusta dibujar?*
B —*Sí, soy artístico(a).*
o: *No, no soy muy artístico(a).*

Estudiante A

Estudiante B

3 A —*¿Eres ordenado(a)?*
B —*Sí, y también soy trabajador(a).*
o: *No, no soy ordenado(a).*

Estudiante A

Estudiante B

Teaching Suggestions

Ex. 2: Remind students that *Estudiante B* must make a logical response to *Estudiante A.*

2 ESTUDIANTE A
a. ¿Te gusta patinar?
b. . . . practicar deportes?
c. . . . tocar la guitarra?
d. . . . ayudar en casa?

ESTUDIANTE B
a.–d. Answers will vary. Look for adjective agreement.

3 Questions and answers will vary. Look for adjective agreement.

Apply

Re-enter / Recycle

Ex. 4: greetings from *El primer paso*

Teaching Suggestions

Ex. 2: You may want to specify the people that students write about; for example, characters in a familiar book or play, TV personalities, sports heroes, other teachers, etc. Set a minimum number of adjectives to be used. In groups, have students read their descriptions so that others in each group can guess the people. Have a group's spokesperson read aloud the best one.

Note that Exs. 3 and 4 are directed to students in Spanish for further comprehension practice in the target language.

Answers: Empecemos a leer y a escribir

1 a. Cenicienta
b. Caperucita Roja
c. Blancanieves

2–3 Answers will vary.

4 Answers will vary, but students may mention: *María Estela es sociable y deportista, pero no muy trabajadora.* (Note: Students may also answer with *eres,* as if they were answering María Estela directly.)

Empecemos a leer y a escribir

Responde en español.

1 Match the following descriptions to the correct fairy tale characters.

Amable, callada, trabajadora.
Ayuda en casa.
Pobrecita ___ .

Atrevida, impaciente, no prudente.
Va a visitar a su abuela.
Pobrecita ___ .

Amable y sociable.
Tiene siete amigos.
Es ___ .

a. Blancanieves

b. Caperucita Roja

c. Cenicienta

2 Write a description of a well-known person like the ones in Exercise 1. See if your partner can tell whom you are describing.

3 ¿Cómo eres? ¿Eres atrevido(a)? ¿Paciente? ¿Perezoso(a)?

4 Eres ...

Options

Strategies for Reaching All Students

Spanish-Speaking Students

Empecemos a leer y a escribir: Ex. 2: Have students write three short sentences describing themselves, then have them read their sentences to the class.

 **Un paso más Ex. 1-D**

Enrichment

Have students list the adjectives that they think *other* people or friends would use to describe them.

 **Practice Wkbk. 1-4**

 **Audio Activity 1.3**

 **Pruebas 1-3, 1-4**

Cultural Notes 

(p. 43, realia)
Looking for a little excitement? A comic book might be just what you're looking for. Easy to read and inexpensive, comic books carry the reader along quickly: the ending is never more than a few pages away. Both the writing and the illustrations are equally enjoyable, making for a literary / visual combination that keeps millions of readers coming back for more. Comic books specialize in adventure stories. This advertisement from Editorial Anaya promises an exciting armchair adventure.

Practice

Teaching Suggestions

The *Comuniquemos* section allows for integrated practice of both vocabulary sections of the chapter.

Exs. 1–2: Have students provide at least five examples of likes and dislikes for activities.

Answers: Comuniquemos

1–2 Dialogues will vary, but look for the correct infinitive used: *ayudar en casa, cocinar, dibujar, escuchar música, estudiar, hablar por teléfono, ir a la escuela, ir al cine, leer, nadar, patinar, practicar deportes, tocar la guitarra, ver la tele(visión).*

3 Dialogues will vary, but look for *eres* + adjective agreement and use of *me / te gusta* + inf.

Comuniquemos

Here's another opportunity for you and your partner to use the vocabulary you've just learned.

1 Find out how many of these activities both you and your partner enjoy. Take turns asking the questions. Be sure to choose only those activities you really like. You should each ask at least three questions.

A —*A mí me gusta escuchar música. ¿Y a ti?*
B —*A mí también me gusta.*
o: *A mí no me gusta.*

Options

Strategies for Reaching All Students

Spanish-Speaking Students

Have Spanish-speaking students describe themselves in four or five sentences, concentrating on telling what activities they like and do well. Ask the class if they understand what the Spanish-speaking students have said.

Students Needing Extra Help

Remind students that *o:* indicates a choice.
Ahora lo sabes: Have students write these sections and keep them as a personal chart in their notebooks. They may use them as part of their portfolios and as review practice come assessment time.

2 Now take turns finding out if you and your partner dislike the same things. Use the pictures in Exercise 1, and this time choose only those activities you *don't* like. Ask at least two questions each.

A —*No me gusta cocinar. ¿Y a ti?*
B —*A mí tampoco me gusta.*
o: *A mí sí me gusta.*

3 What have you and your partner learned about each other? Write a two-sentence description of your partner. Include two words that describe him or her and two activities that he or she likes. Read your description aloud, pausing to let your partner say *Sí* or *No* to your statements.

A —*Tú eres generoso(a) y artístico(a).*
B —*¡Sí!*
A —*Te gusta escuchar música y cocinar.*
B —*¡No! Me gusta más practicar deportes y leer.*
o: *Pues, sí me gusta escuchar música, pero no me gusta cocinar.*

Ahora lo sabes

Using what you have learned so far, can you:

- **ask someone what he or she likes to do?**
- **tell what you like or don't like to do?**
- **find out from someone what he or she is like?**
- **describe yourself?**

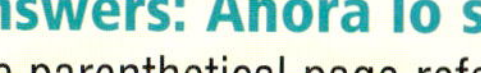

Answers: Ahora lo sabes

The parenthetical page references after the answers refer to the sections in the chapter where this information was first presented. Be sure to tell students to refer to these sections for further practice.

- *¿Te gusta* + inf.? *(pp. 30–31)*
- *(No) me gusta* + inf. *(pp. 30–31)*
- *¿Eres* + adj.? *(pp. 38–39)*
- Answers will vary, but should contain *soy* + adjective agreement. *(pp. 38–39)*

 **Audio Activity 1.4**

 **Writing Activities**

 **Comm. Act. BLMs 1-1, 1-2**

 **Examen de habilidades 1**

Cultural Notes

(pp. 44–45, photos)
Much like their U.S. counterparts, young Latin Americans enjoy going to movies, video arcades, parties, listening to music, and participating in sports during their free time. In many Spanish-speaking countries, family life exerts a strong influence on young people, with siblings often socializing together as part of a larger group of friends. Young people in the U.S. often take on after-school jobs for extra spending money. In Latin America, such jobs are less plentiful, and students are usually expected to devote after-school hours to their studies.

Apply

Background Information

(See the Cross-Curricular Connections at the beginning of the chapter on pp. 26–27 for further activities.
For a complete list of the curricular areas covered in PASO A PASO A, *see p. T23 of this Teacher's Edition.)*

Héroes de la historia provides a cross-curricular connection with social studies. You may want to share the following cultural information: The names of streets in Spanish-speaking countries often reflect historical events or dates. For example, in Mexico City, *Avenida 16 de septiembre* commemorates Mexico's independence from Spain in 1810. In Sevilla, Spain, the *Jardines de Murillo* commemorate the famous Spanish painter Bartolomé Esteban Murillo. In Quito, Ecuador, *Avenida de Francisco de Orellana* commemorates the Spaniard who explored the Amazon River.

Ir al cine provides a cross-curricular connection with math. It also provides practice in using a graphic organizer that applies to many curricular areas. Be sure students understand that although several countries call their currency the *peso,* each is distinct and has, as the chart shows, a different rate of exhange.

Conexiones

These activities connect Spanish with other subject areas you may be studying.

Héroes de la historia

In Spanish-speaking countries, streets are often named after historical figures or other famous people. Simón Bolívar, who liberated Venezuela, Colombia, Ecuador, Perú, and Bolivia from Spain, has streets in several countries named after him.

Think about the street names in your community or in a nearby city. Find out about the people that the streets were named after. If your community doesn't have streets named after famous people, do this activity with towns, schools, or other public buildings. In a group, make posters about these people like the one of Simón Bolívar. Include some words that describe them. Add a photo or a drawing of the person if you can find one.

If you were going to rename the street you live on, whom would you name it for? Why?

Retrato de Simón Bolívar (1859), Arturo Michelena.
Museo Bolivarien, Caracas, Venezuela

Options

Strategies for Reaching All Students

Students Needing Extra Help

(p. 47, realia) Explain the use of the 24-hour clock in the movie times. Ask students what time *Star Trek* is shown using the 12-hour clock: 16:35 (4:35 P.M.); 19:50 (7:50 P.M.); and 22:10 (10:10 P.M.).

Ir al cine: Explain that the "exchange rate" refers to the rate at which money is given in exchange for the currency of a different country. For example, in 1995, one U.S. dollar was equivalent to about six new Mexican *pesos.* The value of the currency of each country fluctuates depending on such factors as economic and political stability. Thus, the rates shown in the chart on p. 47 may not represent the actual value of the currencies.

¿Qué te gusta hacer?: Explain that a Venn diagram uses overlapping circles or rectangles to show the relationship among different groups.

Enrichment

Have students bring in a newspaper or magazine ad that contains something they would like to purchase. Using the exchange rates from p. 47, have them figure out how much that item would cost in three of the listed countries.

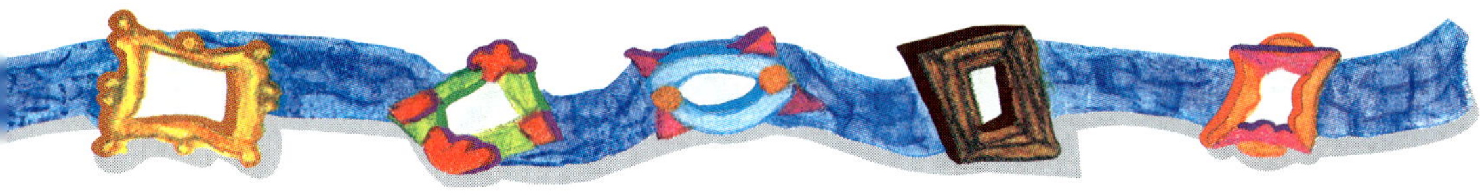

Ir al cine

Where does a movie ticket cost the most? Where does it cost the least? Here are the prices of a movie ticket in six Spanish-speaking cities. Using the exchange rates shown, convert the prices to dollars. Then make a graph showing the cities and the movie ticket prices in order from most expensive to least expensive. Be prepared to tell the city where a movie ticket is most expensive and the city where it is least expensive.

Ciudad	Entrada
Bogotá, Colombia	2,000 pesos *(848 pesos = $1)*
Caracas, Venezuela	300 bolívares *(170 bolívares = $1)*
Madrid, España	450 pesetas *(130 pesetas = $1)*
México, D.F., México	12 pesos *(5.8 pesos = $1)*
Santiago, Chile	2,000 pesos *(413 pesos = $1)*
Montevideo, Uruguay	32 pesos *(5.8 pesos = $1)*

¿Qué te gusta hacer?

Look at these pairs of activities. In a group, find out how many students prefer to do one activity over the other and how many like to do both activities about equally. Draw a Venn diagram.

Label it with one of these pairs of activities.

ir al cine / ver la televisión
dibujar / ir al museo
practicar deportes / ver deportes
tocar música / escuchar música
nadar / patinar

ir al cine — ver la televisión

Then ask everyone in the group to write his or her initials in one of the three areas. Students who prefer one activity should write in the part of the circle that doesn't overlap. Those who like both activities equally should write in the overlapping part.

Teaching Suggestions

You may choose the activities you want your class to do. You may prefer to use the activities as homework, for enrichment, or for your Spanish-speaking students. This material is not part of the testing program, however, it is appropriate for use in student assessment.

For Activity 2 *(Ir al cine)*, check, or have students check, current exchange rates in a newspaper. You may want to review the mathematical process involved in this activity. For example, to convert 2,000 Colombian *pesos* into dollars, students divide 2,000 by 848 (the number of *pesos* to the dollar) to get the answer of $2.36.

Activity 3 *(¿Qué te gusta hacer?)* provides practice in using a graphic organizer that applies to many subject areas. Ask groups of four to combine their data on a large Venn diagram on the chalkboard. Then ask a student to give the results.

Answers: Conexiones

Héroes de la historia: Responses will vary.

Ir al cine: A movie ticket is most expensive in Montevideo ($5.52) and least expensive in Caracas ($1.76).
Montevideo, Uruguay ($5.52)
Santiago, Chile ($4.84)
Madrid, España ($3.46)
Bogotá, Colombia ($2.36)
México, D.F., México ($2.07)
Caracas, Venezuela ($1.76)

Cultural Notes 

(p. 46, photo)
Simón Bolívar (1783–1830) is often called the "George Washington of Latin America" *(el Libertador)*. The South American countries of Venezuela, Colombia, Ecuador, Peru, and Bolivia all trace their successful revolts against Spanish rule to Bolívar's military and political leadership.

(p. 47, realia)
See if students can figure out the titles of these movies in English. *(Dumb and Dumber; 101 Dalmations; Richie Rich; The Professional; Star Trek, the Next Generation)* Point out that in the last frame, *sesión de madrugada* means "midnight show" and *sesión a las 14 horas* means 2:00 show, or "matinee."

Preview

Transparency 10

Teaching Suggestions

This poem serves as a summary of the structures students have been using. As they work through the poem and the questions, students will formulate for themselves the rules given on the following pages. Encourage students to think through the possible rules and then compare them with the explanations they will read later.

Answers

Answers will vary; students may say they'd expect to find adjectives or words that describe the author.

A Answers will vary; students may say they found out that the author is not extremely one way or another, that today she is talkative and tomorrow she may be quiet, for example.

B The poet is female, since almost all of the adjectives end in *-a: generosa, tacaña, callada, graciosa, perezosa.*

C Answers will vary, but may include: Words ending in *-o* refer to males and words ending in *-a* refer to females. Yes; *amable, deportista, impaciente, paciente, prudente, trabajador, sociable.* Words ending in *-e* can refer to males or females.

Gramática en contexto

Here is a descriptive poem entitled "Yo soy yo." What kind of information would you expect to find in such a poem?

Now read the poem.

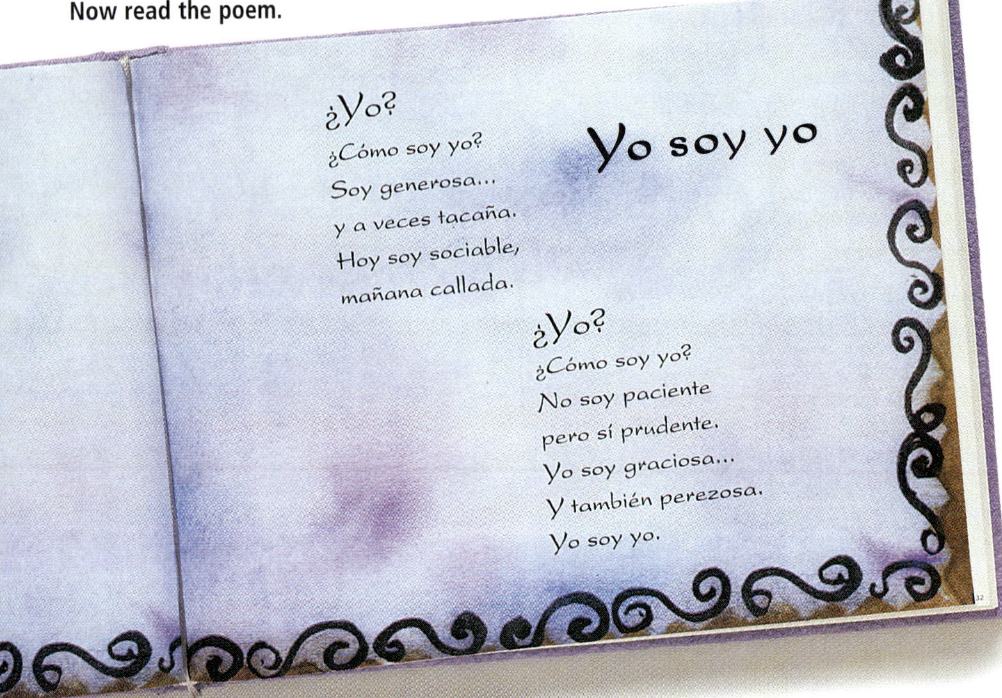

A Think about the predictions you made before you read the poem. Did you find the information that you thought you would find in the poem? What did you find out about the person who wrote it?

B Is the poet male or female? How do you know? Find at least three words that give you that information.

C Think of a rule that could help you decide whether to use the words *generoso* or *generosa* and *callado* or *callada* to describe a person. Are there any descriptive words (adjectives) on pages 38–39 that your rule does not cover? Which ones? Can you think of a rule for these words?

Options

Strategies for Reaching All Students

Students Needing Extra Help

For sections A–C, model aloud so that students hear everyone's responses. Write any responses on the chalkboard for visual learners.

Exs. 1–2: Encourage students to use the Organizer.

Ex. 1: Make sure students understand that they should choose words from the list.

Ex. 2: Point out to students that they can also use negative statements.

Enrichment

Ask for a male volunteer to read the poem aloud, making the necessary changes in adjective forms.

Ex. 1: Have students play a memory game in which they turn over cards with adjectives on them and try to match a feminine adjective with its masculine form (exclude adjectives ending in *-e* and *deportista).* Play with at least ten sets of adjectives (20 cards made prior to the game). A variation of this game is to have students match an adjective with its opposite. (This will be more challenging if separate cards are made for masculine and feminine forms. For example, the correct match for *perezosa* has to be *trabajadora,* not *trabajador.)*

Los adjetivos

Words describing people and things are called adjectives.

- In Spanish, adjectives describing males usually end in *-o*.
- Adjectives describing females usually end in *-a*. However, there are some exceptions, such as *deportista*, which can describe both females and males.
- Adjectives that end in *-e* can describe either females or males. How many examples can you find in the list?

Here are the adjectives you already know:

amable	deportista	impaciente	serio
artístico	desordenado	ordenado	seria
artística	desordenada	ordenada	sociable
atrevido	generoso	paciente	tacaño
atrevida	generosa	perezoso	tacaña
callado	gracioso	perezosa	trabajadora
callada	graciosa	prudente	trabajador

1 Look at the list of adjectives. Seventeen words can be used to describe a boy. Which are they? Which adjectives can be used to describe a girl? How many of the adjectives can be used to describe a boy *or* a girl? Which are they?

2 Students are preparing a who's who that describes each member of the class. Ask your partner what he or she is like. Each of you should choose four or more words from the list to describe yourselves.

A —*¿Cómo eres?*
B —*Soy generosa, trabajadora, paciente y sociable.*
o: *Soy generoso, trabajador, paciente y sociable.*

Present & Practice

Class Starter Review

On the day following the presentation of adjectives, you might begin the class with this activity:
Write these professions in English on the chalkboard: race car driver, politician, salesperson, sculptor, judge, comedian, baseball player, accountant. Ask what adjectives would describe the quality or qualities of a person wanting to enter one of these professions. List the words under the professions and see if the whole class agrees.

Answers

1 Adjectives which are used to describe a boy are: *amable, artístico, atrevido, callado, deportista, desordenado, generoso, gracioso, impaciente, ordenado, paciente, perezoso, prudente, serio, sociable, tacaño, trabajador.* Adjectives which are used to describe a girl are: *amable, artística, atrevida, callada, deportista, desordenada, generosa, graciosa, impaciente, ordenada, paciente, perezosa, prudente, seria, sociable, tacaña, trabajadora.* There are six adjectives which can describe either a boy or a girl: *amable, deportista, impaciente, paciente, prudente,* and *sociable.*

2 Answers will vary, but look for adjective agreement.

Practice

Answers

3 ESTUDIANTE A

a. Yo (no) soy deportista. ¿Y tú?
b. . . . gracioso(a). . . .
c. . . . tacaño(a). . . .
d. . . . generoso(a). . . .
e. . . . prudente. . . .
f. . . . trabajador(a). . . .
g. . . . ordenado(a). . . .
h. . . . artístico(a). . . .
i. . . . serio(a). . . .

ESTUDIANTE B

Answers may vary.
a. Yo (también / tampoco) soy deportista.
b. . . . gracioso(a).
c. . . . tacaño(a).
d. . . . generoso(a).
e. . . . prudente.
f. . . . trabajador(a).
g. . . . ordenado(a).
h. . . . artístico(a).
i. . . . serio(a).

3 How similar are you and your partner? For each of the following pictures, say whether you have that personality trait. Then find out whether your partner has it too.

A —*Yo soy impaciente. ¿Y tú?*
B —*Yo también soy impaciente.*
o: *No, yo no soy impaciente.*

o: A —*Yo no soy impaciente. ¿Y tú?*
B —*Yo tampoco soy impaciente.*
o: *Yo soy (muy) impaciente.*

Options

Strategies for Reaching All Students

Students Needing Extra Help

Ex. 4: Reinforce and review the importance of gender in Spanish grammar.

Enrichment

Ex. 3: As a follow-up, you might have pairs of students act out a job interview in which a supervisor questions the applicant's qualities and the applicant must contradict him or her. For example:
—*¿Eres impaciente?*
—*¡No! No soy impaciente. Soy paciente.*
Make sure students begin the interview with appropriate greetings and introductions. If possible, videotape the interviews as a class project.

4 Take turns with a partner describing these fictional characters. Afterward, compare your descriptions with those of another pair of students.

Scrooge A —¿Cómo es Scrooge?
B —Es muy tacaño.

¡No olvides!

To describe a third person (he or she), use *es*.

Estudiante A

a. Mary Poppins
b. Ricitos de Oro (Goldilocks)
c. Superman
d. Garfield
e. el león de *El Mago de Oz*
f. La Cenicienta (Cinderella)
g. Charlie Brown
h. Lucy
i. Robin Hood
j. Donald Duck

Estudiante B

5 Choose any person, either real or fictional, whom your partner is likely to know about. Tell your partner what the person is like. If necessary, pantomime any other helpful hints. Can your partner figure out whom you are describing?

4 ESTUDIANTE A

a. ¿Cómo es Mary Poppins?
b. . . . Ricitos de Oro?
c. . . . Superman?
d. . . . Garfield?
e. . . . el león de *El Mago de Oz?*
f. . . . La Cenicienta?
g. . . . Charlie Brown?
h. . . . Lucy?
i. . . . Robin Hood?
j. . . . Donald Duck?

ESTUDIANTE B

Answers will vary, but students may mention:

a. Es paciente.
b. Es sociable.
c. Es atrevido.
d. Es perezoso.
e. Es prudente.
f. Es trabajadora.
g. Es serio.
h. Es impaciente.
i. Es generoso.
j. Es gracioso.

5 Responses will vary, but look for adjective agreement.

 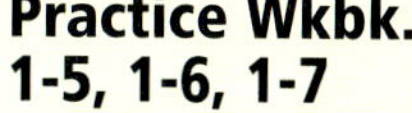

Practice Wkbk. 1-5, 1-6, 1-7

 **Writing Activities**

 **Pruebas 1-5, 1-6**

Cultural Notes 

(p. 51, realia)
If students ask: *agotado,* exhausted; *confundido,* confused; *extático,* ecstatic; *culpable,* guilty; *sospechoso,* suspicious; *enojado,* angry; *histérico,* hysterical; *frustrado,* frustrated; *triste,* sad; *confiado,* confident; *avergonzado,* embarrassed; *feliz,* happy; *malicioso,* wicked; *asqueado,* disgusted; *asustado,* scared; *rabioso,* furious; *apenado,* ashamed; *cauteloso,* cautious; *cómodo,* comfortable; *deprimido,* depressed; *agobiado,* overwhelmed; *esperanzado,* hopeful; *solitario,* lonely; *enamorado,* in love; *celoso,* jealous; *aburrido,* bored; *sorprendido,* surprised; *ansioso,* anxious; *pasmado,* astonished; *tímido,* timid.

Present & Apply

Answers: La cultura desde tu perspectiva

1 Answers will vary.

2 Point out that some of the steps may appear in a different order, depending on how important students perceive the statements. Discuss as a class.
Order of answers will vary, but may include:
You talk to the new student after class.
You work on a school project with the new student.
The new student calls you on the phone for help with an assignment.
You go to the movies with a group of friends, including the new student.
You go out with the new student for a snack after school.
You are invited to the new student's house for lunch.
You invite the new student to your house for dinner.
You are invited to attend the *quince años* (15th birthday) party of the new student's sister.

You become *conocidos* when you and the new student go to the movies with a group of friends, but you don't become *amigos* until you have met each other's families. / Answers will vary.

Sometimes you can tell the difference between a *conocido* and an *amigo* by the way two young people say hello and good-by. *Conocidos* may greet each other warmly by saying *¡Hola!* or *¿Qué tal?*, and they may chat for a while. *Amigos* and family members often hug each other, slap each other on the back, or may even kiss each other on the cheek.

La cultura desde tu perspectiva

1 Turn back to the *¡Piénsalo bien!* section on pages 28–29. Identify the people again and, with a partner, compare your answers with the ones you gave the first time. How does what you have learned about *amigos* change the way you look at the people in the photos?

2 What might be the steps in making a friend (*amigo*) from a Spanish-speaking country? Copy the sentences on the right on strips of paper. Then make a sequence chart by arranging them in an order that makes sense. When you are satisfied with the order, glue or tape the strips to a sheet of paper.

A new Spanish-speaking student joins your class.

- The new student calls you on the phone for help with an assignment.
- You talk to the new student after class.
- You invite the new student to your house for dinner.
- You work on a school project with the new student.
- You are invited to attend the *quince años* (15th birthday) party of the new student's sister.
- You go to the movies with a group of friends, including the new student.
- You go out with the new student for a snack after school.
- You are invited to the new student's house for lunch.

When are you *conocidos?* At what point do you become *amigos?*

In a group, compare your sequence charts. Discuss any differences. Decide on one sequence to share with the class. Were some sentences harder to place than others? Why?

Options

Strategies for Reaching All Students

Spanish-Speaking Students

Ask: *¿Conoces a los padres de un(a) amigo(a)? ¿Has invitado a un(a) amigo(a) a tu casa para celebrar un evento especial?*

 **Un paso más Ex. 1-E**

En Córdoba, Argentina

En Cuernavaca, México

Background Information

For further cultural information on Spanish-speaking countries, you may wish to obtain copies of Culturgram, a publication in newsletter form available from: Kennedy Center Publications / Brigham Young University / P.O. Box 24538 / Provo, UT 84602-4538
(phone: 800-528-6279)

Multicultural Perspectives

Have students make a Venn diagram of similarities, differences, and common interests of young people from a Spanish-speaking culture and of those from the U.S.

As extra credit, students could create posters of these findings. Include the use of visuals with the text for a colorful display for the classroom, hallway, or special school occasion.

Writing Activities

Cultural Notes

(p. 53, photos)
Students in Latin America often wear school uniforms as a way of establishing a sense of community and equality within the student body. Uniforms worn by both private- and public-school students tend to be conservative in appearance. Girls usually wear dark skirts or dresses and boys often wear dark slacks and a tie. Schools usually provide families with a list of uniform items and addresses of locations where they can be purchased. Some schools have periodic inspections to check students' uniforms.

Preview

Transparency 11

Teaching Suggestions

Have students add *sí / tampoco* to their Organizers.

Answers

A No, they do not enjoy playing soccer, because they appear to be hurt, and one is saying *A mí no me gusta el fútbol.*

B *A mí tampoco me gusta* means "I don't like it either."

C Cartoons will vary. Assist as needed in getting students started.

Gramática en contexto

A Do the people in the cartoon enjoy playing soccer? How do you know?

B What does *A mí tampoco me gusta* mean?

C With a partner, create a similar cartoon for an activity that you both dislike. Using the speech balloons above as a model, write speech balloons for your cartoon.

Options

Strategies for Reaching All Students

Students Needing Extra Help

Check students' Organizers and post a corrected copy.

Sí / Tampoco

- Sometimes you want to agree with someone who dislikes something and say you don't like it either. Use *a mí tampoco me gusta.*

  —A mí no me gusta nadar.
  —A mí **tampoco me gusta**.

- Other times you want to say that you *do* like something that someone else *dislikes*. Use *sí* + *me gusta* to make this difference clear.

  —A mí no me gusta hablar por teléfono. ¿Y a ti?
  —A mí **sí me gusta**.

- You may also want to say that you like one thing but dislike something else. Use *sí* + *me gusta* to make this difference clear.

  —No me gusta estudiar, pero **sí me gusta** hablar por teléfono.

1 Read the following conversations. In each set, who agrees with Student A—Student B or Student C? Which student *disagrees* with Student A?

A —*No me gusta nadar.*
B —*A mí sí me gusta.*
C —*A mí tampoco me gusta.*

A —*No me gusta nada cocinar.*
B —*A mí tampoco me gusta.*
C —*A mí sí me gusta mucho.*

2 You and your partner are discussing activities that you like and don't like. Choose five activities that you don't like, and find out whether or not your partner agrees.

A —*No me gusta dibujar. ¿Y a ti?*
B —*Pues, a mí sí me gusta.*
o: *A mí tampoco me gusta.*

Una piscina en Madrid

Present & Practice

Answers

1 In conversation one, Student C agrees with Student A. Student B disagrees with them. In conversation two, Student B agrees with Student A. Student C disagrees with them.

2 ESTUDIANTE A
Questions will vary, but should include *No me gusta* + inf.
ESTUDIANTE B
Answers will vary, but should include *a mí sí me gusta* OR *a mí tampoco me gusta.*

Cultural Notes

(p. 55, photo)
In 1992, the European Economic Community declared Madrid the Cultural Capital of Europe. However, the city offers diversions apart from its famed *café* scene and world-class museums. Public pools are popular spots for cooling off during the summer heat. One such pool is found in Casa de Campo, a public park located on the banks of the Manzanares River and formerly the royal family's hunting preserve.

Present & Practice

Teaching Suggestions

Have students add *ni . . . ni* to their Organizers.

Reinforce and review the importance of gender in Spanish grammar.

Answers

3 1. c
2. a
3. b

Ni . . . ni

- *Ni . . . ni* means "neither . . . nor" or "not . . . or." Use *ni . . . ni* to say that neither of two descriptions fits you. You must include the word *no* in front of the verb.

  No soy **ni** sociable **ni** callada.

  No soy **ni** artístico **ni** deportista.

- You also use *ni . . . ni* to say that you do not like either of two choices. For example:

  No me gusta **ni** patinar **ni** cocinar.

3 Match these sentences with the pictures.

1. Soy deportista pero no gracioso.
2. Soy paciente y prudente.
3. No soy ni generoso ni ordenado.

a. b. c.

Options

Strategies for Reaching All Students

Spanish-Speaking students

Have students write out their responses to Ex. 4 and then have them read a few aloud to the class.

4 Imagine that these are new students in your Spanish class. Tell what each person might say about his or her likes and dislikes.

Susana

Me gusta dibujar y cocinar, pero no me gusta ni leer ni practicar deportes.

a. Jorge

b. Benjamín

c. Cristina

d. Elena

5 Take turns asking and answering questions to find out what your partner is like. Discuss whether your partner is

- *sociable o callado(a)*
- *paciente o impaciente*
- *prudente o atrevido(a)*
- *generoso(a) o tacaño(a)*

A —*¿Eres trabajador(a) o perezoso(a)?*
B —*Soy (muy) trabajador(a).*
o: *Soy perezoso(a).*
o: *No soy ni trabajador(a) ni perezoso(a).*

4 Explain why *y* becomes *e* in item b.

a. Me gusta practicar deportes y leer, pero no me gusta ni ver la tele(visión) ni ayudar en casa.

b. Me gusta escuchar música e ir al cine, pero no me gusta ni nadar ni hablar por teléfono.

c. Me gusta nadar y dibujar, pero no me gusta ni estudiar ni ir a la escuela.

d. Me gusta tocar la guitarra y leer, pero no me gusta ni cocinar ni patinar.

5 Questions and answers will vary, but look for adjective agreement and use of *ni . . . ni* where appropriate.

 **Practice Wkbk. 1-8, 1-9**

 **Audio Activity 1.5**

 **Pruebas 1-7, 1-8**

 **Comm. Act. BLM 1-3**

Apply

Pronunciation Tape 1-3

Todo junto A

Play

Todo junto B

Play

Using the Video

Video segment 3: See the Video Teacher's Guide.

Video Activity C

Background Information

The game commonly known as Charades is called *las adivinanzas* (guessing game / riddles) in Spanish.

Here's an opportunity for you to put together what you learned in this chapter.

1 ¡Jugar a las adivinanzas!

In small groups, take turns acting out your favorite activity. For example, you might pretend that you're playing the guitar or swimming. Group members try to guess the activity. The student who guesses correctly takes the next turn. (You can also try playing *las adivinanzas* with the descriptive vocabulary words on pages 38–39.)

2 Las preferencias

Take a poll to find out which activities your classmates like to do. On a sheet of paper, list the activities mentioned in this chapter. Across the top, write these headings: ***me gusta mucho, me gusta, no me gusta, no me gusta nada.*** First, put a √ next to the activity that you think everyone will like. Put an X next to the one you think the fewest number of people will like. Then interview four classmates, asking about all the activities on the list. Mark the answers on your chart and total the number of votes for each activity under each heading.

	me gusta mucho	me gusta	no me gusta	no me gusta nada
ayudar en casa			ll	ll
patinar	ll		ll	
ver la tele	llll			

Options

Strategies for Reaching All Students

Students Needing Extra Help

Ex. 2: Have students base their chart on the model shown. Remind them that the activities listed are examples, and that they should choose from all the activities presented in the chapter.

Enrichment

Ex. 2: Find out which activity is the class favorite by asking how many students ranked each activity number one. Keep track on the chalkboard. Repeat the procedure to rank the class's descending order of preference. Use ordinal numbers for comprehensible input.

Cooperative Learning

Divide the class into groups of four students. Instruct each student to write his or her name at the top of an index card and then to pass the card to the left. Using an appropriate adjective, each student should write a compliment about the student named on the card. Cards should then be circulated until every student has written a complimentary description for each person

Autorretrato (1930), Frida Kahlo

3 ¿Cómo soy?

Bring to class a photograph or a picture of a person cut out of a magazine. Mount the picture on a sheet of paper. Based on the picture, what do you think this person is like? What are his or her likes and dislikes? Write a four-line caption in which the person describes himself or herself.

Tengo . . . años.	*Me gusta (mucho) . . .*
Soy . . .	*No me gusta (nada) . . .*

In small groups, look at the photos and read the captions. Display the portraits in the classroom.

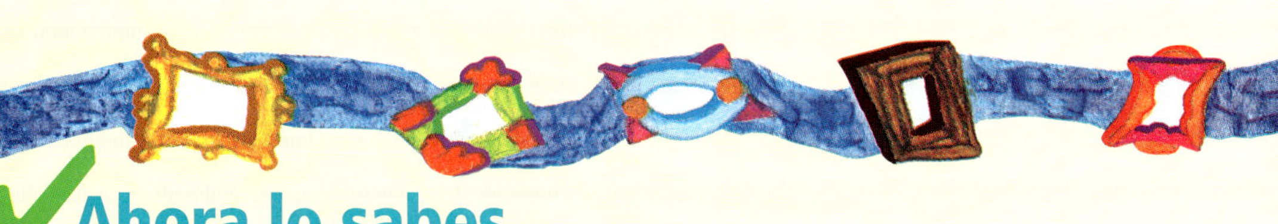

✓Ahora lo sabes

Using what you have learned so far, can you:

- **compare your likes and dislikes with someone else's?**
- **say that you don't like either of two choices?**
- **emphasize that you do like something?**
- **compare and contrast the meaning of the word "friend" in the United States and *amigo* in Spanish-speaking countries?**

Answers: Actividades

1 Student responses will vary.

2 Class poll results will vary.

3 Student captions will vary, but look for adjective agreement and use of *(No) me gusta* + inf.

Answers: Ahora lo sabes

The parenthetical page references after the answers refer to the sections in the chapter where this information was first presented. Be sure to tell students to refer to these sections for further practice.

- Answers will vary. *(pp. 30–31, 55–56)*
- No me gusta ni ___ ni ___. *(p. 56)*
- A mí sí me gusta. *(p. 55)*
- Answers will vary, but students may say that the concept of friendship is taken more seriously in a Spanish-speaking country than in the U.S. *(pp. 36–37, 52–53)*

 **Writing Activities**

 **Comm. Act. BLMs 1-4, 1-5**

 **Examen de habilidades 2**

in the group. Let students read their own cards first, then have them share with the class. If so desired, return them to the students whose names appear on the cards. As an alternate activity, bring to class one intriguing picture of a person and have all the students write captions for this picture. Then have students compare and contrast their captions.

Cultural Notes 

(p. 59, photo)
Since her death, Frida Kahlo (1910–1954) has become one of the most popular artists of the twentieth century. Kahlo is known for her surreal and sometimes disturbing paintings. Many people are fascinated with Kahlo's complicated relationship with her husband, Mexican muralist Diego Rivera. Others are interested in the way she coped with the intense physical discomfort she experienced as the result of an accident. The artist painted numerous self-portraits, which often reflected her emotional state at that time. Several were intended as gifts for loved ones—especially Diego Rivera.

Apply

Process Reading

Make sure students understand the four headings in this section and the tasks they represent:

- *Antes de leer:* pre-reading activity for activating prior knowledge; emphasis on one or more strategies for overcoming the tendency to read slowly, word by word, and instead to focus on receiving the message being communicated in the text
- *Mira la lectura:* scanning / skimming for general ideas or information, looking for cognates, proper nouns, headings, numbered or bulleted items, familiar words, etc.
- *Infórmate:* reading for more detailed information and for comprehension
- *Aplicación:* post-reading activity to transfer new skills or information to a new context or task

Teaching Suggestions

Remind students that they can do several things to check their guesses about the meaning of unknown words. They can ask another student, they can ask a Spanish speaker in the school or community, and they can look the words up in a dictionary or in the glossary at the back of their books.

¡Vamos a leer!

Antes de leer

STRATEGIES ➤ Using prior knowledge / Making predictions

This is the pen pal section of a Mexican young people's magazine. What kinds of information would you expect to find here? Make a list of three things.

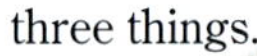

Mira la lectura

STRATEGY ➤ Scanning

Scanning is a strategy to help you quickly make sense of what you are reading. When you scan a selection, you look only for certain information. You do *not* have to read every word. For example, you might scan a bus schedule to find out if there is a five o'clock bus to where you are going.

Scan the pen pal section to see if it includes the three things you expected to find. What, if anything, is missing?

¡HOLA!

María Elena Sánchez Ureña
Niños Héroes Sur No. 734
02400 México D.F.
Edad: 12
Pasatiempos: coleccionar muñecas Barbie, escuchar música, leer libros sobre personas famosas

Raúl Domínguez Verdugo
Av. Kennedy 24
2° piso
44890 Guadalajara, Jal.
Edad: 12
Pasatiempos: leer biografías y libros sobre deportes, nadar y practicar fútbol

Eric Iván Casas
Monterrey 6, Col. Roma
03200 México D.F.
Edad: 13
Pasatiempos: nadar, patinar, fútbol

Laura Torres Pano
Benito Juárez No. 218
Jardines de la Asunción
20260 Aguascalientes, Ags.
Edad: 13
Pasatiempos: practicar vóleibol y béisbol, acampar, escuchar música

- *Niños Héroes* is the name of a street. *Sur* means "south."
- The five-digit number before the name of the city is a postal code like our Zip Code.
- The capital of Mexico is *la Ciudad de México* or, officially, *México D.F. D.F.* stands for *Distrito Federal*. What do you think that means? What city in the United States has a similar abbreviation? What does it stand for?
- *Col.* stands for *colonia* and means "neighborhood" or "area."
- *Jardines de la Asunción* is the name of a residential part of the city, like *Colonia Roma*.
- *Ags.* is an abbreviation for *Aguascalientes*, which is the name of a Mexican state as well as a city.
- *Av.* is an abbreviation for *Avenida*. What do you suppose the word means?
- *2° piso* is an abbreviation for *segundo piso* (second floor).
- *Jal.* is an abbreviation for *Jalisco*, a Mexican state.

Options

Strategies for Reaching All Students

Spanish-Speaking Students

 **Un paso más Ex. 1-F**

Students Needing Extra Help

Do all the activities in *¡Vamos a leer!* as a class or in small groups. The latter might work better at first. Use the Organizer as needed.

Enrichment

Ask students to name the student or students from *¡Hola!* who would most likely get along well with an American student who enjoys music as well as sports (Laura Torres Pano).
Aplicación: You may want to have students create a bulletin-board display with their written responses. Encourage them to use photos.

Infórmate

STRATEGY➤ Using context to get meaning

1 In what order does María Elena Sánchez Ureña provide the following information?

a. address c. hobbies
b. age d. name

2 Where do the writers live? On a separate sheet of paper, write each writer's first name under one of these headings.

Mexico City	Another city

3 Read about the hobbies of María Elena, Eric, Laura, and Raúl. On a separate sheet of paper, list the hobbies that two or more of them share. Then list those that are not shared. Use these headings.

Shared	Not shared

Are there any hobbies whose meaning you cannot understand? If there are, work with a partner to figure them out.

Aplicación

Imagine that your class is going to exchange letters with a class in Mexico or another Spanish class in your city. Attach a recent picture of yourself or a self-portrait to a sheet of paper. Write a caption for your picture. Don't forget to give this information.

- Nombre y dirección
- Edad
- Pasatiempos

Answers

Antes de leer

Answers will vary, but students may say they'd expect to find names, addresses, ages, likes and dislikes, or hobbies.

Mira la lectura

Answers will vary. / Federal District / Washington, D.C. (District of Colombia) / Avenue

Infórmate

1 Order is as follows: name, address, age, hobbies

2 Mexico City: María Elena, Eric Iván
Another city: Laura, Raúl

3 Shared hobbies include: *escuchar música, leer libros, nadar, practicar fútbol.*
Individual hobbies include: *coleccionar muñecas Barbie, patinar, practicar vóleibol y béisbol, acampar.*

Aplicación

Explain that in Spanish, we usually write the street name first, then the number.
You may want to have students create a bulletin board display of their letters. Encourage them to use photos. You may wish to organize a pen-pal program with another Spanish class in your school or in a nearby one. If possible, access the Internet via a computer and on-line service to request "key pals."

Apply

Process Writing

Inform students in advance that their work will be kept in a portfolio of their writing, and that they will be able to select the best examples for assessment. Explain that their portfolio will help them keep a record of their progress throughout the year.

Portfolios represent a systematic process involving both learner and teacher. They document progress toward specific standards by applying clearly stated criteria in selecting, monitoring, and evaluating significant products and performance. (For a more detailed explanation of portfolio writing and assessment, see pp. T40–T44.)

In preparation for the writing assignment, you may wish to briefly review adjective agreement.

Step 3: Remind students about correct accent placement, question marks, and exclamation points. For spelling checks, tell students that they may always refer to the vocabulary sections or the *Resumen del capítulo.*

Step 4: Exhibit the illustrated poems in the classroom or in another part of the school. Have the poems published in the school newspaper.

¡Vamos a escribir!

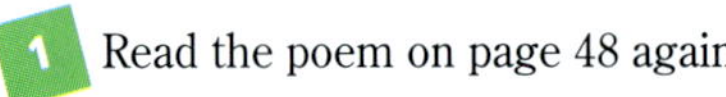

Write a poem about yourself similar to the one on page 48. Follow these steps:

1. Read the poem on page 48 again.

   Look at the vocabulary on pages 38–39 and write down three adjectives that apply to you and three that don't. Use the headings *Soy* and *No soy.*

   Then, using the vocabulary on pages 30–31, write down at least three activities that you like to do and three activities that you don't like to do. Use the headings *Me gusta* and *No me gusta.*

2. Write your poem based on this model and the lists that you made. Use adjectives in lines 3 and 4. Use activities in lines 5 and 6.

   ¿Yo?
   ¿Cómo soy yo?
   Soy ___ y ___ ,
   pero a veces soy ___ .
   Me gusta ___ y también ___ ,
   pero no me gusta ___ .
   Yo soy yo.

   Now show your poem to a partner. Ask which parts of the poem he or she likes and which ones might be changed. Decide whether or not you agree, then rewrite your poem, making any changes that you have decided on.

3. Check for spelling, accents, and punctuation. Note that in Spanish we do not capitalize every line of a poem. We capitalize only the beginning of a sentence and proper nouns. Use this checklist.
   - capital letters at the beginning of a sentence
   - accent marks (*música, teléfono*)
   - question marks at the beginning and end of questions
   - agreement of adjectives (*generoso* or *generosa*)

4. Make a clean copy of your corrected poem. Add drawings or pictures if you like. Share your work with your classmates, with your family, or with Spanish-speaking friends—or acquaintances. You may want to include it in your portfolio.

Options

Strategies for Reaching All Students

Spanish-Speaking Students

To extend the assignment, have students write a poem describing their best friend or an ideal friend. Display the poems in the classroom.

Un paso más Ex. 1-G

Students Needing Extra Help

Step 2: Review the definition of an adjective, reminding students that it is a word that describes someone or something. Have them give examples of adjectives in English to make sure they understand. Refer to the Organizer.
Step 3: Use the Organizer.

Resumen del capítulo 1

¡Qué buen trabajo!

Use the vocabulary from this chapter to help you:

- describe yourself
- find out what other people are like
- talk about what you like and don't like to do
- compare your likes and dislikes with other people's

to talk about activities
ayudar en casa
cocinar
dibujar
escuchar música
estar con amigos
estudiar
hablar por teléfono
 el teléfono
ir a la escuela
ir al cine
 el cine
leer
nadar
patinar
practicar deportes
tocar la guitarra
ver la televisión (la tele)

to ask someone what he or she likes
¿Qué te gusta (hacer)?
¿Te gusta ___?
¿Y a ti?

to say what you like
(A mí) me gusta ___.
(A mí) me gusta mucho ___.
(A mí) me gusta más ___.
(A mí) sí me gusta ___.
A mí también.

to say what you do not like
(A mí) no me gusta ___.
(A mí) no me gusta mucho ___.
(A mí) no me gusta nada ___.
A mí tampoco me gusta ___.

to ask someone what he or she is like
¿Cómo eres?
¿Eres (tú) ___?

to say what you or someone else is like
(Yo) soy ___.
(Tú) eres ___.
es

to describe yourself or others
amable
artístico, -a
atrevido, -a
callado, -a
deportista
desordenado, -a
generoso, -a
gracioso, -a
impaciente
ordenado, -a
paciente
perezoso, -a
prudente
serio, -a
sociable
tacaño, -a
trabajador, -a

to ask if a statement is accurate
¿De veras?

other useful words and expressions
a veces
muy
ni...ni
pero
pues
también
tampoco
y

Summarize

Writing Activities

Mi portafolio

Test Generator

Cultural Notes

(p. 62, photo)
The invention of the telephone has made letter writing out-of-date for many of us. Crafting a letter, though, can still be the best mode of communication where telephone service is costly or unreliable. Besides, nothing beats a hand written message for conveying deeply held emotions. In recent years, computer e-mail has given rise to "electronic" pen pals. More and more, people are turning to writing—in this case, the keyboard—instead of the phone.

CAPÍTULO 2

THEME: SCHOOL

SCOPE AND SEQUENCE Pages 64–103

COMMUNICATION

Topics

School supplies

School subjects

Class schedules

Time-telling

Numbers 32–59

Objectives

To compare school systems in the U.S. and in Spanish-speaking countries

To talk about school subjects and supplies

To tell what people need

To say what something is for

To express possession

To express quantity

To ask for information

To express regret / hesitation

To talk about location

To ask and tell when something takes place / To ask and tell the time

CULTURE

Mexican vs. U.S. school systems

Levels of speech: *tú / Ud. / Uds.*

GRAMMAR

Los pronombres personales

Verbos que terminan en -ar

Los sustantivos

Ancillaries available for use with Chapter 2

Multisensory/Technology

Overhead Transparencies, 12–17

Audio Tapes and CDs

Projects for Proficiency: Blackline Master Spanish Activities for Middle School Learners

Vocabulary Art Blackline Masters for Hands-On Learning, pp. 13–17

Classroom Crossword

Video

CD-ROM

Print

Practice Workbook, pp. 23–32

Writing, Audio & Video Activities, pp. 21–28, 68–70, 102–103

Communicative Activity Blackline Masters

Pair and Small Group Activities, pp. 15–20

Situation Cards, p. 21

Un paso más: Actividades para ampliar tu español, pp. 7–12

Assessment

Assessment Program

Pruebas, pp. 25–28, 33–35

Exámenes de habilidades, pp. 29–32, 36–39

Mi portafolio, pp. 40–41

Test Generator

Video still from Chap. 2

Cultural Overview

Educational Traditions

Although educational goals in Spain, Latin America, and the U.S. are fundamentally the same—most educators, for example, want to develop good citizens—their educational traditions are quite distinct.

Many of the educational traditions of Latin America have their origin in Spanish traditions. The Spanish school system is divided into four different levels of education: 1) preschool, 2) *Educación General Básica* (EGB), which is primary education, 3) *Bachillerato Unificado y Polivalente* (BUP), which is a program of study aimed at university requirements, or *Formación Profesional* (FP) which is high-school-level training in technical fields, and 4) university study. In order to enter a university, the *Curso de Orientación Universitaria* (COU) must be completed.

Children in Spain may enter free preschool programs. Primary schooling begins at age 6 and continues to age 16. *Educación General Básica* provides a background in languages, mathematics, social and natural sciences, and artistic expression. Children receive around 25 hours of instruction a week. Though school books are free in some special cases, Spanish families usually pay for books as well as school supplies, transportation, lunch service, and voluntary extracurricular activities, such as foreign language study or music. This is generally true throughout Latin America as well.

If students complete the EGB before age 16, they receive the certificate of *Graduado Escolar* and may choose to continue their education in either a secondary (BUP) or a technical-training school (FP). Those who do not complete their studies by age 16 receive a certificate of *Escolaridad* and are eligible only for technical-training schools.

BUP is geared toward academics and FP is hands-on training in the areas of science and technology, health-care technology, or business. Evaluation in either option is through exams in each subject area. A final comprehensive exam is given twice a year. Students who wish to continue their studies must pass this exam.

Perhaps the most significant contrast between the U.S. and Spanish educational systems is the "tracking" of students for college. In the U.S., high-school graduates have theoretically received a general academic preparation enabling them to attend any of a variety of post-secondary educational institutions. In Spain, however, secondary education more specifically gears students to either university studies or further technical and business education.

Introduce

Re-entry of Concepts

The following list represents words, expressions, and grammar topics re-entered from *El primer paso* to Chap. 1:

El primer paso
School supplies
Numbers 0–31
School vocabulary

Chapter 1
Activities
Gustar expressions

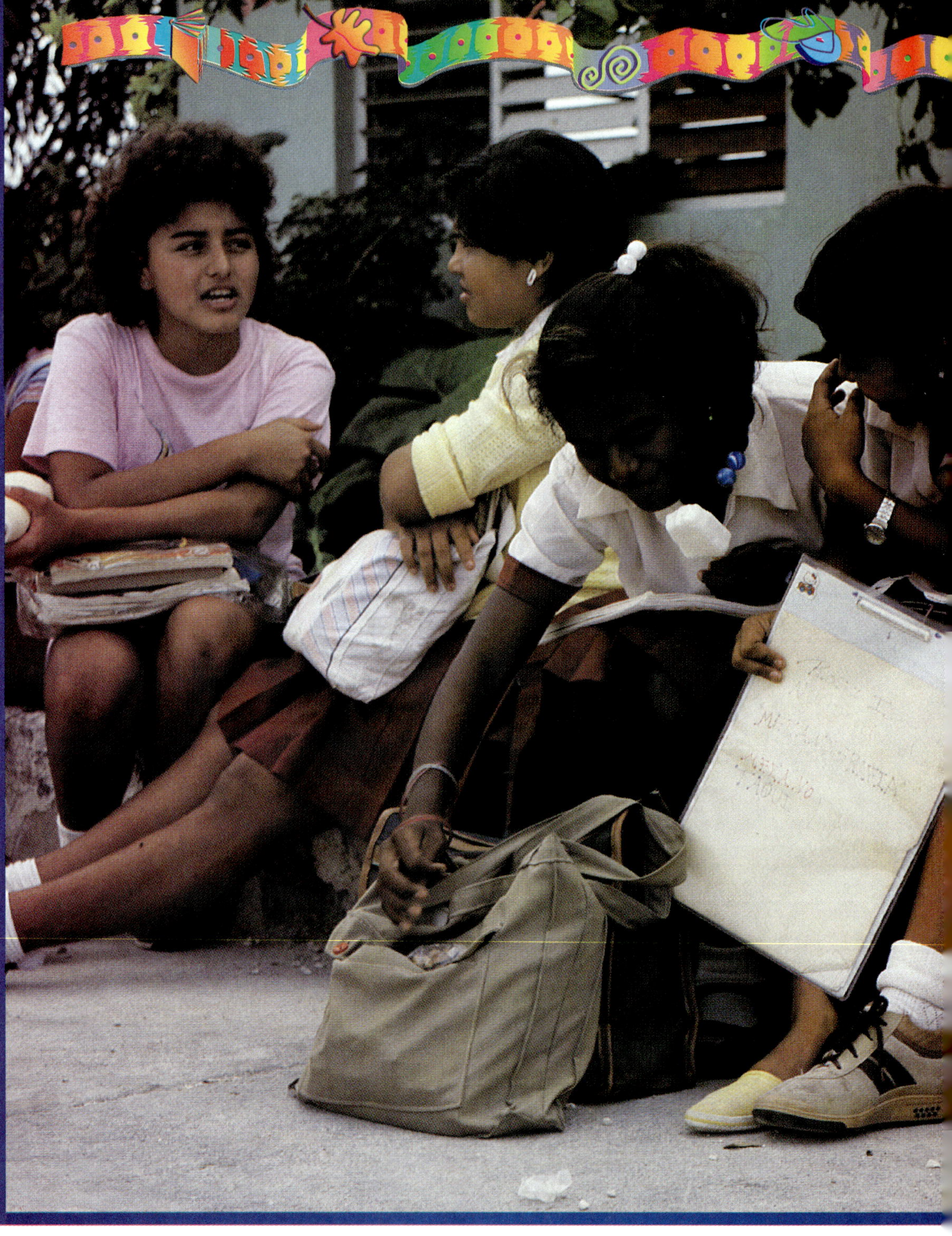

Planning

Cross-Curricular Connections

Math Connection *(p. 68)*

Explain the difference between ordinal and cardinal numbers. Have students be responsible for looking up words for 9th through 20th and then writing them on a poster or on the chalkboard. They may want to make a list for their notebooks. (Point out that, although they exist, the words in Spanish for "eleventh" and greater are generally not used.)

You may also wish to review Roman numerals, along with ordinal numbers in English.

Art Connection *(pp. 76–77)*

Have students plan a study schedule for the afternoon or evening based on their school subjects. Have them design and illustrate the time (beginning and ending) devoted to the study of each subject. Students could draw pictures to illustrate descriptions of activities.

Geography Connection *(pp. 100–101)*

Obtain two maps of Argentina from a travel agency or tourist office. Post one on the wall. From the second, cut out picture features, names of cities and sites, etc. Give pairs of students these cutouts and have them locate and pin them on the map.

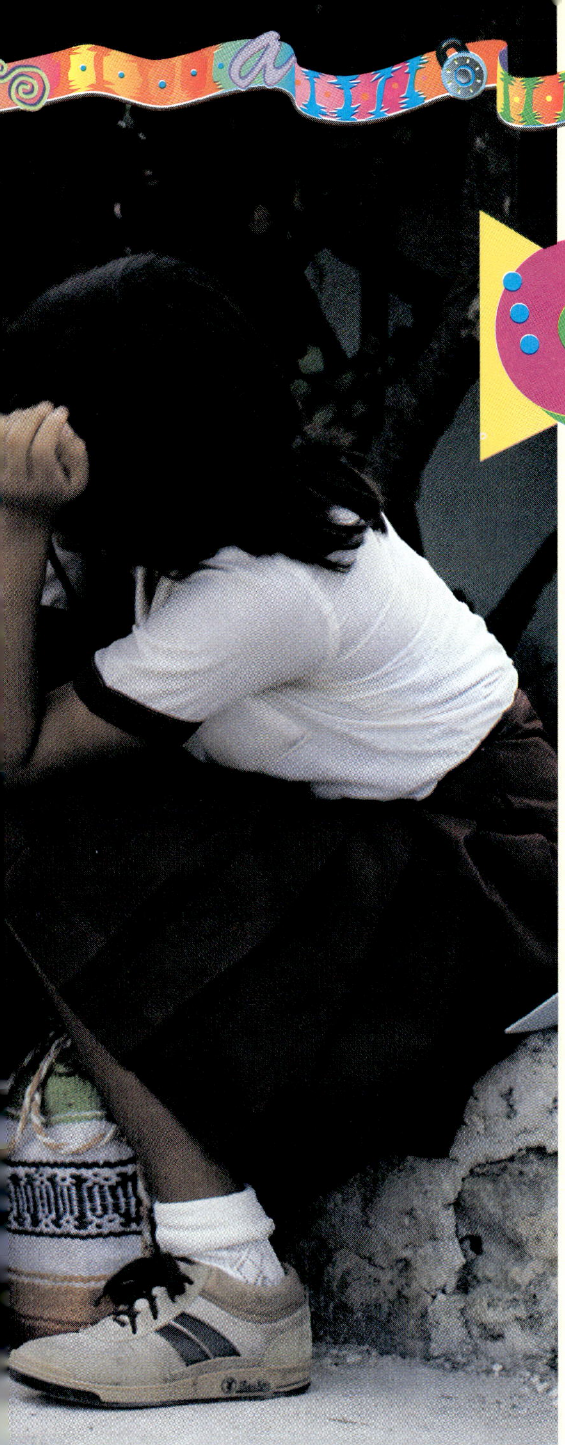

Capítulo 2

¿Qué clases tienes?

OBJECTIVES

At the end of this chapter, you will be able to:

- **describe your class schedule**
- **find out about someone else's schedule**
- **name some school supplies you use**
- **compare your school experience with that of a student in a Spanish-speaking country**

Isla Mujeres, México

Continue by giving each pair a blank map and have them make a pictorial of the area. Have each pair pick one aspect or location and do a brief follow-up paragraph in English.

(For further cross-curricular activities, see the Conexiones *section on pp. 84–85.)*

Spanish in Your Community

Besides in your school, where else in the community is it possible to learn Spanish or other foreign languages? Have students suggest other learning sources. Possible answers might include: community colleges, universities, private language schools, tapes, and libraries. Ask: What languages are taught in our community? What foreign language do you think is the most popular in our community? Discuss reasons why this might be so.

Cultural Notes 

(pp. 64–65, photo)

Isla Mujeres is located about five miles off the Caribbean coast of Yucatán. Students from throughout the island travel into town, *el pueblo,* on the island's northern end, to attend classes. How did this island get its name? One story says the explorer Hernández de Córdoba found wooden images of Mayan goddesses on the island. Another theory claims that Spanish sailors found only women, since the men were out fishing.

Preview

Cultural Objective

- To compare your school experience with that of a student in a Spanish-speaking country

 **¡Piénsalo bien!**

Play

 **Video Activity A**

Using the Video

This chapter's video focuses on school—classes, supplies, and schedules. Students will see our hosts in Madrid visiting a middle school and interviewing students in class.

Since the videos for this chapter and for Chapters 3, 4, 6, 8, and 9 were filmed in Spain, students will hear the forms of *vosotros* and the Castilian accent being used. You may want to prepare your students by reviewing those verb forms.

Show students segment one once through, then ask them to predict what this chapter's tape will be about, based on the chapter's theme. Then have students watch the segment again several times. After the first time, you may wish to have them brainstorm possible vocabulary and expressions they will need to talk about what they

¡Piénsalo bien!

Look at the photos. Are they similar to what you are used to? Are they different in any ways?

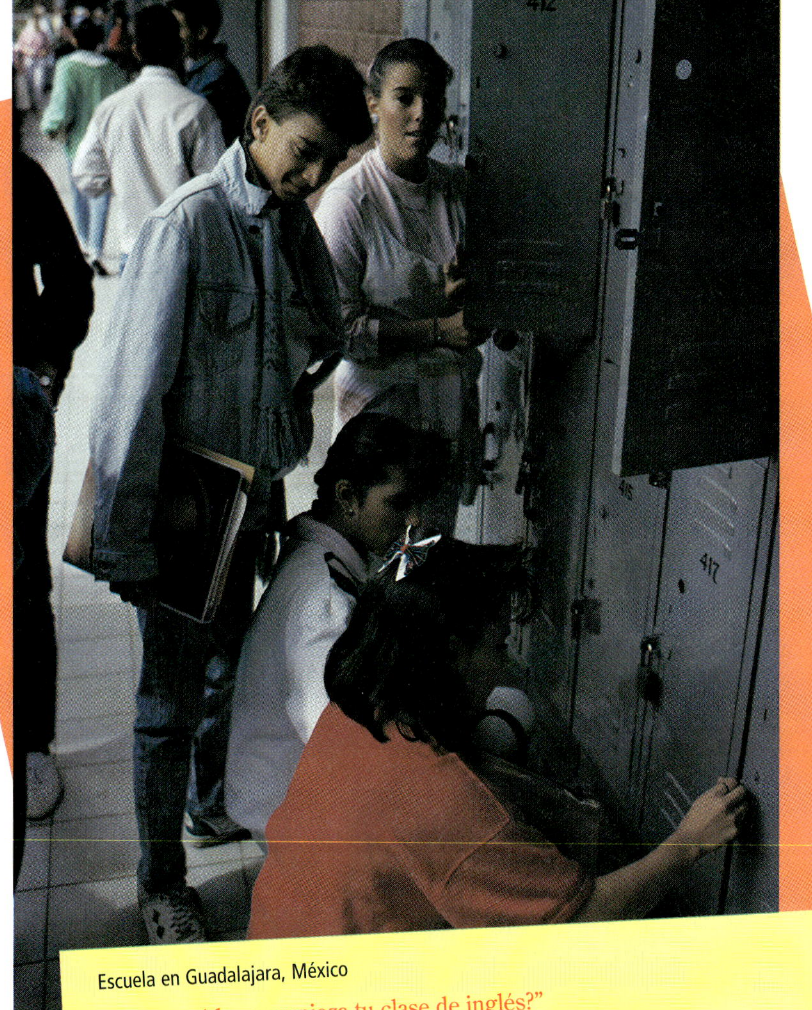

Escuela en Guadalajara, México

"Luz, ¿a qué hora empieza tu clase de inglés?"

Options

Strategies for Reaching All Students

Spanish-Speaking Students

Ask: *¿Qué clases tienes este semestre? ¿Qué necesitas para una clase de matemáticas? ¿Qué necesitas para tus otras clases?*

 **Un paso más Ex. 2-A**

Students Needing Extra Help

Have students first make a list of their classes in English. After the vocabulary presentation on pp. 68–69, ask students to then list their classes in Spanish.

Lima, Perú

"Me gusta mucho tocar en la banda. Yo toco el tambor."

Cuernavaca, México

Estas muchachas tienen mucha tarea.

saw on the video. Ask students to identify: a) things they saw that looked familiar but were somewhat different from what they might see in their own school, and b) anything they saw that they probably would not see in their own school.

Video segment 1: For more teaching suggestions, see the Video Teacher's Guide.

Teaching Suggestions

See the Projects for Proficiency BLMs for activity ideas that you may elect to use throughout the chapter.

Answers: ¡Piénsalo bien!

Answers to inductive questions may vary.

Cultural Notes

(p. 66, photo / p. 67, bottom photo)
The beginnings of life-long friendships are often forged in school. These friends in Guadalajara, Jalisco, meet and exchange a few words at their lockers. Two classmates from Cuernavaca, Morelos, are working together on an assignment, using standard ruled notebooks purchased at a local *librería.*

(p. 67, top photo)
Marching bands are common elements in parades and civic events around the world, including in Lima, Peru. Derived from the French word *bande* (company), modern bands, like this group of *limeño* students, strive to stay in step through precision drills. A marching band usually includes only wind and percussion instruments that can be easily carried and heard afar.

Present

Chapter Theme
School subjects and supplies

Communicative Objectives
- To ask and tell when something takes place
- To talk about school subjects
- To talk about school supplies
- To tell what people need
- To say what something is for
- To express possession
- To express quantity
- To ask for information
- To express regret
- To express hesitation
- To talk about location

Transparencies 12–13

Vocabulary Art BLMs

Pronunciation Tape 2-1

Vocabulario para conversar A

Play

Using the Video
Video segment 2: See the Video Teacher's Guide.

Video Activity B

Sección 1

Vocabulario para conversar

¿Qué clases tienes?

- As your teacher reads the name of each school subject, raise your right hand if you have that class.
- Now, as your teacher reads the name of each school subject, make a thumbs up gesture if you like it and a thumbs down gesture if you don't.
- As your teacher reads the name of each school supply, hold up the item if you have one.

Horario	Primer semestre	Segundo semestre
(1ª) primera hora	inglés	matemáticas
(2ª) segunda hora	educación física	ciencias de la salud
(3ª) tercera hora	matemáticas	educación física
(4ª) cuarta hora	ciencias sociales	inglés
(5ª) quinta hora	almuerzo	almuerzo
(6ª) sexta hora	ciencias	español
(7ª) séptima hora	español	ciencias
(8ª) octava hora	arte	música

Options

Strategies for Reaching All Students

Spanish-Speaking Students
Spanish-speaking students can make their own vocabulary lists with additional classes and supplies, using the words with which they are already familiar. If necessary, help them with spelling.

Enrichment
Enhance the vocabulary presentation by bringing in class schedules, course descriptions, etc., from schools in Spanish-speaking countries.
If students should ask: *novena hora* (ninth period / hour), *décima hora* (tenth period / hour).

Vocabulario para conversar: As a written assignment, have students use adjectives they've learned to describe their behavior in different classes, perhaps pointing out how behavior may vary according to the class they're in. Example: *Soy perezoso(a) en la clase de matemáticas, pero muy trabajador(a) en la clase de ciencias.*

También necesitas . . .

la clase de ____	____ *class*	para	*for*
difícil	*difficult, hard*	tu	*your*
fácil	*easy*	¿Qué?	*What?*
la tarea	*homework*	Lo siento.	*I'm sorry.*
aprender: (yo) aprendo	*to learn: I learn*	A ver...	*Let's see...*
(tú) aprendes	*you learn*	Aquí / Allí está.	*Here / There it is.*
necesitar: (yo) necesito	*to need: I need*		
(tú) necesitas	*you need*		
tener: (yo) tengo	*to have: I have*		
(tú) tienes	*you have*		

¿Y qué quiere decir . . . ?
mucho, -a

¡No olvides!
tú = *you*
tu = *your*

Grammar Preview

Necesito and *necesitas* are presented lexically, as is the use of indefinite articles. The explanation of *-ar* verbs appears in the grammar section on pp. 90–91. Gender of nouns and the use of indefinite articles are on p. 95.

Teaching Suggestions

Formation of plural nouns will be taught in Chap. 4. For now, students will use them, but they will not be expected to form them.

Label classroom supplies and objects around the room. Have students start filling in their Organizers.

Class Starter Review

On the day following initial presentation of vocabulary, you might begin the class with either of these activities:
1) Name a class subject and have students signal *sí* or *no* as you mention school supplies that might be necessary for that class.
2) Have students work in groups and create a collage or poster of school supplies to be used for a particular class or to be stored in a locker. You might want to have other students guess whose class or locker it is.

Learning Spanish Through Action

STAGING VOCABULARY: *Levanten, Muestren, Señalen, Toquen*
1) MATERIALS: transparency of school supplies in the *Vocabulario para conversar* or the actual items
DIRECTIONS: Using the transparency or actual school supplies, have pairs of students touch or point to the items that you mention. If the actual items are available, you may wish to have students raise the item, then ask them *¿Qué tienes?* (Repeat this activity with actual items the next day as a race with volunteers on two teams.)
2) MATERIALS: transparency of school subjects in the *Vocabulario para conversar*
DIRECTIONS: Using the transparency, mention a class subject and have pairs of students touch or point to the appropriate illustration. Continue until each class subject is mentioned.

Practice

Critical Thinking: Classifying Information

As a written activity, have students use the *Vocabulario para conversar* to list the supplies they probably would *never* use in school. Then ask them to list the ones they would use in almost *every* class. Compile this information and write the lists on the chalkboard.

Teaching Suggestions

Ex. 3: If students have these items, ask them to put them on their desks.

Answers: Empecemos a conversar

1 ESTUDIANTE A

a. ¿Tienes mucha tarea en tu clase de ciencias?
b. . . . matemáticas?
c. . . . ciencias sociales?
d. . . . inglés?
e. . . . español?
f. Questions will vary.

ESTUDIANTE B

a.–f. Answers will vary.

Empecemos a conversar

With a partner, take turns being *Estudiante A* and *Estudiante B*. Use the words that are cued or given in the boxes to replace the underlined words in the example. (lightbulb) means you can make your own choices. When it is your turn to be *Estudiante B*, try to answer truthfully.

1 

A —*¿Tienes mucha tarea en tu clase de <u>ciencias de la salud</u>?*
B —*Sí, tengo mucha tarea.*
o: *No, no tengo mucha tarea.*
o: *No estudio ciencias de la salud.*

Estudiante A | Estudiante B

2 

1ª

A —*¿Qué clase tienes en la <u>primera</u> hora?*
B —*¿En la <u>primera</u> hora? Pues, tengo <u>inglés</u>.*

Estudiante A

a. 2ª
b. 3ª
c. 4ª
d. 5ª
e. 6ª
f. 7ª
g. 8ª

Estudiante B

Options

Strategies for Reaching All Students

Spanish-Speaking Students

Pair bilingual with non-bilingual students for Exs. 1 and 2. You may wish to have them write out Ex. 4, using at least three questions. Help them check their spelling.

 **Un paso más Exs. 2-B, 2-C**

Students Needing Extra Help

Ex. 2: Explain that when we speak, we often repeat all or part of the question to be sure we understand what was asked. Model one or two examples in English.

Ex. 3: Explain the responses before moving ahead. Model with as many other school supplies as necessary.

3 

A —*¿Qué necesitas en tu clase de matemáticas?*
B —*Necesito un lápiz, un cuaderno y una carpeta.*

Estudiante A **Estudiante B**

4 A —*¿Tienes un lápiz?*
B —*A ver . . . Sí, aquí está.*
o: *Sí, allí está.*
o: *No, lo siento.*

Estudiante A **Estudiante B**

2 ESTUDIANTE A
a. ¿Qué clase tienes en la segunda hora?
b. . . . tercera hora?
c. . . . cuarta hora?
d. . . . quinta hora?
e. . . . sexta hora?
f. . . . séptima hora?
g. . . . octava hora?

ESTUDIANTE B
a. ¿En la segunda hora? Pues, tengo . . . *(Answers will vary.)*
b. . . . tercera hora? . . .
c. . . . cuarta hora? . . .
d. . . . quinta hora? . . .
e. . . . sexta hora? . . .
f. . . . séptima hora? . . .
g. . . . octava hora? . . .

3 ESTUDIANTE A
a. ¿Qué necesitas en tu clase de matemáticas?
b. . . . arte?
c. . . . ciencias sociales?
d. . . . inglés?
e. . . . español?

ESTUDIANTE B
a.–e. *(Answers will vary.)*
Necesito . . .

4 ESTUDIANTE A
Questions will vary, but should include school supplies. Encourage *Estudiante A* to ask at least three or four questions.

ESTUDIANTE B
Answers will vary depending on whether *Estudiante B* has the object mentioned. Ask students to show the object if they have it.

Apply

Re-enter / Recycle

Ex. 3: *gustar* expressions from Chap. 1

Teaching Suggestions

Ex. 3: Remind students of *ni . . . ni.*

Empecemos a leer y a escribir: For additional practice, have students make a two-column chart. In the left column they should write the heading *Clase* and list their classes. In the right column, have them write the heading *Necesito* and list the school supplies they need next to each class.

If the *Empecemos a leer y a escribir* sections are done in class, you can have students work in groups to figure out the answers, but have each student write his or her answers on a separate sheet of paper. You may prefer to use these sections as homework assignments throughout the chapters.

Ex. 5: Students may enjoy drawing the contents of their backpack and labeling each item.

Options

Strategies for Reaching All Students

Spanish-Speaking Students

Ex. 1: Allow students to list the names of items to which they are already accustomed to using, and to add to the list as they see fit.

Remind them that a Venn diagram uses partially overlapping circles or rectangles to show the similarities or differences between two or more concepts. See the Projects for Proficiency BLMs for a Venn diagram template.

Enrichment

Have students write a list of the school supplies that they were required to have for all their classes at the beginning of the year.

Empecemos a leer y a escribir

Responde en español.

1 Read this list of everyday items and decide where you use them: only at school, only at home, or in both places. Copy the Venn diagram and write the items in the correct areas. If you don't use an item, write it outside the circles.

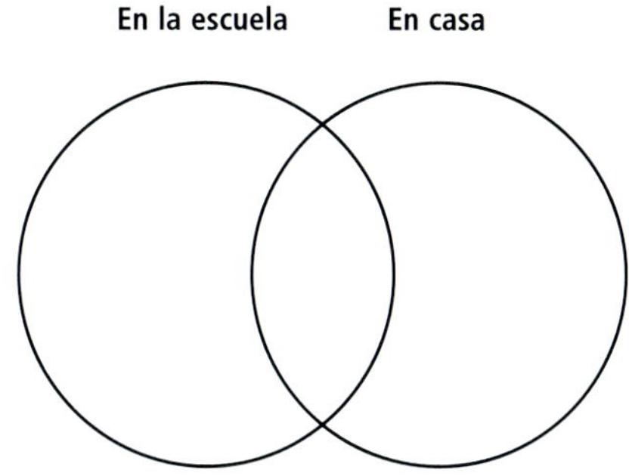

un marcador
una grabadora
un teléfono
un diccionario
una guitarra
una hoja de papel
un pupitre
una regla
un cuaderno
un bolígrafo
una pizarra
un lápiz

2 In two columns, under the headings *Fácil* and *Difícil*, list the subjects you are taking this year.

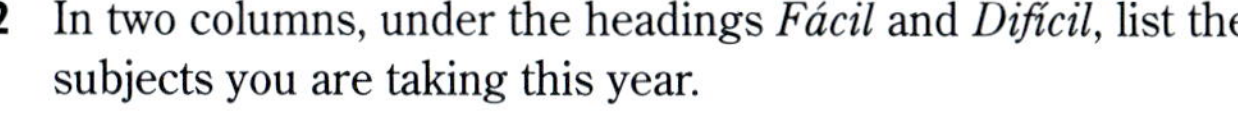

3 ¿Qué te gusta más, hacer la tarea de español o hacer las actividades con tus compañeros en la clase de español?

4 ¿Qué necesitas para tu primera clase?

5 ¿Qué tienes en tu mochila?

Estos estudiantes mexicanos hacen la tarea para la clase de ciencias sociales.

También se dice

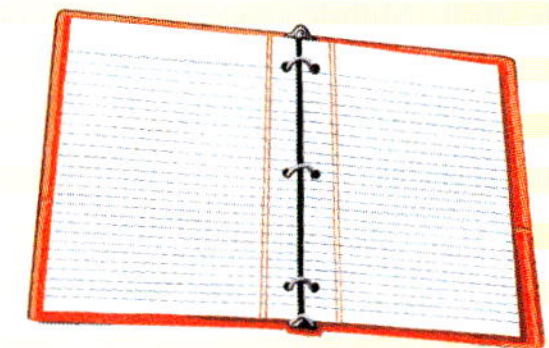

la carpeta de anillas
el archivador

el plumón

Answers: Empecemos a leer y a escribir

1–5 Answers will vary, but look for appropriate school supplies in Exs. 4 and 5.

 **Practice Wkbk. 2-1, 2-2**

 **Audio Activity 2.1**

 **Writing Activities**

 **Pruebas 2-1, 2-2**

 **Comm. Act. BLM 2-1**

Cultural Notes 

(p. 72, realia)
Writing is one of the defining characteristics of civilization. In past centuries only a few people knew how to read, and access to many written texts was restricted to the privileged. In our modern era, writing and literacy are considered basic skills to be acquired by all members of a society. Many countries, such as Chile, invest significant effort into promoting literacy skills to build a strong country.

(p. 73, photo)
These students are studying in the library of the Colegio Tulum in Mexico City. Tulum, which means "City of dawn," is an archaeological site in Quintana Roo on the Yucatán peninsula. Tulum is the only known walled city by the ocean that the Mayas ever constructed.

Present & Apply

Cultural Objective

- To talk about similarities and differences between a Mexican and a U.S. middle school

Background Information

If students ask, these are other classes listed in the schedule: *Ciencias naturales,* Science; *Dibujo técnico,* Drafting; *Libre,* Free period; *Receso,* Break; *Taller,* Workshop (includes woodworking, metal working, and related crafts); *Teatro,* Theater / Drama class.

Point out that there is no lunch break in the schedule, because most students would go home for lunch at 1:00 or 2:00. The class schedule varies from day to day, and there is no passing period, since the teachers move from room to room, not the students.

Children enter kindergarten (*el kinder)* at about age four and spend two years there. Sometimes the term *preprimaria* (preprimary) is used for kindergarten.

Teaching Suggestions

You might wish to prepare a list of additional discussion questions to ask students after they have read the material. Suggestions: Do you think U.S. students spend more or less time on homework than Mexican students? How much

Mira el horario y la foto. ¿Qué ves que es similar o diferente de lo que ves en tu escuela?

Going to school in Mexico City is similar in some ways to going to school in the United States, but there are some important differences. Primary school (*escuela primaria*) goes from the first grade to the sixth grade. Seventh graders begin middle school (*escuela secundaria*) and say they are in first year (*primero de secundaria*). Eighth graders are in second year (*segundo de secundaria*), and ninth graders are in third year (*tercero de secundaria*).

Not all Mexican schools are alike. You might find that any or all of these things happen:

- Uniforms are required at least four days a week.
- Students stay in the same room, and teachers go from class to class.
- When a teacher enters the classroom, the students stand.
- The teacher calls the students by their last names.
- The students address their teacher as *maestro* or *maestra,* without a last name.
- More class time is spent on teacher lectures than on class discussions.
- Students spend from 15 to 30 minutes per class on homework each night.
- Teachers collect the homework the next day rather than reviewing it in class.

As you can see in the schedule, Mexican schools have a mid-morning break *(receso).* Students play games or sports (usually *fútbol),* or they just chat in the schoolyard. They can buy snacks at the school store or from a street vendor who comes into the schoolyard. They can buy sandwiches, ice cream cones, popcorn, soda, and juice.

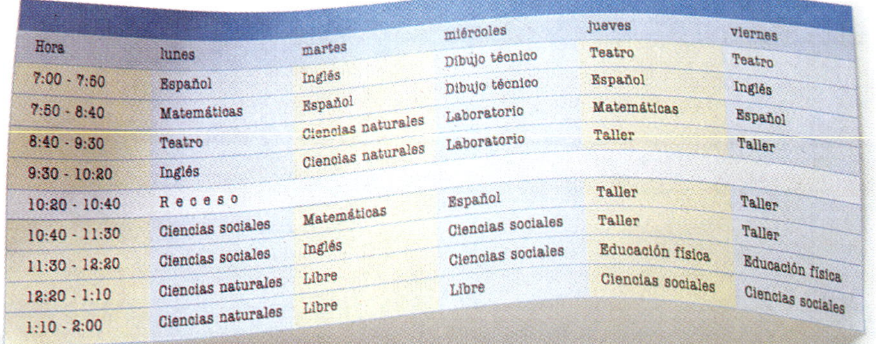

Hora	lunes	martes	miércoles	jueves	viernes
7:00 - 7:50	Español	Inglés	Dibujo técnico	Teatro	Teatro
7:50 - 8:40	Matemáticas	Español	Dibujo técnico	Español	Inglés
8:40 - 9:30	Teatro	Ciencias naturales	Laboratorio	Matemáticas	Español
9:30 - 10:20	Inglés	Ciencias naturales	Laboratorio	Taller	Taller
10:20 - 10:40	R e c e s o				
10:40 - 11:30	Ciencias sociales	Matemáticas	Español	Taller	Taller
11:30 - 12:20	Ciencias sociales	Inglés	Ciencias sociales	Taller	Taller
12:20 - 1:10	Ciencias naturales	Libre	Ciencias sociales	Educación física	Educación física
1:10 - 2:00	Ciencias naturales	Libre	Libre	Ciencias sociales	Ciencias sociales

Receso en Santiago, Chile

Options

Strategies for Reaching All Students

Spanish-Speaking Students

Ask: *¿Te gustaría tener las clases que tiene este estudiante? ¿Qué clases te gustarían más? ¿Deben los estudiantes usar uniformes en la escuela? ¿Por qué?*

Students Needing Extra Help

Have students use their Organizers to help them read the schedule. Give them blank index cards or have them use rulers so they can read straight across the parts of the schedule.

Enrichment

Have students divide a sheet of paper in half and, by making two lists, compare or contrast Mexican and U.S. schools based on the information in the text.

La cultura desde tu perspectiva

1 Which of the things that are done in Mexican schools would you like to see done in your school? Why?

2 Compare the subjects you are taking with those on the schedule. How might your social studies classes be similar to *ciencias sociales?* How might they be different? Are there subjects that students take in Mexico that you wish you could take? Why?

3 What part of your day is like a *receso?* How is it similar? How is it different?

time do you spend on homework each day? Do Mexican schools seem more or less structured than U.S. schools? Do you think Mexican students or U.S. students are more respectful of their teachers? Why?

Have students design a uniform for their school, including colors and style, and describe it to the class. Post the drawings and later vote on the class favorite. You might ask volunteers to wear a type of school uniform to class one day.

Discuss the advantages and disadvantages of school uniforms.

Answers

Answers to inductive question will vary.

Answers: La cultura desde tu perspectiva

1–2 Answers will vary.

3 Answers will vary, but students may say that *receso* is like recess, in which they go out into the schoolyard to relax and be with friends.

Cultural Notes

(p. 75, photo)
These students are leaving their school in Santiago, Chile. Literature, especially poetry, has a strong tradition in Chilean culture. These students will probably study the works of two Chilean Nobel laureates: Gabriela Mistral won the Nobel prize for poetry in 1945 and Pablo Neruda received the same honor in 1971. Mistral is best known for her works *Desolación* and *Los sonetos de la muerte.* Neruda's epic poem *Canto general* is world famous.

Present

Chapter Theme
School: Time-telling

Communicative Objectives
- To talk about school subjects
- To ask and tell when something takes place
- To ask and tell the time

 **Transparencies 14–15**

 **Vocabulary Art BLMs**

 **Pronunciation Tape 2-2**

 **Vocabulario para conversar B**

Play

Step

Using the Video
Video segment 2: See the Video Teacher's Guide.

 **Video Activity B**

Sección 2

Vocabulario para conversar

¿Qué hora es?

- As your teacher says each hour, hold up the corresponding number of fingers. If the hour is higher than the number of your fingers, work with a partner to show the correct number.
- As your teacher reads aloud the time expressions, put your finger on the pictures of the corresponding clocks.
- As your partner points to four different clocks, pantomime an activity that you do at that time of day. Can he or she guess what activity you are demonstrating?

Es la una.

Son las dos.

Son las tres.

Son las cuatro.

Son las cinco.

Son las seis.

Son las siete.

Son las ocho.

Son las nueve.

Son las diez.

Son las once.

Son las doce.

Options

Strategies for Reaching All Students

Spanish-Speaking Students
Ask: *En tu familia, ¿cómo dicen la hora, "dos y cuarto" o "dos y quince"? ¿"Dos y media" o "dos y treinta"?*

Learning Spanish Through Action
STAGING VOCABULARY: *Escriban, Muestren, Vayan*
1) MATERIALS: analog clocks made from paper plates and fasteners (enough for the whole class or groups)
DIRECTIONS: Using a model clock, set a time and then say it out loud. Have a pair of students set the hands of their clocks to the proper positions. Ask students to show their clocks for verification and then show the correct time on your clock before proceeding to the next time.
2) MATERIALS: index cards with various times written on them
DIRECTIONS: Have volunteers go to the chalkboard to complete digital clocks. Say the time while showing the rest of the class the index card. Once the clocks are filled in, students can check their own work against the index cards.

Son las dos y cinco.

Son las dos y cuarto. (Son las dos y quince.)

Son las dos y veinte.

Son las dos y media. (Son las dos y treinta.)

Son las dos y cuarenta y cinco.

Son las dos y cincuenta y ocho.

32 treinta y dos
33 treinta y tres
34 treinta y cuatro
35 treinta y cinco
36 treinta y seis
37 treinta y siete
38 treinta y ocho
39 treinta y nueve
40 cuarenta
41 cuarenta y uno...
49 cuarenta y nueve
50 cincuenta
51 cincuenta y uno....
59 cincuenta y nueve

¡No olvides!
You worked with the numbers 0 to 31 in *El primer paso.*

Un reloj hecho de flores en el Parque Hundido, Ciudad de México

También necesitas . . .

enseñar: enseña	*to teach: (he/she) teaches*	terminar: termina	*to end: it ends*
a	*at*	es	here: *it is*
¿A qué hora?	*At what time?*	¿Qué hora es?	*What time is it?*
empezar: empieza	*to begin: it begins*	¿Quién?	*Who? Whom?*

Grammar Preview
Enseña and *termina* are presented lexically here for communication skills. These will appear in the grammar explanation of *-ar* verbs on pp. 90–91.

Teaching Suggestions
Discuss the system of telling time on the 24-hour clock (8:00 P.M. = 20:00). Note that there are other time-telling formats. For example, 1:40 could be read as *(Faltan) veinte para las dos* or *Son las dos menos veinte.* (Use Transparency 85 to present the concept of telling time.)

Encourage students to listen to a Spanish-speaking radio or TV station to hear how time is given.

Tell students that when we use a number that ends in *-uno* before a masculine noun, we drop the *o: Tengo treinta y un cuadernos.* (Note that *veintiún* has an accent mark.) When a number ending in *-uno* precedes a feminine noun, this ending becomes *-una: Tengo veintiuna carpetas.*

Class Starter Review
On the day following initial presentation of vocabulary, have students form groups of three or four and take turns counting the number of pages in a given chapter, or the number of pencils or pens in their group.

Using Photos
Ask: *¿Qué hora es en la foto?*

Cultural Notes 

(p. 77, photo)
Mexico City's parks, gardens, and monuments provide residents with many opportunities to take a break from the fast pace of life in the largest city in the world. This colorful spot is on the southern extension of the 18.5-mile-long Avenida Insurgentes, one of the city's two main traffic arteries.

Practice

Re-enter / Recycle

Exs. 1–3: numbers 0–31 from *El primer paso*

Teaching Suggestions

As an optional activity, have the class form two teams. Have one student from each team go to the chalkboard. (Use discretion when sending students to the chalkboard. Be aware of some students' sensitivity to "perform" in front of the class.) Say a time. The first student to write it correctly with numbers stays at the chalkboard and the team wins a point. (As an alternate activity, have a student draw a clock or use a pre-made paper-plate clock with an indicated time. Another student then writes the time with words.) Replace the student from the losing team and continue the game.

Exs. 1–3: Point out that these questions all ask about time, but in different ways.

Ex. 2: If necessary, explain why *la clase de ciencias de la salud* is after the verb form in the model (inversion in questions). This explanation comes later in the chapter's grammar presentation of *-ar* verbs.

Ex. 3: Have students use their Organizers.

Empecemos a conversar

1

A —*¿Qué hora es? ¿Son las doce y cuarenta y cinco?*
B —*No, es la una.*

Estudiante A

Estudiante B

Options

Strategies for Reaching All Students

Spanish-Speaking Students

Have Spanish-speaking students write Ex. 1. Pairs of bilingual and non-bilingual students can write Exs. 2–3. Encourage them to expand their answers, where possible.

Un paso más Ex. 2-D

Enrichment

Exs. 1–2: Encourage students to invent mini-dialogues naming other classes and times. Have students act out the dialogues for the class. Classmates should listen for the classes and times given.

2 

A —*¿A qué hora empieza la clase de ciencias de la salud?*
B —*Empieza a las once y termina a las once y cincuenta.*
o: *No tengo clase de ciencias de la salud.*

Estudiante A **Estudiante B**

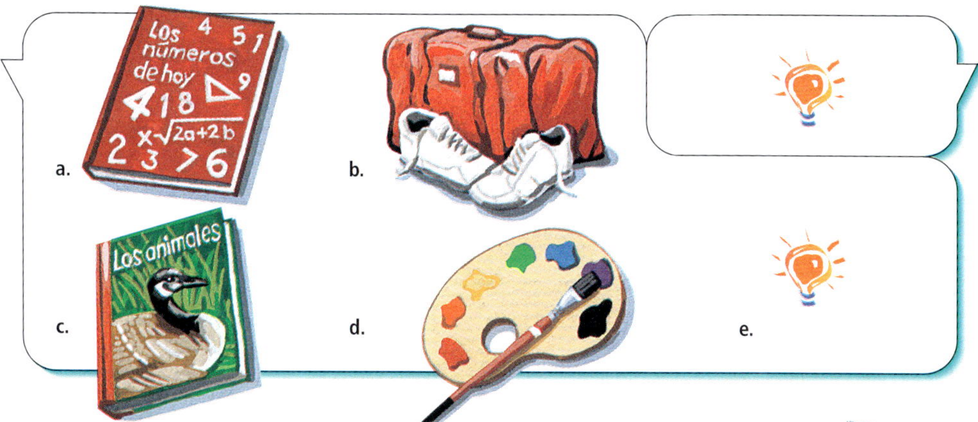

3 A —*¿Cuándo tienes la clase de español?*
B —*A ver. . . . A las nueve y diez.*

A —*¿A qué hora termina la clase?*
B —*A las nueve y cincuenta.*

A —*¿Quién es tu profesor(a)?*
B —*El profesor Soto.*

Estudiante A **Estudiante B**

¡No olvides!

When we use titles such as *señor(a)* or *profesor(a)* to talk about a person, we add *el* or *la*: ***La** señora López enseña español.* But when we are speaking to that person, we do not use *el* or *la*: *¿Cómo está, señora López?*

Answers: Empecemos a conversar

1 ESTUDIANTE A

a. ¿Qué hora es? ¿Es la una y cuarto (quince)?
b. . . . ¿Son las diez?
c. . . . ¿Son las doce y media (treinta)?
d. . . . ¿Son las once?
e. . . . ¿Son las tres y media (treinta)?
f. . . . ¿Son las siete?
g. . . . ¿Son las cuatro?
h. . . . ¿Son las seis y cuarenta y cinco?

ESTUDIANTE B

a. No, es la una y treinta y cinco.
b. No, son las nueve y cincuenta y cinco.
c. No, son las doce y cuarenta.
d. No, son las once y veinticinco.
e No, son las tres y veinte.
f. No, son las siete y diez.
g. No, son las tres y cincuenta.
h. No, son las seis y treinta y cinco.

2 ESTUDIANTE A

a. ¿A qué hora empieza la clase de matemáticas?
b. . . . educación física?
c. . . . ciencias?
d. . . . arte?
e. Questions will vary.

ESTUDIANTE B

a.–e. Answers will vary.

3 Dialogues will vary, but look for appropriate times and names given.

Apply

Re-enter / Recycle
Ex. 1: *gustar* expressions from Chap. 1

Teaching Suggestions
Students should have a copy of their schedule with them for Exs. 2 and 3.

Answers: Empecemos a leer y a escribir
1 a. Ana, b. Federico, c. Ernesto

2–4 Answers will vary.

Multicultural Perspectives
With variances from one Spanish-speaking country to another, many schools have instruction from 9:00 A.M. to 1:30 P.M. before breaking for lunch. Students often go home for their midday meal where they are joined by other family members. The meal may last from 2:00 P.M. until 4:30 P.M. They then return for their afternoon classes, which may last until 7:00 P.M. or later. Ask students familiar with other cultures to share any information they know about school schedules.

Empecemos a leer y a escribir

Responde en español.

1 Read these two dialogues.

FEDERICO: Me gusta mucho dibujar.
ERNESTO: ¿De veras? A mí no me gusta dibujar. No soy nada artístico. Yo soy deportista. Me gusta nadar y patinar.

ANA: Me gusta mucho leer, especialmente libros de historia.
SUSANA: A mí no me gusta leer libros de historia, pero sí me gusta la ciencia ficción.

Who would probably say these sentences?

a. Me gustan mucho las ciencias sociales.
b. En mi mochila tengo muchos lápices, marcadores y hojas de papel.
c. Mi clase favorita es la clase de educación física.

2 ¿Quién es tu profesor(a) favorito(a)? ¿Qué enseña? ¿A qué hora empieza la clase? ¿Cuándo termina?

Estudiantes en una escuela puertorriqueña miran demostraciones en una clase de ciencias.

Options

Strategies for Reaching All Students

Students Needing Extra Help
Ex. 4: Structure this activity for students and give them a model. Tell them that times should include minutes, and that most students' schedules should have at least five classes.

Practice Wkbk. 2-3, 2-4

Audio Activity 2.2

Pruebas 2-3, 2-4

3 Escribe tu horario en una hoja de papel. Usa este modelo.

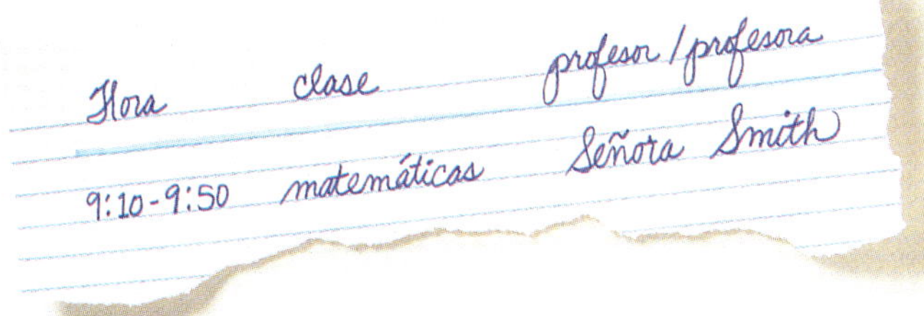

4 En una hoja de papel, escribe tu horario ideal.

Para decir más

Here is some additional vocabulary that you might find useful for activities in this section.

el período de actividades
activity period

novena hora
ninth hour

la clase de economía doméstica
home arts class

la clase de taller
industrial arts class

la clase de computadoras
computer class

Una escuela en la Ciudad de México

"El inglés es muy difícil, ¿no?"

Cultural Notes

(pp. 80–81, photos)
In subjects such as foreign languages or science, the secrets to learning are practice and hands-on experience. Puerto Rican students examine science displays set up in their library. Here students admire projects by pupils of the *tercer* level, before moving on to inspect work by students in *sexto.* Science projects allow students to apply principles and concepts to real materials. Uniformed students in Mexico City practice oral skills, vocabulary, and grammar through dialogues and readings.

Practice

Re-enter / Recycle

Ex. 1: *gustar* expressions from Chap. 1

Teaching Suggestions

Ex. 2: To review vocabulary, have students play Concentration. In small groups, have them prepare two sets of matching index cards. You may want to assign preparation of the cards as homework. Students should write the name in Spanish of all the classroom items and school supplies that they know. (To review these words, they may look at the *Resumen* for *El primer paso* and for this chapter.) Mix up the cards and put them face down on a table. Or, cards could be hole-punched and placed on a pegboard, with the class divided into two teams. One student begins by turning over one of the cards and trying to match it by choosing a second card. If the cards match, the student keeps both cards, says what the item means, and continues. If they don't match, the student replaces the cards face down, and the next person gets a turn. The student with the most pairs wins.

Answers: Comuniquemos

1 ESTUDIANTE A

¿Qué clase te gusta más, . . . ?

ESTUDIANTE B

Answers will vary.

Comuniquemos

Here's another opportunity for you and your partner to use the vocabulary you've just learned.

1 Find out which classes your partner prefers.

A —*¿Qué clase te gusta más, arte o música?*
B —*Me gusta más la clase de música.*

2 You are planning to go shopping for school supplies with a friend. Find out from each other what supplies you need for each class you are taking.

A —*¿Qué necesitas para tu clase de matemáticas?*
B —*A ver... Necesito un cuaderno y una calculadora.*

¡No olvides!

To say that you don't like either of two things, use *ni...ni.*

Options

Strategies for Reaching All Students

Spanish-Speaking Students

Ex. 1: Have students write out the questions they ask their partners about their preferences.

Students Needing Extra Help

Ex. 2: Use the Organizer.
Ahora lo sabes: Have students write this section to keep in their notebooks. Have students check off concepts as they are mastered.

Enrichment

Ex. 1: Have pairs of students vary and extend their dialogues by having *Estudiante A* express surprise, disagreement, or agreement with *Estudiante B*'s reply. Example: *¿De veras? Pues, a mí me gusta más la clase de . . .* or: *¿De veras? A mí también.* Have them act out their dialogues for the class.

3 Make up questions using the words or phrases from the columns below to find out three things about your partner.

¿Qué	tienes	para tu clase de __?
¿Quién	es	tu número de teléfono?
¿Cuándo	necesitas	tu profesor(a) de __?
¿Cuál		la clase de __?
		tu cumpleaños?

Ahora lo sabes

Using what you have learned so far, can you:

- **tell someone what classes you have during certain periods?**
- **ask someone what classes he or she has during certain periods?**
- **tell someone what school supplies you need for a certain class?**
- **ask and tell the time?**

2 ESTUDIANTE A
¿Qué necesitas para tu clase de . . . ?
ESTUDIANTE B
A ver . . . Necesito . . . *(Answers will vary, but may include:* un bolígrafo, una calculadora, una carpeta, una carpeta de argollas, un cuaderno, un diccionario, un lápiz, un marcador, una regla.)

3 Questions and answers will vary.

Answers: Ahora lo sabes

The parenthetical page references after the answers refer to the sections in the chapter where this information was first presented. If necessary, tell students to refer to these sections for further practice. *(Answers will vary.)*

- Tengo ___ en la ___ hora. *(pp. 68–69)*
- ¿A qué hora tienes la clase de ___? *(pp. 68–69, 76–77)*
- Necesito ___ para la clase de ___. *(pp. 68–69)*
- ¿Qué hora es? Es (Son) la(s) ___. *(pp. 76–77)*

 **Audio Activity 2.3**

 **Writing Activities**

 **Comm. Act. BLM 2-2**

 **Examen de habilidades 1**

Cooperative Learning

Have groups of four students prepare an advertisement for a store offering school items for sale. (One student should decide on the items for sale, one should write the prices—previous and discounted, one should draw the poster layout, and another print the information on the poster.) The ad should have a poster display of items with prices clearly marked. Items should be discounted at different times during the day for special sales. Once the display is ready, ask students to give pertinent details. For example: *A las ocho (tengo) carpetas. ¡25 pesos!* Students should be encouraged to include as many school vocabulary items as possible. At the end of the activity the class can select the store most likely to succeed. (If possible, videotape students as they give their presentations so that these can be made into TV commercials.)

Apply

Background Information

(See the Cross-Curricular Connections at the beginning of the chapter on pp. 64–65 for further activities.
For a complete list of the curricular areas covered in PASO A PASO A, *see p. T23 of this Teacher's Edition.)*

If students require information about time zones, tell them the following:
Imagine that every clock in the world showed 6:00 A.M. at the same moment! The sun would be rising over Guayaquil, Ecuador, while it would be directly over Sevilla, Spain. To measure time equally throughout the world, standard time zones were established whereby clocks would show approximately 12:00 noon when the sun was most directly overhead. Most of the world is divided into 24 longitudinal time zones, each 15 degrees wide. New York City (longitude 74 degrees West) and Los Angeles (118 degrees West), for example, are three time zones apart. When it's 12:00 noon in Los Angeles, it's 3:00 P.M. in New York.

Conexiones

These activities connect Spanish with what you are learning in other subject areas.

¿Qué hora es?

Find out if you and your partner understand time zones. Use the time zone map to ask each other questions. For example:

A —Son las ocho (de la noche) en Chicago. ¿Qué hora es en Caracas?
B —Son las diez (de la noche).

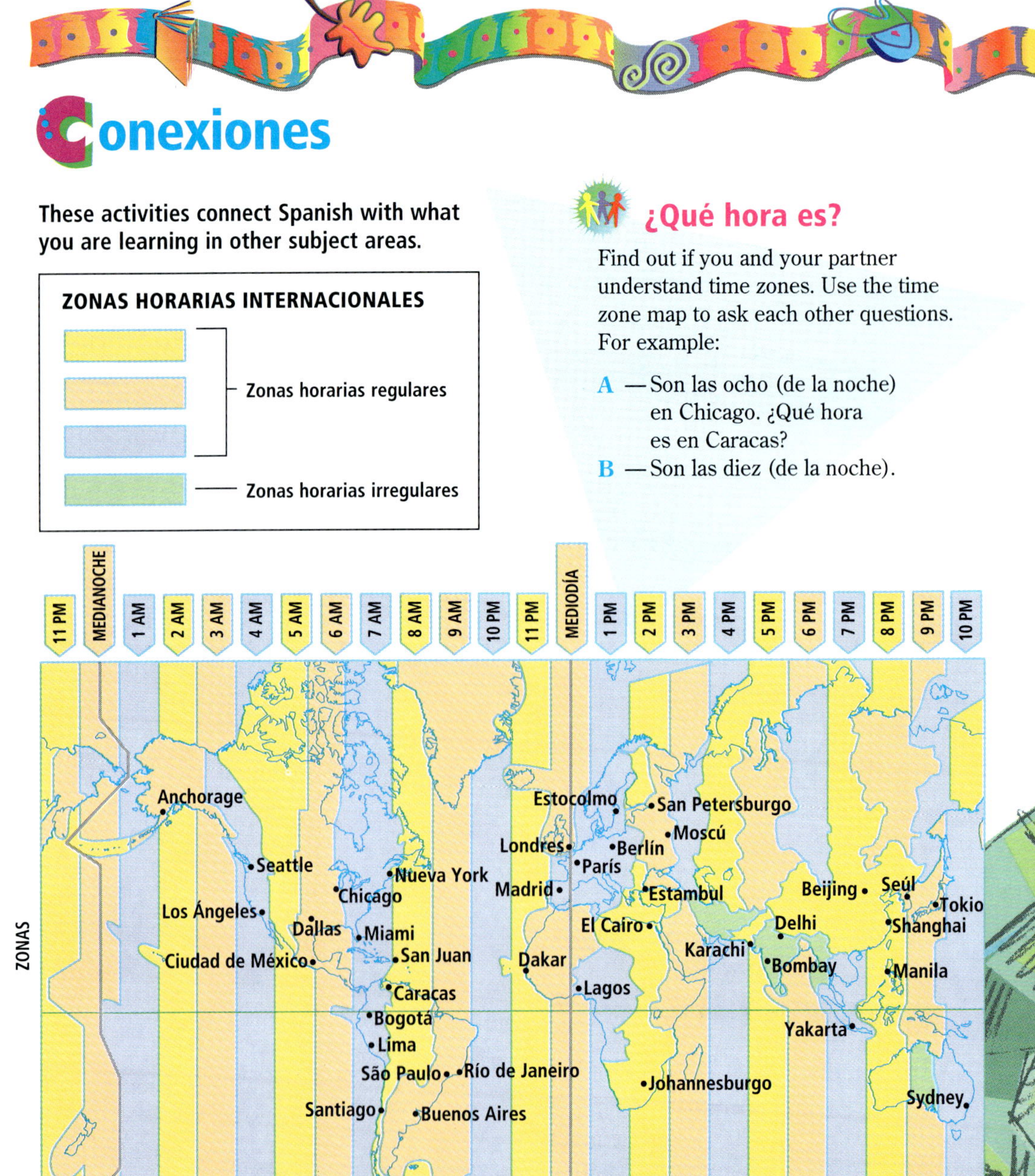

Options

Strategies for Reaching All Students

Spanish-Speaking Students

Say: *Usando el mapa de huso horario* (time zone map), *determina qué hora es en el país de donde es tu familia.*

Students Needing Extra Help

If necessary, demonstrate the concept of time zones using a flashlight and a globe.
¡Buen viaje!: If students ask, tell them that the times indicated on the schedule are shown in local time for that city.

¡Buen viaje!

Imagine that you go to school in Chicago and that your class is taking a trip to San Juan, Puerto Rico. This is your trip schedule:

Use the time zone map and the schedule to figure out how long the flight is. You want to call your family to tell them you had a safe trip. The only time they are all together is at dinner time. What time should it be in San Juan when you call them?

Para pensar

Which word or phrase does not belong in each group?

- marcador, lápiz, grabadora, bolígrafo
- veinte, viernes, treinta, diez
- sala de clases, escuela, cafetería, media
- cuaderno, profesor, compañero, amigo

Create three similar lists and see if your partner can find the word or phrase that does not belong.

Teaching Suggestions

You may choose the number of activities you want your class to do. You may prefer to use the activities as homework, for enrichment, or for your Spanish-speaking students. This material is not part of the testing program, however, it is appropriate for use in student assessment.

The activities *¿Qué hora es? / ¡Buen viaje!* provide a cross-curricular connection with social studies. The activity *Para pensar* provides practice in problem solving and critical thinking that applies to many curriculum areas.

Answers

¡Buen viaje!: The flight is 3 hours and 32 minutes long. / Around 8:00 P.M., provided that dinner is at 6:00.

Para pensar:

- grabadora
- viernes
- media
- cuaderno

Preview

Transparency 16

Answers

Answers will vary. Some examples of non-profit agencies include: Habitat for Humanity, Red Cross, Amnesty International, March of Dimes, and Greenpeace. / The poster serves to encourage the adoption of homeless animals.

A (yo) necesito, (tú) necesitas

B Answers will vary, but students may say the endings are different because they refer to different people.

C *Necesitan;* it ends in *-an*. Students may conclude that the *-an* ending is plural because two dogs are shown in the poster.

Sección 3

Gramática en contexto

This is a poster from a non-profit agency in Santiago, Chile. Can you give an example of a non-profit agency? Without looking at the text, what do you think might be the message of this poster?

A What forms of *necesitar* do you already know?

B When the animals "talk" about themselves, they use the word *necesitamos.* When they talk to the person reading the poster, they use *necesita.* These are two other forms of the verb *necesitar.* Why do you think they are different?

C What other form of *necesitar* do you see in the poster? What is the ending? Why do you think it has that ending?

Options

Strategies for Reaching All Students

Students Needing Extra Help

If necessary, explain the difference between a non-profit agency and one that is in business for profit.

Los pronombres personales

We often use people's names to tell who is doing an action. We also use subject pronouns. They are words that take the place of subject nouns.

Name: John *Subject pronoun*: he
Name: Mary *Subject pronoun*: she

* Most Spanish speakers use *ustedes* when speaking to two or more people. In Spain and in some other areas, however, when they are speaking to two or more people whom they would address individually as *tú*, they use *vosotros* or *vosotras*. We will include these pronouns when we present new verb forms. We will also use them occasionally in situations that take place in Spain. So you should learn to recognize them.

Present

Teaching Suggestions

Explain the use of art with icons in the chart. These pictures indicate about whom we are speaking. (Use Transparency 84 to introduce subject pronouns. Refer to it when teaching verbs, object pronouns, and so on throughout the book.)

Stress the importance of the accent mark on *tú* and *él* by writing *el / él, tu / tú* on the chalkboard along with these sentences: *Él necesita el diccionario. Tú necesitas tu calculadora.* Have a student go to the chalkboard and underline the word for "your" and circle the word for "you." Ask how he or she knew which word was which. Repeat for the words "the" and "he."

Explain that verb forms ending in *-áis*, such as *nadáis*, are used mainly in Spain. We will use them occasionally and students should learn to recognize them. Also, in some areas of Latin America, *vos* is used rather than *tú.*

Show the subject pronoun chart by putting it on the chalkboard or overhead. Explain grammatical terms (pronouns, infinitives, etc.) to avoid discouraging students who have had difficulty with these in English.

Cultural Notes

(p. 86, realia)
Alexander von Humboldt, the famous German explorer of Latin America, said "the civilization of a people can be measured by the way in which they treat their animals." Chile has a long tradition of animal welfare. As early as 1871, don Benjamín Vicuña Mackenna formed the *Sociedad Protectora de Animales* in response to the many deaths of horses from thirst and exhaustion in the streets of Santiago. The *Sociedad,* one of the oldest animal protection societies in the world, rescues hurt, abandoned, or sick animals from the streets. Santiago, with a population of more than three million people, has about 350,000 stray animals. About 7,000 animals find shelter annually at the *Sociedad,* which has ongoing adoption campaigns.

Present & Practice

Teaching Suggestions

Ex. 1: Have students turn to their Organizers to review subject pronouns.

Ex. 2: Use further examples from your school and community to show students the distinction between the three forms of "you."

Show magazine pictures of people of different ages and in different occupations for additional practice.

Point out that if the subject of a sentence in the third person is clearly known, it may be omitted: *Juan estudia en la clase de ciencias.* → *Estudia en la clase de ciencias.*

- *Yo* means "I."

Speaking about yourself: *Yo necesito marcadores.*

- *Tú*, *usted*, and *ustedes* all mean "you."

a. Use *tú* with a family member, a close friend, any other young person or a child, and anyone you call by a first name. Speaking to a friend: *¿Qué necesitas tú?*

b. Use *usted* with an adult or with anyone with whom you would use a title of respect, such as *señor* or *profesora*. *Usted* is usually written as *Ud.* Speaking to your teacher: *¿Necesita Ud. el diccionario, señora?*

c. Use *ustedes* when speaking to two or more people, even if you would call them *tú* individually. We usually write it as *Uds.* Speaking to two friends: *¡Paco! ¡Ana! ¿Necesitan Uds. la grabadora?*

- *Él* means "he." *Ella* means "she."

Speaking about a boy: *Él necesita un lápiz.*
Speaking about a girl: *Ella necesita un bolígrafo.*

- There are two forms for "we" in Spanish: *nosotras* for females, and *nosotros* for males or for a mixed group of males and females.

If you are a girl, speaking about yourself and other girls: *Nosotras necesitamos una calculadora.*

If you are speaking about yourself plus anyone else of the opposite sex: *Nosotros necesitamos una regla.*

- There are also two forms for "they." *Ellos* refers to a group of males or to a mixed group of males and females. *Ellas* refers to a group of females only. We use *ellos* and *ellas* when we are speaking about other people.

Speaking about two or more other people, if any one of them is a male: *Ellos necesitan un cuaderno.*

Speaking about two or more girls: *Ellas necesitan una mochila.*

Options

Strategies for Reaching All Students

Enrichment

Ex. 2: Ask students to name three familiar people they would address as *tú* in Spanish, and three people they would address as *Ud.* or *Uds.*

- In Spanish, we often omit subject pronouns because most verb forms indicate who the subject is.

  Speaking about yourself: *Necesito la grabadora.*
  Speaking about yourself and a friend: *Necesitamos un lápiz.*

- Subject pronouns are usually used for emphasis or contrast, or if the subject is not clear: *Ella es perezosa, pero él es trabajador.*

1 With your partner, take turns telling which subject pronouns Ana would use to speak <u>to</u> these people and which ones she would use to speak <u>about</u> them. (HINT: When Ana is facing them, she is speaking <u>to</u> them. When she is facing you, she is speaking <u>about</u> them.)

a. b. c. d.

e. f. g. h

2 Now tell which form of "you" you would use if you were speaking to these people. Choose from *tú*, *Ud.*, and *Uds.*

a. three classmates
b. an older person sitting next to you on the bus
c. your cousin
d. your mother and sister
e. your teacher
f. the girl next door
g. the principal
h. your father

Answers

1 a. nosotras
b. ellas
c. tú
d. ustedes (Uds.)
e. ellos
f. él
g. usted (Ud.)
h. ella

2 a. Uds.
b. Ud.
c. tú
d. Uds.
e. Ud.
f. tú
g. Ud.
h. tú (Ud.)

Practice Wkbk. 2-5, 2-6

Present & Practice

Answers

3 a. yo
b. ella
c. ellos
d. nosotros
e. ellas
f. él

Class Starter Review

On the day following the presentation of *-ar* verbs, you might begin the class with one of these activities:
1) Prepare a sheet of paper with the personal pronoun icons or use the transparency of pronouns (no words), photocopy a class set, and cut into flashcards. (You may wish to mount these on index cards.) Call out an *-ar* verb. Have pairs of students take turns showing each other their personal pronoun flashcards and saying the correct verb form. Change verbs at regular intervals.
2) Label empty coffee cans with the icons for the subject pronouns or with the actual words. Write *-ar* verbs on slips of paper and distribute among the containers. Have students draw a slip of paper and say the correct verb form.

3 Tell which subject pronoun you would use when talking about these people. Choose from *nosotros, yo, ellos, ellas, él,* or *ella.*

a. yourself
b. your female cousin
c. your parents
d. you and a male friend
e. three female classmates
f. your male pet

Verbos que terminan en *-ar*

A verb usually names the action in a sentence. In Spanish, the last letter or letters of the verb tell you who does the action. We call the verb form that ends in *-r* the infinitive. It means "to ___," and no specific person is doing the action. It is the form you would find in a Spanish dictionary. On the right are some infinitives you already know. We call these *-ar* verbs.

ayudar
cocinar
dibujar
enseñar
escuchar
estudiar
hablar
nadar
necesitar
patinar
practicar
terminar
tocar

nadar

Singular		Plural	
(yo)	nad**o**	(nosotros) (nosotras)	nad**amos**
(tú)	nad**as**	(vosotros) (vosotras)	nad**áis***
(Ud.) (él) (ella)	nad**a**	(Uds.) (ellos) (ellas)	nad**an**

- To change an infinitive to a form that tells who is doing the action, remove the *-ar* and add the appropriate ending.

cocinar	*to cook*
(yo) cocino	*I cook, I am cooking*
(nosotros) cocinamos	*we cook, we are cooking*

- These verb forms are in the present tense. This means that the action takes place regularly or is taking place now.

  Nado en la clase de educación física. ***I swim*** *in phys. ed. class.*

- When you want to say that you do *not* do something, use *no* before the verb form.

  No cocino en la clase de inglés. ***I don't cook*** *in English class.*

*Verb forms ending in *-áis,* such as *nadáis,* are used mainly in Spain. We will use them occasionally, and you should learn to recognize them.

Options

Strategies for Reaching All Students

Spanish-Speaking Students

Ex. 6: Have students write their answers and expand them where possible.

Enrichment

Ex. 4: As a written exercise, have students group the sentences according to their verb endings. Then have them insert subjects into each of these sentences, using personal pronouns or proper nouns as required. They may also change each sentence by turning it either into a negative statement or into a question.
Ex. 7: Have students expand each answer by stating what school supplies they need as they study for each class.

- When we ask a question in Spanish, we usually put the subject after the verb or sometimes even at the end of the sentence.

  ¿Cocina Pedro? ***Does Pedro cook?***

  ¿Estudia mucho **Laura?** ***Does Laura study*** *a lot?*

4 Which of these statements could you use to talk about yourself?

a. Dibuja en la clase de arte.
b. Estudio español.
c. Necesitan un diccionario.
d. Practico deportes.
e. Escuchamos música.
f. Hablo inglés.
g. Habla inglés y español.
h. Necesito una mochila.
i. Tocamos la guitarra.
j. Estudian mucho.

5 Which sentences in Exercise 4 could you use:

a. to talk about one friend?
b. to talk about that friend *and* yourself?
c. to talk about two friends?

6 Name four classmates and tell what school supplies each of them needs for a certain class.

a. Now tell what two of them need for a different class.
b. Tell what you need.
c. Name one classmate and tell what you and that person need.

7 Tell what other subjects you and your classmates are studying.

(nombre)

Julio estudia matemáticas.

a. (nombre)

b. (nombre) y (nombre)

c. (nombre) y (nombre)

d. (nombre) y yo

e. (nombre)

f. yo

Re-enter / Recycle

Ex. 4: activities from Chap. 1

Teaching Suggestions

Exs. 4–5: Have students fill in the verb chart in the Organizer so that they can refer to it when necessary.

Ex. 7: You may want to have students use the Spanish names of their classmates.

Answers

4 b., d., f., h.

5 One friend: a., g.
Friend and yourself: e., i.
Two friends: c., j.

6 Necesita . . . *(Answers will vary for school supplies.)*
a. Necesitan . . .
b. Necesito . . .
c. Necesitamos . . .

7 (Names and classes will vary.)
a. . . . estudia . . .
b. . . . estudian . . .
c. . . . estudian . . .
d. . . . estudiamos . . .
e. . . . estudia . . .
f. (Yo) estudio . . .

Practice Wkbk. 2-7, 2-8

Writing Activities

Pruebas 2-5, 2-6

Comm. Act. BLM 2-3

Present & Apply

Cultural Objective

- To talk about similarities and differences between Mexican and U.S. grading scales

Teaching Suggestions

Some abbreviations used in the report card include: *SEP (Secretaría de Educación Pública)*, *CLAVE CCT* (refers to the school code), *PROM (promedio)* = grade point average.

Answers

Insuficiente is a failing grade.

Answers: La cultura desde tu perspectiva

1 Answers will vary.

2 Answers will vary, but may include suggestions for the exchange student to be prepared to see possible relaxed rules or regulations for the classroom; changes in student-teacher relationships; different treatment of homework, grades, and testing; and differences in the school day with respect to number of courses, class length, and schedules.

Writing Activities

In the United States, grades may be based on tests and quizzes, class participation, projects, homework, and portfolios. But grades in Mexican schools are usually based entirely on test results and homework.

Look at the report card of this student in a Mexican technical middle school. (In a technical school, students prepare to be computer technicians, carpenters, aircraft mechanics, and other kinds of skilled workers.) This is the Mexican grading scale and a list of the roughly equivalent U.S. grades.

Mexico	United States
9, 10	A
8	B
7	C
6	D
5 or lower	F

Students are also graded on behavior, responsibility, cooperation, and appearance. Letter grades are usually given in these areas. Here is one scale ranked from highest to lowest.

- S = sobresaliente
- MB = muy bueno
- B = bueno
- R = regular
- I = insuficiente

Which grade do you think is a failing grade?

La cultura desde tu perspectiva

1. What advantages are there to being graded based only on test results and homework? What are some disadvantages?
2. Based on what you now know about schools in Mexico, list five suggestions that might help an exchange student from Mexico adjust to the way things are done in your school.

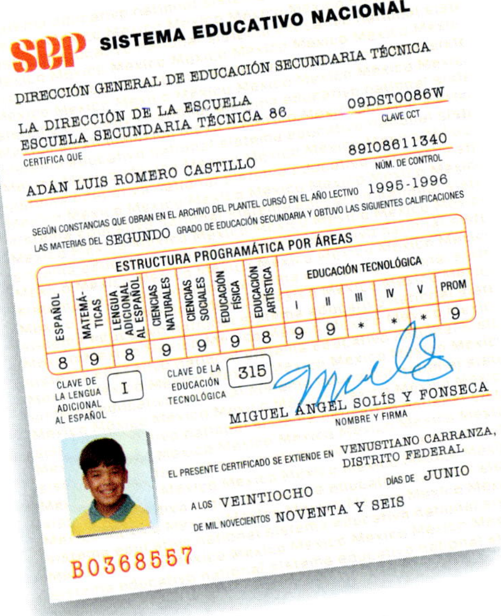

SEP SISTEMA EDUCATIVO NACIONAL

DIRECCIÓN GENERAL DE EDUCACIÓN SECUNDARIA TÉCNICA

LA DIRECCIÓN DE LA ESCUELA
ESCUELA SECUNDARIA TÉCNICA 86 — 09DST0086W (CLAVE CCT)

CERTIFICA QUE

ADÁN LUIS ROMERO CASTILLO — 89I08611340 (NÚM. DE CONTROL)

SEGÚN CONSTANCIAS QUE OBRAN EN EL ARCHIVO DEL PLANTEL CURSÓ EN EL AÑO LECTIVO 1995-1996 LAS MATERIAS DEL SEGUNDO GRADO DE EDUCACIÓN SECUNDARIA Y OBTUVO LAS SIGUIENTES CALIFICACIONES

ESTRUCTURA PROGRAMÁTICA POR ÁREAS

ESPAÑOL	MATEMÁTICAS	LENGUA ADICIONAL AL ESPAÑOL	CIENCIAS NATURALES	CIENCIAS SOCIALES	EDUCACIÓN FÍSICA	EDUCACIÓN ARTÍSTICA	EDUCACIÓN TECNOLÓGICA I	II	III	IV	V	PROM
8	9	8	9	9	9	8	9	9	*	*	*	9

CLAVE DE LA LENGUA ADICIONAL AL ESPAÑOL: I
CLAVE DE LA EDUCACIÓN TECNOLÓGICA: 315

MIGUEL ÁNGEL SOLÍS Y FONSECA
NOMBRE Y FIRMA

EL PRESENTE CERTIFICADO SE EXTIENDE EN VENUSTIANO CARRANZA, DISTRITO FEDERAL A LOS VEINTIOCHO DÍAS DE JUNIO DE MIL NOVECIENTOS NOVENTA Y SEIS

B0368557

Top: Una estudiante en San Cristóbal, Venezuela, escribe el alfabeto en la pizarra. *Inset:* Lima, Perú

Options

Strategies for Reaching All Students

Spanish-Speaking Students

Un paso más Exs. 2-E, 2-F

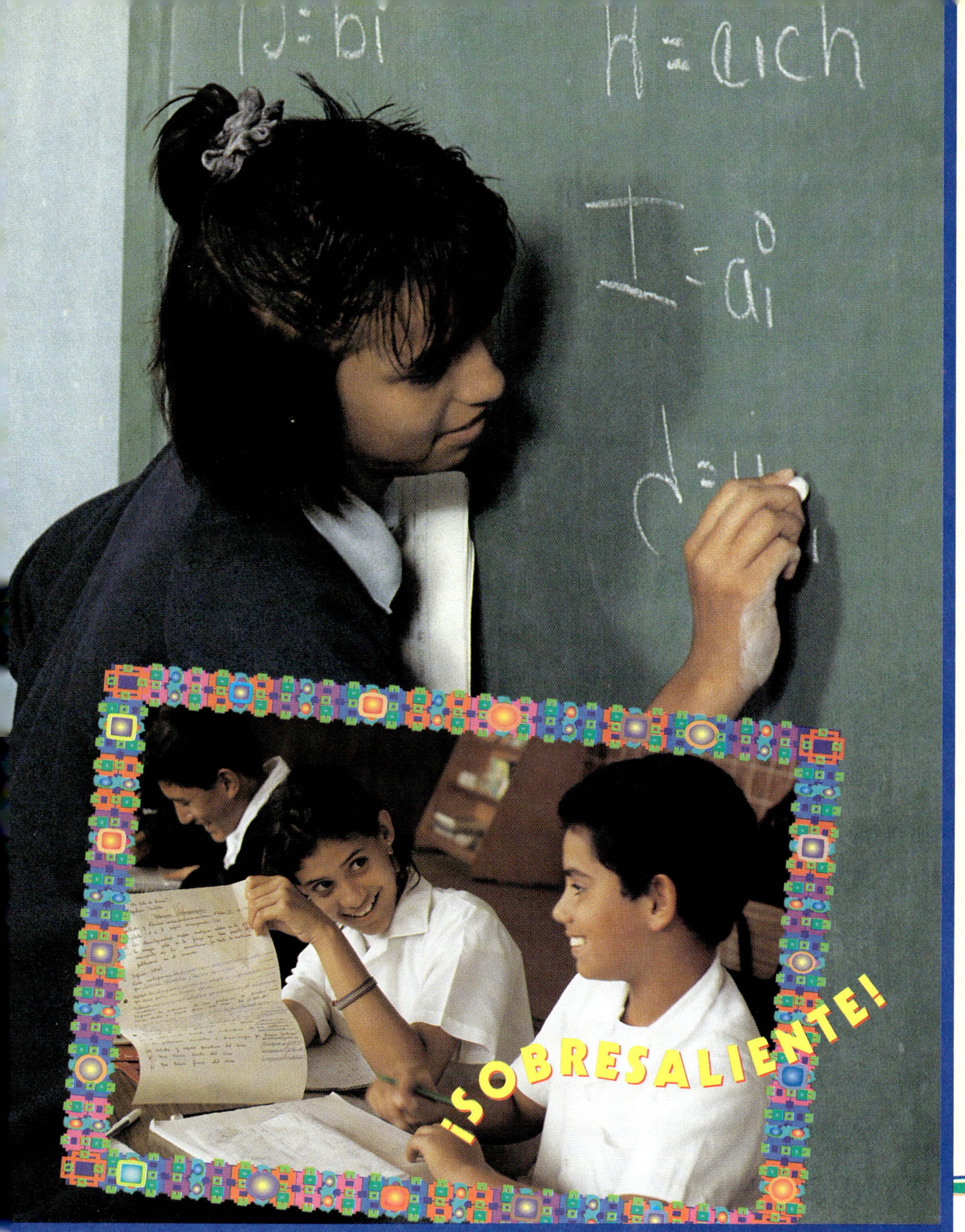

Cultural Notes

(p. 93, photo)
The Spanish writing system (orthography) is closely linked to its sound system (phonetics). This is different from English, for example, which has many words with "silent" letters. English orthography has changed very little in 400 years, but its spoken forms have changed dramatically. Spanish, on the other hand, periodically adopts orthographic changes.
Abecedario is an onomatopoeic synonym for *alfabeto* in Spanish. Both words are commonly used throughout the Spanish-speaking world. Alternative alphabets may be listed as *abecedario Morse, abecedario Braille,* and *abecedario telegráfico.*

(p. 93, inset photo)
This Peruvian student proudly displays her superior grade: a 19. In Peru, students are given number grades between 1 and 20. Scores below 11 are failing, and an above-average grade is in the 14 to 15 range. Top students get a 17 or higher. Other Latin American countries use different systems. Mexico, for example, relies on a 1–10 grading scale. A 6 is sufficient to pass a course, but to move from *primaria* to *secundaria,* a student needs an average of 7.

Preview

Transparency 17

Critical Thinking: Drawing Conclusions from Evidence

Based on the school supplies pictured in the ad, have students determine which classes the owner of the backpack might take and which supplies would be used in each class. Have students present their responses on a grid.

Teaching Suggestions

Have students compare their responses to A, B, and C to the information in the chart and to make any necessary changes in their responses.

Answers

A *-a: una regla, una calculadora; -o: un cuaderno, un diccionario*

B *Un* is used with words ending in *-o; una* is used with words ending in *-a.*

C You would replace the word *un* with *el* and *una* with *la: (la regla, la calculadora, el cuaderno, el diccionario).*

Sección 4

Gramática en contexto

This is a page from a catalogue of school supplies.

A Look at the names of the school supplies. Which ones end in *-a?* Which ones end in *-o?*

B Now look at the use of *un* and *una.* What pattern do you see? Work with a partner to write a rule for when to use *un* and when to use *una.*

C You know the names of some other things you use in school: *el libro, la hoja de papel, la pizarra.* If you were to label the items in the ad using *el* or *la,* how would you know which word to use?

Options

Strategies for Reaching All Students

Students Needing Extra Help

Los sustantivos: Point out that the concept of masculine and feminine in Spanish deals with the spelling of the word, not with the actual definition in English of "masculine" and "feminine."

Los sustantivos

Nouns refer to people, animals, places, and things. In Spanish, nouns have gender. They are either masculine or feminine.

- Most nouns that end in *-o* are masculine. Most nouns that end in *-a* are feminine. For example:

  el libr**o** la calculador**a**

  There are a few exceptions. You know one: *el día.*

- Other Spanish nouns end in *-e* or a consonant. Some of these are masculine, and some are feminine. For example:

  el cin**e** la clas**e**

  el lápi**z** la televisió**n**

- A few nouns can be both masculine and feminine. For example: *el / la estudiante.*
- *El* and *la* are called definite articles and are the equivalent of "the" in English. We use *el* with masculine nouns, *la* with feminine nouns. For example:

  el libro **la** calculadora

  el cine **la** clase

  You need to learn a noun with its definite article, *el* or *la*. In Spanish we often use the definite article where we wouldn't in English:

  Me gusta **la televisión**. *I like television.*

- *Un* and *una* are indefinite articles, like "a" and "an" in English. We use *un* with masculine nouns, *una* with feminine nouns. For example:

  un muchacho **una** muchacha

  un lápiz **una** clase

1 Turn back to page 69. Can you find four masculine nouns and four feminine nouns? Make a list of these words in random order. Leave out the words *el* and *la* or *un* and *una*. Give the list to your partner. Have your partner write the correct definite article in front of each noun. Check the answers.

Present & Practice

Teaching Suggestions

Ex. 1: You may want students to prepare the list of nouns for homework. As enrichment or for extra credit homework, have students rewrite the lists with the correct indefinite article in front of each noun.

Answers

1 masculine: *diccionario, cuaderno, lápiz, marcador;* feminine: *calculadora, carpeta, carpeta de argollas, grabadora, mochila, regla.*

Practice

Re-enter / Recycle

Ex. 3: school supplies from *El primer paso*

Teaching Suggestions

Ex. 3: If students don't have most of the school supplies with them, have them list what they should have brought to class.

Answers

2 Diferente: *el diccionario, la estudiante, el lápiz, la mochila, la pizarra, el profesor*

No diferente: *el bolígrafo, la calculadora, el escritorio, el estudiante, la hoja de papel, el libro, el marcador, el pupitre*
If students ask, eraser is *el borrador.*

3 Be sure that students use indefinite articles in this exercise.

ESTUDIANTE A

a. ¿Tienes un bolígrafo?
b. . . . una regla?
c. . . . una calculadora?
d. . . . un libro?
e. . . . un cuaderno?
f. . . . un diccionario?
g. . . . una carpeta?
h. . . . una carpeta de argollas?

ESTUDIANTE B

a.–h. Sí, tengo. Aquí (Allí) está. / (No, lo siento.)

2 Look at the two pictures of the classroom. Working with a partner, make a list of things that are the same in both pictures and those that are different.

Options

Strategies for Reaching All Students

Students Needing Extra Help

Ex. 2: Have students create a two-column chart with headings *Diferente* and *No diferente* to keep their answers in order.

Practice Wkbk. 2-9

Audio Activities 2.4, 2.5

Pruebas 2-7, 2-8

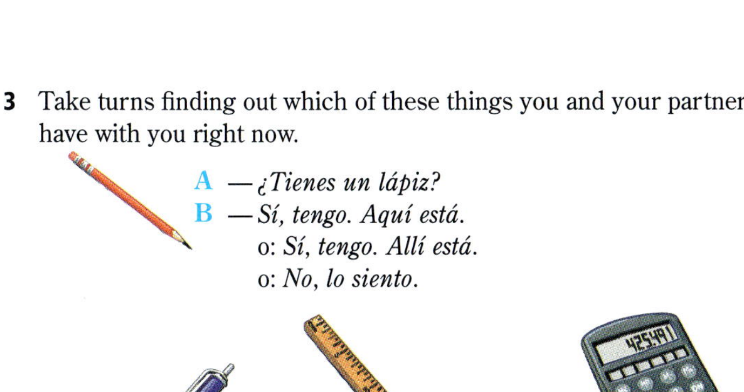

3 Take turns finding out which of these things you and your partner have with you right now.

A —*¿Tienes un lápiz?*
B —*Sí, tengo. Aquí está.*
o: *Sí, tengo. Allí está.*
o: *No, lo siento.*

a. b. c. d.

e. f. g. h.

Después de las clases, Lima, Perú

Cultural Notes 

(p. 97, photo)
Students at a *colegio* in Lima, Peru, gather to converse at the end of the school day. Blue jeans, combined with a navy blue sweater and white shirt, are part of the school uniform. While some private schools may provide transportation, most students walk home or use Lima's public transportation system. Buses are cheap but often crowded. *Colectivos* are "collective-style" taxis or vans that stop for individual passengers but follow specific routes. They are more comfortable than buses yet less expensive than taxis.

Apply

Pronunciation Tape 2-3

Todo junto A

Play

Todo junto B

Play

Using the Video

Video segment 3: See the Video Teacher's Guide.

Video Activity C

Re-enter / Recycle

Ex. 3: school supplies from *El primer paso*

Teaching Suggestions

You may want to change the order of the exercises or have students do only one or two.

As a written assignment, students can list all the class subjects they now know in a chart with two columns: one with the heading *Fácil* and the other with *Difícil.* The next day have the class determine which subject appeared most often in the two lists.

Here's an opportunity for you to put together what you learned in this chapter with what you learned earlier.

1 ¿En qué clases?

In groups of three, take turns asking partners what they do in different classes. For example:

A —*¿Escuchan Uds. música en la clase de español?*
B —*Sí, a veces.*
C —*Nosotros no escuchamos música pero sí hablamos mucho.*

2 Estoy pensando en la clase de . . .

In small groups, take turns thinking of a class. Others in the group will try to guess the class by asking questions. Here are some questions you may want to ask:

Options

Strategies for Reaching All Students

Students Needing Extra Help

Ahora lo sabes: Have students write this section so that they can chart their progress.

3 Las cuatro cartas

In small groups, prepare four index cards in Spanish of all the classroom items and school supplies that you know. (HINT: To review these words, look at the *Resumen* for *El primer paso* and for Capítulo 2.) Mix all the cards and deal them to the players.

The person to the left of the dealer says, for example: *Necesito una calculadora. Marta, ¿tienes una calculadora?* Marta answers either *Sí, tengo una calculadora. Aquí está.* or *No, no tengo.*

If Marta has the card, she hands it over and the student continues asking the other players for cards. If Marta does not have *una calculadora,* the next player gets to ask. Whoever has the most sets of four cards wins the game.

Ahora lo sabes

Using what you have learned so far, can you:

- talk about what you and other people do and don't do regularly?
- ask if someone has a certain thing and answer correctly if he or she asks you?
- speak in an appropriate way to a friend and to a teacher?
- compare and contrast your school experience with that of a student in Mexico?

Ex. 2: Here are other questions students may ask: *¿Tienes mucha tarea? ¿Es fácil o difícil?*

In small groups, have students take turns asking *sí / no* questions to find out what class the leader is thinking of. For example:

A —¿Es tu clase favorita?
B —Sí.
C —¿Tienes mucha tarea?

Answers

1–2 Dialogues will vary.

3 Responses will vary.

Answers: Ahora lo sabes

The parenthetical page references after the answers refer to the sections in the chapter where this information was first presented. If necessary, tell students to refer to these sections for further practice.

- Answers will vary, but look for subject / verb agreement. *(pp. 90–91)*
- ¿Tienes ___ ? Sí, (No, no) tengo ___. *(pp. 68–69, 95)*
- ¿Qué necesitas (tú)? / ¿Necesita (Ud.) el diccionario, profesora? *(pp. 87–89)*
- Answers will vary, but students may cite differences in the grading systems. *(pp. 74–75, 92–93)*

 **Writing Activities**

 **Comm. Act. BLMs 2-4, 2-5**

 **Examen de habilidades 2**

Apply

Process Reading

For a description of process reading, see p. 60.

Multicultural Perspectives

In most Spanish-speaking countries, students may take up to seven courses per school year. These may include: trigonometry, anatomy, history, geography, Spanish, English, French, physical education, and courses in fine arts. Ask students to compare their courses with those taken by their Spanish-speaking counterparts.

Teaching Suggestions

You may wish to assign the tasks in *Antes de leer* and *Mira la lectura* as homework. Check as a whole-class activity.

Antes de leer: Have students brainstorm and list *all* possibilities, not just four.

Aplicación: You may wish to do this as a whole-class activity. To get students started, you may want to model the role play.

¡Vamos a leer!

Antes de leer

STRATEGY ➤ Using prior knowledge

We can often predict the kind of information a document will include. For example, in a menu, we expect to find the names and prices of different dishes. In a bus schedule, we look for arrival and departure times. Here is a report card for a student in Buenos Aires, Argentina. Make a list of four things you might expect to find in a report card.

Mira la lectura

STRATEGY ➤ Scanning

Remember that scanning means reading something quickly just to look for certain information. Scan the report card and put a check mark next to each thing on your list that you found in the report card.

BOLETÍN DE CALIFICACIONES PERTENECIENTE A Josefa Villalba GRADO 2º SECCIÓN B TURNO mañana

	Áreas formativas									Apreciación personal						Control de asistencia			Firmas		
Bimestre	Lengua	Matemáticas	Ciencias de la Naturaleza	Estudios Sociales	Actividades Prácticas	Educación Plástica	Educación Musical	Educación Física	Idioma Extranjero	Colaboración	Responsabilidad	Comportamiento en la escuela	Aseo y presentación	Se destaca en:	Tiene dificultades en:	Asistencias	Inasistencias	Faltas de Puntualidad	Maestro	Director	Padre, tutor o encargado
1º	7	6	9	9	7	5	5	6	9	B	MB	B	B	ciencias y estudios sociales	educación plástica y musical	38	2	0	[illegible]	O. Sánchez	R. Villalba
2º	6	7	9	9	8	6	7	7	8	MB	B	B	B	ciencias y estudios sociales	/	24	6	0	[illegible]	O. Sánchez	R. Villalba
3º	8	9	8	7	6	7	8	9	10	S	MB	MB	MB	idioma y colaboración	actividades prácticas	35	3	1	[illegible]	O. Sánchez	R. Villalba
4º	8	9	8	8	7	9	8	8	9	S	MB	MB	MB	muy buena asistencia y colaboración todo el año		32	4	2	[illegible]	O. Sánchez	R. Villalba

NOTA: Escala conceptual: S, sobresaliente; MB, muy bueno; B, bueno; R, regular; I, insuficiente (2º CICLO).

Escala numérica: 10, sobresaliente; 8 y 9, muy bueno; 6 y 7, bueno; 4 y 5, regular; 1, 2 y 3, aplazado (3er. CICLO)

Este boletín informa sobre el progreso del alumno, teniendo en cuenta el grado de madurez y el ritmo de aprendizaje en las distintas áreas del curriculum así como también la formación de sus hábitos, habilidades y actitudes valorativas dentro del ámbito escolar y sus intereses particulares para las distintas actividades.

SÍNTESIS ANUAL: muy buena

PROMOVIDO A: 3º grado

O. Sánchez

FIRMA Y SELLO DEL D

Options

Strategies for Reaching All Students

Enrichment

If available, bring in additional school documents that you, a friend, or a colleague may have from a Spanish-speaking country to share with the class. Extend this request to Spanish-speaking students in your class.

Infórmate

STRATEGY ➤ Using context clues

As you read, use the words near an unknown word to help you understand it. Look at the words before and after it. For example, in many coupons and school records you will find the words *name*, *address*, and *telephone number* together. If you don't know the Spanish word for "address," its location between the words for "name" and "telephone number" will help you figure it out.

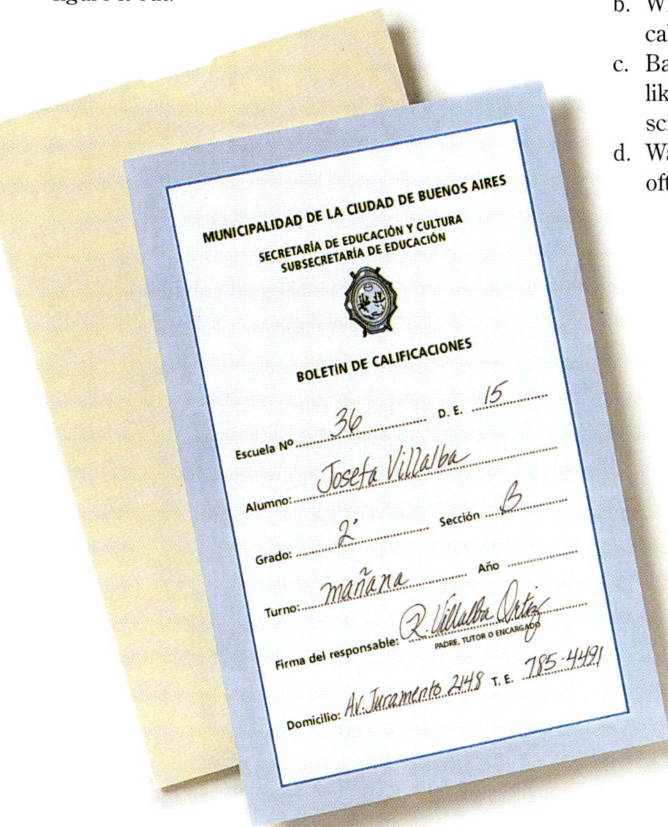

MUNICIPALIDAD DE LA CIUDAD DE BUENOS AIRES
SECRETARÍA DE EDUCACIÓN Y CULTURA
SUBSECRETARÍA DE EDUCACIÓN

BOLETIN DE CALIFICACIONES

Escuela Nº 36 D. E. 15
Alumno: Josefa Villalba
Grado: 2º Sección B
Turno: mañana Año
Firma del responsable: R. Villalba Ortiz
PADRE, TUTOR O ENCARGADO
Domicilio: Av. Juramento 2148 T. E. 785-4491

1 Read the cover of the report card. Which of the following is *not* on the cover?

a. signature of a parent *(padre)*
b. name of the school
c. student's name
d. student's age
e. student's address

2 Read the report card.

a. What would *Áreas formativas* be called in your school?
b. What would *Apreciación personal* be called in your school?
c. Based on this report card, is the student likely to become a better musician or scientist?
d. Was this student late or absent more often?

Aplicación

With a partner, role-play this student showing his or her report card to a parent. Use this model.

PADRE/MADRE: Mmmm.
Necesitas . . . .
Eres muy . . . .

ESTUDIANTE: La clase de . . .
es (muy) . . . .

Answers
Antes de leer

Answers will vary, but students may expect to find the student's name, class schedule, year in school, subjects, teachers' names, grades, and comments in a report card.

Mira la lectura

Answers will vary depending on what the student expected to find in the previous section.

Infórmate

Part 1:
not on the cover:
b. name of the school
d. student's age

Part 2:
a. subjects (classes)
b. personal growth (evaluation)
c. scientist
d. The student was absent more often.

Aplicación

Dialogues will vary.

Cultural Notes

(pp. 100–101, realia)
In Argentine primary schools, promotion to the next higher grade is based on the teacher's and principal's evaluation of the student's classroom performance, including subject matter and maturity.
If students ask, here are the more difficult terms used in the documents: *turno* (session) / *1º, 2º, 3º, 4º: primero, segundo, tercero, cuarto* (1st, 2nd, 3rd, 4th) / *Lengua* (Spanish) / *Actividades Prácticas* (Arts and Crafts) / *Educación Plástica* (Art Theory) / *Colaboración* (Working with others) / *Aseo y presentación* (Personal presentation) / *D.E., Distrito Escolar* (School District) / *T.E., Teléfono del Encargado* (Parent's or Guardian's Telephone Number)

Apply

Teaching Suggestions

You may want to arrange for a pen-pal exchange with a nearby school or another Spanish class in your school using the letters students wrote.

Process Writing

For information regarding writing portfolios, see p. 62.

¡Vamos a escribir!

Write a letter to a Spanish-speaking friend about your school day. Follow these steps.

1. Write out your class schedule. Put a check mark beside two classes in which you have a lot of homework. Underline two classes that you like a lot.

2. Write your letter using the information about your classes. You may use this outline and add two sentences of your own.

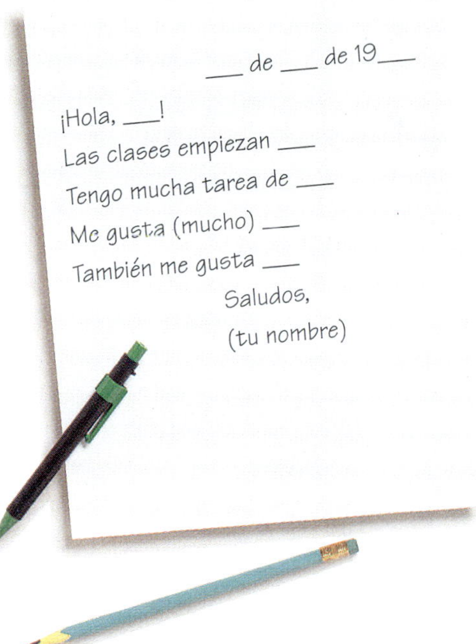

___ de ___ de 19___

¡Hola, ___!
Las clases empiezan ___
Tengo mucha tarea de ___
Me gusta (mucho) ___
También me gusta ___
Saludos,
(tu nombre)

3. Now show your letter to a partner. Ask which parts might be changed. Decide whether or not you agree, then rewrite your letter, making any changes that you have decided on.

4. Check your letter for spelling and punctuation. Use this checklist.
   - capital letters at the beginning of a sentence
   - accent marks
   - correct use of the articles *el*, *la*, *un*, and *una*
   - correct use of *-ar* verbs
   - question marks or exclamation points at the beginning and end of questions and exclamations

5. Make any corrections and recopy. You might send your letter to:
   - a new pen pal
   - a student of Spanish in another school
   - a student in another Spanish class at your school
   - a member of your family or a friend who knows Spanish

You may want to include your letter in your portfolio.

Options

Strategies for Reaching All Students

Spanish-Speaking Students

Have Spanish-speaking students answer the letter of one of the non-bilingual students. They can then compare classes and tell about a favorite one.

 **Un paso más Exs. 2-G, 2-H**

Students Needing Extra Help

Have students use their Organizers to check for spelling and any errors.

Enrichment

Some organizations through which you can arrange pen pals are: International Youth Service / PB 125 / SF-20101 / Turku, Finland; and Worldwide Communications / P.O. Box 634 / Glen Ellen, CA 95442. If your school has access to e-mail or some type of on-line computer service, "key pals" in Spanish-speaking countries would be another option.

Resumen del capítulo 2

Use the vocabulary from this chapter to help you:

- describe your class schedule
- find out about someone else's schedule
- name some school supplies you use

to talk about school subjects
el almuerzo
el arte *(f.)*
las ciencias
las ciencias de la salud
las ciencias sociales
la clase de ___
la educación física
el español
el inglés
las matemáticas
la música
la tarea
difícil
fácil
aprender: (yo) aprendo
(tú) aprendes
enseñar: enseña

to talk about school supplies
la calculadora
la carpeta (de argollas)
el cuaderno
el diccionario
la grabadora
el horario
el lápiz, *pl.* los lápices
el marcador, *pl.* los marcadores
la mochila
la regla

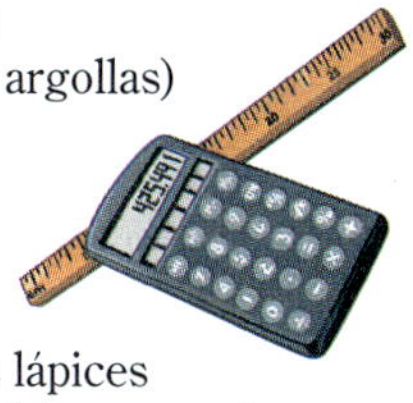

to tell what people need
necesitar: (yo) necesito
(tú) necesitas

to say what something is for
para

to express possession
tener: (yo) tengo
(tú) tienes
tu

to express quantity
mucho, -a
un, -a

to ask for information
¿Qué?

to ask and tell when something takes place
a
¿A qué hora ___?
empezar: empieza
terminar: termina
es
la hora
la primera hora
la segunda hora
la tercera hora
la cuarta hora
la quinta hora
la sexta hora
la séptima hora
la octava hora
el semestre
el primer semestre
el segundo semestre

to ask and tell the time
¿Qué hora es?
Es la una (y ___).
Son las ___ (y ___).
cuarto
media
treinta y dos, treinta y tres, treinta y cuatro . . .
cuarenta, cuarenta y uno . . . , cuarenta y nueve
cincuenta, cincuenta y uno . . . , cincuenta y nueve

to express regret
Lo siento.

to express hesitation
A ver . . .

to talk about location
aquí
Aquí está.
allí
Allí está.

to tell who performs an action
yo
tú
usted (Ud.)
él, ella
nosotros, -as
vosotros, -as
ustedes (Uds.)
ellos, -as
¿Quién?

Summarize

 Writing Activities

 Mi portafolio

 Test Generator

CAPÍTULO 3

THEME: SPORTS AND LEISURE ACTIVITIES

SCOPE AND SEQUENCE Pages 104–143

COMMUNICATION

Topics

Public buildings and places

Seasons

Sports and leisure activities

Objectives

To compare leisure-time activities in Spanish-speaking countries with those in the U.S.

To ask and to tell how someone feels or where someone is

To ask and to tell where someone is going

To talk about activities

To say when and with whom you do an activity

To extend, accept, or decline invitations

To ask for and give an explanation

To express surprise, enthusiasm, or disappointment

To express possession

CULTURE

Leisure-time activities

Parks and *plazas*

GRAMMAR

El verbo ir

Ir + a + *infinitivo*

La preposición con

El verbo estar

Ancillaries available for use with Chapter 3

Multisensory/Technology

Overhead Transparencies, 18–23

Audio Tapes and CDs

Projects for Proficiency: Blackline Master Spanish Activities for Middle School Learners

Vocabulary Art Blackline Masters for Hands-On Learning, pp. 18–22

Classroom Crossword

Video

CD-ROM

Print

Practice Workbook, pp. 33–42

Writing, Audio & Video Activities, pp. 29–36, 71–73, 104–105

Communicative Activity Blackline Masters

Pair and Small Group Activities, pp. 22–27

Situation Cards, p. 28

Un paso más: Actividades para ampliar tu español, pp. 13–19

Assessment

Assessment Program

Pruebas, pp. 42–45, 50–52

Exámenes de habilidades, pp. 46–49, 53–56

Mi portafolio, pp. 57–58

Test Generator

Video still from Chap. 3

Cultural Overview

Leisure-Time Activities

During the week, young people in Latin America participate in a variety of leisure-time activities, such as after-school programs, soccer games, and study groups. When the week is over, however, they look forward to *tardeadas* (chaperoned early evening parties) usually from 6:00 P.M. to 10:00 P.M. for teens and adolescents. These parties, held at schools, nightclubs, or on church grounds, are popular with young people, for this is their chance to dress up, dance, and be with their friends.

An important place to meet friends is the *plaza* in the center of town. In some Mexican towns, after Sunday evening mass, people gather together, and children ride their bicycles around the *plaza.* Couples take their place on the benches, and young men and women stroll around the area. The center of the *plaza* usually features a kiosk or gazebo, where musical entertainment is featured on holidays and special occasions. Sunday evening is the scene of a courtship ritual for adolescents, in which rows made up of four to five males walk clockwise around the kiosk, and females, linked arm in arm, walk counterclockwise around them. From vendors set up at the foot of the kiosk, a young man can buy hollowed-out eggs filled with confetti. With the bravado that his friends impose on him, he can then break the egg over the head of the girl he likes as she passes him by in the *vuelta.* Other times he might buy shimmering balls of tightly rolled streamers that he can throw over the young lady, draping them over her head and shoulders. If she doesn't seem to mind these shows of affection, he can feel safe in asking her the next time around: *¿Te acompaño en esta vuelta?* Later, she may sit down on a bench where the young suitor can stop and speak with her briefly.

Introduce

Re-entry of Concepts

The following list represents words, expressions, and grammar topics re-entered from *El primer paso* to Chap. 2:

El primer paso
Calendar expressions

Chapter 1
Activities
Gustar expressions
Adjectives describing personality

Chapter 2
Time expressions
Personal pronouns

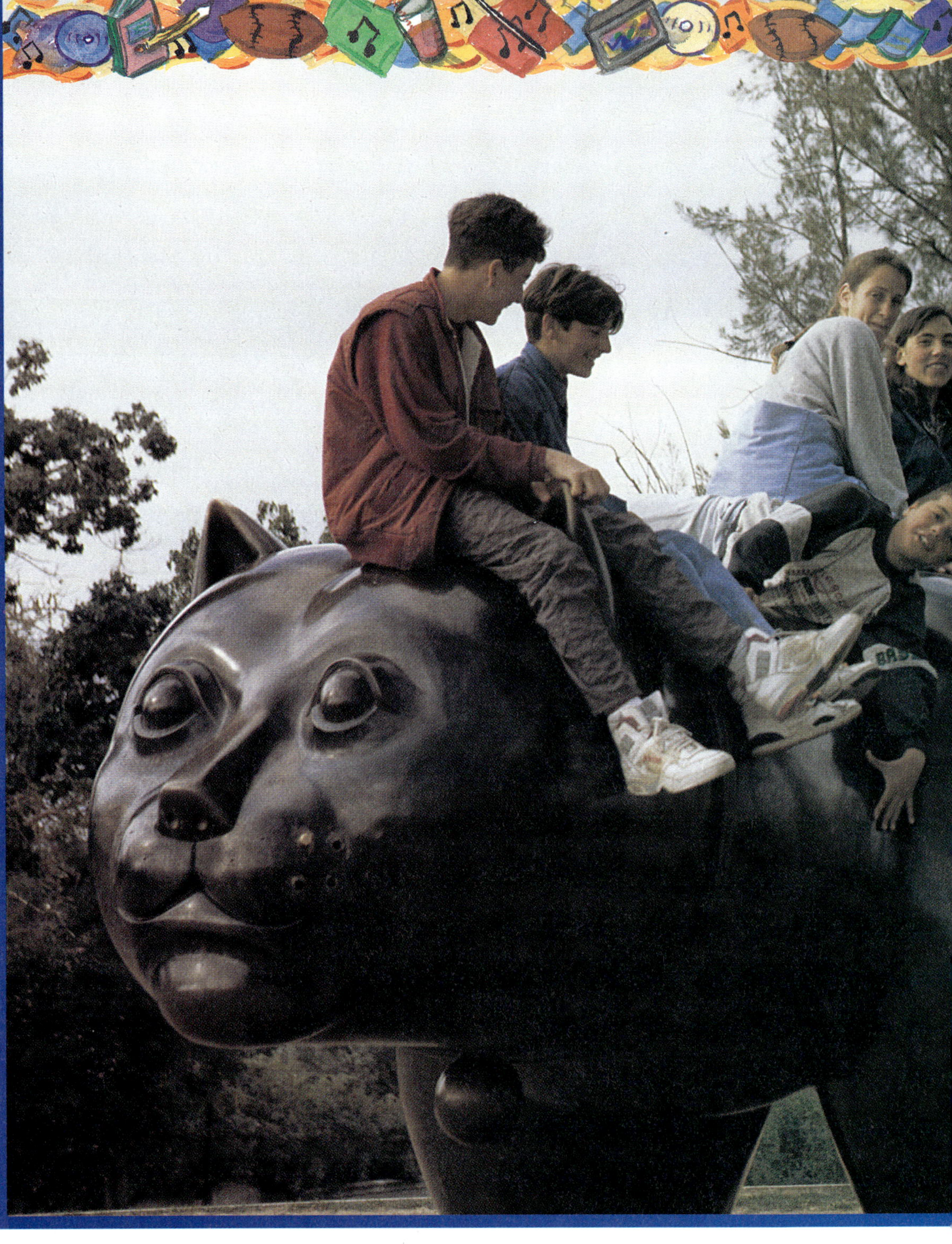

Planning

Cross-Curricular Connections

Physical Education Connection *(pp. 108–109)*
Have students indicate which activities are team sports and which are played by individuals. Ask them to rank the activities by the amount of aerobic exercise or calories burned that they think each one could have. As extra credit, have students verify this information by consulting a health and fitness source or encyclopedia in your library.

Math Connection *(pp. 116–117)*
Have students record on a daily basis the time and location of their activities for an entire week. Using this record as a personal profile, have them develop a schedule for the following week and determine what percentage of their week is spent in school and what percentage in recreational activities.

Geography Connection *(pp. 116–117)*
Have students create a political map of North and South America and write in the current seasons above and below the equator. In pairs, they can select five states or countries from above and below the equator and report on the current temperatures.

(For further cross-curricular activities, see the Conexiones *section on pp. 124–125.)*

Capítulo 3

Los pasatiempos

OBJECTIVES

At the end of this chapter, you will be able to:

- **talk about some of your leisure-time activities**
- **make plans with friends**
- **give, accept, or turn down invitations**
- **compare leisure-time activities in Spanish-speaking countries with those in the United States**

En el parque de la Villa Olímpica, Barcelona

105

Teaching Suggestions
See the Writing, Audio & Video Activities book for Writing Activities that you may elect to use throughout the chapter.

Spanish in Your Community
Which sport in your community (or in the U.S.) has been most greatly influenced by Hispanic culture? Have students choose from the sports listed in the first vocabulary section (p. 108) or suggest any other sport. Have them explain their responses with specific reasons.

Cultural Notes 

(pp. 104–105, photo)
Barcelona hosted the 1992 Summer Olympics and is reaping the benefits of its investments for the games. Young people sit astride a feline sculpture by Colombian artist, Fernando Botero (b. 1932) near the Olympic Village *(Villa Olímpica).* The city has used income generated by the games to complete important civic projects, including the reclamation of coastline that was formerly industrial. Now *barceloneses* and visitors can enjoy more than 25 miles of sandy beach along the coast.

Preview

Cultural Objective

- To compare leisure-time activities in Spanish-speaking countries with those in the U.S.

 **¡Piénsalo bien!**

Play

 **Video Activity A**

Teaching Suggestions

See the Projects for Proficiency BLMs for activity ideas that you may elect to use throughout the chapter.

If available, bring or have students bring several sports or leisure magazines or newspapers from Spanish-speaking countries to class. Share photos of the activities with your students, encouraging a discussion about how these activities compare with theirs.

Discuss other activities that students engage in during weekends.

Using the Video

This chapter's video focuses on sports and leisure activities. Students will see our hosts in Madrid visiting a famous park and interviewing athletes.

¡Piénsalo bien!

Look at the photos. How do the leisure activities of these young people compare to what you and your friends like to do? Which of these would you most likely do with your friends? Read the captions. What do you think a *parque de diversiones* might be? And can you figure out what the *montaña rusa* is?

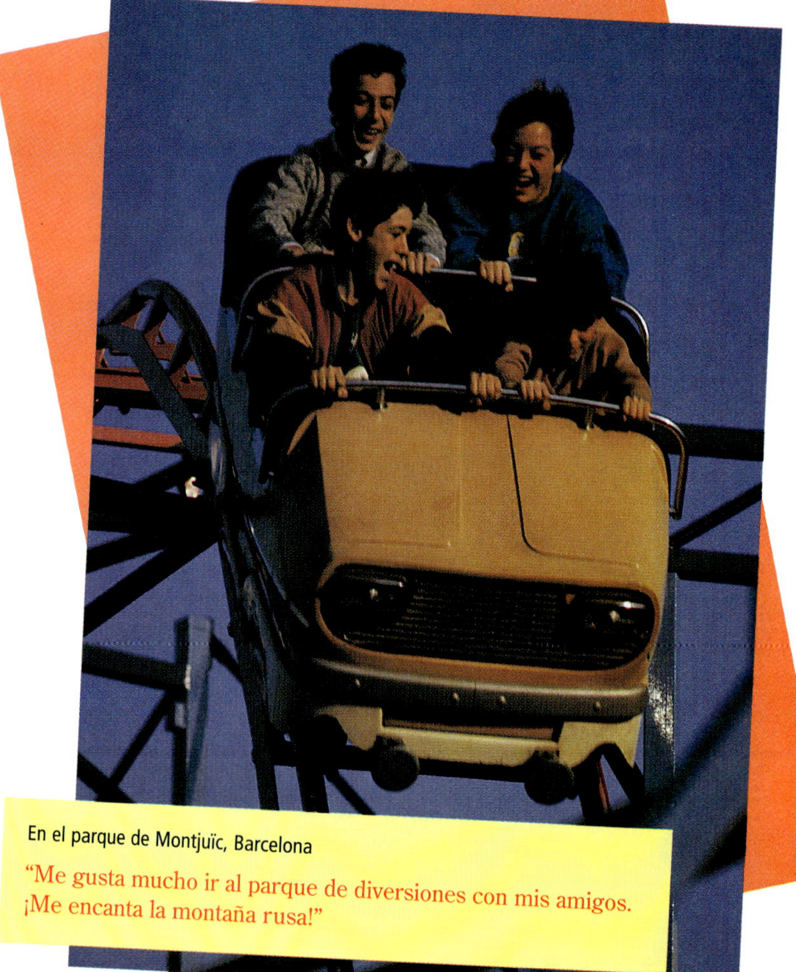

En el parque de Montjuïc, Barcelona

"Me gusta mucho ir al parque de diversiones con mis amigos. ¡Me encanta la montaña rusa!"

Options

Strategies for Reaching All Students

Spanish-Speaking Students

Have students describe what they see in the photos. In addition, ask: *¿Qué te gusta hacer con tus amigos? ¿Cuándo sales con tus amigos? ¿Cuándo vas a fiestas?*

Enrichment

Ask your students if they know any exchange students from Spanish-speaking countries. If they do, have them find out about their leisure-time activities and report back to the class.

Cultural Notes 

(p. 106, photo)
People everywhere enjoy spending time outdoors with friends. In Barcelona, the mountainside park Montjuïc is a great destination on a warm day. Park visitors enjoy outdoor restaurants, museums, gardens, and an amusement park with a large roller coaster. Montjuïc was the site of several Olympic events in 1992.

En la playa Boca Chica, República Dominicana

"¿Te gustaría nadar con nosotros?"

En el patio de una escuela, Lima, Perú

"Después de las clases, Julia y yo practicamos vóleibol. ¿Quién necesita una red?"

Show students segment one once through, then ask them to predict what this chapter's tape will be about. Then have students watch the segment again several times. After the first time, you may wish to have them brainstorm possible vocabulary and expressions they will need to talk about what they saw on the video. Ask students to identify: a) things they saw that were familiar to them, and b) things they saw that they probably would not see in a park where they live.

Video segment 1: For more teaching suggestions, see the Video Teacher's Guide.

Multicultural Perspectives

In many urban Hispanic neighborhoods, *bodegas* (grocery stores) are an informal meeting place for people and for sharing news. Ask students, especially Spanish-speakers, if they know about any other types of informal meeting places from different cultures.

Answers: ¡Piénsalo bien!

Answers to inductive questions will vary. Students should be able to guess from context that a *parque de diversiones* means "amusement park." If they have difficulty with *montaña rusa* (roller coaster), tell them the literal translation ("Russian mountain"), and then see if they can guess the meaning. Have they ever gone on a *montaña rusa?* Where?

(p. 107, top photo)
Three Dominican friends play in the warm waters of Boca Chica, 16 miles east of Santo Domingo, the capital of the Dominican Republic. Boca Chica's sandy beaches stretch for miles along a shallow lagoon. The beach's proximity to Santo Domingo makes it a favorite destination for city dwellers.

(p. 107, bottom photo)
During a break in their school day, these students play ball and chat with friends. Spanish and Quechua are the official languages of Peru, but Spanish is usually the language of instruction in schools. Most indigenous people are bilingual, although Quechua predominates in rural areas. Quechua and related languages, such as Aymará, are spoken by about five million people in the Andean region, which stretches from Ecuador to northern Argentina.

Present

Chapter Theme
Leisure-time activities: Sports

Communicative Objectives
- To tell where someone is
- To talk about activities
- To extend, accept, or decline invitations
- To tell how someone feels
- To tell where someone is going
- To say when and with whom you do an activity
- To ask for an explanation
- To express surprise, enthusiasm, or disappointment

Transparencies 18–19

Vocabulary Art BLMs

Pronunciation Tape 3-1

Vocabulario para conversar A

Play

Using the Video
Video segment 2: See the Video Teacher's Guide.

Video Activity B

Sección 1

Vocabulario para conversar

¿Te gustaría ir conmigo?

- As your teacher reads the name of each activity, put your finger on the corresponding picture.
- As your teacher reads each activity, make a thumbs up gesture if you like it or a thumbs down gesture if you do not. If you like the activity a lot, respond with the Spanish word for "Great!"
- Pantomime for your partner the various activities and see if he or she can point to the ones you are demonstrating.

* The names of all these sports are masculine. For example: *el básquetbol.*

Options

Strategies for Reaching All Students

Spanish-Speaking Students
Ask students to talk about their favorite leisure-time activities.

Un paso más Exs. 3-B, 3-C

Learning Spanish Through Action
STAGING VOCABULARY: *Señalen, Toquen*
MATERIALS: transparency of activities in the *Vocabulario para conversar*
DIRECTIONS: Ask students to touch or point to one of the activities. (As an alternative, have them pantomime activities and ask classmates to guess which ones they are.) Ask: *¿Te gustaría* (name of activity)? Encourage students to use any appropriate response in *También necesitas . . .* for their answers.

También necesitas . . .

estar: (yo) estoy	*to be: I am*	¡Claro que sí!	*Of course!*
(tú) estás	*you are*	¡Claro que no!	*Of course not!*
conmigo, contigo	*with me, with you*	De nada.	*You're welcome.*
¿(A ti) te gustaría ___?	*Would you like ___?*	¡Genial!	*Great! Wonderful!*
(A mí) me gustaría ___.	*I would like ___.*	¡Qué lástima!	*That's too bad! That's a shame!*
poder: (yo) puedo	*can: I can*		
(tú) puedes	*you can*		
querer: (yo) quiero	*to want: I want*		
(tú) quieres	*you want*		
después (de)	*after*		
después de las clases	*after school*		
¿Por qué?	*Why?*		

¿Y qué quiere decir . . . ?

ir: (yo) voy
(tú) vas
con
hoy no
mañana*

* *Mañana* alone means "tomorrow." *La mañana* means "morning."

Grammar Preview

Voy / vas, conmigo / contigo, and *estoy / estás* are previewed here. Their explanation appears in the grammar sections on pp. 127, 135, and 136, respectively.

Background Information

The vocabulary sections for this chapter are in a different order than in *PASO A PASO 1.* Therefore, you will use some ancillaries in a different sequence from the high-school book (Practice Workbook 3-3 before 3-1). The correct sequence of activities is listed in the Teacher's Edition at point of use.

In current usage, native Spanish-speakers omit *a* + definite article after the verb *jugar.*

Class Starter Review

On the day following initial presentation of vocabulary, you might begin the class with this activity: Call out each of the leisure-time activities or use the transparencies. Have students signal (for example, thumbs up or thumbs down) if they like or don't like to do them. Write the activities on the chalkboard or a separate transparency and have students rank them in order of preference.

Practice

Reteach / Review: Vocabulary

Ex. 2: Students can do a variation of this exercise with *Estudiante A* asking *¿Te gustaría . . .?* and *Estudiante B* answering *Me gustaría, pero necesito . . .*

Re-enter / Recycle

Exs. 1–3: activities from Chap. 1

Teaching Suggestions

Empecemos a conversar: Have students continue filling in their Organizers.

Ex. 2: Explain that the Spanish word *y* becomes *e* before a word beginning with *i* or *hi.* For example: *Me gusta nadar e ir a la playa.*

Answers: Empecemos a conversar

1 ESTUDIANTE A

a. ¿Puedes jugar fútbol conmigo?
b. . . . ir al cine . . .
c. . . . ir de pesca . . .
d. . . . estudiar . . .
e. Questions will vary.

ESTUDIANTE B

a.–e. Answers will vary, but may include: *Hoy no; lo siento. Estoy ocupado(a), . . . enfermo(a), . . . cansado(a).*

Empecemos a conversar

With a partner, take turns being *Estudiante A* and *Estudiante B*. Use the words that are cued or given in the boxes to replace the underlined words in the example. 💡 means you can make your own choices. When it is your turn to be *Estudiante B*, try to answer truthfully.

1 

A —*¿Puedes ir de compras conmigo?*
B —*Hoy no; lo siento. Estoy cansado(a).*

Estudiante A | Estudiante B

2 

A —*¿Por qué no quieres jugar fútbol?*
B —*Quiero, pero no puedo. Necesito ayudar en casa.*
A —*¡Qué lástima!*

Estudiante A | Estudiante B

Options

Strategies for Reaching All Students

Spanish-Speaking Students

Ex. 2: Pair bilingual and non-bilingual students. Have them write two or three more responses for *Estudiante B.*

Students Needing Extra Help

Ex. 3: Explain the choice of responses for *Estudiante B.* You may wish to have these written on separate slips of paper so that students can choose them one at a time.

3 A —*¿Te gustaría jugar tenis conmigo?*
B —*¿Contigo? Sí, me gustaría (mucho).*

Estudiante A

Estudiante B

Estos muchachos practican jai alai, el deporte regional del país vasco, en el norte de España.

Los videojuegos son muy populares en Viña del Mar, Chile.

2 ESTUDIANTE A

a. ¿Por qué no quieres jugar vóleibol?
b. . . . jugar fútbol americano?
c. . . . ver la tele(visión)?
d. . . . escuchar música?
e. Questions will vary.

ESTUDIANTE B

a.–e. Answers will vary, but may include: *Quiero, pero no puedo. Necesito ir de compras, . . . cocinar, . . . estudiar, . . . leer.*

3 ESTUDIANTE A

a. ¿Te gustaría ir a una fiesta conmigo?
b. . . . ir al cine . . .
c. . . . ir de compras . . .
d. . . . jugar videojuegos . . .
e. . . . ir de pesca . . .
f. . . . jugar básquetbol . . .
g. Questions will vary.

ESTUDIANTE B

a.–g. Answers will vary. Encourage students to select a different response each time.

Cultural Notes

(p. 111, left photo)
Jai alai, or *pelota vasca,* was first played by Spanish Basques who called the game "merry festival" in *Euskara,* the Basque language. By 1900 the game had been exported to Cuba and from there it became popular in France, Italy, Mexico, the Philippines, Indonesia, and parts of the U.S. An international jai alai federation holds championships every four years.

(p. 111, right photo)
Video arcades, illuminated only by low lights and glowing electronic screens, are a common place for young people to spend time with friends. Conversation is often muted while players concentrate on their games. Such arcades are especially popular in resorts, such as Viña del Mar, Chile, where young vacationers go to relax, test their skills, and meet other people their age.

Apply

Re-enter / Recycle

Ex. 1: adjectives describing personality from Chap. 1

Teaching Suggestions

You may want to use the *Empecemos a leer y a escribir* sections as homework assignments.

Ex. 1: Activate prior knowledge by asking students if they have ever seen a quiz like this in a young people's / teen magazine. Ask if they have ever taken one in English. Before they take the quiz, ask students to work in groups and make a bar graph predicting how many students will be in each category (9–12, 5–8, 1–4). After they take it, ask students to stand in separate parts of the room to indicate which category they are in. Have a student count the total number of students in each category. With these numbers, students can work in the same groups as before and make a bar graph of the predicted number and the true number of students in each category.

Empecemos a leer y a escribir

Responde en español.

1 Toma esta prueba. Escribe las respuestas en una hoja de papel.

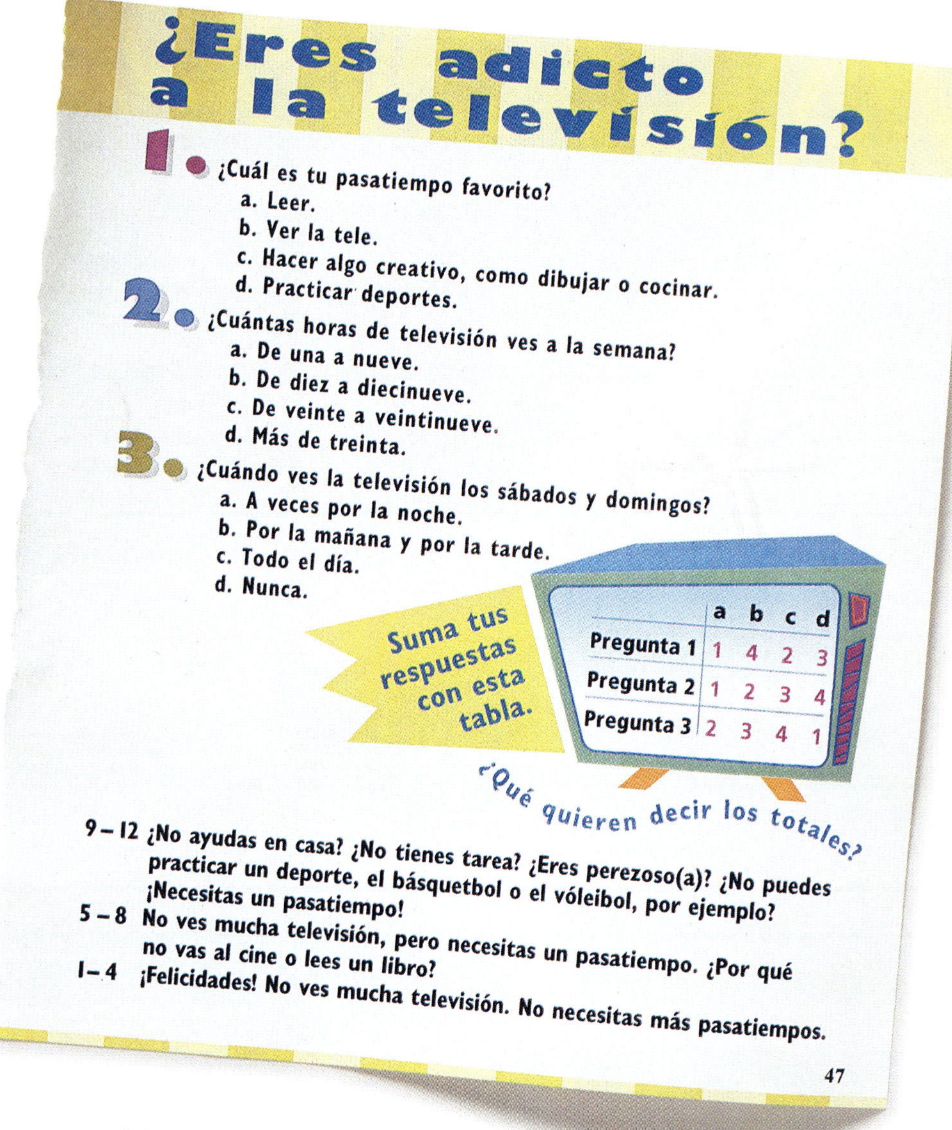

¿Eres adicto a la televisión?

1. ¿Cuál es tu pasatiempo favorito?
- a. Leer.
- b. Ver la tele.
- c. Hacer algo creativo, como dibujar o cocinar.
- d. Practicar deportes.

2. ¿Cuántas horas de televisión ves a la semana?
- a. De una a nueve.
- b. De diez a diecinueve.
- c. De veinte a veintinueve.
- d. Más de treinta.

3. ¿Cuándo ves la televisión los sábados y domingos?
- a. A veces por la noche.
- b. Por la mañana y por la tarde.
- c. Todo el día.
- d. Nunca.

Suma tus respuestas con esta tabla.

	a	b	c	d
Pregunta 1	1	4	2	3
Pregunta 2	1	2	3	4
Pregunta 3	2	3	4	1

¿Qué quieren decir los totales?

9 – 12 ¿No ayudas en casa? ¿No tienes tarea? ¿Eres perezoso(a)? ¿No puedes practicar un deporte, el básquetbol o el vóleibol, por ejemplo? ¡Necesitas un pasatiempo!

5 – 8 No ves mucha televisión, pero necesitas un pasatiempo. ¿Por qué no vas al cine o lees un libro?

1 – 4 ¡Felicidades! No ves mucha televisión. No necesitas más pasatiempos.

47

Options

Strategies for Reaching All Students

Spanish-Speaking Students

(p. 113, realia) Ask: *¿Puedes entender el doble sentido de la oración "Tenemos mucho que ver contigo"?*

 **Un paso más Exs. 3-D, 3-E**

Students Needing Extra Help

Exs. 2–4: Have students refer to their Organizers.

Enrichment

Have students compare the time they spend watching TV with that spent on homework / studying.

Ex. 4: Students may also answer: *¿Qué no te gusta hacer los fines de semana?*

2 Write three excuses that you have learned how to say in this chapter.

3 ¿Qué te gustaría hacer hoy después de las clases?

4 ¿Qué quieres hacer el sábado por la noche?

También se dice

jugar baloncesto

jugar balonvolea

Answers: Empecemos a leer y a escribir

1 Answers will vary.

2 Answers will vary, but may include: *Me gustaría, pero estoy ocupado(a) / enfermo(a) / cansado(a).*

3–4 Answers will vary.

Using Realia

Ask: *¿Qué programa te gustaría ver esta noche? ¿Por qué?*

 **Practice Wkbk. 3-3, 3-4**

 **Audio Activity 3.1**

 **Writing Activities**

 **Pruebas 3-1, 3-2**

 **Comm. Act. BLM 3-2**

Cultural Notes 

(p. 113, realia)
This television station in Spain offers viewers a summer of family entertainment, with game shows such as *La ruleta de la fortuna* (similar to *Wheel of Fortune)* and glimpses into the lives of celebrities in the show *Ricos y famosos. La guardería* (literally, the Day Care Center) is a preschool program in which the hostess, Teresa Rabal, sings and entertains children with hand puppets.

Present & Apply

Cultural Objective

- To talk about parks and leisure-time activities

Teaching Suggestions

Before they read the text, ask students to look at the photos and then discuss any similarities or differences between these parks and those in the area where they live.

Make sure students know the meaning of *Antropología* in the first paragraph, and discuss what might be found in this museum.

Ex. 2: You may want to help students categorize similarities and differences by completing a Venn diagram. See the Projects for Proficiency BLMs for a diagram model.

Critical Thinking: Identifying Evidence

After students have read the text, ask: Which paragraphs provide information that parks in Spanish-speaking countries have a wide variety of family-oriented activities? (Paragraph one mentions a zoo, a botanical garden, several museums, and an amusement park. Paragraph two talks about a puppet show, a concert, and a lake.)

Mira las fotos. ¿Por qué les gusta a las familias visitar estos parques los fines de semana?

El Bosque de Chapultepec in Mexico City is one of the largest city parks in the world. It has a castle, a zoo, a botanical garden, and several museums, including the world-famous Museo Nacional de Antropología. It also has an amusement park, which offers a variety of rides—a roller coaster *(montaña rusa)*, a Ferris wheel *(rueda de feria)*, bumper cars *(carros locos)*, and so on.

El Retiro is the name of Madrid's most famous park. There you can visit the Crystal Palace, where many shows and exhibits are held. You can also watch a puppet show, go to a concert, or row a boat in the artificial lake. Nearby are a botanical garden and one of the world's finest art museums, El Prado.

In Mexico City and Madrid, many families often spend an entire Sunday afternoon at the park.

En el Museo Nacional de Antropología de México

114

Options

Strategies for Reaching All Students

Spanish-Speaking Students

Ask: *¿Dónde está tu parque favorito? ¿Cómo es? ¿Con quién vas allí? ¿Cómo son los parques cerca de tu casa o tu escuela? ¿Cómo sería tu parque ideal?* Responses may be oral or written and shared with other students.

Cultural Notes 

(p. 114, photo)
This colossal stone head at Mexico's Museo Nacional de Antropología is an example of the distinctive sculpturing style of the Olmecs, the first Mesoamerican people to work with large blocks of stone. They carved huge, helmeted heads with high foreheads, flaring nostrils, and thick, down-turned lips. The museum opened in 1964 and today contains 23 exhibition halls packed wth treasures from Mexico's ancient and current cultures.

El Bosque de Chapultepec

La cultura desde tu perspectiva

1 If you were staying with a family in Madrid or Mexico City, where in El Retiro or Chapultepec would you like to spend the most time? Why?

2 In what ways are parks in Spanish-speaking countries similar to parks that you know? How are they different?

El parque del Retiro

Multicultural Perspectives

The area we now know as Chapultepec Park was developed by the Aztecs in the fourteenth century. In 1325, the Aztecs built the magnificent city of Tenochtitlán on the present-day site of Mexico City. The city, the capital of the Aztec Empire, had a population of around 100,000 in 1519, when the Spanish arrived. Although Chapultepec Park may be enjoyed by everyone today, its use originally was restricted to Aztec emperors. Ask students to share any information that they might have about the Aztecs.

Answers

Answers to inductive questions will vary. Accept any logical answers.

Answers: La cultura desde tu perspectiva

1 Answers will vary.

2 Answers will vary. Similarities may include: gardens, paths, lakes, fountains, monuments, etc. Differences may include: castles, restaurants, and amusement parks. Students should see that parks in Spanish-speaking countries are not limited to just playing sports.

(p. 115, top photo)
El parque de Chapultepec is the largest and most important park in Mexico City. The area is also a very old recreation spot, having been used by Aztec kings as a summer residence. Chapultepec is especially crowded on Sundays, when families come to stroll, picnic, and otherwise enjoy the many attractions the park has to offer. Among them are a world-famous zoo, an amusement park, fountains, lakes, museums, and art galleries.

(p. 115, bottom photo)
El parque del Retiro in Madrid is a large, elegantly planned park. Dating to 1630, it was originally intended to be a *buen retiro* (nice retreat) for Felipe IV. Today it serves that function for people who go there to stroll, picnic, rent rowboats on its central lake (which is graced by a statue of Spain's twentieth-century monarch, Alfonso XII), and enjoy puppet theater, art exhibits, and concerts.

Present

Chapter Theme

Leisure-time activities: Places to go

Communicative Objectives

- To ask and to tell where someone is going
- To ask and to tell where someone is
- To say when and with whom you do an activity
- To talk about activities
- To express surprise, enthusiasm, or disappointment
- To give an explanation
- To express possession

Transparencies 20–21

Vocabulary Art BLMs

Pronunciation Tape 3-2

Vocabulario para conversar B

Play

Step

Sección 2

Vocabulario para conversar

¿Cuándo vas al parque?

- As your teacher reads each place name, hold up one finger if you go to that place often and two fingers if you do *not*.
- As your teacher names each season, point to the picture of an activity you like to do or a place you like to go to during that season.
- As your teacher names each place, indicate when you like to go there. Hold up one finger for *por la mañana*, two fingers for *por la tarde*, and three for *por la noche*.

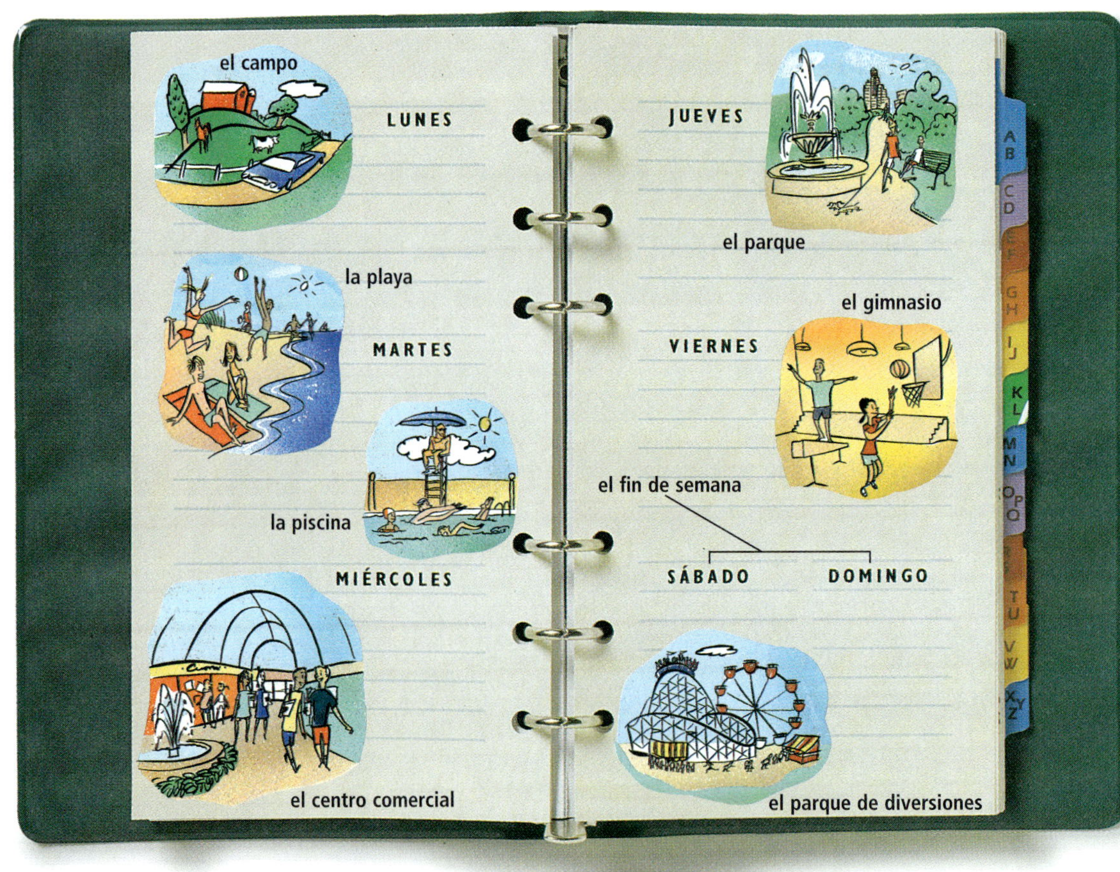

Options

Strategies for Reaching All Students

Enrichment

También necesitas . . . : Reinforce the difference between *mañana* and *por la mañana* by having students tell where they are going tomorrow morning. For example: *Mañana por la mañana voy al (a la) . . .*

Learning Spanish Through Action

STAGING VOCABULARY: *Señalen, Toquen*
MATERIALS: seasons from the Vocabulary Art BLMs or transparency
DIRECTIONS: Have students touch or point to one of the seasons. Then have them name an activity they like to do (or one that cannot be done) in that particular season.

También necesitas . . .

¿Adónde?	*(to) where?*
a	here: *to*
a la, al (a + el)	*to the*
el pasatiempo	*hobby, pastime*
el lunes, el martes . . .	*on Monday, on Tuesday . . .*
los lunes, los martes . . .	*on Mondays, on Tuesdays . . .*
el fin (los fines) de semana	*on the weekend(s)*
(por) la mañana	*(in) the morning*
(por) la tarde	*(in) the afternoon*
(por) la noche	*(in) the evening*
generalmente	*usually, generally*
todos los días	*every day*
porque	*because*
¡No me digas!	*Really? You don't say!*
mi, mis	*my*
tus	*your*

¿Y qué quiere decir . . . ?
¿Dónde?
jugar: (yo) juego
(tú) juegas
el amigo, la amiga
la familia
solo, -a

las estaciones
(*sing.*, la estación)

la primavera

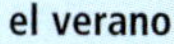
el verano

el otoño

el invierno

¡No olvides!
Do you remember the word *tu?* What do you think the difference is between *tu* and *tus?* When do you think you might use each one? And what is the difference between *tu* and *tú?*

¡No olvides!
¿Por qué? = Why?
porque = because

Using the Video
Video segment 2: See the Video Teacher's Guide.

Video Activity B

Teaching Suggestions
See which season has the birthdays for most students and make this the "class" season.

Class Starter Review
On the day following initial presentation of vocabulary, you might begin the class with this activity: Have students use *¿Cuándo tienes la clase de . . . ?* and *por la mañana / tarde* so that they can take turns asking for and giving information about their school schedules. Use visuals to elicit responses. Make sure that students have their schedules with them for this activity.

Practice

Re-enter / Recycle

Exs. 1–2: calendar expressions from Chap. 1

Teaching Suggestions

Empecemos a conversar: Have students begin filling in their Organizers.

For additional practice, have students make four columns, labeling each one with a season. Using the vocabulary for places (p. 116), have them think about when they usually go there, and write the places in the appropriate columns. (Students can also illustrate the seasons and activities.) Some places will appear in more than one column.

Ex. 1: Have *Estudiante A* add *por la mañana, por la tarde,* or *por la noche* to his or her question.

Exs. 1–2: Remind students that they need *al (a la)* before the location. Explain that *Estudiante B*'s responses are choices and are not to be used in the order given.

Exs. 1–3: Point out that *voy* and *vas* are used to state where someone is going. Explain why *vas* changes to *voy* in the response.

Empecemos a conversar

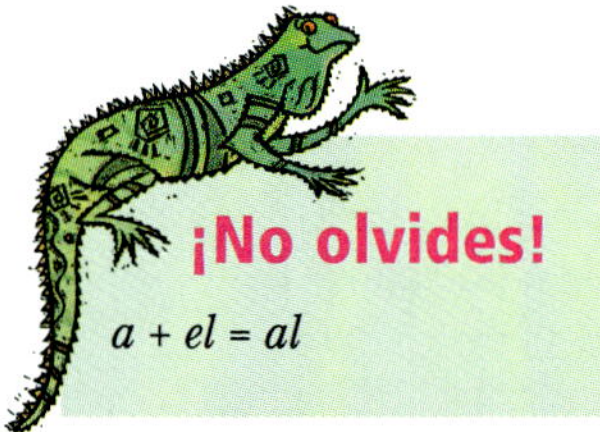

¡No olvides!

a + el = al

1 el domingo

A —*¿Adónde vas el domingo?*
B —*Voy al parque de diversiones.*
A —*¡No me digas! Yo también.*
o: *¡No me digas! Yo voy al cine.*

Estudiante A **Estudiante B**

a. el lunes
b. el martes
c. el miércoles
d. el jueves
e. el viernes
f. el sábado
g. mañana

2

A —*¿Cuándo vas al gimnasio?*
B —*Voy los miércoles y los viernes.*
o: *Pues, generalmente no voy.*

Estudiante A

a. b. c. d. e. f.

Estudiante B

los lunes, los martes . . .
los fines de semana
todos los días
por la mañana / tarde / noche
después de las clases

Options

Strategies for Reaching All Students

Spanish-Speaking Students

Ex. 2: Pair Spanish-speaking students and have them extend the dialogue by having *Estudiante A* ask: *¿Y qué te gusta hacer allí?* or *¿Por qué no vas?*

 **Un paso más Ex. 3-A**

3 

A —*¿Con quién vas al centro comercial?*
B —*Generalmente voy con mis amigos.*
o: *Generalmente voy solo(a).*
o: *No voy al centro comercial.*

Estudiante A | **Estudiante B**

4 

A —*¿Dónde juegas básquetbol?*
B —*En el gimnasio.*
o: *No juego básquetbol.*

Estudiante A | **Estudiante B**

También se dice

la alberca
la pileta

el parque de atracciones

Cursos de inglés.
Sácales el mejor partido.

FSL

Answers: Empecemos a conversar

1 ESTUDIANTE A
a. ¿Adónde vas el lunes?
b. . . . el martes?
c. . . . el miércoles?
d. . . . el jueves?
e. . . . el viernes?
f. . . . el sábado?
g. . . . mañana?

ESTUDIANTE B
a.–g. Answers will vary. Suggested places include: *Voy al parque, . . . al centro comercial, . . . al campo, . . . a la playa, . . . al gimnasio.*

2 ESTUDIANTE A
a. ¿Cuándo vas al parque?
b. . . . a la playa?
c. . . . al campo?
d. . . . al parque de diversiones?
e. . . . a la piscina?
f. . . . al centro comercial?

ESTUDIANTE B
a.–f. Answers will vary.

3 Dialogues will vary.

4 ESTUDIANTE A
a. ¿Dónde juegas vóleibol?
b. . . . béisbol?
c. . . . fútbol?
d. . . . fútbol americano?
e. . . . tenis?

ESTUDIANTE B
a.–e. Answers will vary.

Cultural Notes

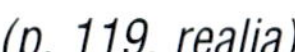

(p. 119, realia)
This advertisement from a Spanish magazine encourages readers to make "the best play of their life" by learning English. The ability to speak English has acquired added value in Europe in recent years, as countries continue to integrate their economies in the European Economic Community. The 900 prefix in the telephone number is for toll-free calls within Spain.

Practice

Reteach / Review: Vocabulary

Ex. 5 *(p. 120):* Elicit another expression that can be used in place of *¡No me digas! (¿De veras?)*

Re-enter / Recycle

Ex. 5: *me / te gusta* from Chap. 1

Answers: Empecemos a conversar

5 ESTUDIANTE A

a. ¿Qué te gusta hacer en la primavera?
b. . . . el verano?
c. . . . el otoño?
d. . . . el invierno?

ESTUDIANTE B

a.–d. Answers will vary. Look for *me gusta* + inf.

5 

A —*¿Qué te gusta hacer en el verano?*
B —*Me gusta ir a la playa porque me gusta nadar.*
A —*¡No me digas! A mí también.*
o: *A mí no (me gusta).*

Estudiante A **Estudiante B**

Viña del Mar, Chile

"En febrero, ¿a quién no le gusta ir a la playa?"

Options

Strategies for Reaching All Students

Enrichment

Ex. 5 *(p. 120):* Students can prepare for this exercise by asking each other: *¿Qué te gusta más, la primavera, el verano, el otoño o el invierno? ¿Cuáles son los meses de la primavera? ¿Y del verano?* etc. Expand this exercise by having students tell with whom they go to that place.

Empecemos a leer y a escribir

Responde en español.

1 Which student is *not* making sense? Identify the student, then rewrite what he or she is saying so that it makes sense.

a. "No soy nada atrevido. Al contrario, soy muy prudente. Generalmente nado en la playa, no en una piscina."

b. "¡Qué lástima! No puedo ir de compras contigo hoy porque estoy enferma."

c. "Soy callada y paciente y me gusta estar sola. Cuando no estoy ocupada los fines de semana, me gusta mucho ir de pesca."

2 Write full sentences telling when you do any four of the activities pictured. You can mention the season, the day of the week, or the time of day. For example:

En el otoño, juego fútbol después de las clases.
En la primavera, voy al campo los domingos.

3 Write questions to ask your partner about when he or she goes to three different places and with whom. Write down your partner's answers.

4 ¿Qué estación te gusta más? ¿Por qué?

5 Generalmente, ¿adónde vas después de las clases? ¿Cuál es tu pasatiempo favorito?

Apply

Teaching Suggestions

Ex. 2: Students can use a sheet of notebook paper folded into four sections. In each section they can write a sentence and then illustrate it.

Ex. 3: Model on the chalkboard. Divide possibilities into interrogatives for people and places. Show students that they have practiced these questions in Exs. 2 and 3 on pp. 118–119.

Answers: Empecemos a leer y a escribir

1 a. "No soy nada prudente. Al contrario, soy muy atrevido. Generalmente nado en la playa, no en una piscina."

2 Sentences will vary, but encourage students to use chapter vocabulary.

3 Questions will vary. Look for *¿cuándo?* and *¿con quién?* along with use of *voy / vas.*

4–5 Answers will vary.

 **Practice Wkbk. 3-1, 3-2**

 **Audio Activity 3.2**

 **Pruebas 3-3, 3-4**

 **Comm. Act. BLM 3-1**

Cultural Notes 

(p. 120, photo)
Viña del Mar is one of Latin America's most famous beach resorts. This small city, just north of the historic Chilean port city of Valparaíso, grows in population during the summer months of December, January, and February when its beaches are filled with vacationers from throughout Latin America and Europe. At this time, many events take place, such as the world-renowned film festival and an international popular music festival. Viña del Mar is noted for its sunshine, good seafood, and scenic beauty.

Practice

Re-enter / Recycle
Exs. 1 and 3: time-telling from Chap. 2

Teaching Suggestions
Ex. 1: You may want to post some of the *¡No olvides!* reminders in the classroom for reference.

Ex. 2: Encourage students to continue this dialogue. For example:
A —*¡Qué lástima! ¿Y el domingo a las dos?*

Ex. 3: Invite several pairs to reenact their conversation for the class.

Answers: Comuniquemos
1–3 Dialogues will vary.

Here's another opportunity for you and your partner to use the vocabulary you've just learned.

1 Your partner wants to get together with you, but you are very busy. Consult the calendar for the week before you reply.

A —*¿Estás ocupado(a) el sábado a las nueve?*
B —*No.*
A —*¿Quieres ir á la playa conmigo?*
B —. . .
o:
A —*¿Estás ocupado(a) el lunes después de las clases?*
B —*Sí. Voy al gimnasio con Enrique.*
A —*¡Qué lastima! ¿Y el martes?*
B —. . .

¡No olvides!
a + el = al

Options

Strategies for Reaching All Students

Spanish-Speaking Students
Pair bilingual with non-bilingual students.

Un paso más Exs. 3-F, 3-G

Students Needing Extra Help
Ex. 3: Model the exercise. Refer to time-telling in Chap. 2.
Ahora lo sabes: Have students write this section so that they can check off what they have mastered.

Cooperative Learning
Supply each student with a blank index card. Divide the class into groups of three. First ask students to write down a season of the year, and then to pass their cards to the right. Next, have them write an activity they like to do, based on the season written on the card they have. Finally, have them pass

2 Make up a dialogue in which you ask a partner to join you in an activity. Your partner will either accept or refuse politely and explain what his or her plans are.

A —*¿Quieres patinar conmigo?*
B —*Sí. ¿Cuándo?*
A —. . .
o:
A —*¿Quieres patinar conmigo?*
B —*Me gustaría, pero no puedo porque voy de compras con mi familia.*

3 You are going to a party Friday night. Find out from a partner

- what time the party begins
- with whom he or she is going

If your partner is going alone, ask if he or she would like to go with you.

Be prepared to present your conversation to the class.

✔Ahora lo sabes

Using what you have learned so far, can you:

- **say what you would like to do after class?**
- **say that you want to do something or go somewhere but cannot?**
- **invite someone to do something with you?**
- **accept or turn down an invitation?**
- **give an excuse or explanation?**

Answers: Ahora lo sabes

- Me gustaría ___ después de las clases. *(pp. 108–109, 116–117)*
- Quiero + *inf.*, pero no puedo. *(pp. 108–109)*
- ¿Quieres + *inf.* conmigo? *(pp. 108–109)*
- Gracias, pero (no puedo, no quiero). *(pp. 108–109)*
- *Answers will vary, but may include:* Me gustaría, pero estoy ___. *(pp. 108–109)*

 **Audio Activity 3.3**

 **Writing Activities**

 **Examen de habilidades 1**

the cards once more to the right. Tell them to write down an expression of frequency (for example: *todos los días, los sábados, por la mañana,* etc.). Ask a member from each group to summarize. Have the class compile all the information in a chart to find out which seasons, activities, or expressions of frequency were listed the most.

Apply

Background Information

(See the Cross-Curricular Connections at the beginning of the chapter on pp. 104–105 for further activities. For a complete list of the curricular areas covered in PASO A PASO A, *see p. T23 of this Teacher's Edition.)*

You may choose the number of activities you want your class to do. You may prefer to use the activities for homework, for enrichment, or for your Spanish-speaking students. This material is not part of the testing program, however, it is appropriate for use in student assessment.

Teaching Suggestions

Pasatiempos favoritos: Write (or have a student write) this chart on the chalkboard or a transparency. If it is easier to manage, you might ask students to express a preference by raising their hands. Have one student record the results.

Review how to calculate a percentage. (Remind students that we deal with percentages almost daily, with restaurant tips, prices on merchandise marked down, etc.) For example, if 10 out of 25 students choose a pastime, use this formula:
x / 100 = 10 / 25

Conexiones

These activities connect Spanish with what you are learning in other subject areas.

Pasatiempos favoritos

Vamos a hacer una encuesta sobre los pasatiempos. Mira la tabla en la pizarra. Haz una marca (√) junto a tu pasatiempo favorito.

Número total de estudiantes:

Pasatiempos	Número de estudiantes	Porcentaje
ir de compras	√√	
ir al parque de diversiones	√	
ir al cine		
jugar videojuegos		
practicar deportes	√	

En grupo, sumen las marcas. Luego calculen el porcentaje de los estudiantes que prefiere cada actividad.

Para pensar

Marta, Pablo, Pilar y Jorge van a lugares diferentes. Van a la piscina, a la cancha de tenis, a una exposición de arte y a un concierto. ¿Adónde va cada uno?

Marta no es muy deportiva, pero nada bien y le gusta mucho.

Pilar toca la trompeta en la banda y escucha música todos los días.

Pablo dibuja todos los fines de semana porque es muy artístico.

La precipitación en Puerto Rico

Usa los mapas para responder a estas preguntas.

a. ¿Dónde llueve más en Puerto Rico?
b. ¿Dónde llueve más en los Estados Unidos?
c. ¿Cuánto *(How much)* llueve donde tú vives? ¿En qué estación llueve más?

Options

Strategies for Reaching All Students

Students Needing Extra Help

Para pensar: To help organize their answers, have students make a grid with the headings *Piscina, Tenis, Exposición,* and *Concierto,* with Marta, Pablo, Pilar, and Jorge down the left-hand side. Students can then place checkmarks in the corresponding spots on the grid. Explain that this is the type of grid used in math for solving logic problems. Through the process of elimination students can obtain the final name. Have them reread the problem to be sure that their answers do not contradict any of the given conditions. See the Projects for Proficiency BLMs for a template and making a grid / table.

La precipitación en Puerto Rico: See if students can figure out the meaning of *pulgadas* (inches).

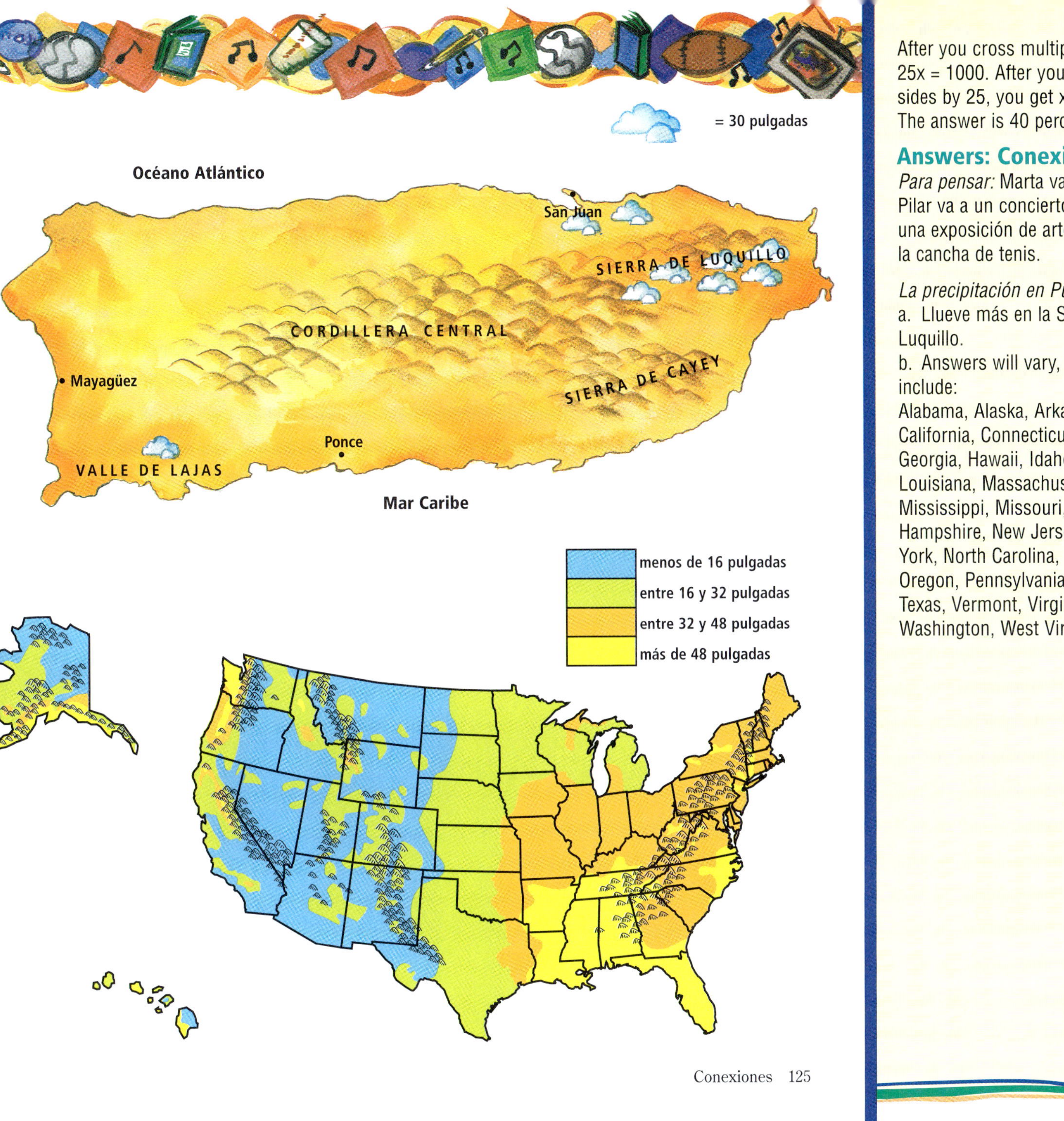

After you cross multiply, you get 25x = 1000. After you divide both sides by 25, you get x = 40. The answer is 40 percent.

Answers: Conexiones

Para pensar: Marta va a la piscina. Pilar va a un concierto. Pablo va a una exposición de arte. Jorge va a la cancha de tenis.

La precipitación en Puerto Rico:
a. Llueve más en la Sierra de Luquillo.
b. Answers will vary, but may include:
Alabama, Alaska, Arkansas, California, Connecticut, Florida, Georgia, Hawaii, Idaho, Kentucky, Louisiana, Massachusetts, Mississippi, Missouri, New Hampshire, New Jersey, New York, North Carolina, Oklahoma, Oregon, Pennsylvania, Tennessee, Texas, Vermont, Virginia, Washington, West Virginia.

Preview

 **Transparency 22**

Teaching Suggestions

Have students fill in the *ir* chart in the grammar portion of the Organizer. Have them brainstorm the kinds of information one might find in such a brochure before they look at the visual.

B: Based on students' explanations, write a rule for the class and post it for future reference. Give some examples in English of the use of (someone) "going to" (do something) to represent future activity. Tenses and their usage may sometimes pose a problem in English.

Answers

Answers to inductive questions will vary, but students may say they'd expect to find information such as location, amenities, and prices.

A swimming, fishing, horseback riding, sunbathing, listening to music, playing sports / *vamos (a)* / *nosotros* / Explanations will vary. Students may say that the *-mos* ending indicates a *nosotros* form.

B Students should be able to guess from context that the sentences read: "(we) are going to go" and "(we) are going to swim." / We use the infinitive.

Gramática en contexto

Look at the brochure describing a family vacation camp. What kind of information would you expect to find? Can you find all that information in this brochure?

Vamos a ir al

CAMPAMENTO BELLA VISTA

¿Por qué no va Ud. con nosotros?

Por la mañana vamos a nadar en la piscina olímpica o vamos a ir de pesca.

Por la tarde vamos a montar a caballo en el campo o a tomar el sol en la playa.

Por la noche vamos a escuchar música o a practicar deportes.

¿No quiere Ud. pasar sus vacaciones en el Campamento Bella Vista?
Para hacer reservas o para obtener más información, llame al 1-800-555-4132.

A What activities does Campamento Bella Vista offer? What verb is used with each pair of activities? What subject pronoun do you think goes with this verb form? Explain your answer to a partner.

B In the brochure, *vamos a* is always followed by a verb. What do you think *vamos a ir* and *vamos a nadar* mean? Based on what you've seen, explain to your partner what form of the verb to use after *vamos a*.

Options

Strategies for Reaching All Students

Students Needing Extra Help

Give some examples in English of when someone is going to do something (We are going to swim).

El verbo ir: Students by now are accustomed to changing verb endings to agree with different subjects in *-ar* verbs *(yo nado, tú nadas),* but this is the first time they are working with irregular verbs. See if they can still see a pattern in the paradigm.

El verbo *ir*

You know that verbs whose infinitives end in *-ar* follow a pattern. The endings show who is doing the action: *(yo) cocino*, *(tú) cocinas*, and so on.

- Verbs that follow certain patterns are called **regular** verbs. Those that do not follow those patterns are called **irregular**. The verb *ir*, "to go," is irregular. Here are its present-tense forms.

(yo)	**voy**	(nosotros) (nosotras)	**vamos**
(tú)	**vas**	(vosotros) (vosotras)	**vais**
(Ud.) (él) (ella)	**va**	(Uds.) (ellos) (ellas)	**van**

- The verb *ir* is often followed by the word *a*.

  Voy a la playa.

  Voy al cine.

1 Based on the chart, with which of the following people would you use the verb form *van?* What forms of *ir* would you use with the other people?

a. Ana y Antonio
b. los muchachos
c. María Luisa
d. Juan Pedro
e. mis amigos
f. Juan Carlos y Jorge

Present & Practice

Class Starter Review

On the day following the presentation of *ir,* you might begin the class with this activity:
Have pairs of students alternate giving subject pronouns and the correct form of the verb *ir.* As a variation, have students make up complete sentences rather than just stating the correct verb form. This activity may be done on the chalkboard or on a transparency.

Answers

1 *van:* a., b., e., f. / *va:* c., d.

 **Practice Wkbk. 3-5**

2 There is a teachers' meeting today and you have the day off from school. Everyone is going to a different place. With a partner, take turns asking and answering questions about where the following people are going.

Anita A —*¿Adónde va Anita?*
B —*Va al centro comercial.*

Estudiante A

a. Gustavo
b. Isabel y Elena
c. Carlos
d. Uds.
e. Felipe y Ramón
f. tú
g. nosotros

Estudiante B

3 Find out from three people where they are going after school today.

A —*¿Adónde vas después de las clases hoy?*
B —*Voy al gimnasio.*

Then tell your partner where each of the three is going. For example:

Ricardo va al gimnasio. Ana María y Patricia van de compras.

Parque de diversiones, Barcelona

Practice

Teaching Suggestions

Ex. 2: Remind students that the verb form changes in some responses. Show how the *a* in *adónde* is shown again in the answers as *al* or *a la.* Practice using *al* or *a la* by reviewing some places prior to doing the exercise.

Ex. 4: Before students begin this exercise, make sure they understand which verb forms to use, especially in the model and item c. Remind them to make choices and to not read straight across the columns.

Answers

2 ESTUDIANTE A

a. ¿Adónde va Gustavo?
b. . . . van Isabel y Elena?
c. . . . va Carlos?
d. . . . van Uds.?
e. . . . van Felipe y Ramón?
f. . . . vas tú?
g. . . . vamos nosotros?

ESTUDIANTE B

Answers will vary, but may include: *al campo, al centro comercial, a la piscina, al parque, al gimnasio.*

a. Gustavo va al (a la) . . .
b. Isabel y Elena van al (a la) . . .
c. Carlos va al (a la) . . .
d. (Nosotros) vamos al (a la) . . .
e. Felipe y Ramón van al (a la) . . .
f. (Yo) voy al (a la) . . .
g. (Uds.) van al (a la) . . .

3 Dialogues will vary.

Options

Strategies for Reaching All Students

Students Needing Extra Help

Ex. 3: Have students write the three responses before reporting back to their partners.

4 Choose one thing from each column in order to make true statements.

mis amigos y yo *Mis amigos y yo vamos de pesca los sábados.*
o: *Mis amigos y yo no vamos de pesca.*

a. mis amigos b. (yo) c. mi familia y yo d. el (la) profesor(a) e. los estudiantes f. nosotros g.		los lunes, los martes . . . los fines de semana en el verano, en el otoño . . . después de las clases por la mañana, por la tarde . . . todos los días

4 a. Mis amigos van . . .
b. (Yo) voy . . .
c. Mi familia y yo vamos . . .
d. El (la) profesor(a) va . . .
e. Los estudiantes van . . .
f. Nosotros vamos . . .
g. Statements will vary.
Suggested places in column 2 include: *ir de compras, el parque de diversiones, ir a la escuela, ir al cine, ir de pesca, el gimnasio.*

Cultural Notes

(p. 128, photo)
Montjuïc, a 630-foot-high mountain in Barcelona, is the site of many attractions, including Parc de Montjuïc, with its craft shops, restaurants, live performances, and impressive garden. The amusement park offers spectacular views of the mountains from its aerial tramway *(los teleféricos).*

Present & Practice

Re-enter / Recycle

Exs. 5–7: activities from Chap. 1

Teaching Suggestions

Ex. 5: Have students write the activities in two columns labeled "Activities that happen regularly" and "Activities that are going to happen tomorrow." This activity is also suitable for homework and for students needing extra help.

Ex. 6: Model, emphasizing the *ir* + *a* + inf. construction. Have students write down their partners' answers for use in Ex. 7.

Ex. 7: Point out that *voy* in the responses for Ex. 6 becomes *va* when referring to another person.

Answers

5 regularly: a., b., c., e.
tomorrow: d., f., g., h.

6 Answers will vary. Look for correct use of *¿Vas a* + inf.? and *Sí, (No, no) voy a* + inf.

7 Statements will vary, but look for correct use of *(no) va (vamos) a* + inf.

 **Practice Wkbk. 3-6**

 **Writing Activities**

 **Pruebas 3-5, 3-6**

Ir + *a* + infinitivo

We also use a form of the verb *ir* + *a* + infinitive to tell what someone is going to do.

Nado los fines de semana. — ***I swim** on the weekends.*

Voy a nadar mañana. — ***I'm going swimming** tomorrow.*

¡No olvides!

Infinitives always end in *-r* in Spanish.

5 Which of these activities happen regularly and which ones are going to happen tomorrow?

a. Patinan.
b. Hablamos.
c. Juego tenis.
d. Va a nadar.
e. Ayudo en casa.
f. Van a estudiar.
g. Vas a jugar béisbol.
h. Vas al parque.

6 With a partner, take turns asking and answering whether or not you're going to do any six of the activities listed.

A —*¿Vas a jugar fútbol mañana?*
B —*Sí, voy a jugar fútbol.*
o: *No, no voy a jugar fútbol.*

ir a una fiesta	jugar básquetbol	ir al cine
estudiar	jugar fútbol americano	ver la tele
ayudar en casa	jugar tenis	ir de compras
ir al centro comercial	jugar vóleibol	leer un libro

7 Based on the answers your partner gave in Exercise 6, tell another student one thing your partner will and will not do tomorrow. For example:

Juan va a jugar fútbol mañana pero no va a ir al cine.

If there is something that both of you—or neither of you—will do, report that too.

(No) Vamos a . . .

Options

Strategies for Reaching All Students

Students Needing Extra Help

Be sure that Organizers are filled in correctly. Have a master one posted.

Enrichment

Ex. 6: As a written assignment, students can tell what they are going to do on each day of the weekend, specifying whether they'll be doing it alone, with family, or with friends.

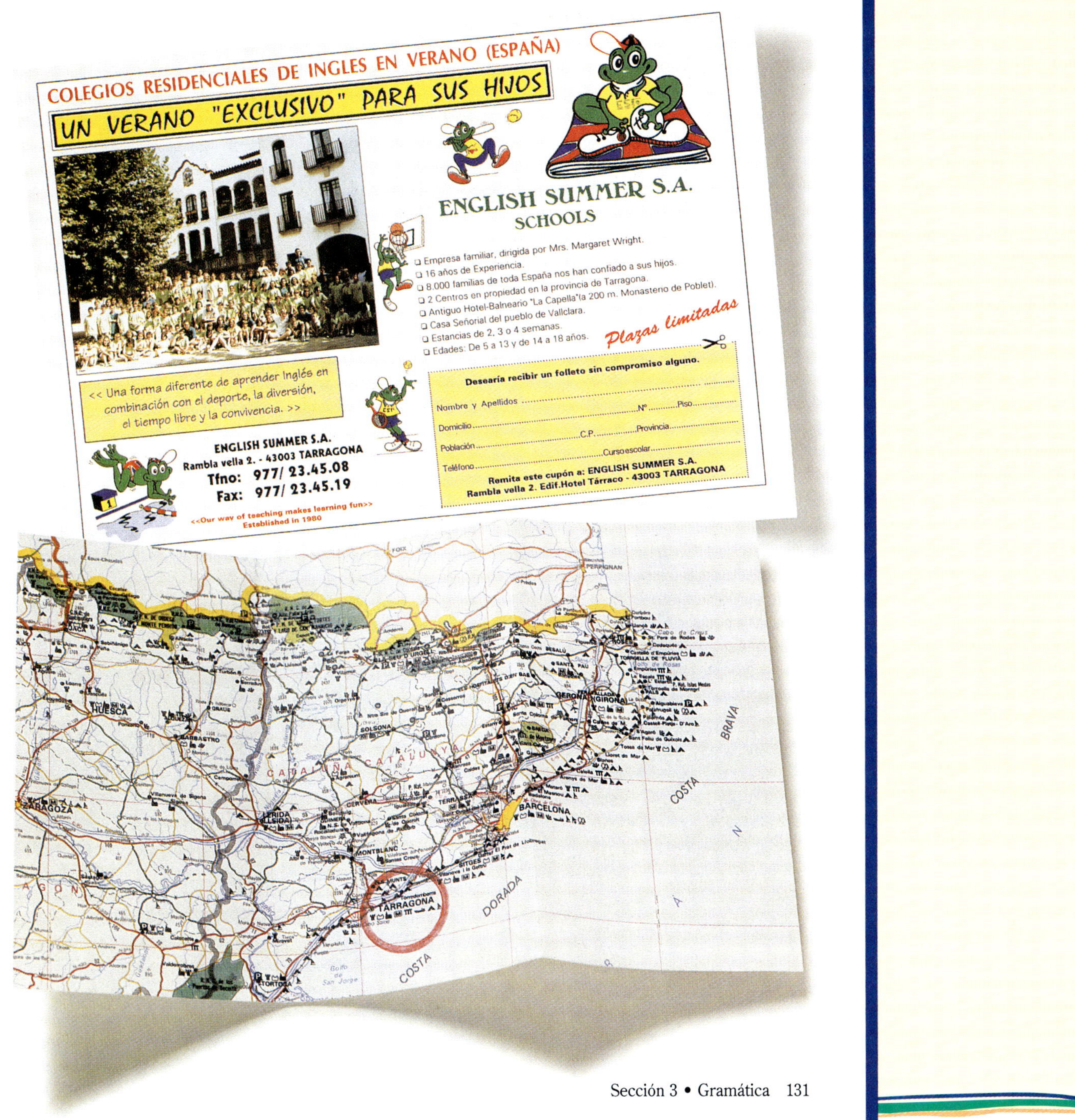

Cultural Notes

(p. 131, realia)
An effective way to learn a foreign language is to be compelled to speak it. Finding a location where another language is spoken does not require travel abroad. Many language schools offer environments in which a second language is obligatory, thereby encouraging learners to dive in and use their new linguistic abilities.

Present & Apply

Cultural Objective

- To talk about plazas

Answers: La cultura desde tu perspectiva

1–2 Answers will vary.

 **Writing Activities**

In small Latin American cities and towns, the main outdoor gathering place is the *plaza,* an area surrounded by the church, government offices, and other important buildings. It may have a small playground. The plaza is where people meet to exchange news and local gossip. Vendors may sell newspapers, magazines, snack food, balloons, and toys. Sometimes there are dance and theater performances. In some plazas you can get your shoes shined or even get your hair cut.

Although the custom is disappearing, in some places almost the whole town may turn out for a late afternoon stroll *(un paseo)* around the plaza. Families walk together. The adults talk, the children play, and the young people chat. It is a pleasant way to socialize and get some fresh air and exercise at the same time.

Some people use the plaza almost as an outdoor family room. They relax, have snacks, and meet their friends. They don't go to the plaza for any specific purpose, but just for the pleasure of being there. The plaza is truly the heart of a town.

La cultura desde tu perspectiva

1. Why do you think people might spend their free time in a plaza? Why might this be fun?
2. Is there a place in your community where people go for the same reasons that people in Spanish-speaking towns go to the plaza? What are the differences? What are the similarities?

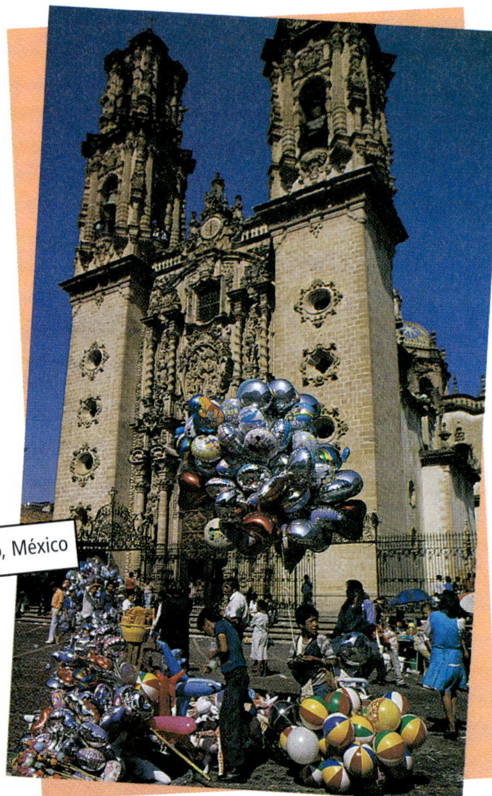

La catedral de Santa Prisca, en la Plaza de Borda, Taxco, México

Options

Strategies for Reaching All Students

Spanish-Speaking Students

 **Un paso más Exs. 3-H, 3-I, 3-J**

Enrichment

As a class activity, have students create a *plaza* with chairs and desks placed in a circle as stores and buildings. (You may wish to have these labeled as such.) Ask volunteers to "walk" around the *plaza* so that they simulate the feeling of being in a Spanish-speaking town. Encourage students who participate to role play accordingly: walking arm in arm, standing close to each other when speaking, and so on. (See p. 103B for details.)

El domingo en la Plaza de Borda

Muchachos y muchachas se divierten en la Plaza de San Fernando, Guanajuato, México.

Cultural Notes

(pp. 132–133, photos)
Much of Latin America's architecture reflects the Moorish heritage of Spain. One element of that influence is the *patio,* so typical of Latin American residences. As a consequence of this building style, the civic *plaza* evolved as a public place for people to rendezvous in their leisure time. *Cafés* and businesses usually surround *plazas.*

Plaza de Borda, the main square or *zócalo,* of Taxco was named for José de la Borda, a French silver merchant, who built *la catedral de Santa Prisca* on the square in gratitude for having found a wealthy vein of silver in Taxco to mine.
Plaza de San Fernando, in the heart of Guanajuato, frequently has book fairs filling its shady area.

Preview

Transparency 23

Answers

A *Estoy ocupado(a). ¿Estás enfermo(a)? / ¿Cómo está Ud.? / estamos / están*

B When you play videogames with me . . . / Answers will vary. Students may mention that they might have expected the word *yo* combined with *con* to mean "with me."

Re-enter / Recycle

Ex. 2: activities from Chap. 1

Teaching Suggestions

La preposición con: Have students fill in this grammar portion of their Organizers.

Ex. 1: Remind students that *conmigo* is answered with *contigo,* just as a verb in the *tú* form is answered with *yo.* Practice with gestures to explain the difference: point toward yourself for *conmigo* and toward a student for *contigo.*

Ex. 2: Show students how a female name is replaced with *ella* and a male name with *él.* Students may need a model to see that *Uds.* becomes *nosotros(as)* in the answer, and that *tú* will become *contigo* and will be answered with *conmigo.* If necessary, provide a model in English first.

Sección 4

Gramática en contexto

Read this ad for a popular new electronic game.

A You already know several forms of the verb *estar*. How would you say "I am busy" and "Are you sick?" How would you ask your teacher "How are you?" Can you predict what the *nosotros/nosotras* form of *estar* would be? And the *Uds./ellos/ellas* form?

B You also know the word *con*. What does *Cuando juegas videojuegos conmigo* mean? How is this use of *con* different from what you might have expected?

Options

Strategies for Reaching All Students

Enrichment

Ex. 1: Encourage students to use a full range of vocabulary in formulating their questions: *¿Quieres ir de compras con nostros mañana? ¿Te gustaría ir al gimnasio el sábado?*

La preposición *con*

The word *con* may be used with the names of people *(con Ana, con Juan)* or in the following ways.

conmigo	**con nosotros / con nosotras**
contigo	**con vosotros / con vosotras**
con Ud. / con él / con ella	**con Uds. / con ellos / con ellas**

1 Take turns asking a partner about doing these things together.

jugar fútbol

A —*¿Quieres jugar fútbol conmigo después de las clases?*
B —*¿Contigo? Claro que sí, gracias.*
o: *Me gustaría, pero no puedo porque . . .*

a. ir de compras	d. ver la tele	g. jugar básquetbol
b. ir al gimnasio	e. estudiar	h. ir a nadar
c. jugar béisbol	f. jugar videojuegos	i.

2 Take turns asking a partner with whom he or she would like to do these activities.

Alicia

A —*¿Con quién te gustaría ir a nadar el sábado?*
B —*Con Alicia.*
A —*¿Con ella?*
B —*Sí, con ella.*

a. Luisa

b. Marta

c. Rafael y Julia

d. Marcela y Graciela

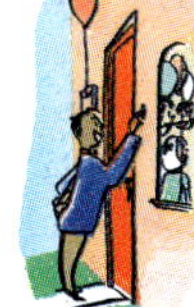
e. Uds.

f. Miguel

g.

Present & Practice

Answers

1 ESTUDIANTE A

a. ¿Quieres ir de compras conmigo después de las clases?
b. . . . ir al gimnasio . . .
c. . . . jugar béisbol . . .
d. . . . ver la tele . . .
e. . . . estudiar . . .
f. . . . jugar videojuegos . . .
g. . . . jugar básquetbol . . .
h. . . . ir a nadar . . .
i. Questions will vary.

ESTUDIANTE B

a.–i. Answers will vary.

2 ESTUDIANTE A

a. ¿Con quién te gustaría ir a patinar el sábado? / ¿Con ella?
b. . . . ir al cine . . . / ¿Con ella?
c. . . . ir de compras . . . / ¿Con ellos?
d. . . . ir al parque de diversiones . . . / ¿Con ellas?
e. . . . ir a una fiesta . . . / ¿Con nosotros(as)?
f. . . . ir al gimnasio . . . / ¿Con él?
g. Questions will vary.

ESTUDIANTE B

a. Con Luisa. / Sí, con ella.
b. Con Marta. / Sí, con ella.
c. Con Rafael y Julia. / Sí, con ellos.
d. Con Marcela y Graciela. / Sí, con ellas.
e. Con Uds. / Sí, con Uds.
f. Con Miguel. / Sí, con él.
g. Answers will vary.

Present & Practice

Answers

3 Statements will vary, but may include: *Me gustaría . . . con . . . el domingo / el sábado / el fin de semana.*

 **Practice Wkbk. 3-7**

Class Starter Review

On the day following the presentation of *estar,* you might begin the class with this activity:
Use the Vocabulary Art BLMs showing the places in the *Vocabulario para conversar* and Transparency 84 (subject pronouns). Have pairs of students alternate saying where different people are.

Teaching Suggestions

You may want to teach this rhyme to your students: "To tell how you feel and where you are, always use the verb *estar.*"

Answers

4 estamos

5 a. ¿Cómo está Juan? / Está enfermo.
b. ¿Cómo está Ud.? / Estoy enfermo(a).
c. ¿Cómo están Uds.? / Estamos enfermos.
d. ¿Cómo estás? / Estoy enfermo(a).

3 Choose any three activities you know and say with whom you would like to do them this weekend, or if you would like to do them alone.

Me gustaría jugar tenis con Pilar el domingo.

El verbo *estar*

Estar ("to be") is an irregular verb. We use it to tell how someone feels or where someone is. Here are its present-tense forms.

(yo)	**estoy**	(nosotros) (nosotras)	**estamos**
(tú)	**estás**	(vosotros) (vosotras)	**estáis**
(Ud.) (él) (ella)	**está**	(Uds.) (ellos) (ellas)	**están**

- In writing, be sure to use the accent mark on all forms except *estoy* and *estamos.*

4 All of these subjects use the same form of *estar.* What is it?

a. Juan y yo
b. tú y yo
c. ellos y yo
d. ella y yo
e. Elisa, Susana y yo

5 Match the questions in column A with the responses in column B.

A	B
a. ¿Cómo está Juan?	Estamos enfermos.
b. ¿Cómo está Ud.?	Estoy enfermo(a).
c. ¿Cómo están Uds.?	Está enfermo.
d. ¿Cómo estás?	

Jugando pato en Argentina

Options

Strategies for Reaching All Students

Students Needing Extra Help

Have students fill in the *estar* chart in the grammar portion of the Organizer.

6 With a partner, take turns asking and answering where these people and pets are.

A —*¿Dónde está Arturo?*
B —*Arturo está . . .*

7 Find out from several classmates how they are feeling today. Take turns asking and answering using *bien*, *enfermo(a)*, or *cansado(a)*.

Keep a log for reporting this information to your teacher. For example:

You ask Juan: *¿Cómo estás hoy?*
He answers: *Estoy cansado.*
You write in your log: *Juan está cansado hoy.*

6 ESTUDIANTE A
Order of questions and answers will vary.
¿Dónde están Pilar y Clara?
. . . está Jaime?
. . . está Sara?
. . . está Nerón?
. . . están Fabián y Sergio?
. . . está Raúl?
. . . está Arturo?

ESTUDIANTE B
Pilar y Clara están en el gimnasio.
Jaime está en el cine.
Sara está en la escuela.
Nerón está en el parque.
Fabián y Sergio están en el campo.
Raúl está en el parque de diversiones.
Arturo está en el centro comercial.

7 Dialogues will vary, but look for correct *estar* forms and adjective agreement.

Practice Wkbk. 3-8, 3-9

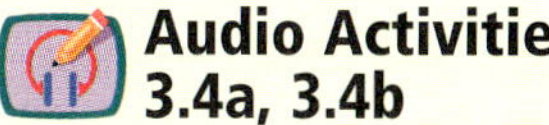
Audio Activities 3.4a, 3.4b

Pruebas 3-7, 3-8

Comm. Act. BLM 3-3

Cultural Notes

(p. 136, photo)
These men are playing a modern-day version of *pato,* a game played by *gauchos* until around 1822. In this game, a duck, a chicken, or some other prize was placed inside a leather pouch, called the *pato*. The *pato* had several stout handles attached to it. Two mounted men from opposing teams would then each grab hold of the handles and pull, until one of them let go. The man with the *pato* would then gallop off as fast as he could, with the opposing team's players trying to catch up to him to grab the handles of the *pato.* The game was eventually outlawed because so many *gauchos* were injured.
In 1937, the game was revived with rules resembling those of basketball, with players facing off on a 650-foot-long field with ten-foot-tall baskets on either end. The object is to get *el pato* (a leather ball with six handles) through the basket.

Apply

 **Pronunciation Tape 3-3**

 **Todo junto A**

Play

 **Todo junto B**

Play

Using the Video

Video segment 3: See the Video Teacher's Guide.

 **Video Activity C**

Re-enter / Recycle

Exs. 1–2: days of the week from *El primer paso*

Teaching Suggestions

Choose the most appropriate activities for your class. You may want to change their order.

¿Cómo soy yo?: Display the collages in the classroom. Save them and have students add to them periodically as they learn more vocabulary. If their are no names on the collages, have classmates guess who the owner is.

Here's an opportunity for you to put together what you learned in this chapter with what you learned earlier.

1 ¿Cómo soy yo?

Make a collage about yourself. You may include drawings or pictures from magazines that show your favorite activities, places where you enjoy spending your free time, people you like to spend time with, and so on. Then get together in a small group to explain your collage and answer any questions. For example:

A mí me gusta mucho ir de compras. Los fines de semana voy al centro comercial con mis amigos.

2 El fin de semana

Tell your partner at least three things that you are going to do this weekend. Say either with whom or when you are going to do each activity. Your partner will ask about the missing information.

A —*Voy a ir al gimnasio el sábado por la mañana.*
B —*¿Con quién?*
A —*Con Pedro.*
o: *Voy solo(a).*

o: A —*Voy a ir al gimnasio con Pedro.*
B —*¿Cuándo?*
A —*El sábado por la mañana.*

Then form a group with another pair, and ask and answer questions about the activities you and your partner are each going to do this weekend. For example:

¿Adónde vas ...?
¿Cuándo ...?
¿A qué hora ...?
¿Con quién ...?

¿Adónde va tu compañero(a)?
¿Cuándo ...?
¿A qué hora ...?
¿Con quién ...?

Be prepared to report to the class about how many students in your group are going to do each activity. For example: *Tres estudiantes van a ir de compras.*

Options

Strategies for Reaching All Students

Spanish-Speaking Students

Pair bilingual and non-bilingual students for the activities in this section.

Students Needing Extra Help

El fin de semana: For extra practice, have students rewrite the two brief dialogues as one longer one.
¿Adónde vas?: Brainstorm for possible places. (See Ex. 2, p. 118.)
Ahora lo sabes: Have students write this section so that they can check off what they have mastered.

Enrichment

Ex. 3: As a variation on this activity, have students choose their favorite place and go to that part of the room. With the other students who are there, students discuss when they go to that place.
A—*¿Cuándo vas a la piscina?*
B—*Generalmente los sábados o los domingos.*

3 ¿Adónde vas?

Of all the places you learned about in this chapter, where do you most like to go when you're not in school? With your teacher, label certain parts of the room as favorite places to go. After the class has divided into two teams, a student from Team A starts by asking a student from Team B a question. For example:

A —*José, ¿vas al gimnasio después de las clases?*

B —*Sí, voy al gimnasio.*
o: *No, voy al parque.*

The person from Team B goes to his or her favorite place, and then asks someone from Team A a question. Questioning continues until everyone has had a turn to ask a question and to go to his or her favorite place.

Afterwards, count how many people are in each place. For example:

Seis estudiantes están en el (la) ...

Which is the favorite place of the largest number of students? How many students are in that place?

✓Ahora lo sabes

Using what you have learned so far, can you:

- **tell where you or someone else is going?**
- **say who is going to do an activity with you?**
- **report how you or someone else feels?**
- **ask and tell where someone is?**

El fin de semana: Have students report on where and at what time group members are going to do the activities. If students ask, here are some additional words to use: *la iglesia* (church); *la mezquita* (mosque); *la sinagoga, el templo* (synagogue, temple).

¿Adónde vas?: To reduce movement, you may want to label the four corners of the room as four popular places to go.

Answers

¿Adónde vas?: Dialogues will vary, but look for correct use of *ir* forms. Places may include: *el campo, el centro comercial, el cine, el gimnasio, el parque, el parque de diversiones, la piscina, la playa.*

Answers: Ahora lo sabes

(Answers will vary.)

- Voy (Vas, Va, . . .) + a + (place). *(pp. 108–109, 116–117, 127)*
- Juana va a patinar conmigo. *(pp.108–109, 116–117, 135)*
- Estoy (Estás, Está, . . . cansado(a). *(pp. 108–109, 136)*
- ¿Dónde está ___ ? / Está ___. *(pp. 116–117, 136)*

 **Writing Activities**

 **Comm. Act. BLMs 3-4, 3-5**

 **Examen de habilidades 2**

Have students keep a tally of their group's responses in order to report on the results of the poll.
A—*¿Cuándo van Uds. a la piscina?*
B—*Tres estudiantes van a la piscina los sábados.*
A—*Miguel y yo vamos a la piscina en el verano.*

Cooperative Learning
Divide the class into groups of four. Have each group brainstorm and prepare a list of activities that they and their friends are going to do this weekend. After a time limit of five minutes, have one member from each group summarize and share the results with the class.

Apply

Process Reading

For a description of process reading, see p. 60.

Multicultural Perspectives

Ball games similar to soccer were popular in the Americas long before the Spaniards arrived. The Mayas played a team game on large stone courts in which the players tried to hit a large rubber ball—with their elbows, hips, or knees—through vertical wood or stone rings placed about 20 feet above the ground. Such games had a religious significance to their participants. Some scholars believe the ball represented the sun and that the two teams fought a symbolic struggle between the forces of light and darkness, or life and death. Ask students to share with the class any information that they might have about games played by other cultures. If possible, have students make a poster or diorama of a game played in Spanish-speaking countries.

Answers
Antes de leer

Answers will vary, but may include: name of player, position, name of team, statistics, and picture of player.

¡Vamos a leer!

Antes de leer

STRATEGY ➤ Using prior knowledge

What kinds of information can you find on a baseball card? Make a list of five things.

Mira la lectura

STRATEGY ➤ Scanning

Read the baseball cards quickly, just to see if you can find the information on your list. Check off the items you found.

140 Capítulo 3

Options

Strategies for Reaching All Students

Students Needing Extra Help

If students ask, help them with the meanings of words in the baseball cards. They should be able to figure out *talla* (height) and *peso* (weight) through context clues, for example.

Enrichment

Have students refer to a weekend sports schedule and invite a classmate to a game listed. The partner should then accept or decline, giving a reason why he or she cannot go.

Infórmate

STRATEGIES **Using cognates**
Using context to get meaning

1 Cognates—Spanish words that look or sound like English words—can be very useful to you in reading. Read the baseball cards and make a list of all the cognates that you can find. Compare lists with a partner, and make a combined list that is as long as possible.

2 Look at the personal information after each player's name and position. Then match these words with the numbers that they might go with.

a. Ligas mayores	175
b. Nació	8
c. Peso	7/13/73
d. Talla	5'10"

3 Now read all the baseball cards carefully. Use what you know about baseball and what you have figured out. Tell a partner the meaning of two words you didn't know before.

Aplicación

1 Choose a famous athlete, and make a sports card for him or her. Make it the size of a small poster. Illustrate it with a photo or drawing. Include this information along with any statistics you can find:

- name
- team
- height and weight
- birthplace and birth date

2 Choose from the word bank to fill in the blanks in these sentences. Not all the words will be used.

a. En la ___ de 1996, Mike jugó su juego número 20.
b. Randy tiene un promedio de .360, el mejor de las ___ mayores.
c. Tom es el mejor robador de ___.
d. ¿Cuál es el nombre de tu ___? ¿Los Leones o los Tigres?

Banco de palabras

bases	lanzador
carreras	ligas
equipo	temporada

Mira la lectura
Answers will vary.

Teaching Suggestions
If possible, bring in or have students bring in baseball cards to compare with the ones in Spanish shown in the text.

Infórmate: Review the concept of cognates from *El primer paso* at this point.

If it is difficult to find information on real players, have students create an imaginary team based on themselves. Display the sports cards in your classroom.

Infórmate
1 Lists may vary:
base, bateador, número, veterano, lesión, parte, consecutivas, líder, victorias, mover, bate, máximo

2 a. Ligas mayores / 8
b. Nació / 7 / 13 / 73
c. Peso / 175
d. Talla / 5'10"

3 Responses will vary.

Aplicación
1 Posters will vary.

2 a. temporada, b. ligas, c. bases, d. equipo

Cultural Notes

(p. 140, realia)
Although invented in the U.S. and considered the quintessential North American game, baseball has fervent fans throughout the Western Hemisphere. The game is particularly popular in the Caribbean in countries such as Cuba and the Dominican Republic. Baseball fans love to follow the pertinent statistics of their heroes, for example, how many home runs a player has hit, how many bases he has stolen, and so on. These cards provide the critical "stats" on players, including the *lanzador* (pitcher) and *jardineros* (outfielders, but literally the "gardeners").

Apply

Process Writing

For information regarding writing portfolios, see p. 62.

Teaching Suggestions

Step 2: Review the letter format in the *¡Vamos a escribir!* section of Chap. 2 on p. 102.

Step 5: Have a group of students decorate a cardboard box to make a mailbox for this activity. Exhibit the letters and the responses to encourage student efforts.

If students ask: mail *(el correo)*, envelope *(el sobre)*, stamp *(el sello)*.

Answers

Steps 1–5: Letters will vary, but encourage students to use the full range of chapter vocabulary.

¡Vamos a escribir!

Imagine that your family is going away for the weekend. Write a letter inviting a friend to join you.

1 Think about what you are going to do while you are away. From the list choose two places that you would like to go and at least one activity that you would like to do in each place.

el centro comercial
- ir de compras
- ir al cine
- jugar videojuegos

la playa
- jugar vóleibol
- nadar

el campo
- ir de camping
- ir de pesca

el parque
- jugar fútbol
- jugar tenis
- jugar básquetbol
- patinar

2 Next, write your letter inviting someone to go with you. Use the format from the *¡Vamos a escribir!* section of Chapter 2, page 102.

3 Show your letter to a partner. Does he or she suggest any changes in the wording, spelling, or punctuation? Recopy your letter and make any changes that you agree with.

4 Use this checklist to check your letter:

- capital letters at the beginning of sentences
- accent marks
- correct use of the verbs *ir*, *ir a*, and *estar*
- question marks and exclamation points at the beginning and end of questions and exclamations

5 Make a clean copy of your letter. Put it in an envelope and "mail" it in a classroom mailbox. Take turns drawing letters from the mailbox and answer the one you pick. You may agree to go, or you may want to make an excuse.

Mira un mapa de España. ¿Por qué crees que la Costa del Sol es un lugar favorito para las vacaciones?

Options

Strategies for Reaching All Students

Spanish-Speaking Students

 **Un paso más Exs. 3-K, 3-L**

Resumen del capítulo 3

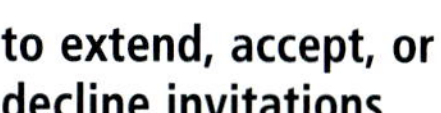

Use the vocabulary from this chapter to help you:

- talk about some of your leisure-time activities
- make plans with friends
- give, accept, or turn down invitations

to ask and to tell how someone feels or where someone is
¿Dónde?
estar: (yo) estoy
(tú) estás

to ask and to tell where someone is going
¿Adónde?
ir: (yo) voy
(tú) vas
a
a la, al (*a+el*)
el campo
el centro comercial
el gimnasio
el parque
el parque de diversiones
la piscina
la playa

to talk about activities
ir a una fiesta
ir de compras
ir de pesca
jugar: (yo) juego
(tú) juegas
jugar básquetbol
jugar béisbol
jugar fútbol
jugar fútbol americano
jugar tenis
jugar videojuegos
jugar vóleibol
el pasatiempo

to say when you do an activity
la estación, *pl.* las estaciones
la primavera
el verano
el otoño
el invierno
el lunes, el martes...
los lunes, los martes...
el fin (los fines) de semana
después de (las clases)
(por) la mañana
(por) la tarde
(por) la noche
generalmente
hoy no
mañana
todos los días

to say with whom you do an activity
con
conmigo, contigo
el amigo, la amiga
la familia
solo, -a

to extend, accept, or decline invitations
¿(A ti) te gustaría ___?
(A mí) me gustaría ___.
poder: (yo) puedo
(tú) puedes
querer: (yo) quiero
(tú) quieres
¡Claro que sí!
¡Claro que no!
De nada.
cansado, -a
enfermo, -a
ocupado, -a

to ask for an explanation
¿Por qué?

to give an explanation
porque

to express surprise, enthusiasm, or disappointment
¡No me digas!
¡Genial!
¡Qué lástima!

to express possession
mi, mis
tus

Summarize

Writing Activities

Mi portafolio

Test Generator

(p. 142, photo)
These swimmers take advantage of the beach in Marbella, Spain, along the Costa del Sol, the southernmost stretch of Spanish coastline in the Mediterranean. The Costa Brava, another site of numerous fine beaches, lies in Northeast Spain, descending south from the French border.

CAPÍTULO 4

THEME: FOOD

SCOPE AND SEQUENCE Pages 144–185

COMMUNICATION

Topics

Foods and drinks

Likes, dislikes, and preferences

Objectives

To talk about eating customs in Spanish-speaking countries

To describe meals and talk about foods and drinks

To express likes or preferences

To indicate frequency

To refer to obligation

To indicate hunger or thirst

To refer to something you cannot name

To express an opinion

To request precise information

To elicit agreement

CULTURE

Meals and mealtimes

GRAMMAR

El plural de los sustantivos

El plural de los adjetivos

Verbos que terminan en -er

Sujetos compuestos

Ancillaries available for use with Chapter 4

Multisensory/Technology

Overhead Transparencies, 24–29

Audio Tapes and CDs

Projects for Proficiency: Blackline Master Spanish Activities for Middle School Learners

Vocabulary Art Blackline Masters for Hands-On Learning, pp. 23–27

Classroom Crossword

Video

CD-ROM

Print

Practice Workbook, pp. 43–52

Writing, Audio & Video Activities, pp. 37–44, 74–76, 106–107

Communicative Activity Blackline Masters

- Pair and Small Group Activities, pp. 29–34
- Situation Cards, p. 35

Un paso más: Actividades para ampliar tu español, pp. 20–25

Assessment

Assessment Program

- Pruebas, pp. 59–62, 67–70
- Exámenes de habilidades, pp. 63–66, 71–74
- Mi portafolio, pp. 75–76

Test Generator

Video still from Chap. 4

Cultural Overview

Revolutionary Foods

Although Columbus and the other European explorers who followed him to the Americas did not find the spices that they sought, they were introduced to a wealth of new foods far more valuable. In time, these foods would not only profoundly affect people's diets, but they would change the course of history.

One of the most important foods cultivated in the Americas was the potato, which today is the world's most widely grown vegetable. Potatoes probably were first grown in the valleys of the Andes by the Incas. In the mid-1500s, Spanish and English explorers introduced the tubers to Europe, where they were initially rejected as a food source because of a widespread fear that root crops caused disease.

Today, potatoes are still an important crop in Andean nations such as Peru, Bolivia, and Chile. They appear in dishes such as Peruvian *papa a la huancaina,* a potato served in a cream sauce.

Corn is another native American crop that revolutionized the diets of people around the world. Along with wheat, rice, and potatoes, corn is considered one of the four most important food crops in the world. Though botanists believe corn may have grown in the Americas as many as 60,000 years ago, Europeans did not know of its existence until Columbus brought back a plant after his first trip to the Americas.

Like the potato, corn is an extremely versatile plant. Besides being relatively easy to grow—it can be planted in soil that is either too wet or too dry for crops such as wheat or rice—corn literally has hundreds of uses. It can be ground into meal or refined into starch, sugar, syrup, or oil. In the form of meal, it is combined with other ingredients to make corn bread, cookies, waffles, and a wide assortment of other foods.

Besides potatoes and corn, many other important foods originated in the Americas. Among them are avocados, pineapples, papayas, peppers, peanuts, tomatoes, and chocolate. These foods have added zest to many national cuisines. The tomato, for example, added a distinct flavor to Mediterranean cooking. And of course, it is well known what effect chocolate had on all of Europe!

Introduce

Re-entry of Concepts

The following topics represent words, expressions, and grammar points re-entered from Chaps. 1 to 3:

Chapter 1
Activities
Gustar expressions
Adjectives to describe personality

Chapter 2
School subjects
School supplies
Possession and need
Time expressions

Chapter 3
Destinations
Pastimes
Adverbs describing when things take place
Invitations (accepting / declining)
Expressions of emotion *(¡Claro que sí!)*

Planning

Cross-Curricular Connections

Geography Connection *(pp. 148–149)*

West of Buenos Aires, the capital of Argentina, is the fertile farming region of the Pampas, which is responsible for most of the nation's food production. Have students research the Pampas and create maps indicating the food products of the region.

Health Connection *(pp. 156–157)*

Have students make a poster of a pyramid of the food groups using cutouts or drawings. Have them write how many portions are recommended and highlight their favorite food from each group.

(For further cross-curricular activities, see the Conexiones *section on pp. 164–165.)*

Spanish in Your Community

What foods from Spanish-speaking countries are available in your community? Have students visit a local Hispanic grocery store or the Hispanic foods section of their supermarket and make a list of at least ten foods sold there. As students share their lists with the class, compile a master list on the chalkboard. If possible, bring the actual items to class.

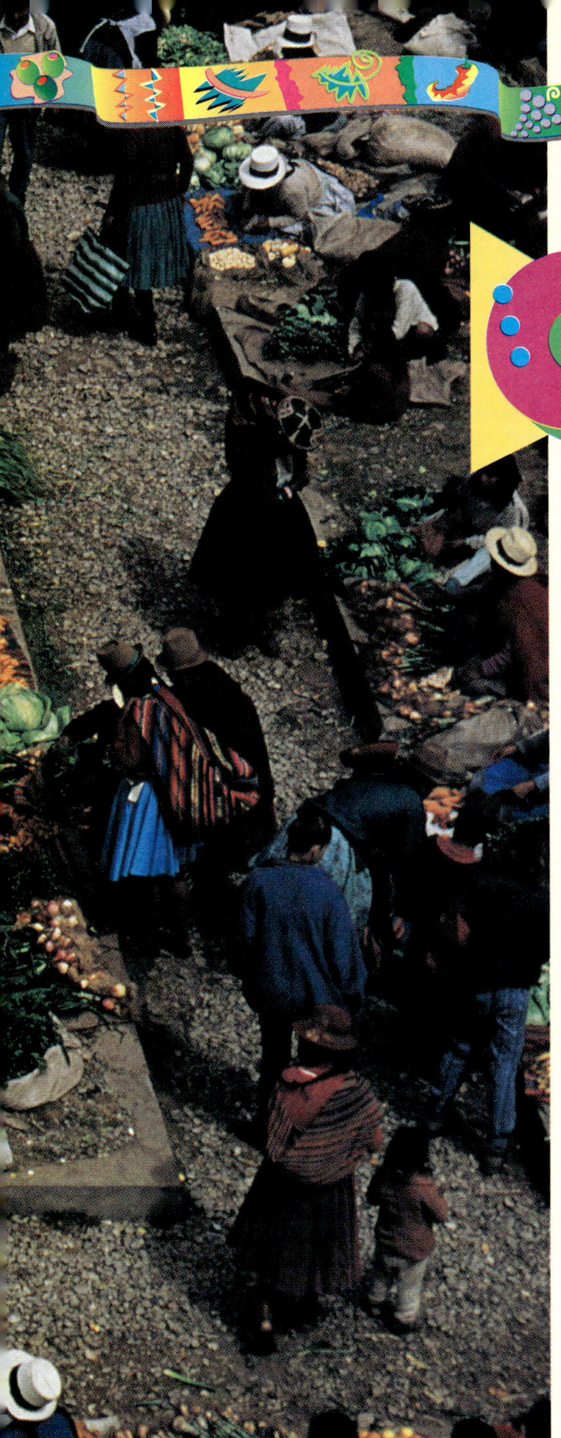

Capítulo 4

¿Qué prefieres comer?

OBJECTIVES

At the end of this chapter, you will be able to:

- **tell what you like and don't like to eat and drink**
- **give reasons for your food and drink preferences**
- **say whether you are hungry or thirsty**
- **compare and contrast eating customs in Spanish-speaking countries and in the United States**

Un mercado en Perú

145

Teaching Suggestions

See the Writing, Audio & Video Activities book for Writing Activities that you may elect to use throughout the chapter.

Cultural Notes

(pp. 144–145, photo)
Las ferias dominicales, or Sunday markets, are commonplace throughout rural Peru. Farmers from small villages carry their produce and other wares to larger towns for the markets, which have both a practical and a social function. Residents stock up on needed items while they meet with friends and relatives to exchange news and conversation. In addition to using traditional *rebozos* (shawls) to carry goods, many women use durable woven plastic bags to carry their purchases home.

Preview

Cultural Objective

- To compare and contrast food in Spanish-speaking countries and in the U.S.

 **¡Piénsalo bien!**

Play

 **Video Activity A**

Using the Video

This chapter's video focuses on food. Students will go with our hosts to the San Miguel Market in Madrid to discover the different types of food for sale there. Show students segment one once through, then ask them to predict what this chapter's tape will be about. Then have students watch the segment again several times. After the first time, you may wish to have them brainstorm possible vocabulary and expressions they will need to talk about what they saw on the video. Ask students to identify: a) things they saw that were familiar to them, and b) things they saw that they probably would not see in a market or grocery store where they live. Video segment 1: For more teaching suggestions, see the Video Teacher's Guide.

¡Piénsalo bien!

Look at the photos. What do you see that is similar to what you are used to? What do you see that's different? What do you suppose the people are doing in the photographs?

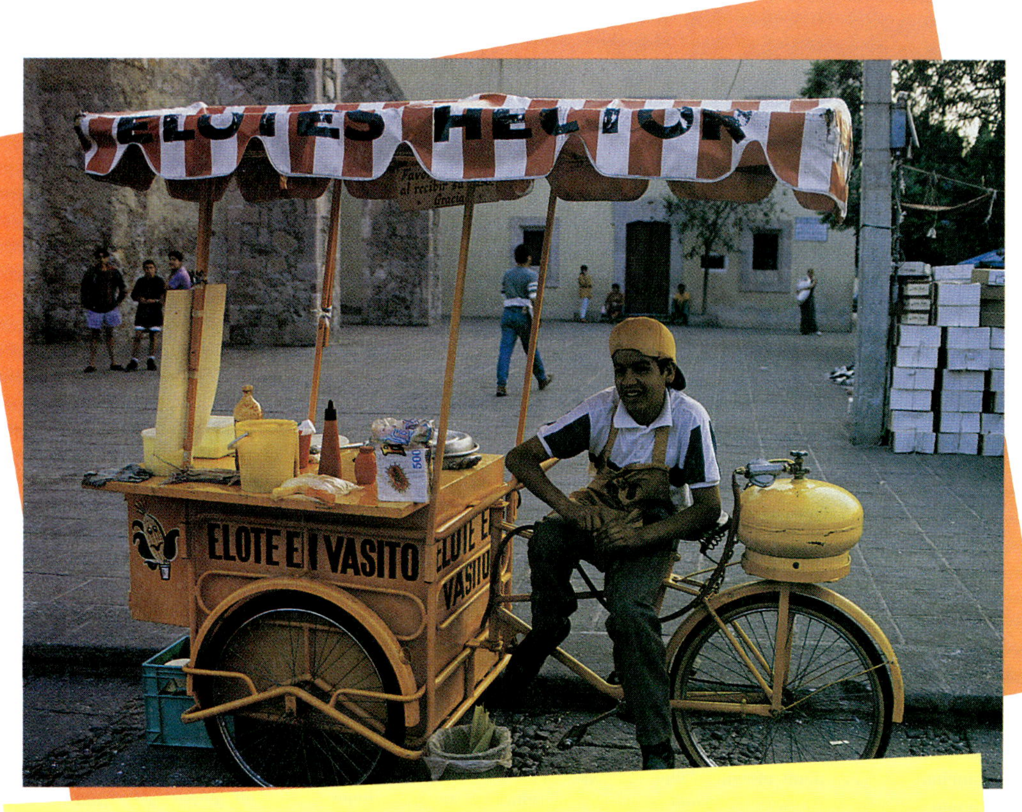

En Aguascalientes, México

Look carefully at the photo. What do you think this boy might be selling? How do you know?

146 Capítulo 4

Options

Strategies for Reaching All Students

Spanish-Speaking Students

Ask: *¿Qué comidas ves aquí? ¿Comes tú las mismas comidas? ¿Qué comen tus abuelos o parientes?*

Students Needing Extra Help

Discuss the mealtimes of your students and typical foods eaten. Compare and contrast this information in a chart form, after presenting the *Perspectiva cultural* sections.

Cultural Notes 

(p. 146, photo)

This boy is selling *elote en vasito,* cooked kernel corn served in a plastic cup, eaten with a spoon. Ears of corn were shucked beforehand, the kernels cooked that same morning, and kept warm throughout the day in the silver container in the cart. The corn is spooned into a cup, sprinkled with lime juice, salt, and your choice of "heat": bottled hot sauce or powdered chili pepper *(chilito piquín).*

"Después, vamos a preparar tortillas."

Un mercado en Cali, Colombia

"¿Qué frutas quieres? ¿Uvas rojas? ¿Uvas verdes? ¿Naranjas?"

Teaching Suggestions

See the Projects for Proficiency BLMs for activity ideas that you may elect to use throughout the chapter.

If possible, bring to class samples of several foods that are eaten regularly in Spanish-speaking countries. Choose nonperishables that can be easily divided and shared with the class. You may wish to collaborate with the home economics teacher to combine your lessons or classes. As an alternative, you might ask student volunteers to bring in food samples at various times during their study of the chapter. Be aware of any food allergies that your students may have.

Answers: ¡Piénsalo bien!

Answers to inductive questions will vary.

(p. 146) We can tell by the picture of the corn on the cart and the corn husks in the pail that the boy is selling corn.

(p. 147, top photo)
Tortillas are a simple, nutritious preparation of corn kernels, slaked lime *(cal,* or calcium hydroxide), and water. The corn is washed, then placed in boiling water with dissolved lime and cooked for two minutes. It stands for several hours, and then the cooked kernels are washed again to remove the hulls, leaving a substance called *nixtamal.* The *nixtamal* is ground and kneaded into tortilla dough that is shaped into a pattie and laid on a griddle to cook.

(p. 147, bottom photo)
Cali is the capital and third-largest city of Colombia's Valle del Cauca department. A department is a governmental entity resembling a state. Many of the products in this photo were probably grown in the subtropical Valle de Cauca, a rich agricultural region especially known for its coffee, sugarcane, cotton, soybeans, beef, and dairy farming.

Present

Chapter Theme
Foods and mealtimes: Preferences

Communicative Objectives
- To describe meals
- To talk about foods
- To express likes or preferences
- To indicate frequency
- To express an opinion
- To elicit agreement

 **Transparencies 24–25**

 **Vocabulary Art BLMs**

 **Pronunciation Tape 4-1**

 **Vocabulario para conversar A**

Play

Using the Video
Video segment 2: See the Video Teacher's Guide.

 **Video Activity B**

Grammar Preview
Como / comes are presented lexically. The presentation of *-er* verbs appears on p. 175.

Sección 1

Vocabulario para conversar

¿Qué te gusta comer?

- As your teacher reads the words aloud, put your finger on the appropriate pictures.
- As your teacher reads the name of a meal aloud, point to a food you like to eat at that meal.
- As your teacher names each food, raise your right hand if you eat it often and your left hand if you seldom eat it.

EL DESAYUNO
el pan tostado
el cereal
el huevo
el jamón

EL ALMUERZO
las frutas
las papas fritas
la hamburguesa
el tomate
los sandwiches
el queso
la ensalada
el sandwich de jamón y queso

Options

Strategies for Reaching All Students

Spanish-Speaking Students
Ask: *¿Qué otras comidas te gustan? Haz una lista.*

 **Un paso más Ex. 4-A**

Learning Spanish Through Action
STAGING VOCABULARY: *Muestren, Pongan*
MATERIALS: Brown (2), pink (1), yellow (1), and red (1) pieces of construction paper, approximately the size of a slice of bread, for each student
DIRECTIONS: Tell students that they are going to make sandwiches. Have them label the brown sheets *el pan tostado,* the pink sheets *el jamón,* the red sheets *el tomate,* and the yellow sheets *el queso.* As you describe a ham, cheese, and tomato sandwich on toast, have students put together their sheets as they would a real sandwich. Expand on this activity by having students create labeled sheets for other sandwich items such as *el bistec, el pollo,* or *el*

También necesitas . . .

comer: (yo) como	*to eat: I eat*	siempre	*always*
(tú) comes	*you eat*	nunca	*never*
la comida	*meal*		
la merienda	*afternoon snack*		
más o menos	*more or less, sort of*		
¡Qué asco!	*Yuk! That's disgusting!*		
¿verdad?	*isn't that so?, right?*		
me encanta(n)	*I love (something)*		

¿Y qué quiere decir . . . ?
en el desayuno / en el almuerzo / en la cena
prefiero, prefieres

Teaching Suggestions

Students who are good in art can prepare drawings of various foods that you can laminate for use as props, flashcards, and so on.

Class Starter Review

On the day following the initial presentation of vocabulary, you might begin the class with this activity:
Have students ask three classmates *¿Qué comes en el desayuno?* Have them record their findings and tally the results for a class graph. On subsequent days, use this activity by substituting *el almuerzo* and *la cena.* After the presentation of the *-er* paradigm, ask volunteers to report their findings to the class.

Multicultural Perspectives

In many Spanish-speaking countries, herbs and spices are important ingredients to season foods. Caribbean dishes may include *coco* (coconut) in the form of oil, meat, or milk. Other important seasonings in Caribbean cuisine include cinnamon, cloves, nutmeg, and mace. *Cilantro* (Chinese parsley or coriander) is used to make several Caribbean curries. Ask students to think about why spices were originally used and valued so highly. Discuss the use of spices in the U.S. as compared with other cultures. If possible, bring some of these spices to class.

pescado. Combine these sheets with the others. After you describe a particular sandwich, have volunteers bring their completed sandwiches to the front of the class to describe their contents from top to bottom. As an alternative to construction paper, use copies of the Vocabulary Art BLMs and have students color them. Add other items when new vocabulary is presented.

Practice

Re-enter / Recycle

Ex. 2: *gustar* expressions from Chap. 1
Ex. 3: *ni . . . ni* from Chap. 1

Answers: Empecemos a conversar

1 ESTUDIANTE A

a. ¿Comes jamón?
b. . . . pollo?
c. . . . pan?
d. . . . pescado?
e. . . . arroz?
f. . . . bistec?
g. . . . sopa de verduras?
h. . . . queso?
i. Questions will vary.

ESTUDIANTE B

a.–i. Answers will vary depending on *Estudiante B*'s preferences.

Empecemos a conversar

With a partner, take turns being *Estudiante A* and *Estudiante B*. Use the words that are cued or given in the boxes to replace the underlined words in the example. 💡 means you can make your own choices. When it is your turn to be *Estudiante B*, try to answer truthfully.

1 
A —*¿Comes huevos?*
B —*Sí, a veces.*

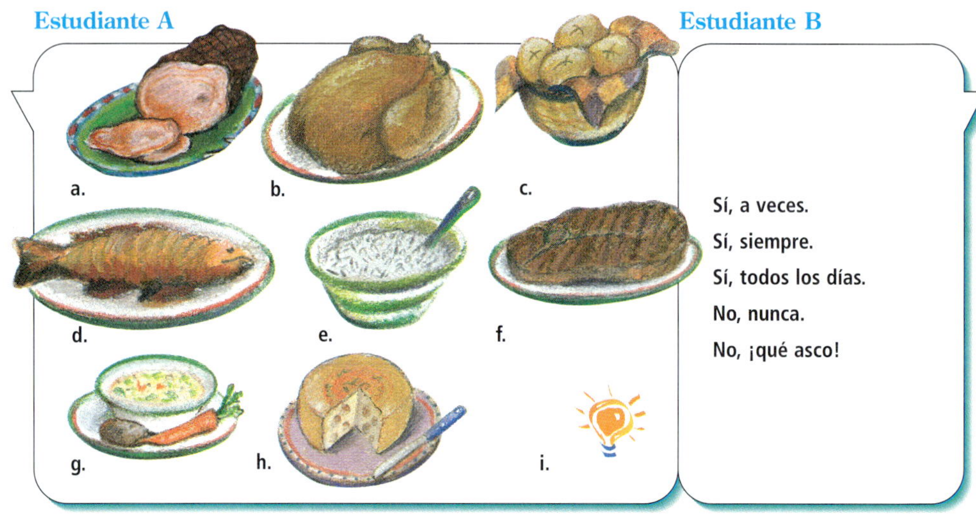

El costeño (n.d.), José Agustín Arrieta

Options

Strategies for Reaching All Students

Spanish-Speaking Students

Try to pair bilingual with non-bilingual students for Exs. 1–3. This will help both. The former will learn to speak clearly and carefully, and the latter will have good models.

 **Un paso más Exs. 4-B, 4-C**

Students Needing Extra Help

Have students begin to fill in their Organizers.
Exs. 1–2: Review the meanings of the responses. Point out that Column B contains choices and that it is not a linear match for answers.

Enrichment

Ex. 2: Do a similar exercise with you taking the place of *Estudiante A* and forming your questions using *te gusta* and singular nouns. Preview the grammar by asking students why you used *te gusta* instead of *te gustan* in your questions. Have them note the difference between *me / te gusta* + inf. and *me / te gusta(n)* + noun by contrasting these sentences: *Me gustan las ensaladas. Me gusta comer ensaladas.* Explain that *las* is not used here after the infinitive.

2  A —*Te gustan las hamburguesas, ¿verdad?*
B —*Sí, me encantan.*

Estudiante A **Estudiante B**

a. b. c. d. e. f.

Más o menos.
Sí, me encantan.
No, no me gustan (mucho).
No, no me gustan nada.
No, ¡qué asco!

3 A —*¿Qué prefieres comer, pollo o pescado?*
B —*Prefiero pollo.*
o: *No me gustan ni el pollo ni el pescado.*

Estudiante A **Estudiante B**

2 ESTUDIANTE A
a. Te gustan las papas fritas, ¿verdad?
b. . . . los tomates . . .
c. . . . las papas al horno . . .
d. . . . las verduras . . .
e. . . . los sandwiches . . .
f. . . . las ensaladas . . .

ESTUDIANTE B
a.–f. Answers will vary depending on *Estudiante B*'s preferences.

3 ESTUDIANTE A
a. ¿Qué prefieres comer, hamburguesas o bistec?
b. . . . sopa de pollo o sopa de tomate?
c. . . . ensalada o sopa de verduras?
d. . . . frutas o verduras?
e. . . . jamón o huevos?
f. . . . papas al horno o papas fritas?
g. . . . huevos o queso?
h. . . . cereal o pan tostado?

ESTUDIANTE B
a.–h. Answers will vary depending on *Estudiante B*'s preferences.

For an additional written assignment, ask small groups to rate the meals at three or four local restaurants with which they are familiar. Students can list the restaurants in one column and then put a check mark under columns with the headings: *Me encanta, Me gusta,* and *¡Qué asco!* or *No me gusta.* Another assignment could be about the time dinner begins and ends at home, with students answering these questions: *¿A qué hora, más o menos, empieza la cena en tu casa? ¿A qué hora termina?*

Cultural Notes

(p. 150, photo)
José Agustín Arrieta (1802–1874) was born in Chiautempan, Tlaxcala, Mexico, into a family of modest means. While not recognized during his lifetime as an accomplished painter, Arrieta is now acknowledged as an important *pintor costumbrista* (painter of local customs and manners). His earliest work reflects nineteenth-century academic painting styles. His later and best works, which depart from the formal canons of the time, depict popular scenes. The best known of these paintings is *El Costeño.* Others include *Puesto de aguas frescas, Interior de pulquería,* and *China poblana con platón de mole.*

Practice & Apply

Answers: Empecemos a conversar

4 ESTUDIANTE A

a. ¿Qué comes en la cena?
b. . . . el almuerzo?
c. . . . el desayuno?

ESTUDIANTE B

a.–c. Answers will vary, but encourage students to use chapter vocabulary.

Multicultural Perspectives

Many foods grown in the Americas today were brought from Europe, Asia, and Africa; others are native to the hemisphere. Corn, tomatoes, papayas, pineapples, and pumpkins were cultivated in the Americas; cocoa was used as a seasoning for foods and as a beverage by the Aztecs. Green beans, onions, lettuce, apples, and grapes were brought to the Americas from Europe. Bananas, okra, coffee, and sugar cane came from Africa. Ask students to plan a menu using only foods found in the Americas.

4 **el desayuno** A —*¿Qué comes en* <u>*el desayuno*</u>*?*
B —*Generalmente como* <u>*cereal y pan tostado*</u>*.*

Estudiante A	Estudiante B
a. la cena b. el almuerzo c. el desayuno	

Options

Strategies for Reaching All Students

Students Needing Extra Help

Ex. 4, p. 152: Have students make three columns labeled *el desayuno, el almuerzo,* and *la cena* so they can organize their answers.

Enrichment

Empecemos a leer y a escribir: You may want to extend Ex. 1 by having students write their own shopping lists and having their partners figure out which meals and / or dishes the ingredients are for.
For Exs. 4–5, ask: *¿A qué hora comes el desayuno (el almuerzo, la cena)?*

Empecemos a leer y a escribir

Responde en español.

1 Read Anita's shopping list. What two meals do you think she is shopping for?

2 What meal is *not* reflected in the shopping list? Copy the list. Then add to it what Anita needs to buy for the third meal.

3 Copy the names of the soups you have learned. Using these as a model, choose other foods from the vocabulary and create three funny soups.

4 Generalmente, ¿qué comes en el almuerzo? ¿Con quién comes?

5 ¿Qué comida prefieres, el desayuno o la cena? ¿Por qué?

También se dice

la tostada

los bocadillos
los emparedados

el bife
el biftec
el filete

las legumbres
las hortalizas

los jitomates

Answers: Empecemos a leer y a escribir

1 Anita is probably shopping for breakfast and lunch.

2 Dinner is not reflected in the shopping list. / Items will vary, but may include: *bistec, pollo, pescado, pan, arroz, papas,* or *verduras.*

3 Sopa de verduras, sopa de tomate, sopa de pollo. / *Answers will vary.*

4–5 Answers will vary.

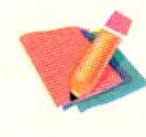 **Practice Wkbk. 4-1, 4-2**

 **Audio Activity 4.1**

 **Writing Activities**

 **Pruebas 4-1, 4-2**

Cultural Notes

(p. 152, realia)
This ad exalts the virtues of oranges and encourages readers to squeeze the orange for all its worth: *sácale todo el jugo.* Readers who fill in the coupon (including all last names!) and send it in have a chance of winning recipe books, hand mixers, and juice extractors.

Present & Apply

Cultural Objective

- To compare and contrast eating customs in Spanish-speaking countries and in the U.S.

Teaching Suggestions

Tell students that words in Spanish that look like and / or sound similar to English words and have the same or similar meaning are called cognates *(hamburguesa, cereal, ensalada, frutas, horrible,* for example). Some Spanish words, though, have a *different* meaning than the English words they resemble. These words are called false cognates. Point out the false cognate in the photo caption at the bottom of p. 155. What do students think *familiar* means? It has two meanings in Spanish: 1) familiar or well known, and 2) related to or pertaining to family. Have students read the caption and look at the photo. Which definition fits? Other false cognates students have encountered so far include *el campo* (countryside), *la estación* (season), and *la carpeta* (pocket folder). You may wish to have them do a quick search through the glossary at the back of their books to look for more cognates or false cognates.

Mira las ilustraciones. ¿Para qué comidas son estos platos? ¿Son similares a o diferentes de platos que tú comes?

In Spanish-speaking countries, as in the United States, there are three main meals—*el desayuno, el almuerzo,* and *la cena.*

El desayuno

El desayuno generally takes place between 7 and 8:30 A.M. It is usually a light meal. It might consist of coffee or *café con leche*, which is half coffee and half hot milk, and bread or rolls with butter and jam. Children and teenagers sometimes drink hot chocolate or chocolate milk instead of coffee.

On weekends, when there is more time to prepare breakfast, people enjoy a variety of foods. The illustrations show two typical Sunday breakfasts in Spanish-speaking regions.

El almuerzo

El almuerzo (called *la comida* in Spain and Mexico) is the largest and most important meal of the day. It is eaten between 1 and 3 P.M. Many businesses and schools close so that families can enjoy *el almuerzo* together at home.

In some countries, for example, Spain, Chile, and Argentina, the midday meal may include several courses. There may be a soup, a meat course with vegetables or a salad, dessert, and coffee. In tropical areas, such as Puerto Rico, the Dominican Republic, and the Caribbean coast, it is usually just one main dish. It is often rice and beans served with a small portion of meat and a drink.

Although this lengthy midday break is still common, more and more businesses are adopting an uninterrupted schedule (*jornada continua*) similar to working hours in the United States. This does not leave time for employees to go home for lunch.

Options

Strategies for Reaching All Students

Students Needing Extra Help

Exs. 3–4: Discuss as a whole class. Answers can also be written for homework.

Enrichment

Eating cold, sweet cereals for breakfast is a custom that has traveled to Spanish-speaking countries from the U.S. Another is eating leftovers from lunch or dinner for breakfast. This is especially true in rural areas, where people need a hearty meal before beginning the day's work.

Un desayuno en un hotel de Asunción, Paraguay

La cultura desde tu perspectiva

1. Look at the photos. Are the people eating a breakfast or lunch that you might eat? What are the similarities? What are the differences?
2. Which meal would you like to try? Why?
3. What might be some of the advantages of a big midday meal in a tropical country? How do you think this custom might affect school and work schedules?
4. How would your day change if families in the United States went home to eat between 1 and 3 P.M.?

Un almuerzo familiar en Santiago, Chile

Critical Thinking: Making Hypotheses

After students read the text, have them speculate as to how the adoption of a *jornada continua* or *horario continuado* in some businesses in large Mexican cities will affect family traditions.

Answers

Huevos rancheros *(eggs with refried beans on a corn tortilla)* y huevos con guineos niños *(finger bananas)* y jamón son para el desayuno; Arroz con habichuelas *(kidney beans)* y papas con verduras son para el almuerzo. / *Answers will vary.*

Answers: La cultura desde tu perspectiva

1–2 Answers will vary, but encourage student discussion by asking for reasons whenever possible.

3 Answers will vary, but students may say that an advantage to consuming a big midday meal is that the body has the rest of the day to burn off the calories. This midday break makes for a longer school and work day.

4 Answers will vary.

Using Photos

Ask students, especially Spanish speakers, if they can identify any of the food items in the photos.

Cultural Notes 

(p. 155, top photo)
This girl is enjoying breakfast in a hotel in Asunción, the capital and largest city of Paraguay. Downtown Asunción is designed in the Spanish colonial style, with a *plaza* surrounded by the business district and important monuments such as *El Panteón de Héroes.*

(p. 155, bottom photo)
Still in their school uniforms, the daughters of a Chilean family join their parents and older sister for dinner. Chileans traditionally eat four meals a day: a light breakfast consisting of coffee and rolls; a large lunch that is the main meal of the day; *once,* a snack of sandwiches and tea served between 5 and 7 P.M.; and a late dinner taken sometime after 9:00 P.M. Chile has a long coastline and fishing is an important industry. Chilean cooking includes numerous seafood dishes.

Present

Chapter Theme
Foods: Fruits, vegetables, and beverages

Communicative Objectives
- To talk about foods and drinks
- To describe meals and foods
- To refer to obligation
- To indicate hunger or thirst
- To refer to something you cannot name
- To express an opinion
- To request precise information

 **Transparencies 26–27**

 **Vocabulary Art BLMs**

 **Pronunciation Tape 4-2**

 **Vocabulario para conversar B**

Play

Step

Using the Video
Video segment 2: See the Video Teacher's Guide.

Sección 2

Vocabulario para conversar

¿Tienes hambre?

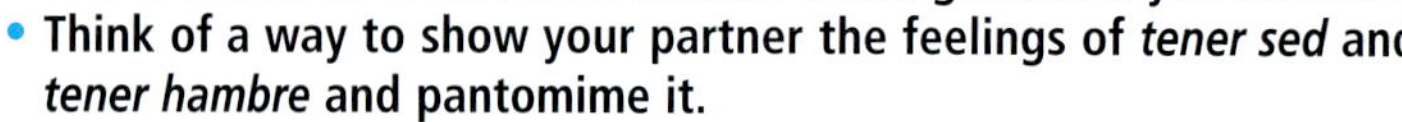

- As your teacher reads each word, make a thumbs up gesture if you like the food or drink and a thumbs down gesture if you do *not* like it.
- Think of a way to show your partner the feelings of *tener sed* and *tener hambre* and pantomime it.
- As your teacher names each fruit, vegetable, or drink, raise your right hand if you ate or drank it yesterday. Raise your left hand if you rarely eat or drink it.

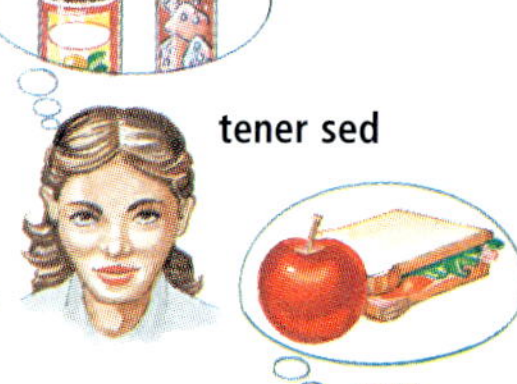

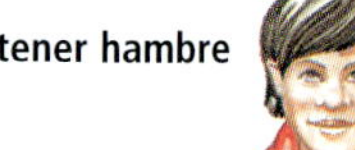

LAS FRUTAS

Options

Strategies for Reaching All Students

Spanish-Speaking Students
Ask: *¿Qué otras frutas y verduras puedes nombrar?* If possible, have volunteers bring in fruits *(mango, papaya, guayaba, jícama,* and *chirimoya,* for example) to show the class.

 **Un paso más Exs. 4-D, 4-E**

Students Needing Extra Help
Have students continue to fill in their Organizers. Be sure to check them for accuracy. Make a master corrected Organizer and post it.

Enrichment
The names of many fruits and vegetables in Mexico are derived from *náhuatl,* an ancient language spoken by the Aztecs in central Mexico and still spoken today in various dialects in Mexico and Central America. Words derived from *náhuatl* are distinguishable by their *-te* (formerly *-tl)* ending: *aguacate* (avocado), *chocolate, cacahuate* (peanut), *tomate, elote* (corn), *ejote* (string bean).

También necesitas . . .

beber: (yo) bebo	*to drink: I drink*	son	*(they) are*
(tú) bebes	*you drink*	unos, unas	*some*
bueno, -a (para la salud)	*good (for your health)*	¿Cuál(es)?	*Which (ones)?*
malo, -a (para la salud)	*bad (for your health)*		
sabroso, -a	*delicious, tasty*		
Creo que sí.	*I think so.*		
Creo que no.	*I don't think so.*		
algo	*something*		
deber: (yo) debo	*ought to, should*		
(tú) debes			

¿Y qué quiere decir... ?

horrible

* *Agua* is a feminine noun. However, we use the article *el* with feminine nouns that begin with stressed *a* or *ha*.

 **Video Activity B**

Grammar Preview

Bebo / bebes and *debo / debes* are presented here lexically. The explanation of *-er* verbs appears on p. 175.

Class Starter Review

On the day following initial presentation of vocabulary, you might begin the class with this activity: As you call out the visualized items in this vocabulary section, ask students to categorize them as *frutas, verduras,* or *bebidas.* Or, divide the class into three groups: *frutas, verduras, bebidas.* Give them five minutes to list all the possible items in their category. When finished, have other classmates see if any items were not listed.

Multicultural Perspectives

Aguas frescas, or flavored waters, are popular beverages in Mexican eating places. Among the selections are *agua de sandía, agua de limón, agua de tamarindo,* and *horchata* (made with rice flour). *Aguas frescas* are sold in restaurants, at market lunch counters, and by street vendors. Invite students to share their knowledge of popular beverages from other cultures. If you have a local Hispanic market, purchase a couple of these beverages so that students can taste them.

Learning Spanish Through Action

STAGING VOCABULARY: *Den, Levántense, Muestren, Pongan*

MATERIALS: Three 8 1/2 X 11" sheets of paper labeled *frutas, verduras,* and *bebidas;* index cards with pictures of all the fruits, vegetables, and beverages in the *Vocabulario para conversar.* If possible, use plastic toys or magazine cutouts.

DIRECTIONS: Have three volunteers go to the front of the class. Give each volunteer one of the sheets, instructing him or her to hold it up for the class. Distribute the index cards to individuals in the class. As you recite each food or beverage, have the student who has the corresponding card for that item get up and give it to the appropriate volunteer. Continue until all of the foods and beverages are properly categorized.

Practice

Re-enter / Recycle

Ex. 1: *tengo / necesito* from Chap. 2, *¿te gustaría?* from Chap. 3

Teaching Suggestions

If possible, obtain plastic fruit and vegetables for manipulatives.

Ex. 1: Explain that *Estudiante A* can also combine statements: *Tengo sed. Necesito beber algo.*

Ex. 3: You may want to brainstorm other appropriate responses such as *Sí, pero no me gustan mucho; Sí, pero no son sabrosas; Sí, pero son horribles;* and *Más o menos.*

Answers: Empecemos a conversar

1 ESTUDIANTE A

Statements will vary. Make sure students correlate *hambre* with *comer* and *sed* with *beber.*

ESTUDIANTE B

Answers will vary, but may include:

¿Te gustaría una manzana?
. . . un plátano?
. . . una naranja?
. . . una zanahoria?
. . . una limonada?
. . . un té helado?
. . . un café?
. . . un refresco?

Empecemos a conversar

1 Necesito beber algo. A —*Necesito beber algo.*
B —*¿Te gustaría un refresco?*

2  A —*¿Debo comer fruta todos los días?*
B —*Creo que sí.*
o: *Creo que no.*

Options

Strategies for Reaching All Students

Spanish-Speaking Students

Exs. 1–2: Pair Spanish-speaking students. For Ex. 2, ask students to explain their answers.

Students Needing Extra Help

Ex. 1: Emphasize that *hambre, comer,* and the foods go together and that *sed, beber,* and the beverages go together.

Enrichment

Ex. 2: Have *Estudiante B* expand his or her answer by saying if the foods named are healthful.

3 A —*Las* *<u>ensaladas</u>* *son buenas para la salud, ¿verdad?*
B —*<u>Sí, y también son sabrosas</u>.*

Estudiante A

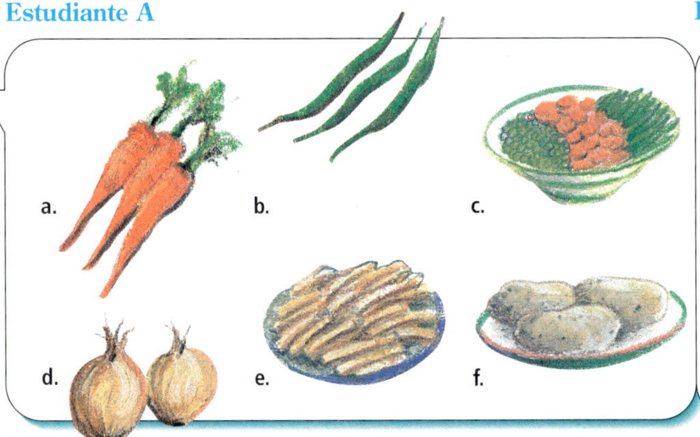

Estudiante B

Creo que sí.

Sí, y también son sabrosas.

No, creo que no.

No, son malas para la salud.

Muchachos comiendo melón y uvas (c. 1650), Bartolomé Esteban Murillo

2 ESTUDIANTE A

a. ¿Debo comer papas fritas todos los días?
b. . . . huevos . . .
c. . . . papas . . .
d. . . . plátanos . . .
e. . . . verduras . . .
f. . . . lechuga . . .
g. Questions will vary.

ESTUDIANTE B

a.–g. Answers will vary.

3 Preview adjective agreement by asking students to predict why *buenas* and *sabrosas* end in *-as*.

ESTUDIANTE A

a. Las zanahorias son buenas para la salud, ¿verdad?
b. Las judías verdes . . .
c. Las verduras . . .
d. Las cebollas . . .
e. Las papas fritas . . .
f. Las papas al horno . . .

ESTUDIANTE B

a.–f. Answers will vary depending on *Estudiante B*'s preferences.

Cultural Notes 

(p. 159, photo)
Bartolomé Esteban Murillo (1617–1682) was a native of Sevilla who became famous throughout Europe for his painting. In keeping with the painting schools of his time, Murillo may well have intended *Muchachos comiendo melón y uvas* (circa 1650) to be an allegory for the sense of taste. The sensations of eating ripe fruit are evoked through carefully rendered textures and use of light and dark contrasts. Allegorical paintings, like this one, often were created as part of a series, so Murillo may have also depicted smell, sight, and the other senses on different canvases.

Apply

Answers: Empecemos a leer y a escribir

1 a. el pato
b. el mono
c. el gato
d. la gallina
e. el cerdo
f. el conejo

Empecemos a leer y a escribir

Responde en español.

1 Unos animales hablan de lo que prefieren comer. ¿Quién dice . . . ?

a. —A ver . . . Me encantan el pan y el agua. Sí, sí. Me gusta mucho beber agua, y como mucho pan en el parque.

b. —En el desayuno siempre como plátanos. En el almuerzo a veces como más plátanos. ¿Y en la cena? Pues . . . generalmente también como plátanos. Son muy buenos para la salud, ¿verdad?

c. —Me gusta la leche, pero prefiero comer pescado.

d. —¿Comer huevos? ¡Ay, no! ¿Huevos? ¡Nunca!

e. —Como mucho todos los días. ¡Pero no puedo comer jamón! ¡Nunca voy a comer jamón!

f. —Yo como muchas zanahorias. ¡A mí me encantan las zanahorias! Me gustaría comer zanahorias en todas las comidas.

Options

Strategies for Reaching All Students

Spanish-Speaking Students

Ex. 4: Ask Spanish-speaking students to find out about their classmates' beverage preferences for breakfast. Then have them write short paragraphs about their findings.
For example: *Pregúntales a tus compañeros qué beben en el desayuno. Luego escribe un párrafo sobre las bebidas más populares.*

Guide students in their writing and provide further questions to be answered in paragraph form.

 **Un paso más Exs. 4-F, 4-G**

Students Needing Extra Help

Ex. 1: Have students use their Organizers.
Ex. 2: Have students draw each dish on a separate paper plate and arrange the four plates in the order of service. Then students can complete the chart.

2 Imagine you are making a dinner menu. Copy the following chart on a sheet of paper.

Primer plato	
Plato principal	
Verdura	
Bebida	

Now read the list of dishes and write them in the correct blanks on your chart.

ensalada de lechuga, tomate, zanahoria y cebolla
té helado
pescado
sopa de pollo

3 ¿Qué verduras te gustan? ¿Cuáles no te gustan?

4 ¿Qué bebida prefieres en el desayuno, en el almuerzo y en la cena? ¿Hay bebidas que no te gustan? ¿Cuáles?

El mercado de Almolonga, Guatemala

También se dice

las bananas
los guineos

las chinas

la chaucha *(sing.)*
las habichuelas verdes
los ejotes

las patatas

las arvejas
los chícharos

el zumo de naranja

2 Menus will vary. Allow students to expand the menu by writing their own favorites. / Primer plato: sopa de pollo; Plato principal: pescado; Verdura: ensalada de lechuga, tomate, zanahoria y cebolla; Bebida: té helado

3–4 Answers will vary.

 **Practice Wkbk. 4-3, 4-4**

 **Audio Activity 4.2**

 **Pruebas 4-3, 4-4**

 **Comm. Act. BLMs 4-1, 4-2**

Enrichment

Ex. 1: Students may enjoy presenting skits based on this exercise.
Ex. 2: Have students create their own dinner menu for a party of six friends. Suggest that they list the courses in the order in which they'll serve them. They should include a soup, salad, and other vegetables.

Cultural Notes 

(p. 161, photo)
Almolonga, Guatemala, lies about three miles south of Quetzaltenango in the Western Highlands of that country. Market days are Wednesdays and Saturdays. The town is particularly well known for its produce and is situated in a fertile farming area. Typically, people selling their produce in Guatemalan markets display their items in attractive arrangements. The women wear the traditional, bright orange *huipiles* (blouses) and headbands of Almolonga.

Practice

Re-enter / Recycle

Ex. 1: *gustar* expressions and *ni . . . ni* from Chap. 1
Ex. 3: *gustar* expressions from Chap. 1.

Teaching Suggestions

Ex. 2: Students may enjoy doing this exercise using props and showing plastic foods as they say the names. Remind students to ask *¿Cómo se dice . . . ?* if they need help. As an alternate activity, students can pretend to be shopping for the items that they need for their meal. Use plastic foods or props marked with prices, paper or plastic bags, and play money.

Ex. 3: Remind students of these affirmative and negative statements and responses to express likes and dislikes:
(A mí) me gusta(n) . . . / A mí también (me gusta). / (A mí) me gusta(n) más . . . / (A mí) me gusta(n) mucho . . . / (A mí) me encanta(n) . . . / A mí sí (me gusta). (A mí) no me gusta(n) . . . / (A mí) no me gusta(n) mucho . . . / A mí tampoco (me gusta). / (A mí) no me gusta(n) nada . . .

Here's another opportunity for you and your partner to use the vocabulary you've just learned.

1 You and a friend are having dinner at a restaurant. Take turns asking each other about your food preferences. Discuss at least two preferences.

A —*¿Prefieres papas al horno o papas fritas?*
B —*Prefiero papas fritas, ¿y tú?*
A —*Yo prefiero papas fritas también.*
o: *Yo prefiero papas al horno.*
o: *A mí no me gustan ni las papas al horno ni las papas fritas.*

Options

Strategies for Reaching All Students

Spanish-Speaking Students

Ask students to answer aloud for the class: *¿Cuáles son tus comidas favoritas? ¿A qué hora cenas? ¿Cena toda la familia junta? ¿Comes algo entre el almuerzo y la cena? ¿Qué comes? ¿Vas con tus amigos a comer después de las clases?*

Cooperative Learning

In groups of four or five, have students plan a complete lunch menu for each day of the school week. Each lunch should include an item from the dairy, meat, vegetable, bread, and fruit groups, a beverage, and some extras. Have a volunteer from each group write the menus on butcher paper, making sure to label each meal with the day on which it will be served. Post the menus on a bulletin board and discuss them. To extend the activity, have student "critics" rate the menus on a scale of 1–5. Set up the scale and define each category beforehand so that everyone is in agreement on the rating system.

2 Imagine that you and your partner are checking out your refrigerator. Suggest a dish for a meal to your partner. Use the picture to help you decide what foods you already have and what you will need to buy.

A —*¿Quieres unos sandwiches para el almuerzo?*
B —*¿Hay jamón?*
A —*Sí, pero necesitamos pan y queso.*

unos sandwiches	el desayuno
una sopa	el almuerzo
una ensalada	la merienda
una ensalada de frutas	la cena

3 Do you remember all the ways you have learned to express your likes and dislikes? For example: *(A mí) me encanta ___, (A mí) no me gusta ___,* etc. Use these expressions in a conversation with your partner about food. Find two foods that you both like and two that you both dislike.

A —*Me encanta la sopa de pollo.*
B —*A mí también me gusta.*
o: *¡No me gusta nada la sopa de pollo!*

✓Ahora lo sabes

Using what you have learned so far, can you:

- **tell what you like and don't like to eat and drink?**
- **say that you are hungry or thirsty?**
- **compare and contrast menus and mealtimes for breakfast and lunch in Spanish-speaking countries and in the United States?**

Answers: Comuniquemos

1 Remind students to include definite articles in their responses if they elect the last option for *Estudiante A.*

ESTUDIANTE A

¿Prefieres agua o limonada?
. . . sopa de pollo o ensalada?
. . . sopa de pollo o sopa de tomate?
. . . té o té helado?
. . . manzanas o plátanos?
. . . leche o café?
. . . guisantes o zanahorias?

ESTUDIANTE B

Answers will vary depending on *Estudiante B*'s preferences.

2–3 Dialogues will vary.

Answers: Ahora lo sabes

- Me gusta(n) ___. No me gusta(n) ___. *(pp. 148–149, 156–157)*
- Tengo hambre. Tengo sed. *(pp. 156–157)*
- Answers will vary, but students may mention the long midday break *(el almuerzo)* during which businesses and schools close. *(pp. 154–155)*

 **Audio Activity 4.3**

 **Writing Activities**

 **Examen de habilidades 1**

Apply

Background Information

(See the Cross-Curricular Connections at the beginning of the chapter on p. 144 for further activities.
For a complete list of the curricular areas covered in PASO A PASO A, *see p.T23 of this Teacher's Edition.)*

Mapas de productos provides a cross-curricular connection with geography.

¿Fruta o verdura? provides a cross-curricular connection with science. You may want to elicit from students such sentences as *La manzana es una fruta. La papa es una verdura.* Here are simplified definitions of fruits and vegetables to help students categorize foods in this chapter. Fruit: The usually edible reproductive body of a seed plant, especially one that has sweet pulp enclosing the seed or seeds. Vegetable: A plant with little or no woody tissue that generally grows for a single season and that is grown for an edible part.

Para pensar provides practice in problem solving and critical thinking that applies to many curriculum areas.

Conexiones

These activities connect Spanish with what you are learning in other subject areas.

Mapas de productos

Here are product maps of Central America and the southwest United States. Use the information on these maps to make a Venn diagram showing which products grow in both areas or in only one of them.

Which products shown on the map of Central America grow in your area? Which grow in another part of the United States? What can you conclude about a region that has crops similar to those in your area? Can you explain why bananas are found in Central America but not in the southwestern part of the United States?

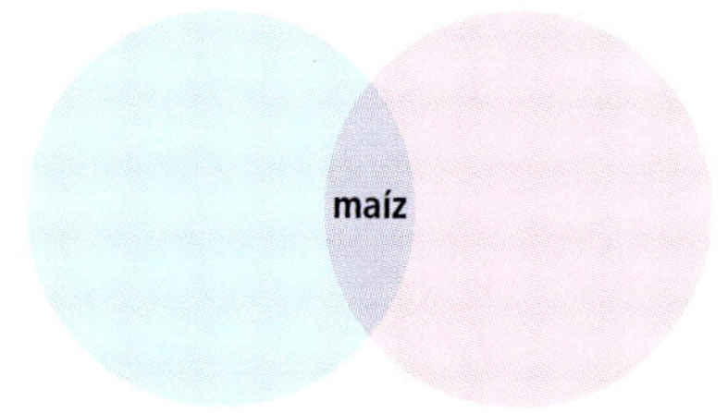

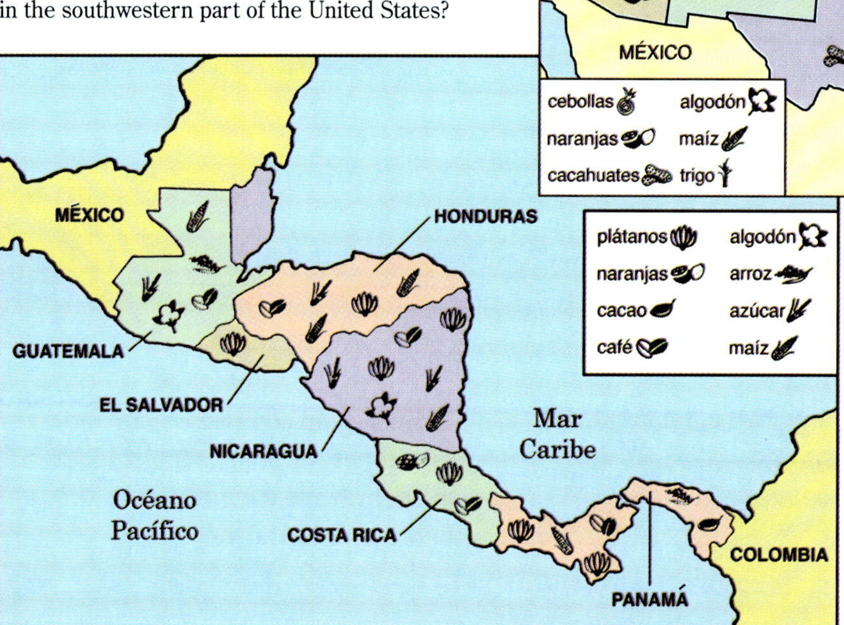

Options

Strategies for Reaching All Students

Students Needing Extra Help

If necessary, point out which countries comprise North and Central America. Some students may not realize or know, for example, that Mexico is part of North America.
For the activities *Mapas de productos* and *Para pensar,* see the Projects for Proficiency BLMs for a Venn diagram template and a grid / chart for solving logic problems.

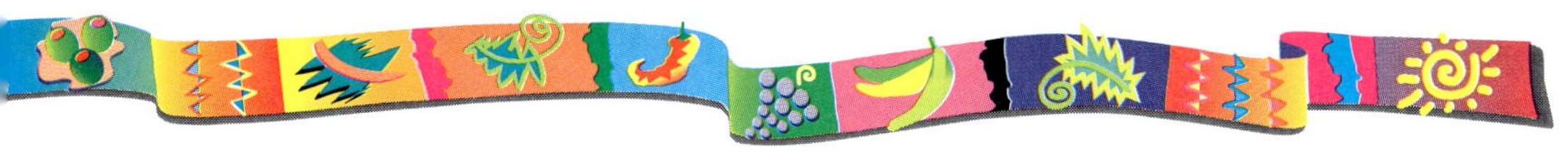

¿Fruta o verdura?

A fruit is the pulp, usually sweet, that surrounds the seed or seeds of a plant. Many fruits grow on trees or vines. A vegetable is a plant that is grown for food. It has little or no woody tissue and generally grows for a single season.

Decide con tu compañero(a) cuáles de éstas son frutas y cuáles son verduras.

- las manzanas
- los tomates
- la lechuga
- los plátanos
- las judías verdes
- las zanahorias

la semilla

Para pensar

Luis, Martín y David comen en la cafetería de la escuela. Uno come una hamburguesa, otro come un sandwich de queso y el otro come una ensalada.

Luis es vegetariano.

A David le gusta comer lechuga.

¿Qué come Luis? ¿Y Martín? ¿Y David?

Teaching Suggestions

You may choose the number of activities you want your class to do. You may prefer to use them as homework, for enrichment, or for your Spanish-speaking students. This material is not part of the testing program, however, it is appropriate for use in student assessment.

Answers: Conexiones

Mapas de productos: Crops grown in Central America include: *plátanos, cacao, café, arroz,* and *azúcar.* / Crops grown in the southwest United States: *cebollas, cacahuates,* and *trigo.* / Crops grown in both regions: *naranjas, algodón,* and *maíz.*

Answers will vary. / Students may mention that *algodón* grows in the south, *maíz* in the midwest, *naranjas* in California and Florida, *azúcar* in Hawaii, and so on. / The region probably has the same type of weather, soil, climate, etc. / Conditions for growing bananas are not right for the southwestern part of the U.S. The topography, geographical location, soil, climate, etc. are all different, as compared to Central America.

¿Fruta o verdura?: Frutas: las manzanas, los tomates y los plátanos; Verduras: la lechuga, las judías verdes y las zanahorias

Para pensar: Luis come un sandwich de queso, Martín come una hamburguesa y David come una ensalada.

Preview

Transparency 28

Teaching Suggestions

A: Compare students' grammar rules for accuracy. Write a rule for the class to use and post it for reference.

Answers

Answers will vary. Discuss more common types of cheese that students may see or buy: American, cheddar, parmesan, Swiss, etc. / See if students can determine that the word *quesos* refers to a plural noun.

A *importados, sabrosos, preparados, franceses, ingleses, suizos, finos* / *americano, suizo* / The words end in an *-s* when they describe *quesos.* / Answers will vary, but look for explanations such as: We add an *-s* to the end of a word to make it plural.

B ¿Te gusta la leche? / ¿Te gustan las papas fritas?

Sección 3

Gramática en contexto

Look at this ad for imported cheeses. How many of these cheeses look familiar to you? Find the word *queso* and the word *quesos*. What do you think is the difference in their meanings?

A Work with a partner or a group.

- List all the words from the ad that describe cheese when it is written *quesos*.
- Find two words that describe cheese when it is written *queso*.
- Compare the two lists. What differences do you see?
- Make up a rule about the way to change words when they describe more than one item.

B Compare the questions *¿Te gustan los quesos importados?* and *¿Te gusta el queso americano?* Tell your partner if you would use *te gusta* or *te gustan* with *la leche* and with *las papas fritas.*

Options

Strategies for Reaching All Students

Students Needing Extra Help

A*:* Review what students have already learned about the plural endings of adjectives. Have them use their Organizers from Chap. 3 to review other adjectives.
B*:* Write a *¿Te gustan . . . ?* question, underlining the plural word.
El plural de los sustantivos: Have students fill in the first section in the grammar portion of their Organizers.

El plural de los sustantivos

- In Spanish, to make nouns plural, we generally add *-s* to words ending in a vowel *(comida → comida**s**)*. We add *-es* to words ending in a consonant *(sandwich → sandwich**es**)*.
- The plural definite articles are **los** and **las**. **Los** is used with masculine plural nouns, **las** with feminine plural nouns.

los plátano**s** **las** manzana**s**

- **Los** is also used with a plural noun that includes both males and females.

  el profesor Sánchez y la profesora Romero = **los** profesores

  Which definite article would you use if the word *muchachos* included both boys and girls?

- When we change singular nouns to plural nouns, we want to keep the stress on the same syllable. Sometimes we have to add or remove an accent mark in the plural.

  el ex**a**men → los ex**á**menes
  el jam**ó**n → los jam**o**nes

- The plural indefinite articles are **unos** and **unas**. They mean "some" or "a few."

  Tengo mucha hambre. Voy a comer **unas** papas fritas y **unos** sandwiches.

- We use *me gust**an*** and *me encant**an*** to talk about a plural noun.

  No me gusta**n** **las** manzana**s** pero me encanta**n** **los** plátano**s**.

¡No olvides!

The singular definite articles are *el* and *la*.

el plátano

la manzana

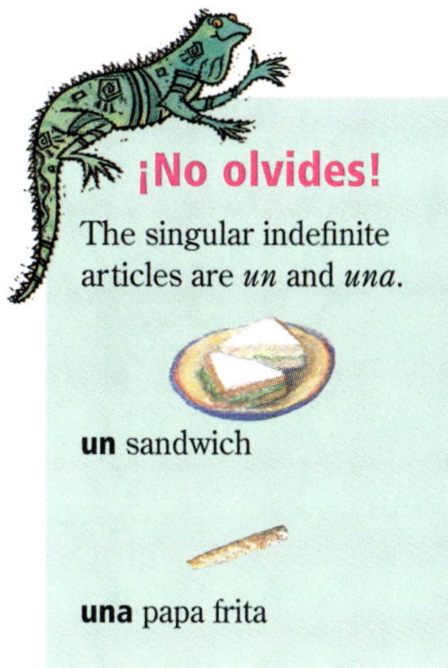

¡No olvides!

The singular indefinite articles are *un* and *una*.

un sandwich

una papa frita

Present

Class Starter Review

On the day following the presentation of the plural of nouns, you might begin the class with this activity:

In pairs, have students alternate asking and answering whether or not they like a particular food or beverage. Look for correct use of *me / te gusta(n)*.

For listening practice, ask students to signal (thumbs up or thumbs down, hands up or down, etc.) if they hear a singular or plural noun as you read a list of words.

Practice

Re-enter / Recycle

Exs. 1–4: *gustar* expressions from Chap. 1

Teaching Suggestions

Ex. 1: Explain the difference in degree between *me gustan* and *me encantan* and how both phrases include the idea of "them." (I like them. / I love them.)

Ex. 3: Review the responses *también* and *tampoco*.

Ex. 4: Review *te gusta* and *te gustaría*.

Reteach / Review: Definite & Indefinite Articles

Ex. 4: Contrast the use of indefinite and definite articles to vary this exercise: *¿Te gustaría comer unas papas al horno? / Sí, me encantan las papas al horno. / No, gracias. No me gustan las papas al horno.*

1 Tell your partner which foods in Column B could go with each expression in Column A.

A	B
a. me gustan	las hamburguesas
b. me gusta	las cebollas
c. me encanta	el pescado
d. me encantan	el jamón
e. no me gustan	los plátanos
f. no me gusta	las frutas
	el jugo de naranja
	las judías verdes

Options

Strategies for Reaching All Students

Spanish-Speaking Students

Ex. 3: Pair bilingual and non-bilingual students for this exercise.

Enrichment

Ex. 2: Have *Estudiante B* expand his or her answer by telling why he or she likes or dislikes the food named.

2 Discuss with a partner whether or not you like the following foods.

A —*¿Te gustan los huevos?*
B —*Sí, me gustan.*
o: *Sí, me encantan.*
o: *No, no me gustan.*

a.

b.

c.

d.

e.

f.

g.

3 These foods might be served in your school cafeteria this week. Take turns with a partner telling whether you like them or not.

A —*Me gustan las papas al horno.*
B —*A mí también.*
o: *A mí no.*

A —*No me gustan las papas al horno.*
B —*A mí tampoco.*
o: *A mí sí.*

a.

b.

c.

d.

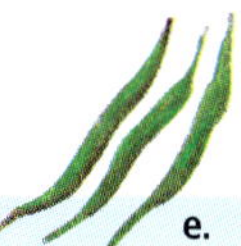

e.

f.

4 Now use the pictures in Exercises 2 and 3 to ask if your partner would like to eat those foods. Pick any five.

A —*¿Te gustaría comer unas zanahorias?*
B —*¡Claro que sí! A mí me encantan.*
o: *No, no tengo hambre. Gracias.*

Answers

1 a. me gustan, d. me encantan, e. no me gustan: las hamburguesas, las cebollas, los plátanos, las frutas, las judías verdes
b. me gusta, c. me encanta, f. no me gusta: el pescado, el jamón, el jugo de naranja

2 ESTUDIANTE A
a. ¿Te gustan los plátanos?
b. . . . las hamburguesas?
c. . . . los guisantes?
d. . . . las verduras?
e. . . . las papas fritas?
f. . . . las zanahorias?
g. Questions will vary.

ESTUDIANTE B
a.–g. Answers will vary.

3 ESTUDIANTE A
a. (No) me gustan los tomates.
b. . . . las naranjas.
c. . . . las uvas.
d. . . . las manzanas.
e. . . . las judías verdes.
f. Statements will vary.

ESTUDIANTE B
a.–f. Statements will vary depending on *Estudiante B*'s preferences.

4 Dialogues will vary.

Practice Wkbk. 4-5

Cultural Notes

(p. 168, realia)
This ad proudly claims that Gallina Blanca instant chicken soup is choice *(selección)*, containing only the finest ingredients. Gallina Blanca makes several varieties of instant soup: broth-based *(sopas)*, cream-based *(cremas)*, and smooth, puréed soups *(purés)*. These soups are used in the preparation of sauces in many Spanish and Latin American kitchens.

Present & Practice

Re-enter / Recycle

Exs. 5–6: adjectives to describe personality from Chap. 1

Teaching Suggestions

El plural de los adjetivos: Have students continue to fill in the first section (adjective endings) in the grammar portion of their Organizers.

El plural de los adjetivos

In Spanish, if a noun is plural, the adjective must also be plural. To make adjectives plural, add *-s* to the final vowel.

La**s** papa**s** frita**s** son sabrosa**s** pero no son buena**s** para la salud.

Lo**s** guisante**s** son bueno**s** para la salud.

Es sabroso.

Son sabroso**s**.

Es sabrosa.

Son sabrosa**s**.

Es horrible.

Son horrible**s**.

- If the adjective ends in a consonant, add *-es.*

  trabajador → trabajador**es**

- When an adjective describes both masculine and feminine nouns, we use the masculine plural ending.

  Los plátan**os** y **las** naranj**as** son sabros**os**.

Options

Strategies for Reaching All Students

Students Needing Extra Help

Ex. 6: Use discretion so that no student feels singled out because of a potentially embarrassing description.

Enrichment

Ex. 5: You may also want students to choose words from the list to describe *un profesor, una amiga,* and *tres muchachos.*

5 Tell your partner all the words you might use from the list to describe *las muchachas.*

a. generosas e. tacaños
b. paciente f. callado
c. sociables g. graciosas
d. seria h. trabajadoras

6 For each of these adjectives, name two famous people or people in your class or school whom the adjective fits. For example: *María y Juan son desordenados.*

artístico, -a	desordenado, -a	serio, -a
atrevido, -a	gracioso, -a	sociable
callado, -a	ordenado, -a	trabajador, -a

Almuerzo al aire libre en Santiago, Chile

Answers

5 a. generosas, c. sociables, g. graciosas, h. trabajadoras

6 Answers will vary, but look for adjective agreement.

 **Practice Wkbk. 4-6**

 **Writing Activities**

 **Pruebas 4-5, 4-6**

Cultural Notes

(p. 171, photo)
Chile enjoys mild winters from June through September. Temperatures in spring and fall days resemble the climate of southern California in the U.S. For much of the year Chilean students can meet with their friends outdoors during their lunch period.

Present & Apply

Teaching Suggestions

If possible, make *licuados de plátano* in class so that everyone can try a small amount.

Answers: La cultura desde tu perspectiva

1–2 Answers will vary.

3 Answers will vary, but students may say that in the U.S., breakfast is eaten around 8 A.M.; lunch around noon; and dinner around 6 P.M.

Writing Activities

La merienda y la cena

In Spanish-speaking countries, people often eat a late afternoon light meal called *la merienda*. It may be like a *desayuno* or like an English tea, with sandwiches, pastries, rolls, *café con leche*, tea, or hot chocolate.

In Chile a late afternoon tea is served between 5 and 6 P.M. People drink tea or coffee in very small cups with little sandwiches and pastries. Young people in Argentina often have fruit shakes (*licuados de fruta)* in the afternoon.

La cena is the evening meal. It may start around 7 o'clock or much later, especially in countries that have a late midday meal. In Spain, *la cena* may start as late as 10 or 11 P.M. Most Spaniards enjoy going out after school or work, and it is customary to wait until all the family members are present before sitting down to eat. *La cena* can be a substantial meal or a light meal. It may include leftovers from the midday meal.

Una merienda en bote, Xochimilco, México

La cultura desde tu perspectiva

1 Do you eat something like a *merienda?* When? What do you eat?

2 Which after-school snack is most popular in your class? Take a class survey. Find out how many students eat these foods for snacks at least twice a week. Then make a bar graph showing the results of the survey.

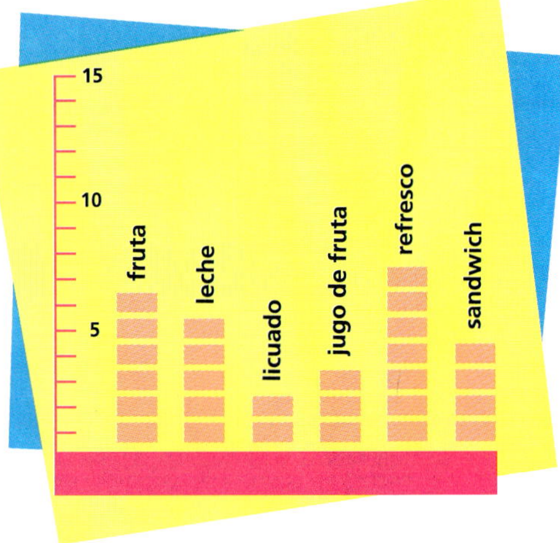

3 What would you tell an exchange student from the Dominican Republic about meals and mealtimes in the United States? Explain the differences that he or she should expect to find.

Options

Strategies for Reaching All Students

Spanish-Speaking Students

Ask: *¿Has probado licuados de otras frutas? ¿Se preparan igual que este licuado de plátano? ¿Qué sabor es tu preferido?*

Un paso más Ex. 4-H

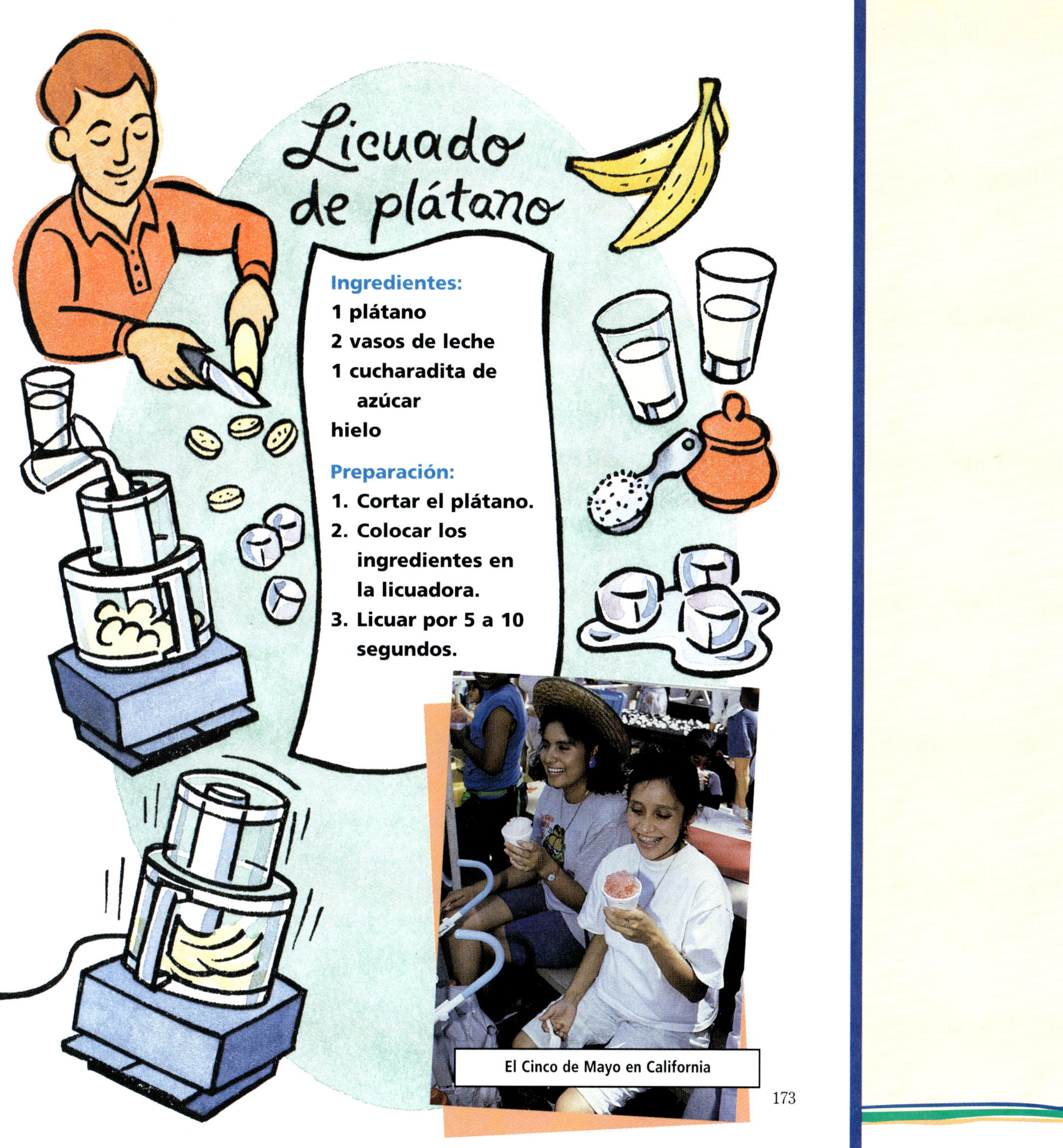

El Cinco de Mayo en California

173

Cultural Notes

(p. 172, photo)
The floating gardens of Xochimilco, Mexico, have flourished since the thirteenth century, when the Chinampaneca Indians established themselves in this area about 13 miles west of what is today the center of Mexico City. A popular attraction for tourists and residents alike, the gardens can be viewed from gondolas like this one, called *trajineras.*

(p. 173, photo)
These two young women are enjoying cool *raspas* (snow cones) on a warm day. Many popular celebrations are in observance of historical events in the Spanish-speaking world. *Cinco de Mayo* commemorates the battle of Puebla, Mexico. While not widely celebrated in Mexico, *Cinco de Mayo* is an important festival for many people of Mexican descent in the U.S., a time to celebrate their heritage. Another holiday from the Spanish-speaking world that is observed by increasing numbers of people in the U.S. is The Day of the Dead *(el Día de los Muertos)*, November 2.

Preview

Transparency 29

Answers

Answers will vary, but students may mention that it is a *salsa* or type of sauce for cooking.

A All three words end in *-mos.* / They begin differently. / We would use *-emos* with *-er* verbs and *-amos* with *-ar* verbs.

B The subject is *Julia y Juana.* / We could use the subject pronoun *ellas.*

Sección 4

Gramática en contexto

Look at this ad for a sensational new food product. What do you think it is? What do you do with it?

A When the parents talk about the whole family, they use the words *comemos, tenemos,* and *cocinamos.* In what way are these three words alike? In what way are they different? Explain to your partner when you would use the *-emos* ending and when you would use the *-amos* ending.

B You already know the difference between *habla* and *hablan.* When the parents use the word *comen,* what is the subject of that verb? What subject pronoun could you use instead?

Options

Strategies for Reaching All Students

Enrichment

After this grammar section, have students return to this page and use the ad as a model to create an original ad of their own for a different food product. They may work in small groups or pairs for this activity. Have them bring in props for a class presentation.

Verbos que terminan en *-er*

You know the pattern of present-tense endings for regular *-ar* verbs. We use the vowel *-a* except in the *yo* form.

HABLAR			
(yo)	habl**o**	(nosotros) (nosotras)	habl**amos**
(tú)	habl**as**	(vosotros) (vosotras)	habl**áis**
(Ud.) (él) (ella)	habl**a**	(Uds.) (ellos) (ellas)	habl**an**

- Another group of infinitives end in *-er.* Some that you know are *beber, comer, leer,* and *deber.* Here are the present-tense forms of the verb *comer.*

COMER			
(yo)	com**o**	(nosotros) (nosotras)	com**emos**
(tú)	com**es**	(vosotros) (vosotras)	com**éis**
(Ud.) (él) (ella)	com**e**	(Uds.) (ellos) (ellas)	com**en**

- How does this pattern differ from that of *-ar* verbs? What clue will help you remember this difference?
- You also know the verb *ver.* It is regular except in the *yo* form, which is *veo.* What would the other forms of *ver* be?

Present

Teaching Suggestions

Verbos que terminan en -er: Have students fill in the verb chart in the grammar portion of their Organizers.

Answers

- The present-tense endings for *-ar* verbs use the vowel *-a;* the present-tense endings for *-er* verbs use the vowel *-e.* By looking at the vowel in the verb ending *(-ar* or *-er),* we can tell what the present-tense pattern will be: vowel *-a* (for *-ar* verbs) or vowel *-e* (for *-er* verbs).
- ves, ve, vemos, (veis), ven

Cultural Notes 

(p. 174, photo)
In Argentina, family members often gather for a leisurely midday meal on weekends and special occasions. Argentina's cuisine shows a variety of influences including Italian, Polish, and Spanish. Beef dishes, however, especially prepared *a la parrilla* (grilled), are perhaps the most typical. *Parrillada* is an Argentine "mixed grill" consisting of various courses of steak, chicken, sausages, lamb, and pork, which are consumed with a crusty bread, a small salad, and wine.

Practice

Teaching Suggestions

Ex. 1: Have students explain how they can identify an *-ar* and an *-er* verb. Ask if they can find the form *(nado)* that does not offer a clue as to whether it is an *-ar* or an *-er* verb. Students may remember that *nadar* is an *-ar* verb.

Ex. 2: Make sure students understand that the subject used in the answer to *e.* is *nosotros;* in *f.* the subject used in the answer is *yo.*

Ex. 3: Model some examples on the chalkboard. There are really three verbs involved in this exercise. Show how the verb in the first sentence becomes an infinitive in the second sentence. Show examples of this construction in English: But she ought to (should) eat vegetables!

Answers

1 *-ar* verbs: c. *hablan,* d. *estudias,* g. *practica,* h. *nado*
-er verbs: a. *debes,* b. *leen,* e. *come,* f. *bebemos*

2 ESTUDIANTE A
a. ¿Qué bebe Julia en el desayuno?
b. . . . beben Raquel y Ramón en el almuerzo?
c. . . . beben Graciela y Juan en la cena?
d. . . . bebe Pablo en el desayuno?
e. . . . beben Uds. en la cena?
f. . . . bebes tú en el almuerzo?

1 Based on the charts on page 175, tell your partner which of the following forms are from verbs that end in *-ar* and which are from verbs that end in *-er.*

a. debes	c. hablan	e. come	g. practica
b. leen	d. estudias	f. bebemos	h. nado

2 With a partner, take turns asking and answering what the following people drink at different meals. Some subjects are plural and some are singular.

tus amigos / el almuerzo

A —*¿Qué beben tus amigos en el almuerzo?*
B —*Beben refrescos.*

a. Julia / el desayuno

b. Raquel y Ramón / el almuerzo

c. Graciela y Juan / la cena

d. Pablo / el desayuno

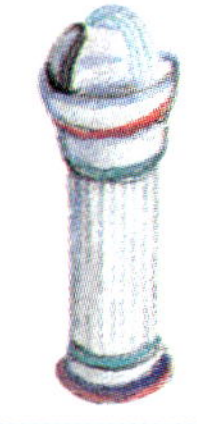

e. Uds. / la cena

f. tú / el almuerzo

Options

Strategies for Reaching All Students

Spanish-Speaking Students

Ex. 3: Have students write the exercise, paying close attention to spelling and the use of accents. Then have them present the exercise orally.

Students Needing Extra Help

Ex. 1: Have students use their Organizers.
Ex. 3: Remind students of adjective agreement: *buenos* for masculine, plural nouns and *buenas* for feminine, plural nouns.

3 These people do not eat certain foods. With your partner, discuss why they should eat them.

Carmen

A —*Carmen no come verduras.*
B —*¡Pero debe comer verduras! Son buenas para la salud.*

a. Arturo y Tomás

b. Ernesto

c. Inés

d. nosotros

e. Victoria y Gloria

f. yo

Cipotes en la marcha por la paz (1992), Isaías Mata

ESTUDIANTE B
a. (Julia) bebe leche.
b. (Raquel y Ramón) beben limonada.
c. (Graciela y Juan) beben té helado.
d. (Pablo) bebe jugo de naranja.
e. (Nosotros, -as) bebemos agua.
f. (Yo) bebo . . . *(Answers will vary.)*

3 ESTUDIANTE A
a. Arturo y Tomás no comen tomates.
b. Ernesto no come papas al horno.
c. Inés no come naranjas.
d. Nosotros no comemos judías verdes.
e. Victoria y Gloria no comen guisantes.
f. Yo no como . . . *(Statements will vary.)*

ESTUDIANTE B
a. ¡Pero deben comer tomates! Son buenos para la salud.
b. . . . debe comer papas al horno! . . . buenas . . .
c. . . . debe comer naranjas! . . . buenas . . .
d. . . . deben comer judías verdes! . . . buenas . . .
e. . . . deben comer guisantes! . . . buenos . . .
f. . . . debes comer . . . *(Statements will vary.)* . . . buenos(as) . . .

Practice Wkbk. 4-7, 4-8

Cultural Notes

(p. 177, photo)
Isaías Mata is a San Francisco muralist whose themes revolve around the life of working people. This section is from his painting *Cipotes* ("kids") *en la marcha por la paz,* covering two walls of a church in the city's Mission District. The depicted individuals are watched over by heroes including Martin Luther King, Jr., Manuel Hidalgo, Sor Juana Inés de la Cruz, and Fray Bartolomé de las Casas. Two archetypal young people are in the lower corner, representing future generations, reminding the viewer that the work we do now will bring fruit in the future.

Present & Practice

Re-enter / Recycle

Exs. 4–5: activities from Chap. 1; pastimes from Chap. 3

Teaching Suggestions

Ex. 5: Students may want to include the name of a friend in *Estudiante A*'s question: *Tú y tu amigo Martín . . .*

Ex. 6: Here is another variation of subject / verb tic-tac-toe. Make cards with plural subjects on them. Have pairs of students play tic-tac-toe by placing the cards on a grid to try to make a row that uses the same verb form.

Sujetos compuestos

- When you talk **about** yourself and someone else, you really mean "we." Therefore, you should use the *nosotros* form of the verb.

  Alejandro y yo (= nosotros) estudi**amos** por la noche.

  Tú y yo (= nosotros) com**emos** a las doce.

- When speaking **to** more than one person—even if you would speak to each of them as *tú*—use the *ustedes* form of the verb.

  Tú y Tomás (= ustedes) practic**an** deportes.

- When you talk **about** more than one person or thing, use the *ellos / ellas* form of the verb.

  Marta y él (= ellos) beb**en** jugo de uva.

  Marta y ella (= ellas) escuch**an** música.

4 Tell your partner which subject pronoun you could use to replace the underlined people in each sentence. Then read the sentence aloud.

Miguel y Ana cantan bien. = Ellos cantan bien.

a. <u>Susana y yo</u> escuchamos música.
b. <u>Juan y Paco</u> patinan en el parque.
c. <u>Tú y Graciela</u> comen mucha fruta.
d. <u>Rosa y ella</u> deben estudiar.
e. <u>Juanita y Dolores</u> practican deportes.
f. <u>Tú y yo</u> bebemos limonada.
g. <u>David y él</u> estudian mucho.

nosotros
nosotras
Uds.
ellos
ellas

Options

Strategies for Reaching All Students

Enrichment

Ex. 4: As a written assignment, students may write sentences using the verb forms not used in this exercise, creating correct subjects for them, and any reasonable variations on the vocabulary in the original sentences.

5 With a partner, take turns asking what each of you might do with a friend on Saturdays. Use the verbs in the list below.

A —*Tú y tu amigo(a) leen libros los sábados, ¿no?*
B —*Sí, leemos libros.*
o: *No, no leemos libros. Patinamos.*

a. ayudar en casa	f. estudiar
b. beber café	g. nadar
c. cocinar	h. leer libros
d. comer sandwiches	i. patinar
e. escuchar música	j. ver la tele

6 Look at this game of tic-tac-toe. Working with a partner, find the row of plural subjects that use the verb *comemos.* Trace the row with your finger.

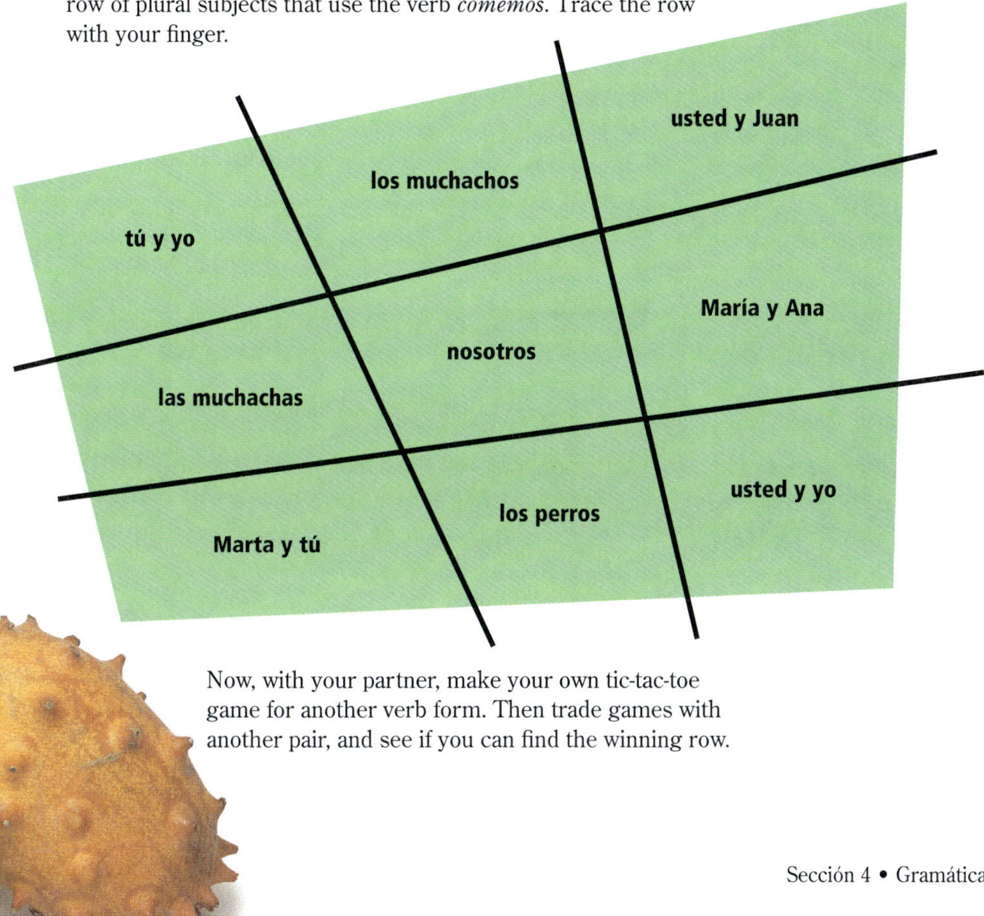

Now, with your partner, make your own tic-tac-toe game for another verb form. Then trade games with another pair, and see if you can find the winning row.

Answers

4 a. Nosotros(as)
b. Ellos
c. Uds.
d. Ellas
e. Ellas
f. Nosotros(as)
g. Ellos

5 Dialogues will vary.

6 The line is traced on a diagonal from the upper, left-hand corner to the lower, right-hand corner: *tú y yo / nosotros / usted y yo.*

 **Practice Wkbk. 4-9**

 **Audio Activity 4.4**

 **Pruebas 4-7, 4-8**

 **Comm. Act. BLM 4-3**

Cultural Notes

(pp. 178–179, background photo)
The names of fruits may differ from country to country, as well as from region to region. Here are some common names in Spanish along with their English translations: *mango* (mango), *limón verde* or *lima* (lime), *naranja* or *china* (orange), *plátanos maduros* or *plátanos morados* (ripe plantains—bottom right), *pitahaya* (pitahaya or horned mellon), a slice of *melón* (cantaloupe), *plátano verde* or *plátano macho* (green plantain—top right), *plátano verde* or *plátano* (green plantain—top left)

Apply

Pronunciation Tape 4-3

Todo junto A

Play

Todo junto B

Play

Using the Video

Video segment 3: See the Video Teacher's Guide.

Video Activity C

Teaching Suggestions

Activity 3: To make the playing board, you will need paper, scissors, paste, food magazines or the equivalent images from the Vocabulary Art BLMs, and paper squares. Have students cut out pictures of chapter vocabulary food from the magazines. (Make sure that these are not from the library or someone's personal collection.) Fold a sheet of 8 1/2 x 11 paper in thirds, like a letter. Then fold the rectangle in thirds. Open out the paper and affix one picture in each of the nine boxes.

Here's an opportunity for you to put together what you learned in this chapter with what you learned earlier.

1 ¿Qué comemos?

You and your partner are at the food court at the mall and are trying to decide what to eat for lunch.

- Ask your partner what foods he or she prefers to eat.
- Tell what you prefer to eat.
- Agree with your partner's suggestions.
  or
  Disagree and tell what *you* prefer to eat.

Keep your conversation going as long as you can. For example:

- Tell *why* you like or don't like to eat these foods.
- Tell *when* you like to eat them.

2 Menús especiales

Your class has been asked to plan some special menus in Spanish for the cafeteria. In groups, choose one of these menus, and plan a main dish, a beverage, and a dessert.

- menú vegetariano
- menú para deportistas
- menú para niños (*children*)

Then, with your group, make a sign announcing the menu. Draw or find pictures to illustrate it. Choose a member of your group to present the sign to the class.

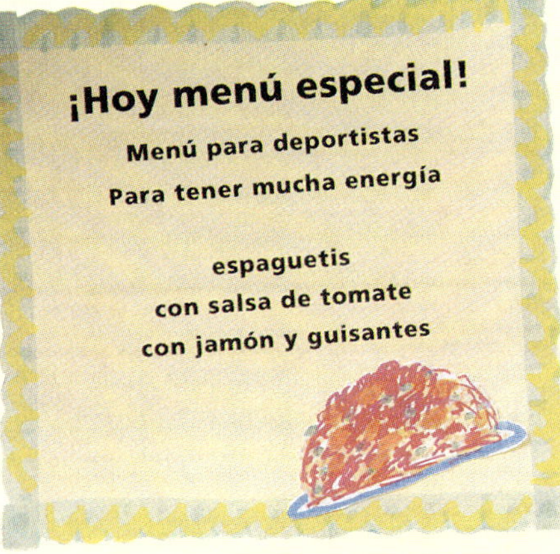

Options

Strategies for Reaching All Students

Spanish-Speaking Students

Ex. 1: Have pairs of students write out the exercise. Then have them present the exercise orally for the rest of the class.

Enrichment

Variants for *Para decir más:* ice cream, *la nieve;* cake, *la torta, el bizcocho, el queque.* You or your students may be more familiar with one or another of the words given.

Cooperative Learning

In groups of three or four, have students compile a list of foods and beverages they like to eat and drink by taking turns and naming them. Then have them decide as a group which food or beverage items are good for them (healthful), or which ones they *should* eat or drink. Model, if neces-

3 Lotería de comida

With your teacher's help, first make a playing board. Then, take some paper squares and you're ready to play!

- When the caller names a food that he or she likes, cover that space with a paper square.

  STUDENT CALLER: *Me gusta el pescado.*

  Cover your picture of fish if you have one on your board.

- When the caller names a food that he or she does *not* like, you do nothing.

  STUDENT CALLER: *No me gusta el pescado.*

  Don't cover your picture of fish, even if you have one on your board.

- Call out "Lotería" when you have covered three spaces in a row horizontally, vertically, or diagonally. You'll be the winner. *¡Buena suerte!*
- The winner must correctly read back the names of the foods that the caller likes. For example:

  Te gusta el pescado. Te gustan las papas fritas. Te gustan las manzanas.

Para decir más

Here is some additional vocabulary that you might find useful for activities in this section.

la pizza
pizza

el perro caliente
hot dog

el tofu
tofu

el yogur
yogurt

el helado
ice cream

la galleta
cookie

el pastel
cake

Ahora lo sabes

Using what you have learned so far, can you:

- **tell what you and your family members eat and drink for dinner?**
- **tell what you like or don't like to eat and drink and why?**
- **describe two foods or drinks?**
- **compare and contrast times and menus for dinner and snacks in Spanish-speaking countries and in the United States?**

Answers: Actividades

1 Dialogues will vary, but look for adjective and verb agreement. Tell students that they also know how to say what they can or cannot and should or should not eat, and they can describe foods. Encourage them to use the full range of chapter vocabulary.

2 Menus will vary, but encourage students to use the full range of chapter vocabulary.

Answers: Ahora lo sabes

- (Yo) como / (Nosotros) comemos ___ en la cena. *(pp. 148–149, 156–157, 175)*
- (No) me gusta comer / beber ___ porque ___. *(pp. 148–149, 156–157)*
- Las judías verdes son buenas para la salud. ¡El café es horrible! *(Answers will vary.) (pp. 148–149, 156–157, 170)*
- Answers will vary, but students may mention that dinner in Spanish-speaking countries generally occurs later in the day than in the U.S. *(pp. 172–173)*

Writing Activities

Comm. Act. BLMs 4-4, 4-5

Examen de habilidades 2

sary: ___ *es bueno(a) para la salud. / Debes comer* ___. Assign the following roles: recorder, reporter, helper, and checker (make sure all students respond in sentences). Ask a member from each group to summarize. Later, have all groups compile a whole-class list. Which items were the most often mentioned?

Apply

Process Reading

For a description of process reading, see p. 60.

Teaching Suggestions

Mira la lectura: Monitor students so that this first reading is not intensive and focuses on confirming their predictions.

Infórmate: Make a chart showing the difference in ingredients between chocolate as prepared by the Aztecs and hot chocolate as prepared by the Europeans. Or make two drawings of the ingredients.

Answers
Antes de leer

Students should recognize the cognate *chocolate* in the title, and the illustrations should provide a clue as to the subject of the reading: the cocoa plant, pods and beans show the history of chocolate; the final illustration shows chocolate as students know it today.

Mira la lectura

Answers will vary.
Picture 1: *cacao;* picture 2: *cacao y varios tipos de chiles;* picture 3: *chocolate en polvo y agua o leche.* / Cognates: *conquistadores, productos, europea, importantes, aztecas, preparan, indios, ceremonias, religiosas, diferente, chocolate, Europa, transforma, líquida, populares, exclusivamente.*

¡Vamos a leer!

Antes de leer

STRATEGIES ➤ **Using prior knowledge**

Using the title and illustrations

Read the title and look at the pictures. What do they tell you about the reading selection? Try to predict what information the selection contains.

Mira la lectura

STRATEGY ➤ **Using cognates**

Read the selection quickly. Don't try to understand every word. Was your prediction based on the title and pictures correct?

Now look at the pictures again. Working with a group, find the words in the paragraph that name the things in the picture.

Look for cognates. With your group, make a list of as many as you can find.

EL CHOCOLATE

En el siglo XV los conquistadores llegan a América. Allí descubren muchos productos nuevos para la comida española y europea. El cacao es uno de los más importantes. Los aztecas usan el cacao para hacer la bebida *tchocolatl* (palabra azteca).

Los aztecas preparan el *tchocolatl* con cacao, maíz y varios tipos de chiles. Es una bebida muy fuerte que los indios beben en sus ceremonias religiosas. Pero el *tchocolatl* azteca es muy diferente del chocolate que bebemos hoy.

En Europa, el *tchocolatl* se transforma en una bebida más líquida y más dulce. En los siglos XVI y XVII el chocolate es una de las bebidas más populares de Europa. Hoy, el chocolate caliente se hace con chocolate en polvo, azúcar y agua o leche. En España, hay chocolaterías, donde sirven chocolate casi exclusivamente.

Options

Strategies for Reaching All Students

Spanish-Speaking Students

Un paso más Ex. 4-I

Students Needing Extra Help

Place the reading in context by reminding students that the chapter theme is food.
Antes de leer: Remind students to use context clues in the text along with the visuals to help them understand the reading.
Mira la lectura: You may wish to provide students with a brief overview of the history of the Mayas and Aztecs. Or, assign as an extra-credit assignment.
Infórmate: Go over the questions with students before you begin the reading. Emphasize that they don't need to know every word in order to understand the text.

Infórmate

STRATEGIES Using the illustrations

Using cognates

Now read the selection using the illustrations and cognates to help you.

1 How did the Aztecs prepare their *tchocolatl?* When did they drink it?

2 How did chocolate change when it was introduced into Europe?

Aplicación

1 Take a survey after school to find five people who like hot chocolate. Ask students of Spanish or other people who speak Spanish. Use the question *¿Te gusta el chocolate?* Write down their names, then report back to your teacher.

2 In your local grocery, find the names of at least three hot chocolate mixes. Choose one of the mixes and list the ingredients. What ingredients have been added since chocolate was introduced to Europe? Why do you think these ingredients were added?

3 Ask three family members or friends if they know where the word *chocolate* came from. Explain it to them if they don't know.

Infórmate

1 The Aztecs prepared *tchocolatl* with cocoa, corn, and different types of chiles. They drank it in religious ceremonies.

2 Answers may vary, but may include that the chocolate differed in taste, appearance, and usage. It was sweeter and not as thick.

Aplicación

1 Surveys will vary.

2 Ingredient lists will vary.

3 The word *chocolate* came from the Aztec word *tchocolatl.*

Multicultural Perspectives

With the influences and infusion of Hispanic cultures within the Americas, many restaurants cater to the varied tastes of their customers. Today, Hispanic cuisine can be classified as traditional or *nouveau,* vegetarian or *con carne,* Tex-Mex or Santa Fe, Salvadoran or Nicaraguan, and so on. Other establishments may feature only traditional Spanish dishes. Invite students to identify and describe other types of Hispanic cuisine.

Enrichment

Bring in a recipe for *mole* and show how it ties in with the Aztec recipe described in the text.

You can make authentic Mexican chocolate with commercial chocolate brands that already contain cinnamon, almond, and vanilla flavorings. Use a *molinillo,* a Mexican wooden beater. Heat two cups of water in an earthenware pot, if possible. As the water comes to a boil, break 3 ozs. of Mexican chocolate into it. Stir until the chocolate has melted. Boil it gently for about five minutes. Remove from the flame. Place the heavy end of the *molinillo* into the pot. Hold the stem between your palms and briskly rub your hands together around the handle, spinning the beater, until the chocolate is frothy.

Apply

Process Writing

For information regarding writing portfolios, see p. 62.

Teaching Suggestions

If possible, bring in a poster of the food groups to show as a model and have students make a poster showing similar items, but with the labels in Spanish. Students may wish to make original drawings or clip photographs from food magazines to make their posters more attractive.

For ease in managing step 4, ask students *not* to put their name on their paper. Have them put a number on their art work and a letter on their paragraph.

Critical Thinking: Synthesizing

Have small groups create an invitation to a dinner party that they will be hosting. Have other groups accept or decline the invitation. (Review Chap. 3 vocabulary related to accepting or declining invitations.)

Answers: ¡Vamos a escribir!

Paragraphs will vary. Check for correct use of verb forms and adjectives.

¡Vamos a escribir!

Imagine that you could have anything you wanted for a special birthday meal. What foods that you have learned would you choose? Afterward you will write a paragraph about such a meal.

1 First, think about the different courses of your meal and what you are going to drink. Copy the following chart on a sheet of paper and fill in the dishes you have chosen.

Primer plato	
Plato principal	
Verdura	
Bebida	

2 Now use your chart to help you write a first draft. The following expressions may be helpful to you as you write.

mi comida favorita
me gusta(n) / me encanta(n)
prefiero
voy a comer
sabroso(a)
primero, segundo

Show your draft to a partner. Listen to his or her suggestions for changes, and decide whether you agree.

3 Make a clean copy of your paragraph. Copy edit it using the following checklist:

- spelling
- capital letters
- punctuation
- adjective endings, for example: *Las naranjas son buenas para la salud.*

4 To share your work, make a collage or poster that shows the meal you have written about. Display all the artwork together and all the paragraphs together. Try to match the paragraphs to the collages and posters.

You might include your work in your student portfolio.

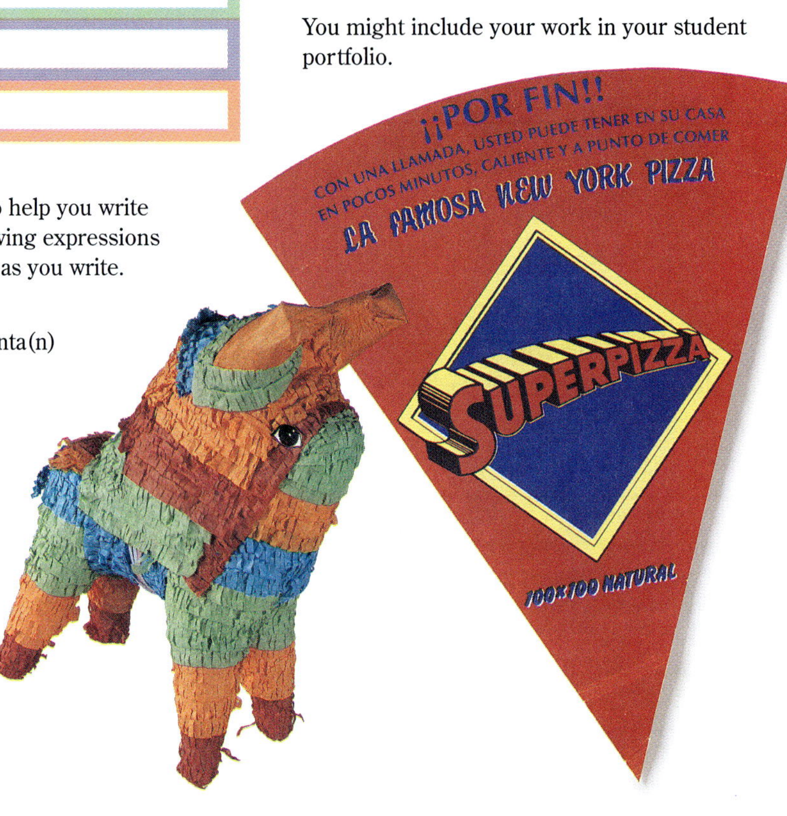

Options

Strategies for Reaching All Students

Spanish-Speaking Students

 **Un paso más Exs. 4-J, 4-K**

Students Needing Extra Help

Step 3: Have students use their Organizers to check spelling.

Resumen del capítulo 4

Use the vocabulary from this chapter to help you:

- tell what you like and don't like to eat and drink
- give reasons for your food and drink preferences
- say whether you are hungry or thirsty

to indicate hunger or thirst
tener hambre
tener sed

to describe meals
beber: (yo) bebo
(tú) bebes
comer: (yo) como
(tú) comes
el almuerzo
la cena
la comida
el desayuno
la merienda
en el desayuno / en el almuerzo / en la cena

to talk about foods
el arroz
el bistec
el cereal
la ensalada
las frutas
la manzana
la naranja
el plátano
la uva
la hamburguesa
el huevo
el jamón
el pan
el pan tostado
la papa
las papas al horno
las papas fritas
el pescado
el pollo
el queso
el sandwich (de jamón y queso)
la sopa
la sopa de pollo
la sopa de tomate
la sopa de verduras
las verduras
la cebolla
los guisantes
las judías verdes
la lechuga
el tomate
la zanahoria

to talk about drinks
las bebidas
el agua *(f.)*
el café
el jugo de naranja
la leche
la limonada
el refresco
el té
el té helado

to describe foods
bueno, -a (para la salud)
horrible
malo, -a (para la salud)
sabroso, -a

to express likes or preferences
más o menos
me encanta(n)
preferir: (yo) prefiero
(tú) prefieres

to express an opinion
Creo que sí.
Creo que no.
¡Qué asco!

to elicit agreement
¿verdad?

to refer to obligation
deber: (yo) debo
(tú) debes

to indicate frequency
nunca
siempre

to refer to something you cannot name
algo

to request precise information
¿Cuál(es)?

other useful words
son
unos, unas

Resumen 185

Summarize

Writing Activities

Mi portafolio

Test Generator

Cultural Notes

(p. 184, realia)
This take-out pizza menu from Barcelona proclaims that *barceloneses* can finally enjoy famous New York-style pizza, delivered hot in just a few minutes. The people at Superpizza only make pizza that is *cien por ciento natural.*

CAPÍTULO 5

THEME: FAMILY

SCOPE AND SEQUENCE Pages 186–227

COMMUNICATION

Topics

Family members

Personal physical characteristics

Age

Numbers 60–100

Objectives

To explain how names are formed in Spanish-speaking countries

To refer to family members

To ask and tell what someone's name is

To ask and tell how old someone is

To show possession

To tell what someone likes

To indicate number

To refer to people

To describe people, animals, and things

To name animals

CULTURE

The family

Spanish last names

GRAMMAR

El verbo tener

El verbo ser

Los adjetivos posesivos

Ancillaries available for use with Chapter 5

Multisensory/Technology

Overhead Transparencies, 30–35

Audio Tapes and CDs

Projects for Proficiency: Blackline Master Spanish Activities for Middle School Learners

Vocabulary Art Blackline Masters for Hands-On Learning, pp. 28–32

Classroom Crossword

Video

CD-ROM

Print

Practice Workbook, pp. 53–63

Writing, Audio & Video Activities, pp. 45–52, 77–79, 108–109

Communicative Activity Blackline Masters

Pair and Small Group Activities, pp. 36–41

Situation Cards, p. 42

Un paso más: Actividades para ampliar tu español, pp. 26–31

Assessment

Assessment Program

Pruebas, pp. 77–80, 85–87

Exámenes de habilidades, pp. 81–84, 88–91

Mi portafolio, pp. 92–93

Test Generator

Video still from Chap. 5

Cultural Overview

Family Ties

Strong family ties and allegiances are central to the social structures of many Spanish-speaking countries. The structure of family surnames, which contain both the mother's and the father's family names, reflects the great importance of the family unit. For example, if Sr. David Ramírez Tejeda is married to Sra. Ángela Díaz Contreras, their children will use the surname Ramírez Díaz.

Although strict gender-defined roles are gradually disappearing, vestiges of a patriarchal family structure can still be found in the different treatment of young men and women within some families. In working-class families, it is often assumed that the girls will help with their younger brothers and sisters and do other domestic work. Boys are largely exempt from these expectations. Boys often receive more education than girls do and have greater independence at an earlier age.

Until recent years, divorce was illegal in several Latin American countries. Although divorce is now possible, it remains socially unacceptable in many places and is often granted with stipulations, as the Church plays an integral part in the social outlook about remarriage. In Mexico, for example, a divorce judgment may stipulate that one or both parties may not remarry for a year or more. The Mexican Civil Code specifies such a restriction because marriage is viewed as the foundation of the family and is not to be entered into lightly or abandoned easily.

In many Spanish-speaking countries, it is considered a duty to spend time with one's family. People would almost never consider missing an important family event such as a baptism, wedding, or birthday. A family member's *compadre* / *comadre* and *padrino* / *madrina* would likely attend these events. Parties span several generations with all family members attending. Everyone from babies to grandparents can be seen at a party on Saturday night.

Good friends are also included in many family events. In many cases, friends are considered part of the family. Friendship ties, like family bonds, are strong. Relatives and friends will help each other out and are regularly a part of the daily lives of each other's families.

Introduce

Re-entry of Concepts

The following list represents words, expressions, and grammar topics re-entered from *El primer paso* to Chap. 4:

El primer paso
Calendar expressions
Numbers 0–31
Greetings

Chapter 1
Activities
Gustar expressions
Adjectives describing personality

Chapter 2
School supplies
School subjects
Numbers 32–59
Possession and need

Chapter 3
Pastimes
Destinations
Adverbs describing when things take place

Chapter 4
Likes or preferences
Opinions
Adjective agreement

Planning

Cross-Curricular Connections

Science Connection *(pp. 200–201)*

Have students list characteristics that they think are probably inherited (e.g., *ojos grises)* and not inherited *(antipático)*. They should verify the accuracy of their lists with the science teacher.

Math Connection *(pp. 200–201)*

Have students first predict then calculate the percentage of students in class that have brown (blue, green, etc.) eyes.

(For further cross-curricular activities, see the Conexiones *section on pp. 208–209.)*

Spanish in Your Community

Have students obtain a copy of a Spanish-language newspaper published in your community (if available). Ask them to look through the society section of this paper and find an announcement of a wedding, baptism, or funeral. Have them determine the family relationships mentioned in the article. As an alternative, have students look through the local phone book to see how

Capítulo 5

¿Cómo es tu familia?

OBJECTIVES

At the end of this chapter, you will be able to:

- **describe family members and friends**
- **ask and tell what someone's age is**
- **tell what other people like and do not like to do**
- **explain how last names are formed in Spanish-speaking countries**

Mural en San Francisco

Teaching Suggestions

See the Writing, Audio & Video Activities book for Writing Activities that you may elect to use throughout the chapter.

many people in their community have common Spanish surnames such as González, García, and Pérez. Have students discover more surnames as they look through the phone book. (Bring in any phone directories printed in Spanish as well.) Ask students to compile and compare the results to see how many names they found and which ones were common to everyone's lists.

Cultural Notes 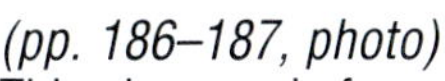

(pp. 186–187, photo)
This close-up is from Michael Ríos' 1982 mural, *ABC,* one of numerous murals in San Francisco's Mission District. Murals function at many levels in ethnic communities. They teach history, mark important events, build a sense of community, and lay a foundation for civic and personal pride. In this painting, Ríos constructs a positive message about the future. At the bottom is a line of people, partially depicted in this illustration, of all ages and races. Three giant, stacked ABC blocks tower above the people, surrounded by other images of human endeavor. Education, peace, and harmony without prejudice, suggests Ríos, are the building blocks of a great future.

Preview

Cultural Objective
• To talk about family members

 **¡Piénsalo bien!**

Play

 **Video Activity A**

Using the Video
This chapter's video focuses on family. Students will join our host in her own Guadalajara home and meet her family. Then they will accompany her to meet a family in nearby Tlaquepaque.

Show students segment one once through, then ask them to predict what this chapter's video will be about. Then have students watch the segment again several times. After the first time, have them brainstorm possible vocabulary and expressions they will need to talk about what they saw on the video. Ask students to identify: a) ways in which the Mexican families were similar to their own family, and b) ways in which the families were different from their own family. Use discretion if you use the latter (item b).

Video segment 1: For more teaching suggestions, see the Video Teacher's Guide.

¡Piénsalo bien!

Look at the photos and compare the families to your own. How many people are in your family? Which family members do you think make up a family? Do you consider your grandparents, uncles, aunts, and cousins as your "family" or are they just "relatives"? Do you all get together sometimes?

"Somos de Guatemala y todos los miembros de mi familia trabajan juntos."

Options

Strategies for Reaching All Students

Spanish-Speaking Students
Ask: *¿Qué es una familia? ¿Cómo es tu familia? ¿Es grande o pequeña? ¿Quiénes son?*

 **Un paso más Ex. 5-A**

Cultural Notes 

(p. 188, photo)
Mayan farmers believe that human life is nurtured by the natural world. The Mayas plant only the crops they will need to sustain themselves and their community. They take care to protect any trees, plants, and animals near their *milpa* or cornfield. A ceremony of thanks is performed at every harvest. Since the arrival of the Europeans nearly 500 years ago, the Mayas have

"Me llamo Juan Pablo y soy de México. Aquí estoy con mi familia para celebrar el cumpleaños de mi abuelo. Tiene 67 años."

Who do you think the *abuelo* is? Why do you think so?

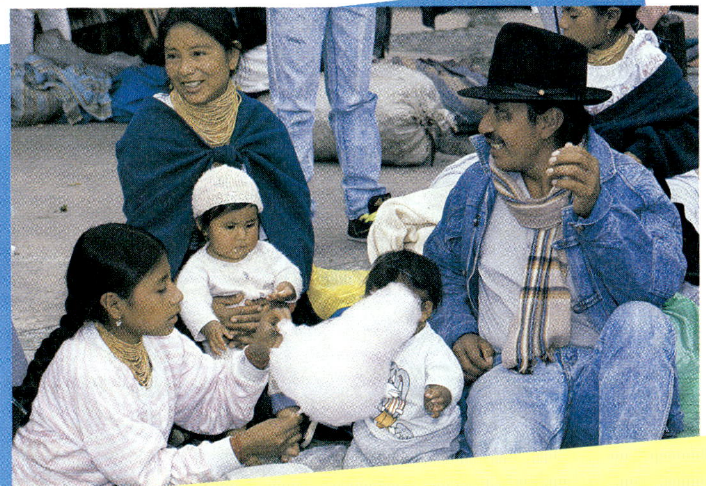

Otavalo, Ecuador

"A mis hermanitos les gusta mucho el algodón de azúcar. Son gemelos y tienen quince meses. Soy la hija mayor. Tengo trece años."

Teaching Suggestions

See the Projects for Proficiency BLMs for activity ideas that you may elect to use throughout the chapter.

To enhance the discussion of families, bring to class photographs of families from a variety of different cultures. Ask students to clip photos from old magazines and newspapers. Help them develop a bulletin-board display of the pictures, complete with Spanish captions.

Background Information

Be sensitive to the fact that many of your students' families may not be typical. Discuss what an American family today may look like: single parent, stepsisters and half brothers, and so on. Not all students will want to discuss this issue. Imaginary families or the family they would like to have when they become adults are alternative topics. Have students bring in magazine photos of a family. They then choose to be one of the people in the photo and base answers about their "family."

Answers: ¡Piénsalo bien!

(p. 188) Answers to inductive questions will vary.

(p. 189, top photo) See if students can guess the meaning of *abuelo* (grandfather) by using context clues. Can they associate *67 años* with the eldest man in the photo?

lost much of their native land. Presently in Guatemala, although around half of the population is indigenous, approximately 2 percent of the country's population owns about 78 percent of the land, creating an inequitable distribution of wealth. Many Mayan people must migrate to find work. During part of each year, they leave their native villages for employment on *fincas,* or ranches, near the coast.

(p. 189, bottom photo)
Otavalo, a village 59 miles north of Quito, bustles with activity at daybreak Saturday mornings as residents from the surrounding villages of Peguche, Agato, and Iluman gather to sell their hand-woven goods. Traditionally, bargaining in the market was expected to be conducted in a whisper. Shouting was strictly forbidden. All things change, however, and buyers and sellers today engage in raucous exchanges.

Present

Chapter Theme
Identifying family members

Communicative Objectives
- To refer to family members
- To ask and tell what someone's name is
- To ask and tell how old someone is
- To show possession
- To tell what someone likes
- To indicate number

Transparencies 30–31

Vocabulary Art BLMs

Pronunciation Tape 5-1

Vocabulario para conversar A

Play

Using the Video
Video segment 2: See the Video Teacher's Guide.

Video Activity B

Vocabulario para conversar

¿Cómo se llama tu hermano?

- Look at the family tree. Put your thumb on the picture of Raquel. As your teacher names each family member *(la abuela de Raquel)*, stretch your forefinger to touch that person's picture.
- When your teacher reads the age of one of the people, put your finger on the appropriate picture.
- Imagine that you are *yo* in the family tree. As your teacher describes a family relationship, such as *la hermana de tu padre*, point to the person who fits that description.

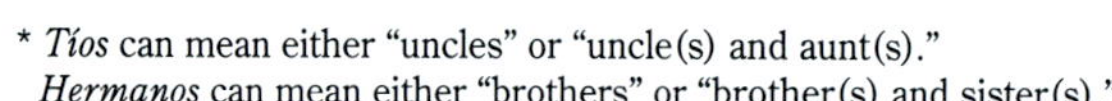
* *Tíos* can mean either "uncles" or "uncle(s) and aunt(s)."
Hermanos can mean either "brothers" or "brother(s) and sister(s)."

Options

Strategies for Reaching All Students

Students Needing Extra Help
Check to see that organizers are filled in correctly. Create a model organizer, and post it for availability.
Students often have difficulty reading a family tree, especially the reference to *yo*. Show them how the relationships change when *yo* becomes another person. For example, if Ana becomes *yo*, then Guadalupe becomes *la madre* and Dolores becomes *la tía*, and so on.

Enrichment
También necesitas. . . : Elicit from students the English word for which *único(a)* might be a cognate. Explain that *único(a)* has two meanings in Spanish: "only," as in *hijo(a) único(a)* and "unique," as in *¡Eres único(a)!*

Learning Spanish Through Action
STAGING VOCABULARY: *Nombren, Señalen*
MATERIALS: transparency of family tree in the *Vocabulario para conversar*
DIRECTIONS: Using the transparency, have pairs of students take the part of Raquel by pointing at the relative as you mention the relationship.

60 sesenta
61 sesenta y uno . . .
70 setenta
71 setenta y uno . . .
80 ochenta
81 ochenta y uno . . .
90 noventa
91 noventa y uno . . .
100 cien

¡No olvides!

Solo, -a = alone: *Generalmente voy al parque solo(a).*

Sólo = only: *María sólo va al parque.*

También necesitas . . .

el hijo / la hija	*son / daughter*
el hijo único / la hija única	*only child*
¿Cómo se llama?	*What is his / her name?*
Se llama ___.	*His / her name is ___.*
¿Cómo se llaman?	*What are their names?*
Se llaman ___.	*Their name(s) is (are) ___.*
el nombre	*name*
¿Cuántos años tiene ___?	*How old is ___?*
Tiene ___ años.	*He / she is ___ years old.*
su	*his, her*
de	*of*
sólo	*only*

¿Y qué quiere decir . . . ?
los hijos
(A él / ella) le gusta(n) ___.
(A él / ella) le encanta(n) ___.

Grammar Preview

Su and *de* are presented here lexically. The explanation of possessive adjectives appears in the grammar section on p. 219.

Teaching Suggestions

Point out the similarities between *abuelo / abuela, tío / tía,* etc.

También necesitas . . . : Point out that *único(a)* is used with nouns and age is expressed with *tener*—to "have" so many years. Mention that after *ser,* the article *el / la* is not used with *hijo(a) único(a).*

Class Starter Review

On the day following initial presentation of vocabulary, you might begin the class with one of these activities:

1) Use the transparency of a family tree with one person labeled *yo.* (You may wish to use the family tree from the Projects for Proficiency BLMs.) Point to other members of the family and ask individual students who these relatives are in relation to *yo.* On the following day, label a different person *yo.* On the third day, arrange pictures of famous people or families from TV programs in a family tree on the chalkboard and do the same activity.

2) Have pairs of students find out the name of at least one member of each other's family.

Practice

Re-enter / Recycle
Ex. 2: numbers 0–31 from *El primer paso,* numbers 32–59 from Chap. 2

Reteach / Review: Definite & Indefinite Articles
Do a quick practice exercise to review definite articles by naming a noun and calling on individuals to give the correct definite or indefinite article.

Teaching Suggestions
Point out to students that they will be using the family tree on p. 193 for Exs. 1–2.

Answers: Empecemos a conversar
1 ESTUDIANTE A

a. ¿Cómo se llama el hermano de Raquel?
b. . . . el tío . . .
c. . . . la tía . . .
d. . . . el abuelo . . .
e. . . . el primo . . .
f. . . . la prima . . .
g. Questions will vary.

ESTUDIANTE B

a. Se llama Marcos.
b. . . . Juan Carlos.
c. . . . Guadalupe.
d. . . . Andrés.
e. . . . Jaime.
f. . . . Ana.
g. Answers will vary.

Empecemos a conversar

With a partner, take turns being *Estudiante A* and *Estudiante B*. Use the words that are cued or given in the boxes to replace the underlined words in the example. [lightbulb] means you can make your own choices. When it is your turn to be *Estudiante B*, try to answer truthfully.

1 la hermana
A —*¿Cómo se llama la hermana de Raquel?*
B —*Se llama Carolina.*

Estudiante A | **Estudiante B**

a. el hermano
b. el tío
c. la tía
d. el abuelo
e. el primo
f. la prima
g. 

¡No olvides!
Use *el* with a masculine noun and *la* with a feminine noun.

2 Marcos
A —*¿Cuántos años tiene Marcos?*
B —*Tiene diez años.*

Estudiante A | **Estudiante B**

a. Jaime
b. la madre de Ana
c. la hija de Juan Carlos
d. el hijo de Guadalupe
e. el padre de Raquel
f. el hermano de Carolina
g. 

Options

Strategies for Reaching All Students

Spanish-Speaking Students
Exs. 1–2: Pair bilingual and non-bilingual students.

Students Needing Extra Help
Ex. 1: Some students may need a review for family relationship words in English. Go over these words before doing the exercise.

Enrichment
Ex. 2: After completing this exercise, have pairs of students ask and tell each other their names and ages.

2 ESTUDIANTE A

a. ¿Cuántos años tiene Jaime?
b. . . . la madre de Ana?
c. . . . la hija de Juan Carlos?
d. . . . el hijo de Guadalupe?
e. . . . el padre de Raquel?
f. . . . el hermano de Carolina?
g. Questions will vary.

ESTUDIANTE B

a. Tiene catorce años.
b. . . . cuarenta y ocho . . .
c. . . . dieciséis . . .
d. . . . catorce . . .
e. . . . cuarenta y dos . . .
f. . . . diez . . .
g. Answers will vary.

Options

Strategies for Reaching All Students

Spanish-Speaking Students
Exs. 3–4: Pair bilingual and non-bilingual students.

In Exercises 3 and 4, ask each other about your own family members, or make up families to talk about.

3 A —*¿Tienes hermanos?*
B —*Sí, tengo un hermano y una hermana.*
o: *No, no tengo hermanos. Soy hijo(a) único(a).*

A —*¿Cómo se llama(n)?*
B —*Mi hermano se llama Julio y mi hermana se llama Marta.*

Estudiante A **Estudiante B**

4 A —*¿Qué le gusta hacer a tu primo?*
B —*Le gusta jugar videojuegos.*
o: *Le encanta jugar videojuegos.*

Estudiante A **Estudiante B**

5 A —*¿Qué les gusta hacer a tus tíos?*
B —*Les gusta jugar tenis.*
o: *Les encanta jugar tenis.*

Estudiante A **Estudiante B**

Practice

Re-enter / Recycle

Exs. 4–5: activities from Chap. 1, pastimes from Chap. 3

Answers: Empecemos a conversar

3–5 Dialogues will vary.

Cultural Notes

(p. 194, realia)
Mi familia covers the 1920s, 1950s, and 1980s as it recounts the history of a family. The story begins with José Sánchez arriving in California from Mexico. He meets and marries María, who is also from Mexico, and they start a family. María becomes a U.S. citizen, but she is wrongfully deported to Mexico. Carrying her new baby, she makes a harrowing trip back to her family in California. By the 1950s, José and María's children have entered adulthood, following different life paths. In the 1980s the family continues to deal with the complexities of life, including a jail sentence for the youngest son.

Apply

Re-enter / Recycle

Ex. 3: activities from Chap. 1, pastimes from Chap. 3
Ex. 5: numbers 0–31 from *El primer paso*

Teaching Suggestions

Ex. 1: If students need help in determining the words for family relationships, have them refer to the family tree on p. 190 for a visual.

Answers: Empecemos a leer y a escribir

1 a. hermano, b. abuelos, c. primo, d. tías, e. abuela, f. prima

2 Family trees and paragraphs will vary.

Empecemos a leer y a escribir

Responde en español.

1 On a sheet of paper, complete each sentence with the correct word.

a. El hijo de mis padres es mi ___ .
b. Los padres de mi madre son mis ___ .
c. El hermano de mi prima es mi ___ .
d. Las hermanas de mi madre son mis ___ .

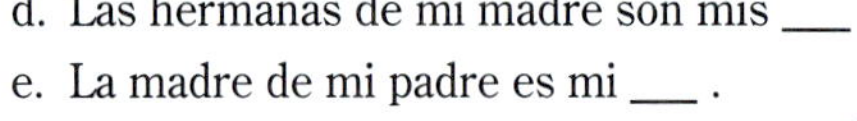

e. La madre de mi padre es mi ___ .
f. La hija de mi tía es mi ___ .

2 Look at the photograph and read the names and descriptions of the people. Imagine that these are members of your family. Make a family tree showing how you fit in, then write a brief paragraph describing your relationship to at least three of the people.

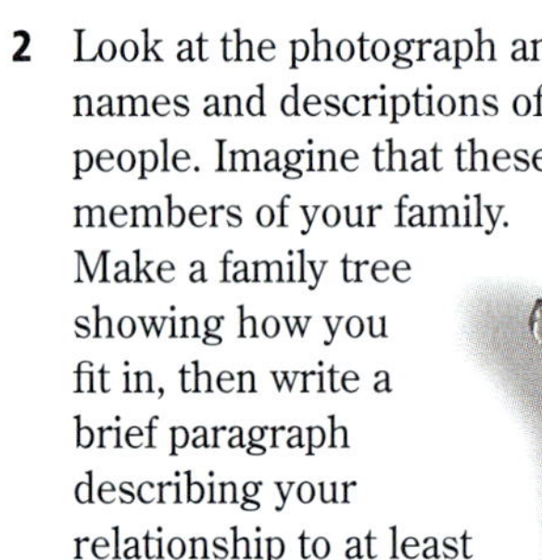

a. Nora (32), madre
b. Ernesto (34), padre
c. María Teresa Girón de Hernández (65), abuela
d. Jesús Hernández (69), abuelo
e. Leonardo (4), hijo
f. Úrsula María (6), hija

Options

Strategies for Reaching All Students

Spanish-Speaking Students

Ask volunteers to bring in family photos and describe the people to their classmates. Or, have them make a collage of these photos.

 **Un paso más Ex. 5-B**

Students Needing Extra Help

Ex. 5: For additonal practice, have students write how many family members they have in these categories: *tíos, primos, abuelos.*

Enrichment

Ex. 3: To extend this exercise, have students write about three things that they and another family member *don't* like to do.

3 Mention at least three interests you share with another family member. For example:

A mi hermana le gusta practicar deportes. A mí también.

4 ¿Hay un hijo único en tu familia? ¿Quién es?

5 ¿Tienes primos? ¿Cómo se llaman? ¿Cuántos años tienen?

También se dice

"Aquí ves el Palacio de Cristal, uno de mis lugares favoritos en El Retiro."

3–5 Responses will vary, but encourage students to use chapter vocabulary.

 **Practice Wkbk. 5-1, 5-2**

 **Audio Activity 5.1**

 **Writing Activities**

 **Pruebas 5-1, 5-2**

 **Comm. Act. BLM 5-1**

Cultural Notes

(p. 197, photo)
El Parque del Retiro in Madrid covers more than 350 acres of land. The *estanque* (ornamental lake) within the park is a favorite place for families to visit and rent rowboats. Around the lake's shoreline are the Crystal Palace and Velázquez exposition centers. The Crystal Palace was built in 1887 in the *art nouveau* style, to honor the Philippines, then a possession of Spain. Also along the rim of the lake is a monument (circa 1922) erected to honor King Alfonso XII.

Present & Apply

Cultural Objective

- To explain how names are formed in Spanish-speaking countries

Answers

Answers to inductive questions will vary, but students may mention that the order of the names is similar (first name, last name) and that the names themselves seem common: Mariela, Ramón, Philip, etc. Surnames are Cohen, Shade, Aramburu, Jiménez; Baby's surnames: Cohen Shade; Father's surnames: Cohen Aramburu; Mother's surnames: Shade Jiménez; Paternal grandfather's surname: Cohen; Paternal grandmother's surname: Aramburu; Maternal grandfather's surname: Shade; Maternal grandmother's surname: Jiménez; Surnames of witnesses: Padilla Ramírez, Uriel Sierra; Judge's surnames: González Salgado.

Answers: La cultura desde tu perspectiva

1 First names for the twins will vary, but their last name would be Bernal Rodríguez.

Mira los nombres del bebé y de sus padres en el acta de nacimiento. ¿En qué son similares a tu nombre y a los nombres de tus amigos(as)? ¿En qué son diferentes?

Which names on the birth certificate do you think are surnames? (Your last name is your surname.) Here are some of the main differences between the system used for naming people in the United States and the one used in Spanish-speaking countries.

In Spanish-speaking countries, a person's full name consists of a first name *(nombre)* followed by two surnames—the father's surname *(apellido paterno)* and then the mother's surname *(apellido materno)*. For example, in the case of this baby, Mariela is her *nombre*, Cohen is her *apellido paterno*, and Shade is her *apellido materno*.

A person's full name is used on all official documents: birth certificates, school records, passports, and identification cards. However, if you met Mariela at a party, she would probably introduce herself as just Mariela Cohen. In some cases, though, it is important to know both last names. For example, a phone book could include several people with the same first and last names. The only way to tell them apart is by looking at their *apellidos maternos*.

La cultura desde tu perspectiva

1 Imagine that Carolina Rodríguez Garza and Julio Bernal Ávalos got married and had twins, a boy and a girl. Think of a name for each, and write out their full names.

2 Using the naming method described, tell what your full name would be. What are some ways this naming method might be helpful?

Madre campesina (1929), David Alfaro Siqueiros

Options

Strategies for Reaching All Students

Students Needing Extra Help

Students will need an extra visual to understand the concept of adding and dropping names. Either make an invitation on cardboard or on the chalkboard, color-coding the names that carry through or that are dropped. Or, ask volunteers to hold up name cards on which you have written the Spanish first and last names of an imaginary married couple. Then, ask students to write the names of any children this couple may have.

Cultural Notes 

(p. 198, photo)
David Alfaro Siqueiros (1896–1974) is often cited as one of the three greatest Mexican muralists of this century, the others being Diego Rivera and José Clemente Orozco. Siqueiros was part of a group of socially committed artists working in Mexico and the U.S. in the 1930s. While Siqueiros experi-

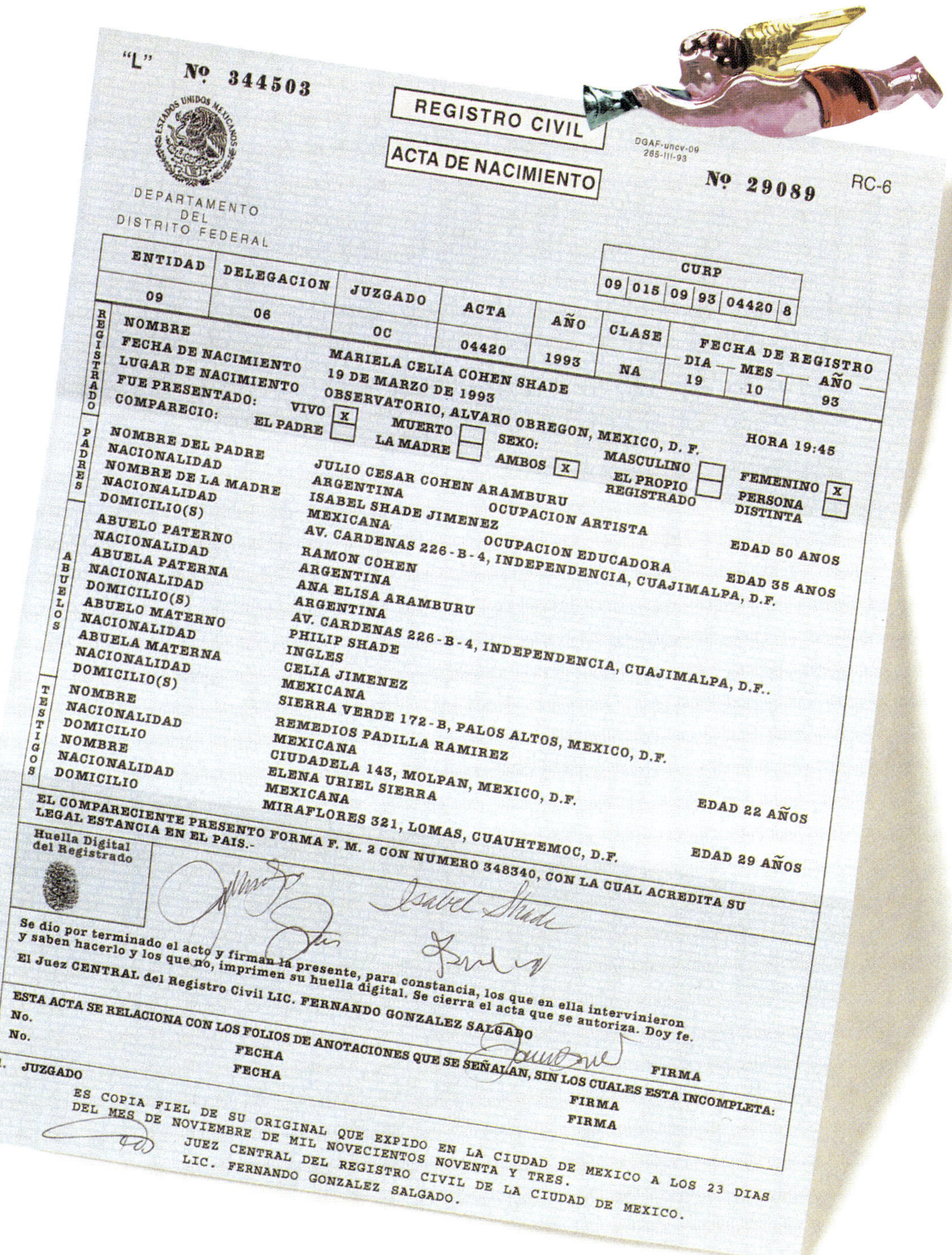

"L" Nº 344503

ESTADOS UNIDOS MEXICANOS

DEPARTAMENTO DEL DISTRITO FEDERAL

REGISTRO CIVIL

ACTA DE NACIMIENTO

DGAF-uncv-09 285-III-93

Nº 29089 RC-6

ENTIDAD	DELEGACION	JUZGADO	ACTA	AÑO	CLASE	FECHA DE REGISTRO DIA	MES	AÑO
09	06	OC	04420	1993	NA	19	10	93

CURP 09 015 09 93 04420 8

REGISTRADO

NOMBRE MARIELA CELIA COHEN SHADE
FECHA DE NACIMIENTO 19 DE MARZO DE 1993
LUGAR DE NACIMIENTO OBSERVATORIO, ALVARO OBREGON, MEXICO, D.F. HORA 19:45
FUE PRESENTADO: VIVO [X] MUERTO [ ] SEXO: MASCULINO [ ] FEMENINO [X]
COMPARECIO: EL PADRE [ ] LA MADRE [ ] AMBOS [X] EL PROPIO REGISTRADO [ ] PERSONA DISTINTA [ ]

PADRES

NOMBRE DEL PADRE JULIO CESAR COHEN ARAMBURU
NACIONALIDAD ARGENTINA OCUPACION ARTISTA EDAD 50 ANOS
NOMBRE DE LA MADRE ISABEL SHADE JIMENEZ
NACIONALIDAD MEXICANA OCUPACION EDUCADORA EDAD 35 ANOS
DOMICILIO(S) AV. CARDENAS 226-B-4, INDEPENDENCIA, CUAJIMALPA, D.F.

ABUELOS

ABUELO PATERNO RAMON COHEN
NACIONALIDAD ARGENTINA
ABUELA PATERNA ANA ELISA ARAMBURU
NACIONALIDAD ARGENTINA
DOMICILIO(S) AV. CARDENAS 226-B-4, INDEPENDENCIA, CUAJIMALPA, D.F..
ABUELO MATERNO PHILIP SHADE
NACIONALIDAD INGLES
ABUELA MATERNA CELIA JIMENEZ
NACIONALIDAD MEXICANA
DOMICILIO(S) SIERRA VERDE 172-B, PALOS ALTOS, MEXICO, D.F.

TESTIGOS

NOMBRE REMEDIOS PADILLA RAMIREZ
NACIONALIDAD MEXICANA
DOMICILIO CIUDADELA 143, MOLPAN, MEXICO, D.F. EDAD 22 AÑOS
NOMBRE ELENA URIEL SIERRA
NACIONALIDAD MEXICANA
DOMICILIO MIRAFLORES 321, LOMAS, CUAUHTEMOC, D.F. EDAD 29 AÑOS

EL COMPARECIENTE PRESENTO FORMA F. M. 2 CON NUMERO 348340, CON LA CUAL ACREDITA SU LEGAL ESTANCIA EN EL PAIS.-

Huella Digital del Registrado

Se dio por terminado el acto y firman la presente, para constancia, los que en ella intervinieron y saben hacerlo y los que no, imprimen su huella digital. Se cierra el acta que se autoriza. Doy fe.

El Juez CENTRAL del Registro Civil LIC. FERNANDO GONZALEZ SALGADO

ESTA ACTA SE RELACIONA CON LOS FOLIOS DE ANOTACIONES QUE SE SEÑALAN, SIN LOS CUALES ESTA INCOMPLETA:

No. FECHA FIRMA
No. FECHA FIRMA
1. JUZGADO FIRMA

ES COPIA FIEL DE SU ORIGINAL QUE EXPIDO EN LA CIUDAD DE MEXICO A LOS 23 DIAS DEL MES DE NOVIEMBRE DE MIL NOVECIENTOS NOVENTA Y TRES.
JUEZ CENTRAL DEL REGISTRO CIVIL DE LA CIUDAD DE MEXICO.
LIC. FERNANDO GONZALEZ SALGADO.

2 At your discretion, allow students to use other surnames, for example, in case of adoption or remarriage. / Answers will vary, but students may say that having two surnames would help distinguish between people that have the same name. Including both parents' surnames stresses the importance of the mother in the family.

Using Realia

Point out to students that the main part of the birth certificate deals with information on the child, parents, grandparents, and witnesses. See if they can pick out cognates in the document. Can they find the words meaning "fingerprint"? *(huella digital)*

mented freely with technique and imagery during his long career, most of his work revolved around his political ideals. *Madre campesina* refers to the indigenous or *mestizo* peoples of Mexico. He uses a monumental style intended to evoke a feeling of solidness and sculptural form.

(p. 199, realia)
According to the Mexican civil code *(El Código Civil)*, a birth must be reported to the local magistrate *(Juez del Registro Civil)* at the local registry *(el Registro Civil)* no later than six months after the date of birth. The birth certificate *(Acta de nacimiento)* must include the signatures of two witnesses to confirm the date, time, and place of birth. Each official copy of a birth certificate must include a notarized statement of verification at the end of the document.

Present

Chapter Theme
Describing friends and family

Communicative Objectives
- To refer to family members
- To refer to people
- To describe people, animals, and things
- To name animals
- To refer to animals and things
- To show possession
- To indicate number

Transparencies 32–33

Vocabulary Art BLMs

Pronunciation Tape 5-2

Vocabulario para conversar B

Play

Step

Using the Video
Video segment 2: See the Video Teacher's Guide.

Video Activity B

Sección 2

Vocabulario para conversar

¿Cómo es tu abuelo?

- As your teacher reads each description, put your finger on the corresponding person or animal.
- As your teacher reads each eye or hair color, raise your hand if it matches yours.
- As your teacher reads each description, make a thumbs up gesture if the description fits you and a thumbs down gesture if it does not.

Options

Strategies for Reaching All Students

Learning Spanish Through Action
STAGING VOCABULARY: *Dibujen, Señalen*
1) MATERIALS: transparency of people in the *Vocabulario para conversar* or pictures from magazines
DIRECTIONS: Using the transparency or magazine pictures, have students point to the person as you describe eye and hair color and other physical characteristics.
2) MATERIALS: colored chalk
DIRECTIONS: Have volunteers go to the chalkboard to draw people as you describe them. Use pictures of famous people as models for your descriptions.

También necesitas . . .

mayor, *pl.* mayores	*older*	ser	*to be*
menor, *pl.* menores	*younger*	tener	*to have*
guapo, -a	*handsome, good-looking*		
cariñoso, -a	*affectionate, loving*		
simpático, -a	*nice, friendly*		
tiene	*he / she has*		
todos, -as (*pl.*)	*everyone*		
(no . . .) nadie	*nobody*		
que	*that, who*		
¿Quiénes?*	*Who?*		

¿Y qué quiere decir . . . ?
la persona
antipático, -a
atractivo, -a
inteligente

*We usually use *¿Quiénes?* instead of *¿Quién?* if we know or expect that the answer will be more than one person.

Grammar Preview

Tiene is presented here lexically. The complete paradigm of *tener* appears on p. 211.

Teaching Suggestions

Explain that although *hombre* and *mujer* are the terms for man and woman, Spanish speakers usually say *un señor* and *una señora* when speaking about someone whom they don't know.

In addition to the adjectives presented in this chapter, review the adjectives from Chap. 1.

Tell students that we say *Tiene el pelo rubio, castaño, negro,* etc., but we say *Es pelirrojo(a).*

Explain that *ojos negros* literally means "black eyes," but the phrase refers to eyes darker than brown. Likewise, this also refers to hair color: *pelo negro.*

One way of approaching this vocabulary is to categorize it in the Organizer under "Words That Describe People" according to eyes, hair, etc., or by opposites.

Class Starter Review

On the day following initial presentation of vocabulary, you might begin the class with this activity: Have students state descriptions of two people in their families, including hair and eye color and personality traits. For further practice, have students describe their classmates in the same manner, without identifying them. Have others guess who they are.

Practice

Reteach / Review: Adjectives

Do a quick drill in which you name an adjective and call on individual students to give you its plural form.

Teaching Suggestions

Ex. 2: Before doing this exercise, ask students similar questions about their families. Explain responses.

Ex. 4: Before students do this exercise, have them describe each other. Then, to provide a model, describe for students someone in the family tree in the first *Vocabulario para conversar*. Finally, have students describe their family members.

Answers: Empecemos a conversar

1 ESTUDIANTE A

a. ¿Cómo se llaman los gemelos?
b. ¿Cómo se llama el hombre joven?
c. ¿Y cómo se llama la mujer vieja?
d. ¿Quiénes tienen ojos azules? ¿Cómo se llaman?
e. ¿Quién tiene pelo canoso? ¿Y pelo castaño?
f. ¿Quiénes tienen pelo rubio?
g. ¿Quién tiene ojos marrones?
h. ¿Cómo es Bandido? Y Muñeca, ¿cómo es?
i. ¿Es grande o pequeño Tigre? Y Nico, ¿cómo es?
j. ¿Cómo es Alicia?

Empecemos a conversar

1

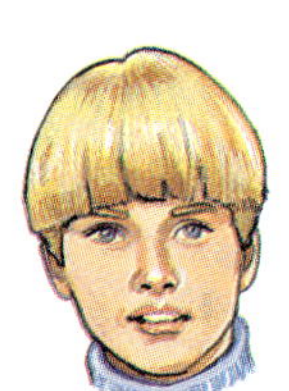

Pablo y Pedro

Adela

¡No olvides!

To make an adjective plural, add *-s* if it ends in a vowel and *-es* if it ends in a consonant:
inteligente → *inteligentes*
menor → *menores*

Bandido

Muñeca

Evangelina

Verónica y Mónica

Santiago

Tomás

Nico

Tigre

Alicia

Estudiante A

a. ¿Cómo se llaman los gemelos?
b. ¿Cómo se llama el hombre joven?
c. ¿Y cómo se llama la mujer vieja?
d. ¿Quiénes tienen ojos azules?¿Cómo se llaman?
e. ¿Quién tiene pelo canoso? ¿Y pelo castaño?
f. ¿Quiénes tienen pelo rubio?
g. ¿Quién tiene ojos marrones?
h. ¿Cómo es Bandido? Y Muñeca, ¿cómo es?
i ¿Es grande o pequeño Tigre? Y Nico, ¿cómo es?
j. ¿Cómo es Alicia?

Estudiante B

Options

Strategies for Reaching All Students

Students Needing Extra Help

Have students use their Organizers from previous chapters.

Enrichment

Ex. 4: Have students also ask each other about other classmates and teachers.
Use the grid template from the Projects for Proficiency BLMs and create a "scavenger hunt" game card in which students can draw and color people with different eye and hair color, height, and so on.

2 **ojos negros** A —*En la clase, ¿quiénes tienen ojos negros?*
B —*María y Luis.*
o: *Nadie (tiene ojos negros).*

Estudiante A **Estudiante B**

a. ojos verdes
b. ojos marrones
c. pelo castaño
d. pelo rubio
e. pelo canoso
f. 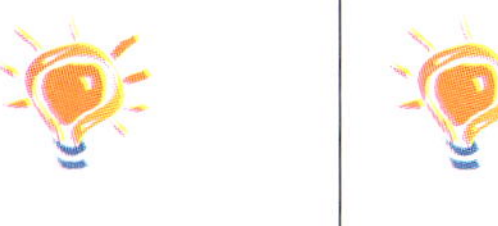

3 **gemelos(as)** A —*¿Hay gemelas en la clase?*
B —*Sí, Clara y Claudia.*
o: *No, no hay.*

Estudiante A **Estudiante B**

a. personas rubias
b. personas pelirrojas 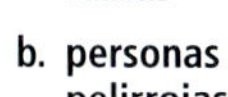
c. 

¡No olvides!

You have already seen *hay* in the expression *¿Cuántos(as) ___ hay?*

In Exercise 4, ask your partner about five family members or pets, real or imaginary.

4 A —*¿Cómo es tu hermano mayor?*
B —*Es alto, inteligente y simpático. Es pelirrojo y tiene ojos verdes.*
o: *No tengo hermanos.*

Estudiante A **Estudiante B**

ESTUDIANTE B
a. Se llaman Pablo y Pedro y Verónica y Mónica.
b. Se llama Santiago.
c. Se llama Evangelina.
d. Los gemelos tienen ojos azules. / Se llaman Pablo y Pedro, y Verónica y Mónica.
e. Evangelina tiene pelo canoso. / Tomás tiene pelo castaño.
f. Santiago, Pablo y Pedro tienen pelo rubio.
g. Santiago tiene ojos marrones.
h. Es un perro feo. / Es un perro bonito.
i. Es grande. / Nico es un gato pequeño.
j. Tiene ojos grises y pelo negro.

2 ESTUDIANTE A
a. En la clase, ¿quién(es) tiene(n) ojos verdes?
b. . . . ojos marrones?
c. . . . pelo castaño?
d. . . . pelo rubio?
e. . . . pelo canoso?
f. Questions will vary.

ESTUDIANTE B
a.–f. Answers will vary.

3 ESTUDIANTE A
a. ¿Hay personas rubias en la clase?
b. ¿Hay personas pelirrojas . . .
c. Questions will vary.

ESTUDIANTE B
a.–c. Answers will vary.

4 Dialogues will vary, but look for adjective agreement.

Apply

Answers: Empecemos a leer y a escribir

1 a. no, b. sí, c. no

2–4 Statements will vary, but encourage students to use the full range of chapter vocabulary. Look for adjective agreement.

 **Practice Wkbk. 5-3, 5-4**

 **Audio Activity 5.2**

 **Pruebas 5-3, 5-4**

 **Comm. Act. BLM 5-2**

Empecemos a leer y a escribir

Responde en español.

1 Elena wrote this letter to introduce herself to a cousin she had never met. On a separate piece of paper, write *sí* or *no* in response to the statements about the letter.

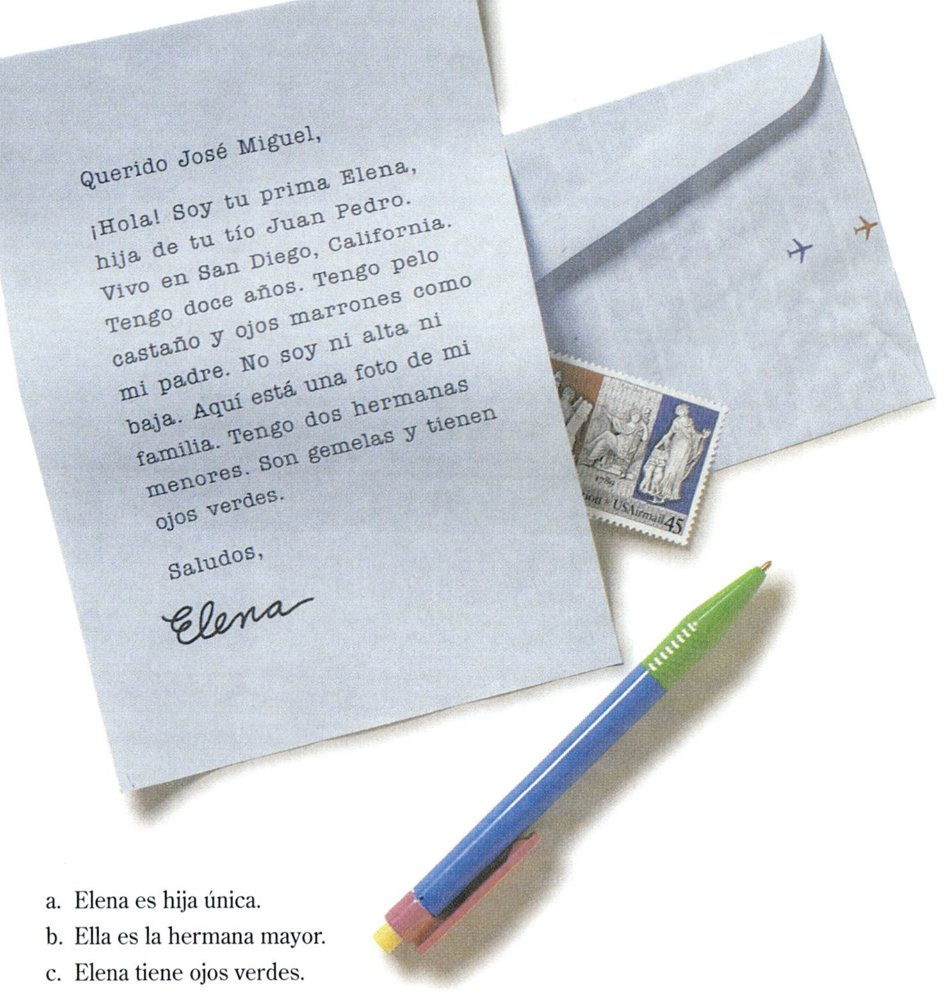

Querido José Miguel,

¡Hola! Soy tu prima Elena, hija de tu tío Juan Pedro. Vivo en San Diego, California. Tengo doce años. Tengo pelo castaño y ojos marrones como mi padre. No soy ni alta ni baja. Aquí está una foto de mi familia. Tengo dos hermanas menores. Son gemelas y tienen ojos verdes.

Saludos,

Elena

a. Elena es hija única.
b. Ella es la hermana mayor.
c. Elena tiene ojos verdes.

Options

Strategies for Reaching All Students

Spanish-Speaking Students

Ask students to write a letter introducing themselves to the class.

 **Un paso más Exs. 5-C, 5-D, 5-E**

2 Imagine that you are one of Elena's cousins and that you have a brother and sister. Reread Elena's letter, then answer it giving similar information about yourself and your brother and sister.

3 Describe a un(a) compañero(a). Menciona su edad, color de pelo, color de ojos y dos características personales.

4 Ahora describe a una persona famosa que admiras: *La persona que admiro se llama . . .*

Una familia mexicana

También se dice

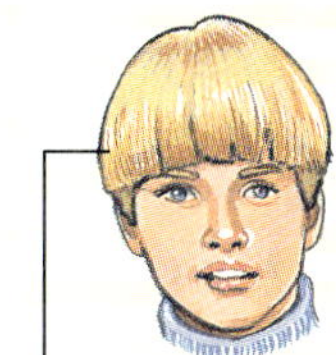

güero, -a

los ojos de color café

colorín, colorina

Practice

Teaching Suggestions

Ex. 1: Model a second example. Put paper numbers on some students in class. Have the rest of the class describe them according to the example.

Answers: Comuniquemos

1 a. A —¿Cómo es George King?
B —Tiene ojos marrones y pelo castaño.
A —¡Ah! George es el número noventa y cuatro.

b. A —. . . Juan Enríquez?
B —. . . ojos azules y pelo negro.
A —. . . Juan . . . cincuenta y cinco.

c. A —. . . John Green?
B —. . . ojos grises y pelo castaño.
A —. . . John . . . ochenta y nueve.

d. A —. . . Hal Jensen?
B —. . . ojos azules y pelo rubio.
A —. . . Hal . . . setenta y dos.

e. A —. . . Sean Morrow?
B —. . . ojos verdes y es pelirrojo.
A —. . . Sean . . . setenta y ocho.

f. A —. . . Felipe del Castillo?
B —. . . ojos marrones y pelo negro.
A —. . . Felipe . . . sesenta y siete.

g. A —. . . Matt Brown?
B —. . . ojos marrones y pelo rubio.
A —. . . Matt . . . ochenta y dos.

Here's another opportunity for you and your partner to use the vocabulary you've just learned.

1 These pictures of the football team are for the school yearbook. Before you can write the captions, you must identify the people in the pictures. Call the coach for help. Take turns with your partner playing the roles of the yearbook writer (A) and the coach (B).

Raja Patel

A —*¿Cómo es Raja Patel?*
B —*Tiene ojos negros y pelo negro.*
A —*¡Ah! Raja es el número sesenta y tres.*

a. George King	b. Juan Enríquez	c. John Green

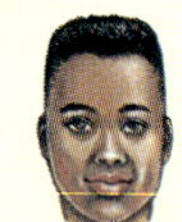

d. Hal Jensen	e. Sean Morrow	f. Felipe del Castillo	g. Matt Brown

Options

Strategies for Reaching All Students

Spanish-Speaking Students

Ex. 1: Have pairs of students work together on this exercise and then present it to the whole class.
Ex. 2: Pair bilingual and non-bilingual students.

 **Un paso más Exs. 5-F, 5-G**

Students Needing Extra Help

Ex. 2: Have pictures of dogs and cats available to describe with true statements. Then make up some false statements. Keep them separate at first.
Have students use their Organizers for *perezoso, prudente,* etc. (Chap. 1); *ir de pesca, la piscina,* etc. (Chap. 3); *hambre, sed, bistec, pescado,* etc. (Chap. 4). Model the responses.
Ahora lo sabes: Have students write this section so that they can keep track of their progress. Expand on these concepts.

2 Describe either the cat or the dog to your partner. To make sure your partner is listening, make two or three false statements. Your partner will correct you. Then your partner will describe the other animal to you. For example:

Se llama . . . *(No) es . . .* *(No) le gusta . . .* *Tiene . . .*

3 Help your partner fill in a chart like this one by telling about a real or imagined relative. Your partner will report to the class:

El primo de Juana se llama Mark. Tiene...

	Nombre	Edad	Color de pelo	Color de ojos	Característica personal
Primo	Mark	12	castaño	azules	alto

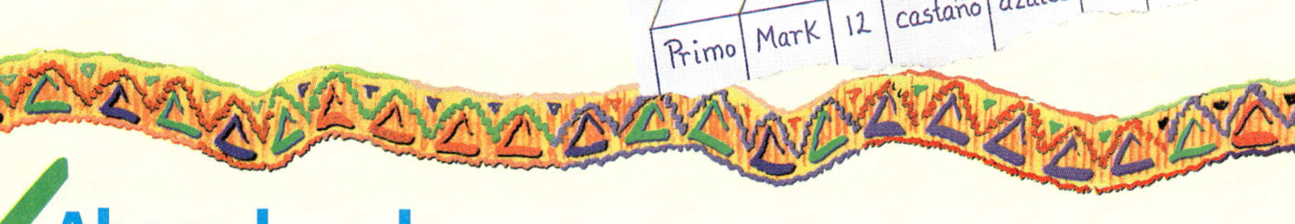

✓Ahora lo sabes

Using what you have learned so far, can you:

- **tell who and how old the members of your family are?**
- **describe the members of your family?**
- **tell what they like and don't like to do?**

2 *Statements will vary, but may include:* Se llama Chispa. Es grande (feo, marrón, inteligente, cariñoso, atrevido). No es prudente. Le gusta nadar (el bistec). Tiene ojos azules (hambre, dos años).

Se llama Michi. Es pequeño (bonito, guapo, negro, prudente). No es inteligente. Le gusta el pescado. Tiene ojos verdes (cuatro años).

3 Statements will vary.

Answers: Ahora lo sabes

(Answers will vary.)

- Mi abuelo Andrés tiene 75 años. *(pp. 190–191)*
- Mi hermana es baja. Tiene ojos negros y pelo castaño. *(pp. 190–191, 200–201)*
- A mi hermano le encanta el fútbol pero no le gusta el béisbol. *(pp. 190–191)*

Audio Activity 5.3

Writing Activities

Examen de habilidades 1

Enrichment

As a written assignment, have students tell what each member of their family likes to do on the weekend, where they go to do it, and with whom they go.

Cooperative Learning

On poster board, have groups of three or four students develop family trees for a famous person. Have the groups discuss possible choices and then vote for their favorite one. After students choose their personality, assign each group member a specific role. In groups of three, for example, the roles could be researcher, writer / artist, and presenter. Provide feedback as groups work independently. Have groups present their trees to the whole class.

Apply

Background Information

(See the Cross-Curricular Connections at the beginning of the chapter on pp. 186–187 for further activities.
For a complete list of the curricular areas covered in PASO A PASO A, *see p. T23 of this Teacher's Edition.)*

Choose the number of activities you want your class to do. Use the activities for homework, for enrichment, or for your Spanish-speaking students. This material is not part of the testing program, however, it is appropriate for use in student assessment.

Teaching Suggestions

You may wish to use the survey / poll sheet in the Projects for Proficiency BLMs for the second activity.

Conexiones

These activities connect Spanish with what you are learning in other subject areas.

Carlos IV y su familia (1800), Francisco de Goya

Las familias en el arte

Look at these paintings. Pick one to describe to a partner in Spanish. Your partner will put his or her finger on the appropriate family member. Then think about what the artist is trying to tell you about the people in the painting. Describe the personality of at least two members of the family in the painting you chose.

Sandía / Watermelon (1986), Carmen Lomas Garza

Options

Strategies for Reaching All Students

Students Needing Extra Help

For the third activity, assist students as needed with calculating the percentages. Remind them to set up the problem as a fraction. For example: 100% / 511 total vowels and consonants = x% / 226 vowels. Cross multiply and divide to obtain the percentage of vowels (44 percent).

Enrichment

Have volunteers bring in family photos and repeat the first activity.

¿De qué color son tus ojos?

Prepara una tabla en una hoja de papel. En la primera columna escribe una lista de los colores de ojos y de pelo. Observa a diez compañeros. En la segunda columna, indica cuántos(as) tienen los ojos y el pelo de cada color *(each color)*.

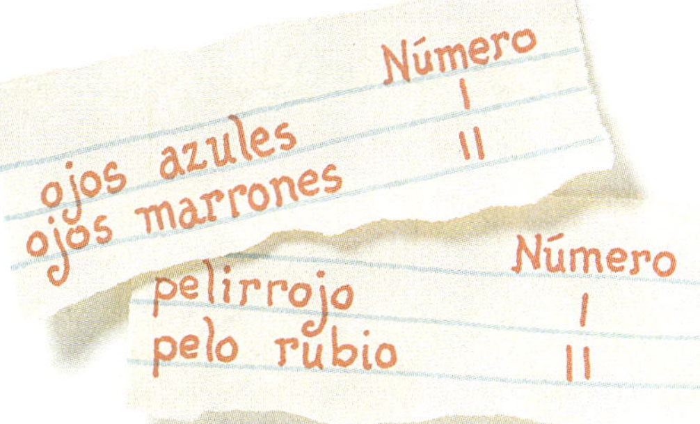

¿Qué color de ojos es el más común en la tabla? ¿Qué color de pelo? Compara tu tabla con las tablas de dos o tres compañeros(as). ¿Son similares o diferentes los resultados? ¿Cómo se explican los resultados? Habla con tu profesor(a) de ciencias para más información.

Vocales y consonantes

Look at this class list from a school in a Spanish-speaking country. Are there more vowels or more consonants in the list? In a group, estimate the percentage of vowels and consonants. Then calculate the exact number. Make a pie chart to show the percentage of vowels compared to consonants.

Bermúdez Bischoff, Mario
Camacho Sánchez, Luisa
Colón Vega, Javier
De Diego D'Amico, Francisco J.
Del Valle Olmo, Lis Anette
Franco Weissman, Carolina
González Matos, Claudia
Hernández Cáceres, Anelys
Juliá Savarit, Ana Rita
Lázaro Collazo, Lionel E.
Lázaro Martínez, Laura M.
León García, Rosalinda
Liberatore Gallardo, Katia
Martínez Colón, Ángel
Mendoza Rosich, Arístides
Nieves Sánchez, Juan Carlos
O'Reilly Martínez, Ofelia
Pérez Colón, Marisol
Pérez Pérez, Rafael
Quiñones Rodríguez, José A.
Ramos Junqueva, Martín
Rigaud Colón, Pilar
Ríos Marini, Viviana
Ríos Ortiz, Michelle
Ríos Ortiz, Marta
Schumacher Saavedras, Rebeca

vocales

consonantes

Now repeat this activity for *your* class list. Estimate first, then calculate and make a pie chart. Compare the two pie charts. What hypothesis can you make about the number of vowels and consonants in Spanish names compared with the names of your classmates?

Answers: Conexiones

Las familias en el arte / ¿De qué color son tus ojos?: Responses will vary.

Vocales y consonantes: Some sources classify the *h*—when it doesn't follow the letter *c*—as neither a consonant nor a vowel, because it is a silent letter. In addition, the *y* is sometimes classified as a vowel or a consonant, depending on the sound produced. The following answers list the *h* as a consonant and the *y* as a vowel, since most students will probably list them as such from their background in English-language skills.
The list has 285 consonants (56 percent) and 226 vowels (44 percent). Students may conclude that most names in Spanish will contain more consonants than vowels.

Cultural Notes

(p. 208, top photo)
Goya rendered this painting of Carlos IV (1748–1819), King of Spain (1788–1808) and his wife, Queen María Luisa, shown here surrounded by family members. The King's eldest son Ferdinand, in blue, stands to the left. The woman next to Ferdinand, with her face averted, represents his yet-to-be-chosen bride. María Luisa is flanked by her youngest children. Goya has included himself in the background, to the left of the painting, behind an easel.

(p. 208, bottom photo)
Carmen Lomas Garza (b. 1948) bases many of her paintings, etchings, and lithographs on memories of growing up in an extended Mexican American family in Kingsville, Texas, near the Mexican border. Lomas Garza says she decided to be an artist at thirteen. In 1990 she published *Family Pictures,* a bilingual children's book illustrating routine or traditional activities from her childhood. In this painting, the artist remembers how various generations of her family would sit out on the porch in the warm summer air enjoying a cool slice of watermelon handed out by her father.

Preview

Transparency 34

Answers

Answers will vary, but students may mention that they would expect to find background information about the star, such as age, family information, and so on.

A In Spanish, age is expressed as "having" so many years with *tener.*

B Sara is described as being very serious and hardworking, and at times she is funny and lazy. / *es* (from *ser)*

C *somos* / It ends in *-mos.* It means "we are."

Gramática en contexto

This is a page from a Mexican magazine article about TV star Sara Sánchez. What kind of information would you expect to find in the captions?

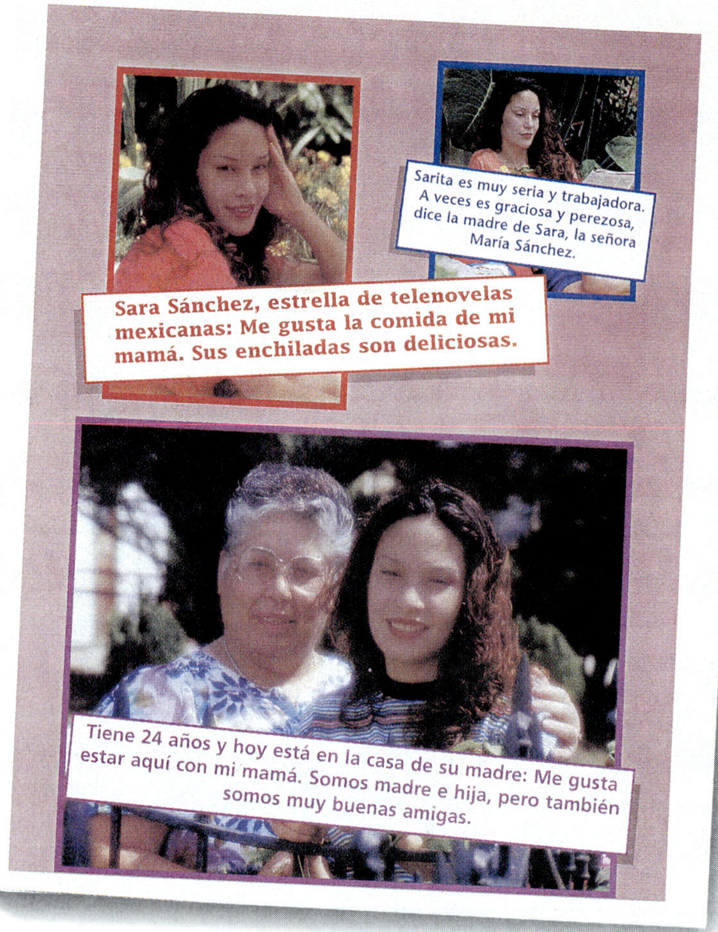

Sarita es muy seria y trabajadora. A veces es graciosa y perezosa, dice la madre de Sara, la señora María Sánchez.

Sara Sánchez, estrella de telenovelas mexicanas: Me gusta la comida de mi mamá. Sus enchiladas son deliciosas.

Tiene 24 años y hoy está en la casa de su madre: Me gusta estar aquí con mi mamá. Somos madre e hija, pero también somos muy buenas amigas.

A Sara's age is one fact that is given. Look at the verb in the expression that tells her age. Make a rule for expressing age in Spanish.

B How does Sara's mother describe her daughter? What verb form does she use?

C Look at the caption in which Sara describes her relationship with her mother. What verb form does she use? Explain to a partner how you recognize this as a *nosotros(as)* verb form. What do you think it means?

Options

Strategies for Reaching All Students

Students Needing Extra Help

C: Write the verb forms in a paradigm, using the pronouns. Then students can see that you have used all the forms except for "we." Remind them that they already know this setup from *-ar* verbs.

El verbo *tener*

The verb *tener*, "to have," follows the pattern of other *-er* verbs. However, most of the forms of *tener* are irregular. Here are all of its present-tense forms.

(yo)	**tengo**	(nosotros) (nosotras)	**tenemos**
(tú)	**tienes**	(vosotros) (vosotras)	**tenéis**
(Ud.) (él) (ella)	**tiene**	(Uds.) (ellos) (ellas)	**tienen**

- You have already seen some of these verb forms. In what ways is *tener* irregular?

¡No olvides!

Remember that *tener* is sometimes used where in English we use a form of the verb "to be": *tener sed / hambre / años.*

1 Based on the chart, tell which form of the verb *tener* you would use:

a. to talk about what one person has
b. to talk about what more than one person has
c. to talk about what you have
d. to talk about what you and a friend have
e. to tell what a friend of yours has

Una familia en La Paz, Bolivia

211

Present & Practice

Teaching Suggestions

El verbo tener: Ask students to identify what *tener* has in common with other *-er* verbs. What is different? Students may then complete the *tener* chart on their Organizers.

Explain that in a negative sentence, we generally don't use the indefinite article after the verb *tener* unless there is an adjective. *(No tengo lápiz. / No tengo un lápiz azul.)*

Class Starter Review

On the day following the presentation of *tener,* you may wish to begin the class with this activity: Give various classroom objects or school supplies to students. Then ask who has a specific item *(¿Quién tiene un(a) . . . ? Miguel, ¿tienes un(a) . . . ?* etc.). Or, ask who has a certain eye or hair color: *¿Quién tiene pelo rubio?*

Answers

1 a. tiene
b. tienen
c. tengo
d. tenemos
e. tienes

Cultural Notes

(p. 211, photo)
This family is walking to school up a cobblestone street in La Paz, Bolivia. La Paz is the highest capital city in the world, situated around 12,000 feet above sea level. The La Paz airport is named, appropriately, El Alto.

Present & Practice

Re-enter / Recycle

Ex. 2: school supplies from Chap. 2
Ex. 4: singular and plural adjective agreement from Chaps. 1 and 4, adjectives describing personality from Chap. 1

Answers

2 Order of dialogues will vary.
A —¿Quién tiene los cuadernos?
B —Elisa y Dolores.
A —¿Cuántos cuadernos tienen?
B —Tienen dos.

A —. . . las reglas?
B —Pablo.
A —¿Cuántas reglas tiene?
B —Tiene dos.

A —. . . los bolígrafos?
B —Marta y Esteban.
A —¿Cuántos bolígrafos tienen?
B —Tienen cuatro.

A —. . . los lápices?
B —Manuel.
A —¿Cuántos lápices tiene?
B —Tiene cinco.

A —. . . los marcadores?
B —Eva.
A —¿Cuántos marcadores tiene?
B —Tiene tres.

A —. . . las carpetas?
B —Luz.
A —¿Cuántas carpetas tiene?
B —Tiene tres.

2 A class is getting ready to start a project. Several students have gathered the supplies they need. Find out who has them and how many they have.

libros
A —*¿Quién tiene los libros?*
B —*Víctor.*
A —*¿Cuántos libros tiene?*
B —*Tiene cuatro.*

3 Find out the ages of four students in your class. Then ask about the number of aunts and uncles and brothers and sisters they have. On a sheet of paper, copy the grid below. As you ask students the questions, write their names and the information you receive. While talking to them, notice their eye and hair color and write this information in the appropriate columns.

A —*¿Cuántos años tienes, David?*
B —*Tengo 13 años.*
A —*¿Cuántos tíos tienes?*
B —*Tengo nueve tíos.*
o: *No tengo tíos.*

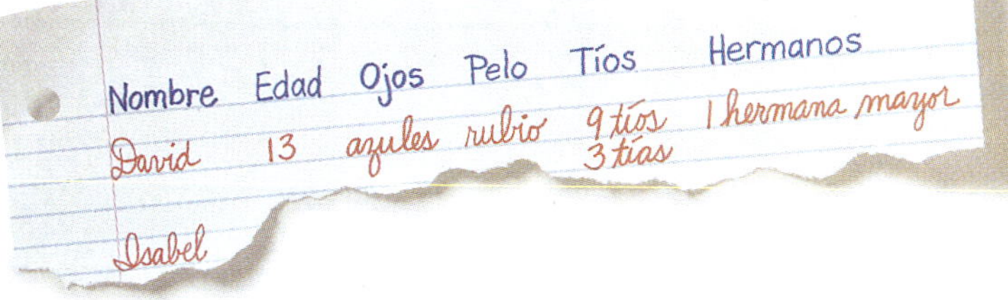

Options

Strategies for Reaching All Students

Spanish-Speaking Students

Ex. 3: Have students write this exercise.

Students Needing Extra Help

Ex. 4: Model different combinations.
El verbo ser: Have students fill in the chart in the grammar portion of their Organizers.

Enrichment

Ex. 3: As a written assignment, have students make up questions to interview a classmate regarding whether he or she has cats or dogs at home. Encourage students to be as thorough and creative in their questions as possible. For example, if the interviewee has no dogs or cats at home,

4 Using the information from Exercise 3, compare yourself with at least three classmates. Write as many statements as you can about similarities or differences in age, appearance, and number of aunts and uncles and brothers and sisters. Then report to the class.

David y yo tenemos 13 años. Tenemos el pelo rubio. Tenemos una hermana mayor, pero yo tengo también dos hermanos menores. o: *Él tiene 13 años, pero yo tengo sólo 12 años. Etc.*

El verbo *ser*

The verb *ser*, "to be," is also an irregular verb. We use *ser* with adjectives to tell what someone or something is like.

- You already know some forms of *ser*. Here are all of its present-tense forms.

(yo)	**soy**	(nosotros) (nosotras)	**somos**
(tú)	**eres**	(vosotros) (vosotras)	**sois**
(Ud.) (él) (ella)	**es**	(Uds.) (ellos) (ellas)	**son**

5 Which of the sentences in Column B could be used to describe the people in Column A? Look for verb and adjective clues. Some of the sentences in Column B can be used more than once.

A	B
Arturo	Es inteligente.
Clara	Somos simpáticos.
Yo	Son altos.
Clara, Arturo y yo	Soy amable.
Tú	Eres prudente.
Uds.	
Arturo y Clara	

3 Dialogues will vary, but encourage students to use chapter vocabulary.

4 Reports will vary, but practice making the adjectives agree in number and gender.

A follow-up activity might include one student standing and reading a statement such as, *Daniel y yo tenemos 12 años.* All other students about whom the statement is true also stand. Then all students sit down. Another student stands and reads: *Sara y yo no tenemos hermanos.* All students about whom the statement is true also stand. Continue with other statements.

Practice Wkbk. 5-5

Class Starter Review

For the day after *ser* is presented: Using adjectives that students have learned, ask: *¿Quién (no) es . . . ? ¿Eres . . . ? ¿Son Uds. . . . ?* etc. Be aware of students' sensitivity to answering this type of question. You might use the names of famous personalities instead of those of your students. Draw these people on the chalkboard and have students describe them.

Answers

5 Arturo, Clara: Es inteligente. / Yo: Soy amable. / Clara, Arturo, y yo: Somos simpáticos. / Tú: Eres prudente. / Uds., Arturo y Clara: Son altos.

students might turn their line of questioning to whether the interviewee likes cats or dogs, or whether they would like to have them but can't because another family member dislikes them. If there are cats or dogs at home, students can ask how many of each there are, their names and ages, what the pets are like, and what they like to do.

Practice

Re-enter / Recycle

Exs. 6–8: singular and plural adjective agreement from Chaps. 1 and 4, adjectives describing personality from Chap. 1.

Answers

6 a. Alicia y María son graciosas, pero Felipe es serio.
b. José es bajo, pero Miguel y tú son altos.
c. Laura y Rita son tacañas, pero Jaime es generoso.
d. Pablo y yo somos trabajadores, pero Mateo es perezoso.
e. Duque y Manchi son grandes, pero Rex es pequeño.
f. Turquesa y Condesa son bonitas, pero Barrabás es feo.
g. Marcos y Miguel son desordenados, pero tú eres ordenada.

6 In each of these groups, two people are alike in some way and the third is different. Describe their similarities and differences.

Luisa / Ana y yo

Luisa es artística, pero Ana y yo somos deportistas.

a. Alicia y María / Felipe

b. José / Miguel y tú

c. Laura y Rita / Jaime

d. Pablo y yo / Mateo

e. Duque y Manchi / Rex

f. Turquesa y Condesa / Barrabás

g. Marcos y Miguel / tú

Options

Strategies for Reaching All Students

Spanish-Speaking Students

Ex. 7: Pair bilingual and non-bilingual students.

7 Think of three pairs of famous people who are alike in at least one way. Find out if your partner can tell you how they are alike. You may want to use the list of adjectives to help you.

A —*¿Cómo son Gloria Estefan y Madonna?*
B —*Son bonitas.*

alto, -a	atrevido, -a	feo, -a	joven	simpático, -a
amable	bajo, -a	generoso, -a	ordenado, -a	sociable
antipático, -a	bonito, -a	gracioso, -a	pelirrojo, -a	tacaño, -a
artístico, -a	cariñoso, -a	guapo, -a	perezoso, -a	trabajador, -a
atractivo, -a	desordenado, -a	inteligente	serio, -a	viejo, -a

8 Now ask your partner in what way you and a classmate are alike or different. Repeat with two other classmates.

A —*¿Cómo somos Roberto y yo?*
B —*Uds. son trabajadores.*
o: *Él es trabajador, pero tú eres perezoso.*

"Muchas veces voy al parque los fines de semana. Aquí estoy con mi familia en Chapultepec."

7–8 Dialogues will vary, but look for verb and adjective agreement.

 **Practice Wkbk. 5-6, 5-7**

 **Writing Activities**

 **Pruebas 5-5, 5-6**

Cultural Notes

(p. 215, photo)
In many Latin American countries, including Mexico, families spend a great deal of time together. Most people almost never consider missing an important family event such as a graduation or a baptism. Gatherings are multigenerational, with everyone from grandparents to babies in attendance.

Present & Apply

Cultural Objective

- To explain how names are formed in Spanish-speaking countries

Critical Thinking: Understanding Points of View

Tell students that married women in the U.S. were at one time almost exclusively formally addressed with the first name of their husbands (for example: Mrs. John Smith). Although some women may still prefer this form of address, this practice is deemed inappropriate to many women in the U.S. today. Discuss with students why many women would be offended if addressed by their husband's name.

Answers

Rebeca Romero Salinas / García Mendoza

Look at the names of the three family members. What was the mother's name before her marriage? What is the father's surname?

When a woman marries, she may

- **keep her full name unchanged; for example, Rebeca Romero Salinas**
- **add *de* and her husband's surname; for example, Rebeca Romero Salinas de García**
- **add *de* and her husband's surname and drop her *apellido materno;* for example, Rebeca Romero de García**

You would address her as Sra. Romero de García or Sra. García. But she would never be addressed as Sra. José Luis García.

Una familia mexicana en el parque

Options

Strategies for Reaching All Students

Spanish-Speaking Students

Ask volunteers to share the complete names for their family members: parents, grandparents, and so on.

 **Un paso más Ex. 5-H**

Enrichment

Point out that in Spanish-speaking countries, a woman's widowhood is also indicated in her name. If the husband of Sra. Guerra de Olivas dies, she becomes Sra. Guerra, vda. *(viuda)* de Olivas.

Una boda tradicional de bombero en Costa Rica

La cultura desde tu perspectiva

1 Think of a married woman you know, and explain what her name might be if she lived in a Spanish-speaking country.

2 Name one advantage of the naming system in Spanish-speaking countries.

Una boda en Xochimilco, México

Answers: La cultura desde tu perspectiva

1 Answers will vary.

2 Answers will vary, but students may say that this naming system might help distinguish between people having similar names. The inclusion of the mother's surname emphasizes the importance of both parents in a person's identity.

Writing Activities

Cultural Notes

(p. 217, top photo)
This jubilant occasion appropriately marks the wedding of a *bombero* in San José, Costa Rica, with arching streams of water. Firefighters in the U.S. and Costa Rica share a common goal of extinguishing fires and increasing awareness of public safety. Unlike their counterparts in the U.S., however, *bomberos* in Costa Rica work for the Instituto Nacional de Seguros, a national agency; they are not contracted by municipalities.

(p. 217, bottom photo)
Mexican weddings, like this one in Xochimilco, are often lavishly planned affairs, including as many family members and friends as possible. A very special role in Mexican weddings is played by the bride and groom's godparents, who drape a garland of beaded pearl leaves around the shoulders of the wedding couple, encircling them as they exchange vows. After the wedding mass the newlyweds bring a gift of roses and pray to the Virgen de Guadalupe, Mexico's patron saint.

Preview

Transparency 35

Answers

A su casa

B su

C tu libro / su libro

Gramática en contexto

Look at these pages from a Mexican music magazine. Vidal is a member of a popular singing group.

A Find the words in the photo caption that mean the same as *la casa de Vidal.*

B Vidal has two favorite colors. If he had only one, the caption would talk about *color favorito.* What else in the phrase *sus colores favoritos* would change?

C You already know how to talk about something that belongs to you *(mi libro).* How would you refer to a book that belonged to the person to whom you were speaking? How about a book that belonged to someone about whom you were speaking?

Options

Strategies for Reaching All Students

Students Needing Extra Help

Remind students that possessive adjectives in Spanish agree in number and gender with the modified object, not the person to whom it belongs. They might need extra practice with certain forms, such as *su(s),* when these words modify singular or plural nouns. Use visuals to help reinforce this concept.

Los adjetivos posesivos

To tell what belongs to someone or to show relationships, we use *de* + noun. For example:

Tengo el cuaderno **de** Felipe.
La hermana **de** María es amable.

- Another way to tell what belongs to someone and to show relationships is to use possessive adjectives. You already know some of them.

mi hermano	**mis** hermanos
tu abuela	**tus** abuelas
su hijo	**sus** hijos

- The possessive adjective must be singular if the noun is singular and plural if the noun is plural.

Mi prima es alta. Mi**s** prima**s** son alta**s**.

1 Match the following questions and answers.

¿Cómo es el amigo de Mónica?	Mi amigo es simpático.
¿Cómo es tu amigo?	Sus amigos son simpáticos.
¿Cómo son los amigos de Mónica?	Su amigo es simpático.

En Cuernavaca, México

Present & Practice

Teaching Suggestions

Have students fill in the grammar portion of their Organizers. Remind them of the information from Section B on the previous page. Discuss the idea of one owner, one thing; and one owner, two things. The *-s* in *mis, tus,* and *sus* automatically signals the plural form. Give a few models.

Discuss the English use of apostrophes to show ownership and how this concept is not used in Spanish. Give students a formula: object + *de* + person. Emphasize the word order: In Spanish the object is first, followed by the person. Have students give examples.

Class Starter Review

On the day following the presentation of possessive adjectives, you might begin the class with this activity:
Go around the classroom, pointing to objects on students' desks, asking: *¿De quién es este libro?* Students should answer in complete sentences: *El libro es de Mario. / Es el libro de Mario.*

Answers

1 ¿Cómo es el amigo de Mónica? Su amigo es simpático. / ¿Cómo es tu amigo? Mi amigo es simpático. / ¿Cómo son los amigos de Mónica? Sus amigos son simpáticos.

Cultural Notes

(p. 218, photo)
This photo, from the magazine *Furia musical,* is part of a spread featuring photos of the homes belonging to members of the Mexican musical group Campeche Show. This group gained popularity in the 1980s as part of the *onda grupera,* a musical trend featuring groups which play *cumbia* dance music.

(p. 219, photo)
As this photo of Mexican boys in football uniforms indicates, there is a strong American influence in Cuernavaca, the capital of the state of Morelos. Its cool climate and lush vegetation have made it an appealing home to Mexicans and foreigners since colonial times. Today Cuernavaca has a community of about 20,000 U.S. residents, and attracts many more *norteamericanos* with its numerous language schools.

Options

Strategies for Reaching All Students

Students Needing Extra Help

Ex. 3: Again, be aware of students' sensitivity to discussing their family. Allow them to use the names of friends or those of an imaginary family.

Cultural Notes 

(p. 220, realia)
American-made films are among the most popular seen by movie-goers in Spain. Hollywood blockbuster films often appear soon after their U.S. release dates. In many cases, U.S. films are dubbed in Spanish. Other films rely on subtitles, which especially appeal to viewers who enjoy listening to English.

2 Using the family tree on page 193, make three true and three false statements about Raquel's family. Your partner will look at the family tree and respond *sí* if the statement is correct. If it is incorrect, your partner will respond *no* and correct it.

A —*La hermana de Raquel tiene 17 años.*
B —*Sí, su hermana tiene 17 años.*
A —*Los primos de Raquel se llaman Jaime y Luz.*
B —*No, sus primos se llaman Jaime y Ana.*

3 With your partner, take turns telling about three of your family members.

Mi abuela Rosa tiene 67 años. Mis tíos se llaman Jorge y Cecilia. Tienen dos hijos que se llaman Roberto y Ramón. Mi tía Cecilia es pelirroja y tiene ojos verdes. Etc.

Form a group with another pair. Each of you will report what you have learned about your partner's family.

La abuela de Roberto ... Sus tíos ...

Esta familia vive en las montañas de Guatemala.

Practice

Re-enter / Recycle

Exs. 2–3: numbers 0–31 from *El primer paso,* numbers 32–59 from Chap. 2
Ex. 3: singular and plural adjective agreement from Chaps. 1 and 4, adjectives describing personality from Chap. 1

Teaching Suggestions

Ex. 2: Have students do two true and one false statement. First do all true statements. Then write false statements on the chalkboard. They may have to write these to show how possessive adjectives work. In the example, show how *la* becomes *su,* and *de Raquel* disappears.

Answers

2–3 Dialogues will vary, but encourage students to use the full range of chapter vocabulary.

 **Practice Wkbk. 5-8, 5-9, 5-10**

 **Audio Activity 5.4**

 **Pruebas 5-7, 5-8**

 **Comm. Act. BLM 5-3**

(p. 221, photo)
This Mayan woman, wearing a tie-dyed skirt *(corte jaspeado),* and her children walk near the remote village of Nebaj in the Guatemalan *altiplano.* The *altiplano* is the mountainous region in western Guatemala where the majority of indigenous people live and is primarily comprised of the departments of El Quiché, Sololá, Quetzaltenango, Huehuetenango, and Totonicapán. Tourists rarely visit Nebaj and its neighboring villages of San Juan Cotzal and Chajul even though it is a beautiful area for hiking. During the political tensions of the 1980s, Nebaj was the site of fighting between Government troops and many local residents.

Apply

 **Pronunciation Tape 5-3**

 **Todo Junto A**

Play

 **Todo Junto B**

Play

Using the Video

Video segment 3: See the Video Teacher's Guide.

 **Video Activity C**

Teaching Suggestions

Other words your students may want to know: *divorciado, -a* (divorced); *casado, -a* (married); *soltero, -a* (unmarried, single).

For the first activity, you may wish to see the "coat of arms" sheet from the Projects for Proficiency BLMs for more information.

Answers

Activities 1–3: Encourage students to use the full range of chapter vocabulary. Look for verb and adjective agreement.

Todo Junto

Para decir más

Here is some additional vocabulary that you might find useful for activities in this section.

el esposo, la esposa
husband, wife

el nieto, la nieta
grandson, granddaughter

el pariente, la parienta
relative

el padrino
godfather

la madrina
godmother

crespo, -a
curly (hair)

lacio, -a
straight (hair)

largo, -a
long (hair)

corto, -a
short (hair)

Here's an opportunity for you to put together what you learned in this chapter with what you learned earlier.

1 Escudo de armas

Create a poster-sized family coat of arms based on the characteristics and hobbies of your family. For example, you might include a basketball to stand for a brother or sister who really loves that sport. Use drawings and pictures cut from magazines.

Then present your coat of arms to a group, and explain the meaning of the symbols. For example:

Mi hermana juega básquetbol todos los días.
A mi madre le gusta cocinar.
A mí me encantan los videojuegos.

Options

Strategies for Reaching All Students

Spanish-Speaking Students

 **Un paso más Exs. 5-I, 5-J**

Cooperative Learning

Divide the class into groups of three or four students. Have each individual write the name of one sports or entertainment personality on a notecard. Students should not see each other's cards. Now, have each group play "Guess the Personality." Designate one student in each group to serve as the moderator. Taking turns, each student gets to ask the moderator one question about the celebrity on the moderator's card. For example: *¿Es un hombre? ¿Tiene pelo rubio?* After each question, the moderator answers either *sí* or *no.* Students record the information on a piece of paper. Students alternate asking questions. Play continues until someone guesses the celebrity. Assign a new moderator and personality for the next round.

2 ¿Quién es?

Bring to class a picture of a person cut from a magazine. Write a description of the person on a separate piece of paper. Then work with a partner.

- Read your description aloud. (Do not show your partner the picture.)
- Your partner will draw the person you are describing.
- Compare the drawing to the picture.

Then form groups and mix all your group's pictures, drawings, and written descriptions. Exchange them with those of another group, and try to match all three pieces: the pictures, the drawings, and the written descriptions.

3 La familia ideal

Do you prefer a small family or a large one? Create an ideal family from pictures you cut from magazines. (You can include pets and as many family members as you want.) Paste or tape the pictures to heavy paper. Write descriptions under the pictures. Include:

- relationships *(madre, hijo,* etc.)
- ages
- personal descriptions and personality characteristics
- favorite pastimes

Present your ideal family to a group.

Ahora lo sabes

Using what you have learned so far, can you:

- **tell what someone has?**
- **ask and tell how old someone is?**
- **describe someone?**
- **tell what belongs to someone?**

Multicultural Perspectives

Riddles and rhymes are an integral part of all cultures. They often are learned at home from parents or siblings and are passed from one generation to another. A rhyme common to many Hispanic families is one that is recited while preparing tortillas or gathering eggs: *Tortillas de pan y de vino / pasa papá que viene en camino. Tortillitas de pan y de queso / pasa papá que va de regreso.* Some riddles reflect upon the wonders of nature and explain a natural occurrence or phenomenon. Invite students to share with the class a riddle or rhyme that has been in their families for many years.

Answers: Ahora lo sabes

(Answers will vary.)

- Elisa tiene dos gatos. *(p. 211)*
- ¿Cuántos años tiene tu hijo? / Tiene siete años. *(pp. 190–191, 211)*
- Mi hermano es alto y tiene ojos verdes. *(pp. 190–191, 200–201, 211, 213)*
- Ana tiene el libro de su hermano. *(p. 219)*

 **Writing Activities**

 **Comm. Act. BLMs 5-4, 5-5**

 **Examen de habilidades 2**

Apply

Process Reading

For a description of process reading, see p. 60.

Teaching Suggestions

Antes de leer: Have students explain why they would use certificates for each occasion.

Answers
Antes de leer

Responses will vary, but all answers apply.

Mira la lectura

Mother's Day

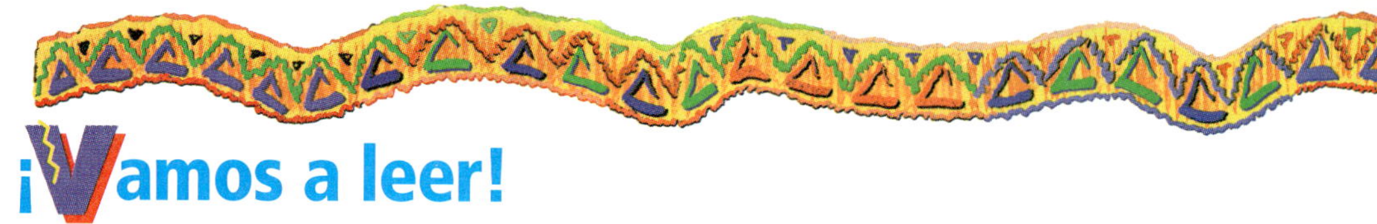

¡Vamos a leer!

Antes de leer

STRATEGY ➤ Using prior knowledge

When might you receive a certificate? Working with a partner, choose the occasions from this list. (There is more than one answer.)

a. when you are born
b. when you enter middle school
c. when you win a prize in a school contest
d. when you graduate
e. when you have done something special

Mira la lectura

STRATEGY ➤ Skimming

Read this certificate quickly just to find out what holiday it might be for.

What occasion do you think this certificate is for?

Options

Strategies for Reaching All Students

Enrichment

Have students design and write a certificate on a computer word-processing program. They then can decorate the final copy with artwork of their choosing.

Infórmate

STRATEGY **Using context to get meaning**

1 Read the certificate carefully. Make a list of words you don't know. Work with a partner to figure them out. Use what you know about certificates and holidays to help you. If you are having trouble, take this quiz to help you.

1. En una **votación unánime**, ¿quiénes votan sí?
   a. Todos votan sí.
   b. Muchos votan sí.
   c. Nadie vota sí.
2. ¿Quién **otorga** los diplomas en una graduación?
   a. Un(a) estudiante.
   b. Un(a) profesor(a).
   c. El director/la directora de la escuela.
3. ¿Quiénes **nombran** al presidente del club de español?
   a. Los profesores de español.
   b. Los padres de los estudiantes.
   c. Los miembros del club.
4. Estoy enfermo. **Por eso** ___ .
   a. estudio mucho.
   b. practico deportes después de las clases.
   c. no puedo ir a la escuela.

2 Which of these responses do you think the person who receives this certificate might give?

a. Muchas gracias.
b. ¿Cuántos años tienes?
c. Tengo que ayudar en casa.
d. ¡Qué lástima!

Aplicación

1 Tell a partner three new words you learned from this reading.

2 Design and write a *Certificado de Excelencia* for a family member or for the principal, a teacher, or a student.

Infórmate

1 Lists will vary.
1. a.
2. c.
3. c.
4. c.

2 a.

Aplicación

1 Responses will vary.

2 Certificates will vary, but encourage students to use the full range of previously learned vocabulary.

Cultural Notes 

(p. 225, realia)
An arrangement of flowers is a gift for many occasions. For Mother's Day in Colombia, customary gifts include red and pink roses which symbolize love and tenderness. Pink *rosas* are also common for the *quinceañera.* Children celebrating their first communion typically receive white roses, which stand for innocence. In Nicaragua, white flowers are often found at funerals. For *el Día de los Enamorados* in Mexico, it's popular to give *azucenas* (white lilies), *margaritas* (daisies), and *gladíolos* (gladiolus).

Apply

Process Writing
For information regarding writing portfolios, see p. 62.

Teaching Suggestions
Step 2: Students have enough vocabulary so that they could expand on these words.

Answers
Cards will vary, but encourage students to use the full range of chapter vocabulary.

¡Vamos a escribir!

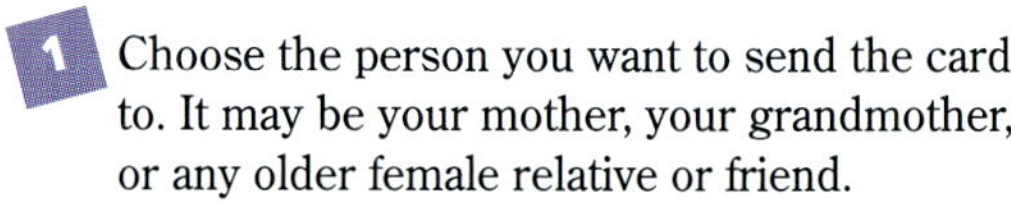

Mother's Day is an important holiday in Latin America. In Puerto Rico it falls on the same day as in the United States, the second Sunday in May. In Mexico, it is on May 10; in Argentina, on the third Sunday in October. Make a Mother's Day card in Spanish.

1 Choose the person you want to send the card to. It may be your mother, your grandmother, or any older female relative or friend.

Read the covers of the sample cards. How would you complete those thoughts? Think of other ideas for the wording of your message. Use the ideas in the *Certificado de Excelencia* from *¡Vamos a leer!* to help you.

2 Fold a piece of paper like a card. Write the draft of your message, and sketch the illustration.

You may want to use some of these expressions.

dar las gracias *to thank*
un beso *a kiss*
un abrazo *a hug*
con todo mi corazón *with all my heart*
¡Feliz Día de las Madres! *Happy Mother's Day!*

Show your card to a partner. Listen to his or her suggestions for changes, and decide whether you agree.

3 Fold another piece of paper, and make a clean copy of your card. Copy edit it using the following checklist:

- spelling
- capital letters
- punctuation
- correct use of the verbs *tener* and *ser*
- correct use of possessive adjectives

Complete the illustration for your card. It may be a photo, a picture cut from a magazine, a drawing, or anything you like.

4 Send your card to the person you chose.

Options

Strategies for Reaching All Students

Students Needing Extra Help
Under special circumstances, allow students to choose another family member, relative, or friend for whom they can make the card.

Resumen del capítulo 5

Use the vocabulary from this chapter to help you:

- describe family members and friends
- ask and tell what someone's age is
- tell what other people like and do not like to do

to refer to family members
los abuelos: el abuelo
la abuela
los hermanos: el hermano
la hermana
los hijos: el hijo
la hija
los padres: el padre
la madre
los primos: el primo
la prima
los tíos: el tío
la tía
el hijo único, la hija única
los gemelos, las gemelas

to ask and tell what someone's name is
¿Cómo se llama(n) ___?
Se llama(n) ___.
el nombre

to ask and tell how old someone is
¿Cuántos años tiene ___?
Tiene ___ años.
sesenta (sesenta y uno . . .)
setenta (setenta y uno . . .)
ochenta (ochenta y uno . . .)
noventa (noventa y uno . . .)
cien

70 81 100

to refer to people
el hombre
el muchacho, la muchacha
la mujer
la persona
que
¿Quiénes?

to describe people, animals, and things
alto, -a
antipático, -a
atractivo, -a
bajo, -a
bonito, -a
cariñoso, -a
feo, -a
grande
guapo, -a
inteligente
joven
mayor, *pl.* mayores
menor, *pl.* menores
pequeño, -a
simpático, -a
viejo, -a
ser + *adjective*
el pelo: canoso
castaño
negro
rubio
pelirrojo, -a  
los ojos: azules
grises
marrones
negros
verdes

to name animals
el gato
el perro

to show possession
de
su, sus
tener

to tell what someone likes
(A + *person*) le gusta(n) ___.
(A + *person*) le encanta(n) ___.

to indicate number
(no . . .) nadie
sólo
todos, -as

to refer to animals and things
que

Summarize

 Writing Activities

 Mi portafolio

 Test Generator

CAPÍTULO 6

THEME: CLOTHING

SCOPE AND SEQUENCE Pages 228–271

COMMUNICATION

Topics

Clothing

Colors

Prices

Numbers 101–199

Objectives

To compare where people shop for clothes in Spanish-speaking countries and in the U.S.

To identify articles of clothing and describe clothes

To talk about colors

To discuss prices

To assist customers in a store

To indicate a specific item or items

To address people

To start a conversation

To talk about shopping and places to shop for clothing

To tell when something happened

To indicate location

CULTURE

Shopping for clothes

Types of clothing stores

GRAMMAR

La posición de los adjetivos

Los adjetivos demostrativos

El complemento directo: Los pronombres

Ancillaries available for use with Chapter 6

Multisensory/Technology

Overhead Transparencies, 36–41

Audio Tapes and CDs

Projects for Proficiency: Blackline Master Spanish Activities for Middle School Learners

Vocabulary Art Blackline Masters for Hands-On Learning, pp. 33–37

Classroom Crossword

Video

CD-ROM

Print

Practice Workbook, pp. 64–72

Writing, Audio & Video Activities, pp. 53–60, 80–82, 110–111

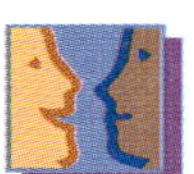
Communicative Activity Blackline Masters

- Pair and Small Group Activities, pp. 43–48
- Situation Cards, p. 49

Un paso más: Actividades para ampliar tu español, pp. 32–37

Assessment

Assessment Program

- Pruebas, pp. 94–97, 102–104
- Exámenes de habilidades, pp. 98–101, 105–108
- Mi portafolio, pp. 109–110

Test Generator

Video still from Chap. 6

Cultural Overview

Shopping

Throughout Latin America and Spain, people traditionally have shopped for clothing in small neighborhood specialty stores or at public marketplaces. These shopping habits are changing in many cities, however, as large department stores are becoming more commonplace.

Popular department stores include Colombia's San Andresito and Spain's El Corte Inglés, Galerías Preciados, and Galerías Primero. Shopping malls such as Mexico City's Perisur are also becoming more commonplace. Perisur, like malls in the U.S., features a variety of chain store branches *(sucursales).* Among them are Liverpool, a fashionable clothing store, and Sanborn's, a department store and favorite lunch spot. Perisur has become a central place for friends to meet and spend time together as well as to shop. *Puntos de fábrica* (factory outlet stores) are becoming increasingly popular places to buy clothing.

Local indoor and outdoor markets still exist in many communities throughout Latin America. At El Mercado Oriental, a market that covers dozens of square blocks in Managua, Nicaragua, one can buy almost anything. In many smaller cities and towns in Mexico, *el día de plaza,* a once- or twice-weekly event, draws people from many surrounding communities. Vendors may travel from town to town depending on where the market will take place that day. Local residents rely on the market to supply them with clothes and other items. Customers can pay for their merchandise with cash or by credit without using a credit card. The merchant writes down the name of the client and how much she or he owes. For example, in Mexico, *botas de piel Alcalá* (fine leather boots) are very expensive. A person can put a down payment on the boots and take them home. Every week the customer pays off a portion of the debt until the boots have been paid for.

Another common way of shopping is to wait for the *mercado a ruedas* (market on wheels) and *vendedores ambulantes* (door-to-door salespeople) to make a stop on the block. Shoppers appreciate the convenience as well as the congenial, personal service from familiar vendors.

Introduce

Re-entry of Concepts
The following list represents words, expressions, and grammar topics re-entered from *El primer paso* to Chap. 5:

El primer paso
Numbers 0–31
Calendar expressions

Chapter 1
Gustar expressions
Activities
Adjective agreement

Chapter 2
Numbers 32–59
School supplies
Expressing need

Chapter 3
Places and buildings

Chapter 4
Food
Expressing likes and preferences
Adjective agreement

Chapter 5
Numbers 60–100
Family and friends
Adjectives describing physical characteristics
Possessive adjectives
Tener

Planning

Cross-Curricular Connections

Economics Connection *(pp. 232–233)*
Have students find out today's value of a currency from a Spanish-speaking country and convert the prices on p. 232. Have students then compare amounts among the different currencies.

Geography Connection *(pp. 242–243)*
Have students complete a Venn diagram with clothing items. (See the Projects for Proficiency BLMs for a template.) Label one circle Argentina and the other Puerto Rico. The whole diagram should have a label that reads: *¿Qué ropa llevas en julio?* Ask students to fill in the circles with appropriate clothing items.

Math Connection *(p. 252)*
Have pairs of students create an ad for a shop in a Spanish-speaking country showing three or four featured items and the prices in that country's currency and in U.S. dollars. They should name the store and write any other pertinent advertising information. Display the ads around the room.

(For further cross–curricular activities, see the Conexiones *section on pp. 250–251.)*

Capítulo 6

¿Qué desea Ud.?

OBJECTIVES

At the end of this chapter, you will be able to:

- **describe the color, fit, and price of clothes**
- **ask about and buy clothes**
- **tell where and when you bought clothes and how much you paid for them**
- **compare where people shop for clothes in Spanish-speaking countries and in the United States**

Tres generaciones llevan ropa tradicional, Guatemala

229

Teaching Suggestions

See the Writing, Audio & Video Activities book for Writing Activities that you may elect to use throughout the chapter.

Multicultural Perspectives

The indigenous people of Mexico and Central America may be seen wearing unique clothing. A *huipil* is an embroidered blouse. An *enredo* is a long, wrapped skirt. A *rebozo* is a shawl that can serve as a fashion accessory, as a head covering, or to cradle a baby. Men wear *sarapes* (ponchos), *huaraches de seis agujeros* (sandals with two rows of three eyelets, laced with leather cords) and *sombreros de palma* (straw hats). The patterns embroidered on the fabric of the clothing often contain information about community, marital status, or family affiliation. If you have students from other countries, ask them to share information about their traditional clothing, and, if possible, wear this clothing to class one day. Perhaps your students also know someone who has traveled to Mexico or Central America and can bring in these articles of clothing.

Cultural Notes

Spanish in Your Community

Have students look at their clothing labels at home and at clothes in stores to determine how many of them are made in Hispanic countries. In addition, have them bring in clothing items purchased and made in Spanish-speaking countries.

(pp. 228–229, photo)
The Mayas are a traditional people. Knowledge of customs and beliefs is passed from generation to generation through stories and conversations. A mother teaches her daughter to wear her full costume consisting of a *corte* (skirt), a *huipil* (blouse), and a *perraje* (shawl). Some costumes also include *fajas* (woven sashes) or *tocados* (headdresses). Women are often trained by their mothers and grandmothers as weavers. In addition, it is often the women who take produce and other products to regional markets to sell.

Preview

Cultural Objective

- To compare where people shop for clothes in Spanish-speaking countries and in the U.S.

 **¡Piénsalo bien!**

Play

 **Video Activity A**

Using the Video

This chapter's video focuses on shopping for clothing. Students will search for clothing bargains with our hosts in Madrid, visiting a major women's clothing store and a popular street market. Show students segment one once through, then ask them to predict what this chapter's tape will be about. Then have students watch the segment again several times. After the first time, have them brainstorm possible vocabulary and expressions they will need to talk about what they saw on the video. Ask students to identify: a) things they saw that were familiar to them, and b) things they saw that they might not see in a clothing store in their home town or city.

Video segment 1: For more teaching suggestions, see the Video Teacher's Guide.

¡Piénsalo bien!

Look at the photographs. How do the stores in these pictures compare with those that you are familiar with?

Una estatua de San Francisco está en el centro del mercado de El Parián, Puebla, México.

"Me encanta ir de compras en un mercado tradicional. ¡Cuántas gangas hay!"

230 Capítulo 6

Options

Strategies for Reaching All Students

Spanish-Speaking Students

Ask: *¿Tienen las mismas tiendas en el centro comercial por donde vives tú? ¿Cuánto cuestan los artículos que ves en las fotos? ¿Vas a los centros comerciales con tus amigos? ¿Qué hacen allí?* Share this information with your other students in class.

 **Un paso más Ex. 6-A**

Cultural Notes 

(p. 230, photo)

A sensory blur of color, sounds, and smells swirls around shoppers in an open-air market. *Papeles picados* (cut paper designs) are strung above the *puestos* (booths). Shoppers can purchase *artesanía* (handmade crafts), household goods, clothing, shoes, food, furniture, and more in a large market. Vendors carefully monitor their wares, which are hung from the canopies, organized on shelves, and attractively arranged on display tables.

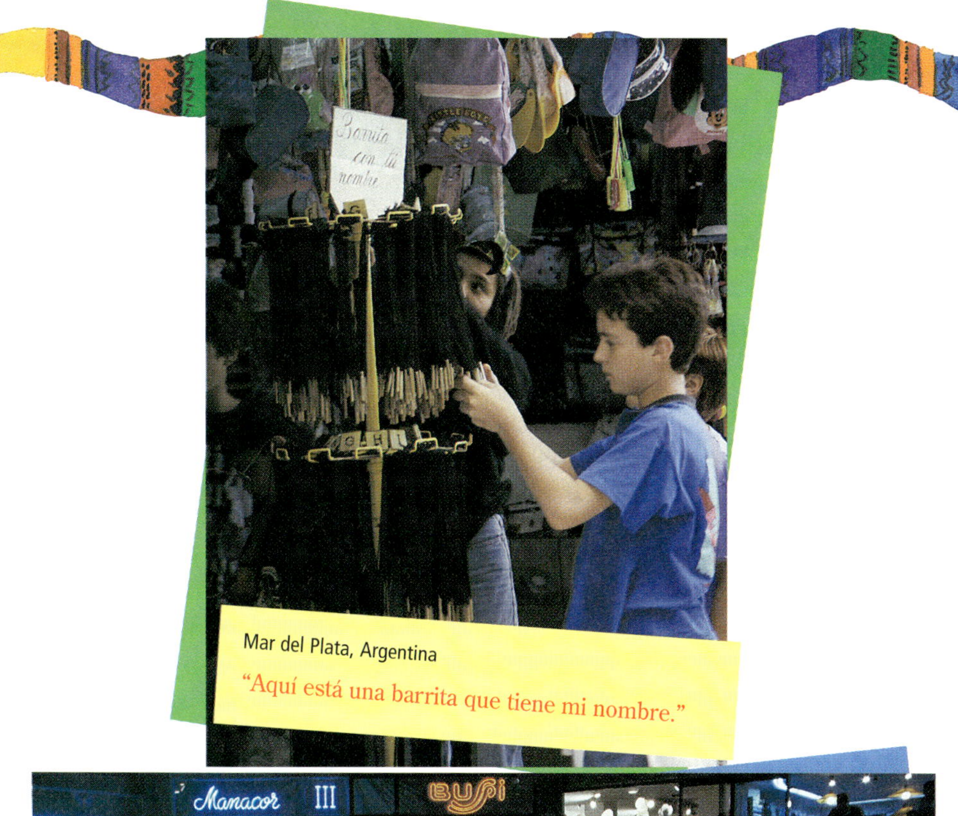

Mar del Plata, Argentina

"Aquí está una barrita que tiene mi nombre."

Centro comercial en Zaragoza, España

"Yo prefiero los centros comerciales, donde hay muchas tiendas diferentes."

Teaching Suggestions

See the Projects for Proficiency BLMs for activity ideas that you may elect to use throughout the chapter.

Critical Thinking: Evaluating Information

Ask small groups of students to prepare lists of factors they consider when making a clothing purchase. Lists might include price, brand name, size, quality, style, and so on. After students have prepared their lists, have them rank the factors according to importance. Discuss the lists.

Answers: ¡Piénsalo bien!

Answers will vary, but students may say that some stores sell similar merchandise as stores in the U.S.

Using Photos

(p. 231, top photo) Explain that *barritas* are cords with metallic bars at the end, engraved with a person's first name. They were very popular in Argentina a few years ago. Young people wore them around their necks. Ask students if they can think of a similar clothing fad that they have known and that is no longer popular (jerseys, overalls, etc.).

(p. 231, top photo)
This boy is browsing through a sidewalk display of *barritas* in one of the many retail outlets that dot the streets of downtown Mar del Plata. Located approximately 180 miles southeast of Buenos Aires, Mar del Plata, with its seaside resort and bustling downtown, is a popular tourist attraction. During the summer months of January and February, many *porteños,* or residents of Buenos Aires, travel down the coast to see the many attractions the city has to offer.

(p. 231, bottom photo)
Shopping malls are now commonplace in most Spanish-speaking countries. Not only do they have clothing stores, bookstores, and fast-food restaurants, many of them have supermarkets as well. At the Alcampo mall in Zaragoza, Spain, shoppers can eat in their favorite restaurant, look at the latest fashion designs, and buy their groceries, all without leaving the complex.

Present

Chapter Theme
Clothing and colors

Communicative Objectives
- To identify articles of clothing
- To talk about colors
- To discuss prices
- To describe clothes
- To talk about shopping
- To indicate a specific item or items
- To assist customers in a store
- To address people
- To start a conversation

Transparencies 36–37

Vocabulary Art BLMs

Pronunciation Tape 6-1

Vocabulario para conversar A

Play

Using the Video
Video segment 2: See the Video Teacher's Guide.

Video Activity B

Vocabulario para conversar

¿Cuánto cuesta la camisa?

- As your teacher reads the name of an article of clothing, point to that item if you are wearing it.
- As your teacher reads the name of each color, hold up or point to something that is that color.
- Your teacher will read the name of an article of clothing together with the name of a color. If you are wearing that article of clothing in that color, stand up.

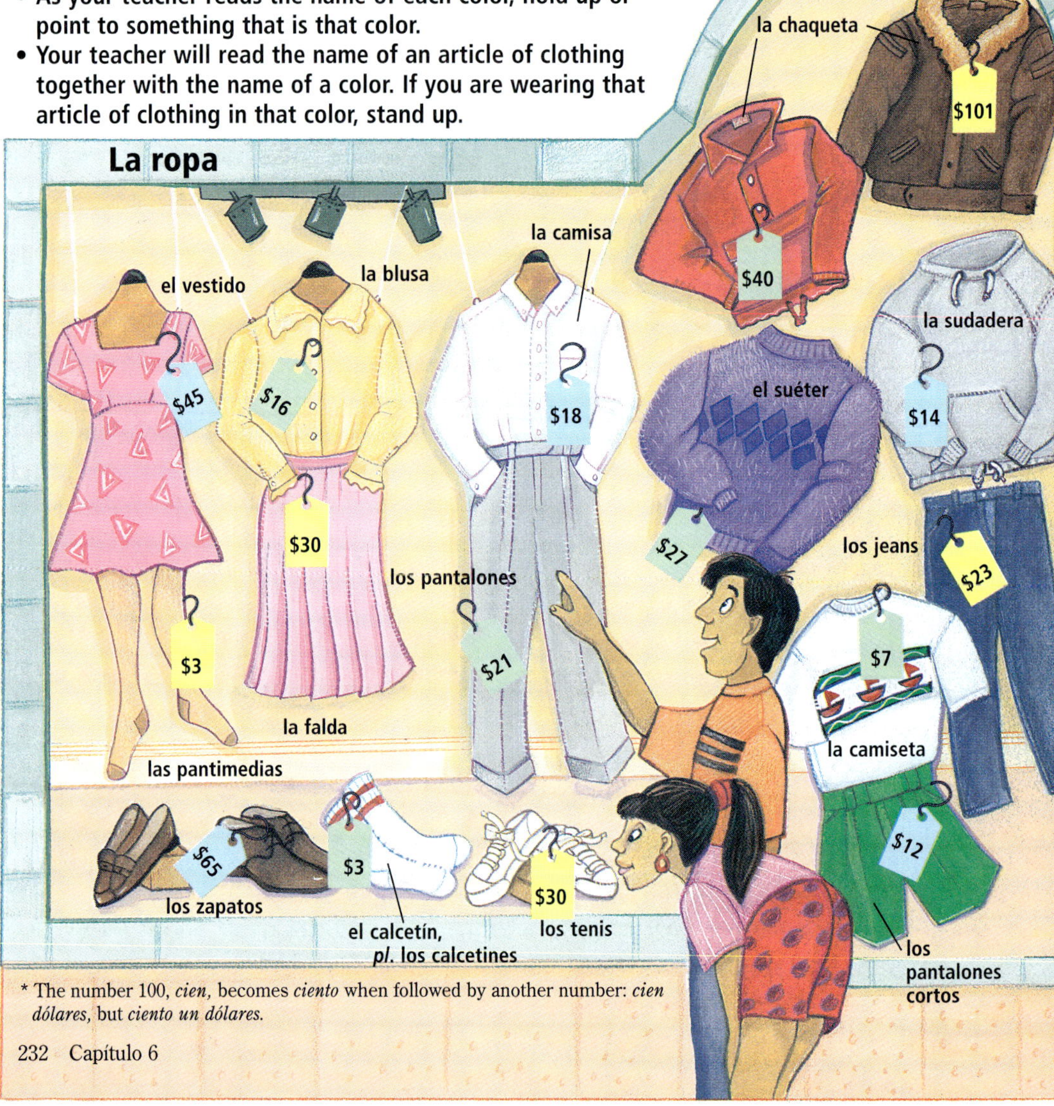

* The number 100, *cien*, becomes *ciento* when followed by another number: *cien dólares*, but *ciento un dólares*.

Options

Strategies for Reaching All Students

Enrichment
Bring in pictures of clothing from magazines and mail-order catalogues. Have individuals or small groups present pictures to the class, naming the item of clothing, its price, and color. As a follow-up conversation, elicit opinions about the items from individual students, asking questions such as: *¿Te gusta(n) . . .? ¿Qué te gusta más? ¿Qué no te gusta nada? ¿Cuesta(n) mucho o poco . . .?*

Learning Spanish Through Action
STAGING VOCABULARY: *Levántense, Siéntense, Señalen, Toquen*
1) MATERIALS: transparency of clothing from the *Vocabulario para conversar*
DIRECTIONS: Using the transparency, point to an article of clothing. Ask students who are wearing that item to stand. While students remain standing, state a color. Students wearing that color may then sit down. Continue naming colors (or have a volunteer do so) until all students are seated, and then repeat with another article of clothing.
2) MATERIALS: none
DIRECTIONS: Ask students to touch or point to articles in the room as you mention a color.

También necesitas...

¿Cómo te queda(n)?	*How does it (do they) fit you?*	los, las	*them*
Me queda(n) bien.	*It fits (They fit) me well.*	¿Cuánto?	*How much?*
¿De qué color?	*What color?*	costar: cuesta(n)	*to cost: it costs (they cost)*
buscar	*to look for*	¿Qué desea (Ud.)?	*May I help you?*
comprar	*to buy*	joven	*young man, young woman*
llevar	*to wear*		
para mí	*for me, to me*		
para ti	*for you, to you*		
este, esta	*this*		
ese, esa	*that*		
lo, la	*it*		

¿Y qué quiere decir . . . ?
el dólar
corto, -a
perdón

* When you talk about colors without a noun, use the masculine definite article: *Me gusta el rojo. No me gusta el anaranjado.*

Grammar Preview
Demonstrative adjectives and direct object pronouns are previewed here. The explanation appears in the grammar sections on pp. 255 and 261.

Teaching Suggestions
Point out that *marrón, verde, gris,* and *azul* do not change form in the feminine.

Remind students that they have seen *joven* as an adjective in Chap. 5. Explain that it can mean both "young man" and "young woman," and *jóvenes* can mean "young people," but as a form of address, *joven* is used mainly with males. *Señorita* is used when addressing a young, unmarried female.

Class Starter Review
On the day following initial presentation of vocabulary, begin the class with this activity:
Make flashcards of the fruits and vegetables from the Vocabulary Art BLMs (Chap. 4) or from grocery store ads. Color them in or have students do so. Have students say the name of the item and its color: *Esa manzana es roja. Esta lechuga es verde.*

Practice

Reteach / Review: Vocabulary

Ex. 3: Have students review the vocabulary for family members by naming other relatives for whom they're shopping.

Re-enter / Recycle

Exs. 1–2: numbers 0–31 from *El primer paso,* numbers 32–59 from Chap. 2, numbers 60–100 from Chap. 5

Teaching Suggestions

Explain the difference between the definite articles and direct object pronoun use of *la, los,* and *las.*

Exs. 1–2: Explain the use of *cuesta(n)* with singular and plural nouns.

Ex. 3: Before beginning this exercise, review noun and adjective agreement. Do a few of these aloud.

Answers: Empecemos a conversar

1 ESTUDIANTE A

a. Perdón, ¿cuánto cuesta el suéter?
b. . . . el vestido?
c. . . . la chaqueta?
d. . . . la blusa?
e. . . . la falda?
f. . . . la sudadera?

ESTUDIANTE B

a. Cuesta veintiséis dólares.
b. . . . cuarenta y tres . . .

Empecemos a conversar

With a partner, take turns being *Estudiante A* and *Estudiante B.* Use the words that are cued or given in the boxes to replace the underlined words in the example. 💡 means you can make your own choices. When it is your turn to be *Estudiante B,* try to answer truthfully.

1 

A —*Perdón, ¿cuánto cuesta la camisa?*
B —*Cuesta veintidós dólares.*

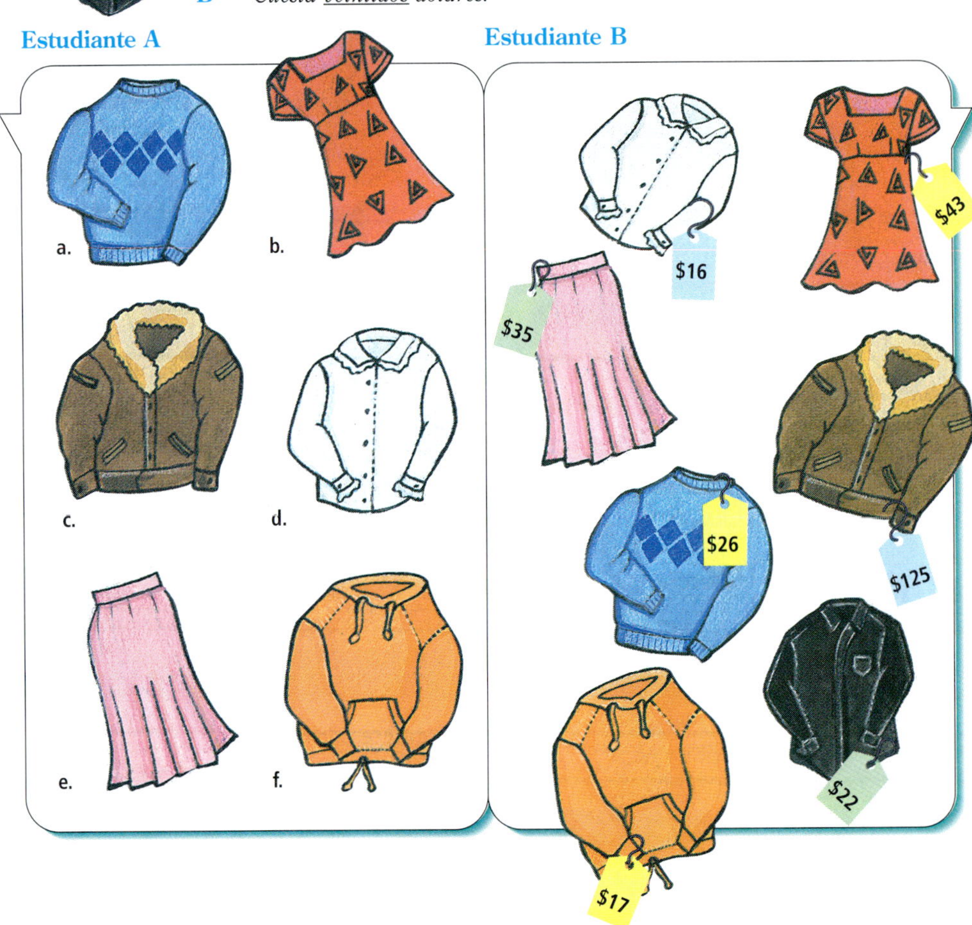

Options

Strategies for Reaching All Students

Spanish-Speaking Students

Exs. 1–3: Pair bilingual with non-bilingual students.

 **Un paso más Ex. 6-B**

Students Needing Extra Help

Have students begin filling in their Organizers.

Remind students that the nouns for articles of clothing do not change gender to match their owner. For example, a shirt *(una camisa)* is always feminine, whether a boy or girl is wearing it.

Enrichment

Ex. 1: To practice *cien* and *ciento*, have students redo the entire exercise with prices ranging from $100 to $199.

Have students bring in magazines, catalogues, or supplements from the Sunday newspaper and do Ex. 1 using the clothing items and prices in the ads as a guide.

2  A —*Perdón, ¿cuánto cuestan los zapatos?*
B —*Cuestan sesenta dólares.*

Estudiante A **Estudiante B**

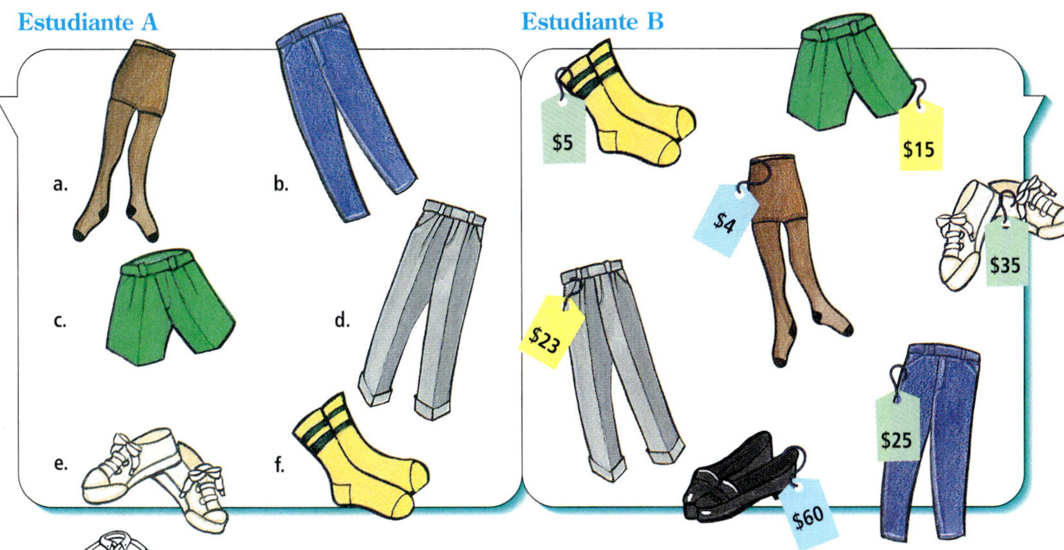

3  A —*¿Qué desea, señor (señora / joven / señorita)? ¿Una camisa?*
B —*Sí, busco una camisa azul para mí y una camisa rosada para mi hermana.*

Estudiante A **Estudiante B**

c. . . . ciento veinticinco . . .
d. . . . dieciséis . . .
e. . . . treinta y cinco . . .
f. . . . diecisiete . . .

2 ESTUDIANTE A
a. Perdón, ¿cuánto cuestan las pantimedias?
b. . . . los jeans?
c. . . . los pantalones cortos?
d. . . . los pantalones?
e. . . . los tenis?
f. . . . los calcetines?

ESTUDIANTE B
a. Cuestan cuatro dólares.
b. . . . veinticinco . . .
c. . . . quince . . .
d. . . . veintitrés . . .
e. . . . treinta y cinco . . .
f. . . . cinco . . .

3 ESTUDIANTE A
a. ¿Qué desea, señor (señora / joven / señorita)? ¿Una camiseta?
b. . . . ¿Una sudadera?
c. . . . ¿Unos jeans?
d. . . . ¿Unos calcetines?
e. . . . ¿Un suéter?
f. Questions will vary.

ESTUDIANTE B
a. Sí, busco una camiseta azul para mí y una camiseta anaranjada para mi hermana.
b. . . . una sudadera anaranjada . . . una sudadera anaranjada . . .
c. . . . unos jeans marrones . . . unos jeans negros . . .
d. . . . unos calcetines blancos . . . unos calcetines rojos . . .
e. . . . un suéter anaranjado . . . un suéter verde . . .
f. Answers will vary.

Practice

Re-enter / Recycle

Ex. 5: adjectives describing physical characteristics from Chap. 5

Background Information

Exs. 4–5 have been controlled so that students can preview the use and placement of direct object pronouns (feminine, singular *la* and masculine, plural *los)* before they are presented in the grammar section. If students can handle using a greater variety of direct object pronouns, add additional items to these exercises, presenting appropriate, revised models as well.

Teaching Suggestions

Ex. 5: Isolate the two possible responses and show how they work with the pictures. Once students understand the process, add more pictures for further practice.

Answers: Empecemos a conversar

4 In the model, note that the name of the color, *amarillo,* is a noun, and that there is no agreement: *¿La tiene en amarillo?*

ESTUDIANTE A

a. Me encanta esa camiseta. ¿La tiene en amarillo?
b. . . . chaqueta . . .
c. . . . blusa . . .
d. . . . falda . . .
e. . . . camisa . . .

4 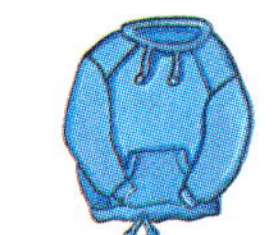

A —*Me encanta esa* <u>*sudadera*</u> *azul. ¿La tiene en amarillo?*
B —*¿Esta* <u>*sudadera*</u>*? Sí, aquí la tiene.*
o: *No, no la tenemos en amarillo.*

No insista. No los vendemos por separado. Lo sentimos. Aquí no puede escoger muslo o pechuga. Aquí, o se lleva la parejita, o no hacemos nada. Por más diferentes que le parezcan o aunque prefiera mil veces el izquierdo al derecho, los Twins no se venden por separado. Y porque, fíjese, así juntitos, da gloria de verlos. A cuál más bonito. ¿Lo toma o lo deja?

Options

Strategies for Reaching All Students

Spanish-Speaking Students

Ex. 4: Pair bilingual with non-bilingual students.

Students Needing Extra Help

Ex. 4: Point out that the first response will be used if the requested color is there, and the second response if it isn't.

Enrichment

Ex. 4: To preview the grammar, ask students the meaning of *esa / esta.* Make this preview more concrete by picking up pairs of objects and placing them so that you can touch one and point to the other to illustrate the difference between *esta / esa, este / ese.* Try not to place anything very far away so as to avoid *aquel(la).*

5 A —*¿Cómo te quedan* *los jeans?*
B —*Me quedan bien. Los compro.*
o: *No me quedan bien. Son muy grandes (pequeños).*

Estos jóvenes españoles buscan tenis nuevos.

ESTUDIANTE B
a. No, no la tenemos en amarillo.
b. ¿Esta chaqueta? Sí, aquí la tiene.
c. No, no la tenemos en amarillo.
d. ¿Esta falda? Sí, aquí la tiene.
e. ¿Esta camisa? Sí, aquí la tiene.

5 ESTUDIANTE A
a. ¿Cómo te quedan los tenis?
b. . . . los pantalones cortos?
c. . . . los zapatos?
d. . . . los pantalones?
e. . . . los calcetines?

ESTUDIANTE B
a. Me quedan bien. Los compro.
b. Me quedan bien. Los compro.
c. No me quedan bien. Son muy pequeños.
d. No me quedan bien. Son muy grandes.
e. No me quedan bien. Son muy pequeños.

Cultural Notes

(p. 236, realia)
As stated in the ad, you cannot buy only one oxford; shoes must be purchased as "twins." Footware made in Spain is world-renowned for its high quality. The town of Elche (in the region of Valencia) and Palma de Mallorca are especially famous for the production of *calzados.*

(p. 237, photo)
Young Spaniards reviewing a selection of athletic shoes. Jogging is one of the most popular forms of exercise, especially in cities where access to large parks provides scenic running paths. Health clubs with well-equipped facilities for joggers are also flourishing.

Apply

Re-enter / Recycle

Ex. 4: *gustar* expressions from Chap. 1

Teaching Suggestions

You may prefer to use the *Empecemos a leer y a escribir* sections as homework assignments.

Ex. 2: Share students' choices and discover the most popular colors. Create a class color for each item, then choose a day and see how many students wear those colors.

Ex. 3: For additional practice, tell students that they have $100 to spend on clothes at the shopping mall. Ask them to write a sentence telling what items they would like to buy and their cost: *Me gustaría comprar . . . .*

Answers: Empecemos a leer y a escribir

1 b: ¿Por qué no? Combina jeans con un suéter gris y unos zapatos negros. Él lleva jeans, un suéter rojo, blanco y azul y una chaqueta grande.
c: En la casa él lleva jeans, una camiseta blanca y una camisa roja. Ella está muy elegante en sus pantalones negros, blusa azul y suéter blanco.

Empecemos a leer y a escribir

Responde en español.

1 Two of these catalogue captions have errors. Find them and write the corrected sentences on a sheet of paper.

Options

Strategies for Reaching All Students

Spanish-Speaking Students

Ex. 3: Ask: *¿Qué llevas los fines de semana?* For listening practice, have bilingual and non-bilingual students ask and answer the same question.

Students Needing Extra Help

Ex. 2: Review colors and adjective endings for colors not ending in *-o.*

2 Choose three of the following articles of clothing and say which colors you prefer for each one.

Prefiero las chaquetas negras.

- las chaquetas
- los tenis
- los calcetines
- las sudaderas
- los jeans
- los pantalones cortos

3 ¿Qué ropa vas a llevar mañana? ¿De qué color es?

4 ¿Qué colores te gustan más? ¿Hay colores que no te gustan nada? ¿Cuáles son?

También se dice

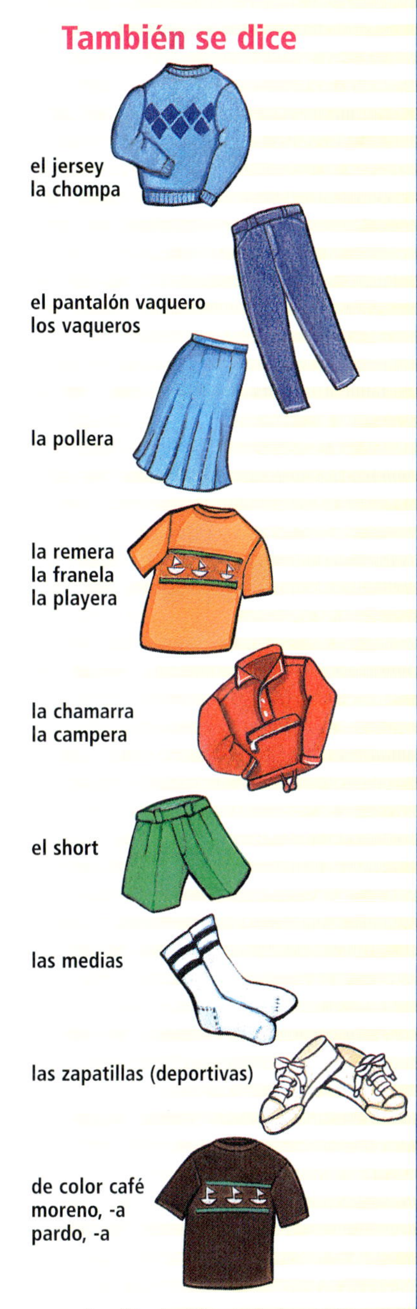

2 Answers will vary, but check for adjective agreement: *Prefiero los tenis blancos.*

3 Answers will vary: *Voy a llevar un suéter mañana. Es azul.*

4 Remind students that they will need the article *el* before each color. Responses will vary, but check for adjective agreement: *Me gustan el azul y el amarillo más. No me gusta el marrón.*

 **Practice Wkbk. 6-1, 6-2**

 **Audio Activity 6.1**

 **Writing Activities**

 **Pruebas 6-1, 6-2**

 **Comm. Act. BLM 6-1**

Present & Apply

Cultural Objective

- To compare where people shop for clothes in Spanish-speaking countries and in the U.S.

Teaching Suggestions

The idea of specialized stores where you buy just one type of product may be unfamiliar to many students. Explain this concept to them. Point out that, to some extent, we also have types of specialized stores, such as sporting goods stores, shoe stores, and so on.

Critical Thinking: Synthesizing

Have students imagine they are owners of a small clothing store. Ask: How can you increase business in your store? Using learned vocabulary, have small groups of students create ads to attract customers of large stores to their small ones. Ask them to also create an inventory list of the merchandise their stores should carry. These ads and lists might be considered as part of your student assessment.

Perspectiva CULTURAL

Hay muchos tipos de tiendas y de centros comerciales en las grandes ciudades de Hispanoamérica.

Although the concept of the shopping mall originated in the United States, many countries have adopted the idea and have sometimes improved on it by creating indoor shopping centers of great beauty.

Young people in Spanish-speaking countries like to window-shop at malls, just as you probably do. There is a wide variety of clothing available in the stores because people everywhere like to be up to date in what they wear.

In Spanish-speaking countries, there are also tailors and dressmakers who make clothing at affordable prices. Instead of renting a tuxedo or buying a beautiful dress in a store, a young person may wear custom-made formal clothing to a wedding or other special event.

Una zapatería en Caracas, Venezuela

Cerca de San Sebastián, España

Options

Strategies for Reaching All Students

Spanish-Speaking Students

Ask: *¿Hay tiendas pequeñas en tu comunidad que vendan productos de otros países? ¿Qué productos de otros países puedes comprar allí?*

Enrichment

If there is a sizable Hispanic population in your area, visit Hispanic neighborhood stores as a class trip. If this is not possible, you may wish to videotape your visit and then show it later to the class. Give students a topic on which to prepare a brief report, such as the products carried, the people who work and shop there, or how long the stores have been in existence.

Cultural Notes 

(p. 240, top photo)
Caracas, Venezuela, is only two and one-half hours by air from Miami, and only four and one-half hours from New York City. Perhaps because of its proximity to the U.S., Caracas has a strong North American influence in food, fashion, and architecture. Shopping malls are common, with some of the best known including Centro Ciudad Comercial Tamanaco, Concresa, and Centro Comercial Chacaíto.

Centro comercial en Buenos Aires

La cultura desde tu perspectiva

1 Do you think you would be able to find your favorite brands of clothing in the stores pictured? Why or why not?

2 When might young people in Latin America wear something that was made especially for them? If a visiting Latin American teen asked you why you didn't have a special outfit made for a party, how would you explain?

Answers: La cultura desde tu perspectiva

1 Answers will vary.

2 Students may mention a wedding or some other type of special event. / Answers may vary, but students may say that, here in the U.S., one doesn't usually have special outfits made for parties.

Multicultural Perspectives

Although bargaining once was a common practice in the U.S., this method of procuring goods and services is used on a much smaller scale today. In Latin America, however, it is a part of everyday life. In markets such as the one in Chichicastenango, Guatemala, both locals and tourists bargain with shop owners and vendors to establish prices. A unique aspect of these markets is that the sellers actually expect potential buyers to bargain. If they don't, the sellers may think that the buyer does not value the product! Ask students to think of examples of when they or someone in their family has used bargaining to buy something (flea markets, antique stores, garage sales, etc.). Discuss why they think bargaining is still popular in some areas, and have them brainstorm advantages and disadvantages to bargaining.

(p. 240, bottom photo)
The Spanish Basque country, Euskadi, is a region of about three million persons whose culture and language set them apart from the rest of Spain. *El país vasco* straddles the Spanish and French border west of the Pyrenees Mountains. About one-quarter of Basque people speak the Basque language, *Euskara.* The neon sign in this photograph, however, is written in Castilian.

(p. 241, photo)
Shopping malls in Spain and Latin America can offer the same attractions found in U.S. malls, with the exception that many stores often emphasize a regional or national specialty. At Galería Pacífico, the Buenos Aires mall shown here, shoppers can find bargains for renowned Argentine merchandise, such as leather goods, wool clothing, and high-quality jewelry.

Present

Chapter Theme
Clothing stores

Communicative Objectives
- To talk about shopping and places to shop for clothing
- To identify articles of clothing
- To describe clothes
- To indicate a specific item or items
- To tell when something happened
- To indicate location

 **Transparencies 38–39**

 **Vocabulary Art BLMs**

 **Pronunciation Tape 6-2**

 **Vocabulario para conversar B**

Play

Step

Using the Video
Video segment 2: See the Video Teacher's Guide.

Sección 2

Vocabulario para conversar

¿Cuánto pagaste por el suéter?

- As your teacher names each article of clothing, point to the picture of the store in which you would most likely buy it.
- As your teacher says how much he or she paid for a certain item, make a thumbs up sign if you think it is the truth and a thumbs down sign if you think it is a joke.
- As your teacher tells you where he or she bought a certain item, make a thumbs up sign if this is a logical place to purchase it and a thumbs down sign if it is not.

Options

Strategies for Reaching All Students

Enrichment
Have students work in small groups. One student says: *Voy a* + store. *¿Qué voy a comprar?* The group gets three guesses: *Vas a comprar . . .* If the group guesses within three chances, the student poses an additional question: *¿De qué color?*

Learning Spanish Through Action
STAGING VOCABULARY: *Señalen, Vayan*
MATERIALS: cards with pictures of stores, transparency of stores, or "shoe box" stores (see note on the next page under Teaching Suggestions)
DIRECTIONS: Project the transparency or place the cards on the walls of the classroom. Ask students to point or go to the store as you call out each one. In addition, ask each student: *¿Qué vas a comprar?* or *¿Qué compraste?*

También necesitas...

la ganga	*bargain*	pagar:	*to pay:*
barato, -a	*inexpensive*	(yo) pagué	*I paid*
caro, -a	*expensive*	(tú) pagaste	*you paid*
nuevo, -a	*new*	por	*for*
¡Qué + *adjective!*	*How ___!*	estos, estas	*these*
comprar:	*to buy:*	esos, esas	*those*
(yo) compré	*I bought*	otro, -a	*another, other*
(tú) compraste	*you bought*	hace + (dos semanas)	*(two weeks) ago*
		por aquí	*around here*

 **Video Activity B**

Grammar Preview

Demonstrative adjectives are previewed here. The explanation appears in the grammar section on p. 255. *Aquel(los) / aquella(s)* are presented in *PASO A PASO B.*

Teaching Suggestions

También necesitas . . . : Show students how *qué* + adjective works. Teach *compré / compraste* as vocabulary only, not as a grammar point. Do the same with *hace* + time expression.

To reinforce vocabulary, have students make a "store front" by drawing the store on paper and wrapping it around a shoe box. Put together several stores to create *el centro comercial* to be used in front of the class for vocabulary practice.

Class Starter Review

On the day following initial presentation of vocabulary, begin the class with this activity:
Have pairs of students ask their partners where they purchased certain clothing items and how much they paid for them. (If students are reluctant to discuss this topic, bring in department store catalogues to elicit the information.)

Practice

Re-enter / Recycle

Ex. 2: numbers 0–31 from *El primer paso,* numbers 32–59 from Chap. 2, numbers 60–100 from Chap. 5

Reteach / Review: Spelling

Ex. 3: Stress the importance of the accent mark on *mí* by writing *mí / mi* on the chalkboard with these sentences: *Para mí esa camisa es muy cara. Yo compré mi camisa en un almacén.*

Teaching Suggestions

Ex. 3: Review the formation of plural nouns. Explain that because of the expense, the customer is looking for another store to see if the prices are better.

Answers: Empecemos a conversar

1 ESTUDIANTE A

a. ¿Dónde compraste esos calcetines nuevos?
b. . . . jeans . . .
c. . . . pantalones . . .
d. . . . pantalones cortos . . .
e. . . . tenis . . .

ESTUDIANTE B

a.–e. Answers will vary, but should include: *el almacén, el centro comercial, la tienda de ropa, la zapatería,* or *la tienda de descuentos.*

2 ESTUDIANTE A

a. ¿Cuánto pagaste por el vestido? / ¡Qué barato (caro)!

Empecemos a conversar

1 A —*¿Dónde compraste esos zapatos nuevos?*
B —*Los compré en el centro comercial.*

2 A —*¿Cuánto pagaste por la chaqueta?*
B —*Pagué doce dólares.*
A —*¡Qué barata (cara)!*

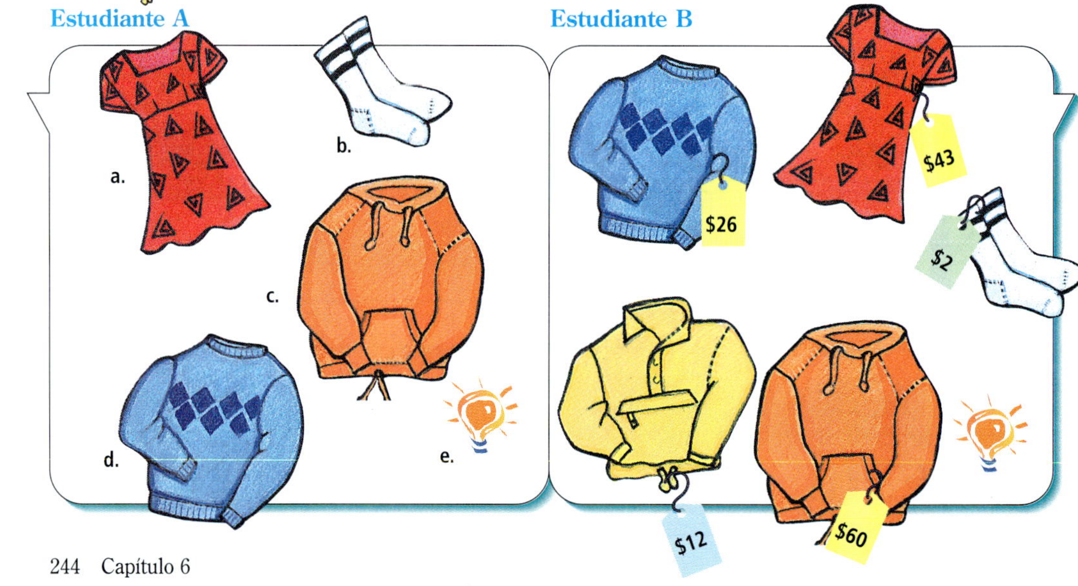

Options

Strategies for Reaching All Students

Spanish-Speaking Students

Exs. 1–4: Pair bilingual with non-bilingual students.

 **Un paso más Ex. 6-C**

Students Needing Extra Help

Exs. 1–3: Point out that *Estudiante B*'s response is not directly across from *Estudiante A*'s clue.
Ex. 2: Keep in mind that the responses *¡Qué barato(a)!* or *¡Qué caro(a)!* are subjective, as either might be deemed correct by students.

Enrichment

Ex. 2: Pairs of students can extend this dialogue by having *Estudiante A* contrast what he or she paid for the item in question. Example: *¡Qué barato (caro)! Pues, por mi suéter, yo pagué . . . . Estudiante B* can then ask where *Estudiante A* bought the item. Model sentences for students.

3 

A —*Estos pantalones cortos son caros, ¿verdad?*
B —*Sí, para mí son muy caros. ¿Hay otro almacén por aquí?*

Estudiante A **Estudiante B**

4 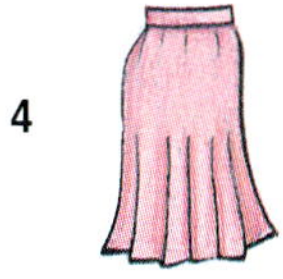

A —*Esa falda es muy bonita. ¿Es nueva?*
B —*Sí. La compré hace dos días.*
o: *No, es vieja. La compré hace un año.*

Estudiante A **Estudiante B**

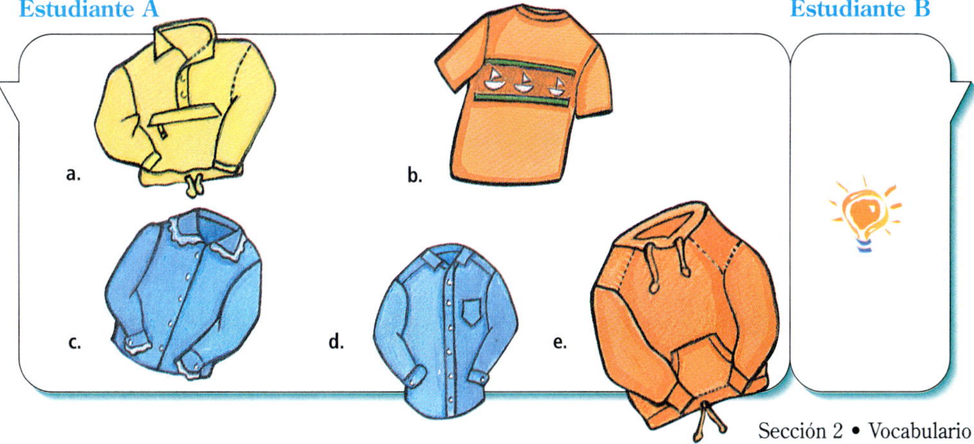

b. . . . los calcetines? / ¡Qué baratos (caros)!
c. . . . la sudadera? / ¡Qué barata (cara)!
d. . . . el suéter? / ¡Qué barato (caro)!
e. Questions will vary.

ESTUDIANTE B

a. Pagué cuarenta y tres dólares.
b. . . . dos . . .
c. . . . sesenta . . .
d. . . . veintiséis . . .
e. Answers will vary.

3 ESTUDIANTE A

a. Estos (dos) suéteres son caros, ¿verdad?
b. . . . (dos) vestidos . . .
c. . . . calcetines . . .
d. . . . zapatos . . .
e. . . . tenis . . .

ESTUDIANTE B

a. Sí, para mí son muy caros. ¿Hay otro centro comercial por aquí?
b. . . . otra tienda de descuentos . . .
c. . . . otra tienda de ropa . . .
d. . . . otra zapatería . . .
e. . . . otra zapatería . . .

4 ESTUDIANTE B

a. Esa chaqueta es muy bonita. ¿Es nueva?
b. . . . camiseta . . .
c. . . . blusa . . .
d. . . . camisa . . .
e. . . . sudadera . . .

ESTUDIANTE B

a.–e. Sí. La compré hace . . . / No, es vieja. La compré hace . . . *(Answers will vary.)*

Apply

Re-enter / Recycle

Ex. 1: *gustar* expressions from Chap. 1
Ex. 5: calendar expressions from *El primer paso*

Answers: Empecemos a leer y a escribir

1 Answers given indicate the order of the person, from left to right.
a. 3
b. 2
c. 4
d. 6

Empecemos a leer y a escribir

Responde en español.

1 Four people are describing their clothing likes and dislikes. Read these descriptions. Then match the quotations with the people in the picture. (Two people will be left over.)

a. Me gusta la ropa conservadora. Llevo camisa blanca y pantalones grises a la escuela.
b. Me encanta la ropa atrevida. Siempre llevo ropa de color negro. A mis padres no les gusta mi ropa.
c. A mí me gustan todos los colores. ¡Mira! Hoy llevo pantalones rojos con una camisa amarilla y anaranjada.
d. En el verano siempre llevo pantalones cortos y camisetas. Mis amigos y yo sólo necesitamos ropa para practicar deportes.

Options

Strategies for Reaching All Students

Enrichment

Ex. 4: Have pairs of students invent a dialogue in which they go shopping. Encourage them to describe their favorite shopping companion. If students don't shop with anyone or don't like to go shopping, have them say so and describe reasons as best they can for their shopping habits or preferences. You might wish to videotape their presentations.

Hold a "white elephant" sale in class. Ask students to bring in at least one small item (a book, toy, etc.). Half the class can be buyers and the other half sellers. Use play money and encourage students to bargain in Spanish.

2 List your three favorite items of clothing. Include their color and say how they fit you.

3 ¿Dónde puedes comprar . . .

- zapatos para la escuela?
- ropa para una fiesta?
- chaquetas para el invierno?

4 Cuando vas de compras, ¿buscas gangas o no? ¿Por qué?

5 ¿Compraste algo esta semana? ¿Qué compraste? ¿Qué compraste hace un mes? ¿Y hace dos o tres meses? Describe uno de los artículos que compraste.

2–5 Answers will vary, but encourage students to use the full range of chapter vocabulary.

Multicultural Perspectives

Latin American currencies tell much about the histories and cultures of the countries. The official currency of Venezuela, the *bolívar,* is named after Simón Bolívar, the great liberator who led the fight for independence in South America between 1810 and 1824. The *quetzal*—the official unit of money in Guatemala—is named after a rare, exotic bird found only in Central American rain forests. Encourage students to bring in and explain other foreign currencies.

 **Practice Wkbk. 6-3, 6-4**

 **Audio Activity 6.2**

 **Pruebas 6-3, 6-4**

Cultural Notes

(p. 247, realia)
Ad for the Miami International Mall. Cubans make up Miami's oldest and largest Hispanic community. They first came to Miami in large numbers in 1960 as exiles from the government of Fidel Castro. Today, Miami has other large Hispanic groups, notably Nicaraguans, who like the first group of Cubans, fled political unrest in their homelands.

(p. 247, realia)
As with U.S. dollars, *pesetas (ptas),* the currency of Spain, come in different denominations. Coins are of different sizes, shapes, and weights, depending on their worth. *Monedas* have the value of 1, 5, 10, 25, 50, 100, 200, and 500 *pesetas.* A one *peseta* coin (the silver coin on the far, top right) is smaller and lighter than the 500 *peseta* coin (the coin on the bag). Bills with different sizes and colors have denominations of 1,000, 2,000, 5,000, and 10,000 *pesetas.*

Practice

Re-enter / Recycle

Ex. 1: activities from Chap. 1, places and buildings from Chap. 3
Ex. 2: numbers 0–31 from *El primer paso,* school supplies from Chap. 2
Ex. 3: numbers 0–31 from *El primer paso,* numbers 32–59 from Chap. 2, numbers 60–100 from Chap. 5

Teaching Suggestions

Ex. 2: As a warm-up before this exercise, have students suggest a logical price for each item or use a store ad.

Ex. 3: Distribute mail-order catalogues, store leaflets, or advertising supplements from Sunday newspapers that you or students have brought in.

Answers: Comuniquemos

1 ESTUDIANTE A
Questions will vary: *¿Qué ropa llevas cuando vas al cine? (. . . al parque? / . . . al centro comercial? / . . . a la escuela? / . . . al parque de diversiones? / . . . al campo? / . . . a una fiesta?* etc.)
ESTUDIANTE B
Answers will vary: *Generalmente llevo pantalones cortos y tenis. / Nunca voy al cine.*

Here's another opportunity for you and your partner to use the vocabulary you've just learned.

¡No olvides!
a + el = al

1 Find out what your partner wears to at least four different places.

A —*¿Qué ropa llevas cuando vas al gimnasio?*
B —*Generalmente llevo . . .*
o: *Nunca voy al gimnasio.*

Options

Strategies for Reaching All Students

Spanish-Speaking Students

Ex. 1: Have students write part of the exercise: *Escribe seis oraciones que describan lo que llevas a diferentes lugares.*
Ahora lo sabes: Ask students to answer these questions aloud so that others can listen.

 **Un paso más Ex. 6-D**

Students Needing Extra Help

Ex. 1: Have students use their Organizers for this chapter and from Chap. 3 to review the places.
Ex. 2: Have students use their Organizers from Chap. 2 for school supplies.
Ahora lo sabes: Have students write this section so they can track their progress.

Cooperative Learning

Divide the class into groups of three or four students. Using vocabulary from the *Vocabulario para conversar,* have each student prepare a list of the clothing they are wearing and their colors. (As an alternative, students can list their favorite colors.) Have one student in each group collect the lists and record the colors of one type (shoes, socks, etc.) of clothing. Have another stu-

2 Find out how much your partner paid for at least five of his or her school supplies.

A —*¿Cuánto pagaste por el diccionario?*
B —*Pagué cinco dólares, más o menos.*

3 You want to buy something special to wear this summer. You have a budget of $75. Decide on three items you would like and what colors they should be. Your partner will estimate how much each item costs and tell you the total. Can you buy what you want?

A —*Me gustaría comprar unos pantalones grises.*
B —*Cuestan $25.*
A —*También debo comprar (quiero/necesito)...*

Ahora lo sabes

Using what you have learned so far, can you:

- **describe the clothes you wear?**
- **ask and tell how much something costs?**
- **tell where you bought something and how much you paid for it?**

2–3 Dialogues will vary, but encourage students to use the full range of chapter vocabulary.

Answers: Ahora lo sabes

(Answers will vary.)

- Generalmente llevo jeans y tenis blancos. *(pp. 232–233)*
- ¿Cuánto cuesta esa blusa? / Cuesta veinte dólares. *(pp. 232–233)*
- Compré una falda en el centro comercial por veintiséis dólares. *(pp. 232–233, 242–243)*

 **Audio Activity 6.3**

 **Writing Activities**

 **Examen de habilidades 1**

dent record colors for another type of clothing. Repeat until each type of clothing is recorded. Collect the responses and tally them. Before putting the results on the chalkboard, ask: What do you think is the most popular shoe color? The most popular color of jeans? and so on. (Combine some of the clothing categories for this exercise. For example, shoes / sneakers, pants / jeans.)

Apply

Background Information

(See the Cross-Curricular Connections at the beginning of the chapter on pp. 228–229 for further activities. For a complete list of the curricular areas covered in PASO A PASO A, *see p. T23 of this Teacher's Edition.)*

Choose the number of activities you want your class to do. Use the activities for homework, for enrichment, or for your Spanish-speaking students. This material is not part of the testing program, however, it is appropriate for use in student assessment.

Los colores de las banderas: This activity provides a cross-curricular connection with math and social studies. Have students draw or make various flags and use them for class or hallway decorations. Make sure students can identify the countries and their locations.

¡Qué ganga!: This activity provides a cross-curricular connection with math. Have students create additional questions based on the ad. Here are the equivalents of some unknown vocabulary from the ad: *trajes:* suits; *americanas:* suit or sport jackets; *jerseys:* sweaters; *batas:* robes; *albornoces:* hooded bathrobes; *ropa interior:* underwear; *pañuelos:* handkerchiefs; *bolsos de mano:* tote bags;

Conexiones

These activities connect Spanish with what you are learning in other subject areas.

Argentina | Bolivia | Chile
Colombia | Costa Rica | Cuba
Ecuador | El Salvador | España
Guatemala | Honduras | México
Nicaragua | Panamá | Paraguay
Perú | Puerto Rico | República Dominicana
Uruguay | Venezuela

Los colores de las banderas

These are flags of the Spanish-speaking countries. Estimate which color is the most frequently used. Estimate which color is the least used. Work with a partner. Count to 5 slowly while your partner studies the flags. Your partner will write down his or her guesses. Then switch roles.

Working with your partner, tally the number of times the colors are used. Use a chart like this one.

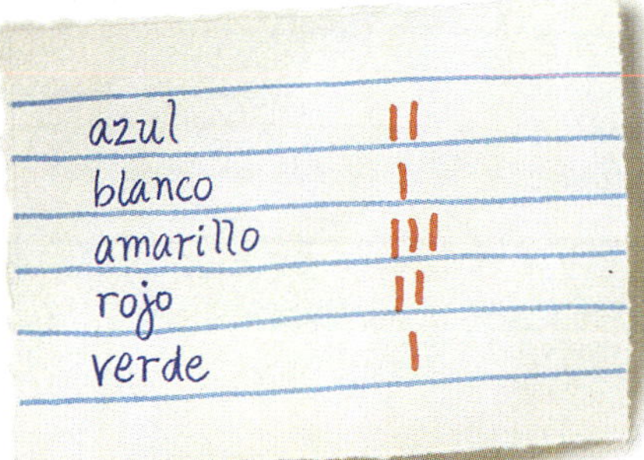

Make a bar graph showing the result of your tally.

Check your original estimates against the information shown in the graph.

Options

Strategies for Reaching All Students

Students Needing Extra Help

¡Qué ganga!: Review how to calculate percentages.

¿Qué llevan?: Remind students that they can obtain the answers by the process of elimination and logical reasoning. Be sure they use a grid in working through this problem. (See the Projects for Proficiency BLMs for a template.)

Flags of Spain and Latin America

Argentina: Blue and white worn by patriots who fought off British invaders in 1806 and 1807.
Bolivia: Red represents blood of heroes; yellow, gold; green, vegetation.
Chile: White star, progress and honor; red, blood of heroes; white, snow of Andes; blue, sky.
Colombia: Yellow represents New World; red, the blood of heroes; blue, the ocean.
Costa Rica: Coat of arms shows three volcanoes, the Caribbean, and seven stars, each representing a province.
Cuba: Star represents independence.
Ecuador: Yellow represents New World; red, the blood of heroes; blue, the ocean.
El Salvador: Blue stripes represent unity; white, peace.
España: Shield represents Aragón, Castilla, and other historic kingdoms of Spain.
Guatemala: Blue stripes represent the Atlantic and Pacific; coat of arms has *quetzal* with scroll bearing date of independence.
Honduras: Stars represent the five Central American republics that formed a union in early 1800s.
México: Coat of arms in the center. Green, independence; white, religion; red, union.

¡Qué ganga!

For what holiday do you think this ad was planned? What day of the week do you think it appeared in the newspaper? Now work with a partner to answer these questions about the ad.

a. Si unos calcetines cuestan $2.50 el domingo, ¿cuánto van a costar el lunes?

b. Si una camisa cuesta $12 el martes, ¿cuánto va a costar el miércoles?

c. Si el precio normal de unos pantalones es $34, ¿cuánto van a costar en liquidación *(on sale)*?

¿Qué llevan?

David, Martín, Mónica y Susana llevan ropa nueva. Uno de ellos lleva unos tenis nuevos, otro lleva unos jeans nuevos, otro una camiseta nueva y otro una chaqueta nueva.

Mónica: Mi tienda favorita es la zapatería.
David: A mí me gustan sólo los pantalones cortos.
Martín: ¡Qué ganga! Pagué sólo tres dólares.

¿Qué ropa nueva lleva cada uno?

cinturones: belts; *bisutería:* costume jewelry; *marroquinería:* leather goods; *prendas de sport:* sportswear; *corbatas:* ties; *pijamas:* pajamas; *sombreros y gorras:* hats and caps.
HOY TAMBIÉN en la VAGUADA: Today at our la Vaguada store also (la Vaguada is a shopping mall in Madrid)
GALERÍAS Marcando estilo: GALERÍAS setting the pace in fashion.

Tell students that normally the word *ti* is spelled without an accent mark. Explain the difference in meaning with *mi / mí.*

If students ask, tell them how to say "cents" *(centavos).* However, as is the case in item a., we generally would say *cuestan dos cincuenta* and avoid saying *dólares* and *centavos,* as we would in English.

Answers: Conexiones

Los colores de las banderas: white / green / (tallies don't include coat of arms) blue: 16; white: 16; red: 14; yellow: 5; green: 2

¡Qué ganga!: Father's Day / Sunday
a. Van a costar $2.00.
b. Va a costar $15.00.
c. Van a costar $27.20.

¿Qué llevan?: David, una chaqueta / Martín, una camiseta / Mónica, unos tenis / Susana, unos jeans

Flags of Spain and Latin America, cont'd.

Nicaragua: Coat of arms features volcanoes representing Central American union; triangle, equality; rainbow, peace; cap, liberty.
Panamá: Blue star, honesty and purity; red star, authority and law.
Paraguay: Red, white, and blue stripes honor French ideals. Coat of arms on front; treasury seal with a lion and liberty cap on back.
Perú: Symbols represent abundant animal, plant, and mineral resources.
Puerto Rico: Resembles Cuban flag recalling 1890s when both countries opposed Spanish rule.
República Dominicana: Blue, liberty; white, salvation; red, blood of heroes.
Uruguay: Stripes represent political division at time of independence. The sun represents independence.
Venezuela: Red, blood of heroes; blue, Atlantic; yellow, prosperity. Stars represent original states that united to proclaim independence.

Preview

Transparency 40

Teaching Suggestions

Have students find the three times *precio(s)* is used in the ad *(precios altos, precios mucho más bajos, precio razonable).* Using context clues, have them figure out the meaning of this word. Then have them find the adjectives that describe *precio(s).* Ask if their explanation about noun / adjective word order is consistent with these uses.

Be sure students understand the difference between *esta* and *está,* and *estas* and *estás.* Point out that this is an example of the importance of accent marks and why they must be aware of them.

Answers

Joven de Hoy / Answers will vary. Students may mention the prices and clothes.

A *precio, gangas / razonable, extraordinarios* / They follow the noun. / No. Unlike in English, in Spanish most adjectives follow nouns.

B *Este* is used with masculine, singular nouns, and *esta* is used with feminine, singular nouns. / Use *este* with a masculine noun and *esta* with a feminine noun. / *Esta falda es bonita. Este suéter es muy grande.* (Answers will vary.)

Gramática en contexto

Here is a clothing store ad. What is the name of the store? What are the advantages of shopping for clothes here?

A The ad says *un precio razonable* and *gangas extraordinarias.* What are the nouns in these expressions? What are the adjectives? Where do the adjectives come in relation to the nouns? Is this like English? Explain your answer to a partner.

B You know that *este* and *esta* mean "this." Find these words in the ad. Are the nouns they are used with masculine or feminine? Explain to a partner how to decide whether to use *este* or *esta.* Give your own example for each.

Options

Strategies for Reaching All Students

Spanish-Speaking Students

Ex. 2: Have students write part of the exercise. *Escribe oraciones para estos artículos (estas prendas). Incluye tus colores preferidos.*

Students Needing Extra Help

Ex. 2: If *Estudiante B* chooses the second response, he or she will have to determine the color. Have students use the Organizer.

¡No olvides!: Emphasize the terms singular / plural, masculine / feminine, rather than number and gender.

La posición de los adjetivos

In Spanish, adjectives usually come after the noun they describe.

Me gusta **la camisa blanca**. = *I like **the white shirt**.*

Tenemos **un perro grande y feo**. = *We have **a large, ugly dog**.*

In English, where do adjectives usually come?

1 In the following four sentences, use your finger to tap each adjective and to circle the noun it describes.

a. Prefiero las faldas azules.
b. No me gusta el vestido blanco.
c. La chaqueta amarilla me queda bien.
d. Pagué $20 por este suéter verde.

2 You and your partner are shopping. Look at the items pictured and tell your partner which ones you like. Your partner will respond with his or her choices.

A —*Me gusta la camisa azul.*
B —*A mí también.*
o: *A mí no. Prefiero una camisa verde.*
o:
A —*No me gusta la camisa azul.*
B —*A mí tampoco.*
o: *A mí sí.*

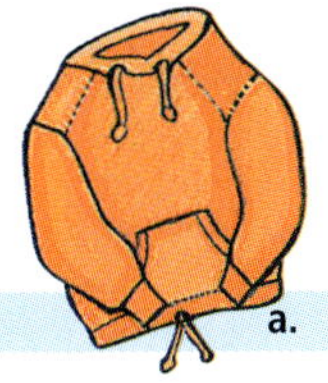
a.
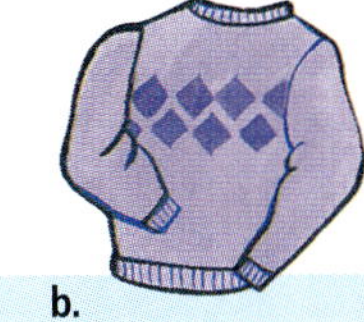
b.
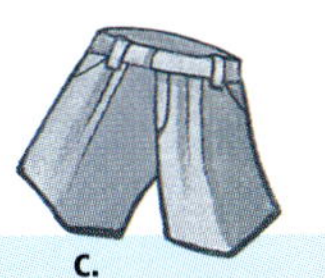
c.

d.
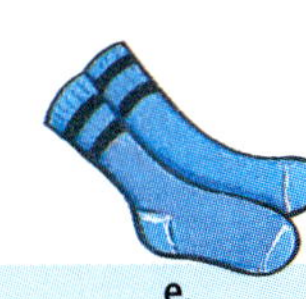
e.

f.

g.

h.

¡No olvides!

Adjectives agree in number (singular / plural) and gender (masculine / feminine) with the nouns they describe: *una chaqueta negra, un vestido rojo.*

Present & Practice

Re-enter / Recycle

Ex. 2: *gustar* expressions from Chap. 1, adjective agreement from Chaps. 1 and 4

Teaching Suggestions

La posición de los adjetivos: Have students start to fill in the grammar portion of their Organizers.

Write the example sentences (both Spanish and English) on the chalkboard or a transparency. Label the nouns and adjectives.

Answers

1 *adjectives:* a. azules, b. blanco, c. amarilla, d. verde
nouns: a. faldas, b. vestido, c. chaqueta, d. suéter

2 ESTUDIANTE A
a. (No) Me gusta la sudadera anaranjada.
b. . . . gusta el suéter morado.
c. . . . gustan los pantalones cortos grises.
d. . . . gustan los zapatos rojos.
e. . . . gustan los calcetines azules.
f. . . . gusta la camiseta blanca.
g. . . . gusta la chaqueta marrón.
h. . . . gustan los pantalones negros.

ESTUDIANTE B
a.–h. Statements will vary depending on *Estudiante B*'s preferences. Look for adjective agreement and placement.

Practice

Re-enter / Recycle

Ex. 3: adjective agreement from Chaps. 1 and 4, family and friends from Chap. 5
Ex. 5: *gustar* expressions from Chap. 1, adjective agreement from Chap. 4

Teaching Suggestions

Ex. 3: Point out the choices in the first line for *Estudiante A*. For the first *Estudiante B* response, review the indefinite articles. Model an example using a singular article of clothing.

Ex. 5: This exercise may be made more realistic by bringing in actual items of clothing or doll clothes. This will help them visualize the difference between *este* and *ese.*

Answers

3 ESTUDIANTE A
a.–h. ¿Qué desea, joven (señor / señora / señorita)? / ¿Para Ud.?
ESTUDIANTE B
a. Busco una sudadera . . . / *Statements will vary for* Estudiante B*'s second part.*
b. . . . unos calcetines . . .
c. . . . una chaqueta . . .
d. . . . un suéter . . .
e. . . . un vestido . . .
f. . . . unos pantalones . . .
g. . . . una camiseta . . .
h. Statements will vary.

Practice Wkbk. 6-5

3 Take turns with your partner playing the roles of a salesperson and a customer. The salesperson should find out what item the customer is looking for and for whom. The items can be for yourself or a person of your choice. You decide the color you want.

A —*¿Qué desea, joven (señor / señora / señorita)?*
B —*Busco unos pantalones cortos grises.*
A —*¿Para Ud.?*
B —*Sí, para mí.*
o: *No, para . . .*

a.

b.

c.

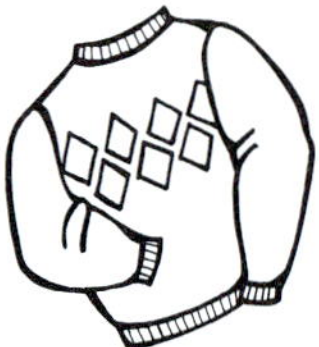
d.

e.

f.

g.

h.

En Guatemala

Options

Strategies for Reaching All Students

Spanish-Speaking Students

Exs. 3 and 5: Pair bilingual with non-bilingual students.

Students Needing Extra Help

For the demonstrative adjectives, see if students can think of any other mnemonic devices to help them remember these words. For example: In Spanish, "this" and "these" have the "t's" *(este / estos).*

Enrichment

Ex. 5: Pairs of students can vary and extend this dialogue by having *Estudiante B* name an item that he or she prefers. Encourage students to specify *ese* as well as *este* along with colors when they name the preferred item: *¿Te gusta esta sudadera rosada? / No, prefiero ese suéter azul.*

Los adjetivos demostrativos

We use demonstrative adjectives to point out people and things. Just as in English, they come before the noun. Like all adjectives in Spanish, they have the same gender and number as the nouns that follow them.

SINGULAR	PLURAL
este vestido *(**this** dress)*	**estos** vestidos *(**these** dresses)*
esta blusa *(**this** blouse)*	**estas** blusas *(**these** blouses)*
ese suéter *(**that** sweater)*	**esos** suéteres *(**those** sweaters)*
esa sudadera *(**that** sweatshirt)*	**esas** sudaderas *(**those** sweatshirts)*

4 With which words in this list would you use the demonstrative adjectives *este* and *ese?* With which words would you use *estos* and *esos? Esta* and *esa? Estas* and *esas?*

a. blusas	e. zapatos	i. ganga
b. pantalones cortos	f. vestido	j. sudaderas
c. tienda	g. suéteres	k. calcetín
d. ropa	h. camisas	l. pantimedias

5 While shopping with a friend, you pick up and look at several items. Find out if your partner likes them.

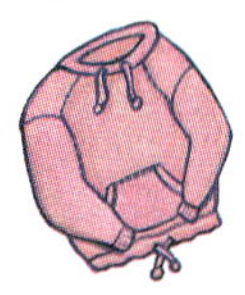

A —*¿Te gusta esta sudadera rosada?*
B —*Sí, me gusta mucho.*
o: *No, no me gusta nada.*

¡No olvides!

Me gusta esta sudadera.

Me gustan estas sudaderas.

a. b. c.

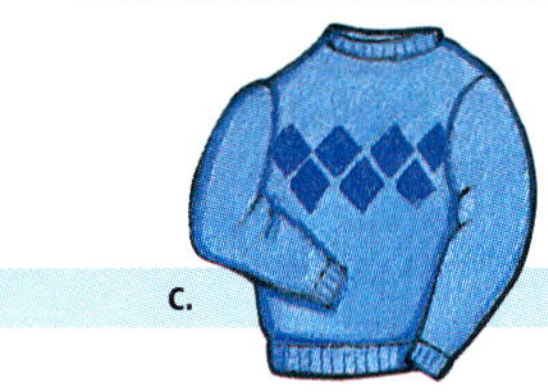

d. e. f.

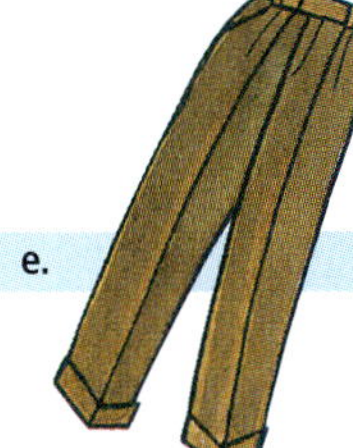

Present & Practice

Teaching Suggestions

Have students fill in the chart in the grammar portion of their Organizers. The concept of "this," "that," "these," and "those" may be confusing for students. (Color-coding these words in sentences written on a transparency can help.) Associating the four letters in *este* with the four letters in "near" and the three letters in *ese* with the three in "far" also helps many students.

Ex. 5: Ask students to bring in actual items of clothing or magazine pictures, flashcards, or doll or baby clothes.

4 este / ese: f., k.
estos / esos: b., e., g.
esta / esa: c., d., i.
estas / esas: a., h., j., l.

5 **ESTUDIANTE A**
a. ¿Te gusta esta chaqueta roja?
b. ¿Te gusta este suéter verde?
c. ¿Te gusta este suéter azul?
d. ¿Te gustan estas blusas anaranjadas?
e. ¿Te gustan estos pantalones marrones?
f. ¿Te gustan estos zapatos amarillos?
ESTUDIANTE B
a.–f. Answers will vary.

Cultural Notes

(p. 254, photo)
The Guatemalan Highlands encompass the central and western areas of that country, and have maintained a significant native weaving tradition dating from early Mayan culture (A.D. 300–1000). Mayan women often use the traditional back strap loom to weave cotton fabrics for their family. Men use the treadle loom to produce cotton and wool textiles for the commercial market. The young vendor in this photo is wearing a *huipil,* or blouse.

Practice

Re-enter / Recycle

Ex. 6: numbers 0–31 from *El primer paso,* numbers 32–59 from Chap. 2, numbers 60–100 from Chap. 5, *tener* from Chap. 5
Ex. 7: school supplies from Chap. 2

Teaching Suggestions

Ex. 6: Have students use their Organizers from previous chapters. Review *se llama(n)* and how to talk about age.

Have students bring in photographs or pictures from magazines of family gatherings and answer similar questions.

Ex. 7: Collect an assortment of school supplies from your students and hold them up, one at a time, as you ask the question. Listen for the correct use of *ese* or *esa.*

Answers

6 Dialogues will vary.
A —¿Cómo se llama esa muchacha alta y rubia? / ¿Cuántos años tiene?
B —Marisol. / Trece.

A —. . . se llama ese hombre bajo? / . . . tiene?
B —Ramón. / Treinta y cinco.

A —. . . ese muchacho callado? / . . . tiene?
B —Luisito. / Nueve.

6 You are at a family party at a friend's house and you want to know who the guests are. Find out from your partner their names and ages.

A —*¿Cómo se llama esa mujer alta y pelirroja?*
B —*Alicia.*
A —*¿Cuántos años tiene?*
B —*Veintiocho.*

Marisol, 13
Ramón, 35
Alicia, 28
Luisito, 9
etc. etc. etc.
etc. etc. etc.
María y Marta, 16
Pablo y Pedro, 14
Rosa, 75

7 Get together in small groups. Each person should put at least two of his or her school supplies in a pile. Take turns holding up items and trying to find out to whom each one belongs.

A —*¿De quién* (Whose) *es esta carpeta? ¿Es de (nombre)?*
B —*Sí, esa carpeta es de Miguel.*
o: *No, esa carpeta no es de Miguel.*

Options

Strategies for Reaching All Students

Spanish-Speaking Students

Ex. 6: Pair bilingual with non-bilingual students.

España: Tels. (93) 4100393/4100394

Una línea de zapatos inimitable, incluso hoy en día hechos a mano.

Zapatos de Tennis según Superga.

(lino, algodón, cuero)

Fabricante desde 1911.

SUPERGA

A —. . . se llama esa mujer con pelo canoso? / . . . tiene?
B —Rosa. / Setenta y cinco.

A —. . . se llaman esos gemelos sociables? / . . . tienen?
B —Pablo y Pedro. / Catorce.

A —. . . se llaman esas muchachas con pelo castaño? / . . . tienen?
B —María y Marta. / Dieciséis.

7 Dialogues will vary. Look for adjective agreement.

Using Realia

Have students identify the "mis-spelled" word in the ad *(Tennis).* Ask them why they think this word was spelled in English. (The English spelling was used to add emphasis to the foreign appeal of the product.)

 **Practice Wkbk. 6-6**

 **Writing Activities**

 **Pruebas 6-5, 6-6**

Cultural Notes

(p. 257, realia)
The shoemaker *Superga,* according to this ad, has "interpreted" tennis shoe creations in much the same way an artist "interprets" the world to create a great work of art. In Western art we have a strong tradition of still-life painting that lovingly portrays objects we deem precious. The status of these tennis shoes is elevated by their juxtaposition with precious objects. The English loan-word, *tennis,* within the Spanish text further sets the ad apart.

Present & Apply

Cultural Objective

- To compare clothing in Spanish-speaking countries and in the U.S.

Critical Thinking: Identifying Stereotypes

Guatemala is famous for the colorful textiles that are typical of the clothing worn by its many indigenous groups that comprise the majority of Guatemala's population. These textiles are very popular with tourists who often buy them in large quantities to sell in Europe and the U.S. Ask: How have these textiles become associated with Guatemala? How do you think a student at the University of Guatemala dresses?

When we see pictures of people in foreign countries, they are often wearing colorful clothing that may seem unusual to us. Sometimes it is their everyday wear. Sometimes it is special-occasion clothing. Sometimes it is a costume. How can you tell?

One way is to look at what the people are doing. If they are at their job, doing housework, or just relaxing, their clothing probably is everyday wear. On the other hand, if they are attending a wedding or a religious celebration, they are probably wearing special-occasion clothing. If they are performing for an audience, the clothing is likely to be a costume.

In family groups, another clue is the pose. If it is a formal pose, the people are probably wearing special-occasion clothing. If it is an informal pose, the clothing is more likely to be everyday wear.

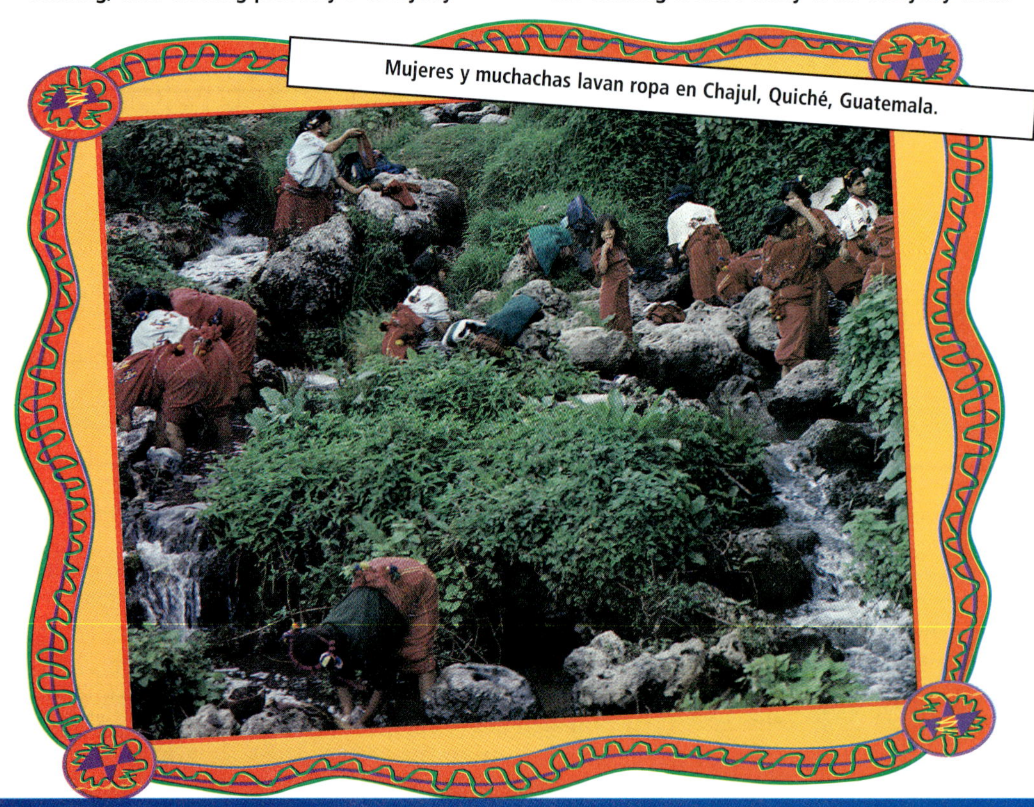

Mujeres y muchachas lavan ropa en Chajul, Quiché, Guatemala.

Options

Strategies for Reaching All Students

Spanish-Speaking Students

 **Un paso más Ex. 6-E**

El Ballet Folklórico de México

La cultura desde tu perspectiva

1 Work with a partner to categorize the clothing that the people in the photos are wearing as (a) everyday wear, (b) special-occasion clothing, or (c) costumes.

2 Now look at these photos taken in the United States. How might someone who has never been to the United States misinterpret them? How does your answer help explain why we sometimes misinterpret the clothing worn by people in other countries?

Answers: La cultura desde tu perspectiva

1 *p. 258:* everyday wear; *p. 259 (top photo):* costumes, *(bottom photos)* Answers will vary.

2 Answers will vary, but students may mention that someone who has never been to the U.S. may think that this is the way people dress here all the time. / We sometimes think the same about the clothing worn by people in other countries, because we don't have enough background information about why they are wearing those particular clothes.
Ask students how they think people in Spanish-speaking countries see us portrayed, based on movies or TV programs from the U.S.

 **Writing Activities**

Cultural Notes

(p. 258, photo)
Chajul lies in the northern section of the Guatemalan department of Quiché, in what is referred to as the "Ixil Triangle," drawn by the three neighboring towns of Chajul, Nebaj, and San Juan Cotzal. These communities are inhabited by the Ixil Maya, who speak a unique language and maintain their rich culture.

(p. 259, top photo)
Supported in part by the Mexican Department of Tourism, the Ballet Folklórico de México is one of Mexico's premier cultural institutions. It was founded by choreographer Amalia Hernández in 1952 and had eight dancers at that time. Now the company has two troupes: one that performs in Mexico and another that tours abroad.

Preview

 **Transparency 41**

Answers

A The letter *m.* / *La* refers to the letter.

B *un huevo* / *Lo* refers to *un huevo.* / Use *lo* to refer to masculine, singular nouns and *la* to refer to feminine, singular nouns.

Sección 4

Gramática en contexto

Read these riddles from a children's book.

A The answer to the first riddle is a letter (*una letra*) of the alphabet. Which one do you think it is? In the third line, what do you think *la* refers to?

B The answer to the second riddle is something you eat. What do you think it is? In the third line, what do you think *lo* refers to? With a partner, decide on a rule about when to refer to something as *lo* or *la*.

Options

Strategies for Reaching All Students

Students Needing Extra Help

Ask students where the direct object pronoun is placed in the following English sentences: I have them. / I didn't buy it. (after the verb) Where is it placed in Spanish? *Los tengo.* / *No lo compré.* (before the verb) Have students copy the Spanish and English examples and underline the pronouns and circle the verbs.

El complemento directo: Los pronombres

A direct object tells who or what receives the action of the verb.

Quiero **esa falda.**	*Esa falda* tells what I want.
Compré **los zapatos.**	*Los zapatos* tells what I bought.

To avoid repeating a direct object noun, we often replace it with a direct object pronoun ("it" or "them").

— ¿Cuándo compraste **la falda?**
— **La** compré hace dos días.

— Isabel, ¿tienes **mi suéter?**
— No, no **lo** tengo. Creo que Manolo **lo** tiene.

Which direct object pronoun replaces *la falda?* Which replaces *mi suéter?*

SINGULAR		PLURAL	
lo	*it* (masculine)	**los**	*them* (masculine)
la	*it* (feminine)	**las**	*them* (feminine)

- The direct object pronoun usually comes right before the verb. If the verb is negative, the pronoun comes between *no* and the verb.

  — ¿Compras **esos pantalones?**
  — Sí, **los** compro.
  o: No, no **los** compro.

- When we have a verb followed by an infinitive, the direct object pronoun is usually placed right before the main verb (not the infinitive).

  — ¿Quieres comprar **esa falda?**
  — Sí, **la** quiero comprar.

  In the sentence *Necesito llevar un suéter*, which is the main verb? Which is the infinitive? How would you restate this using a direct object pronoun?

- Direct object pronouns have the same gender (masculine or feminine) and number (singular or plural) as the nouns they are replacing.

  — Me gusta mucho **esa blusa**. **¿La** tiene en azul?

- When the pronoun replaces both a masculine and a feminine direct object noun, we use *los*.

  — ¿Cuándo compraste **la falda y el vestido?**
  — **Los** compré el sábado.

Present

Teaching Suggestions

1. Discuss what students already know about direct objects from English: they answer the question "who" or "what" of the verb, or receive the action of the verb.
2. Pronouns replace nouns. Once we have stated the noun, we usually replace it with "it" or "them."
3. Using familiar Spanish nouns, have them decide which object pronoun will replace each noun.
4. Using examples from the book and then creating others, have two students stand in front of the classroom, one holding a card that reads *Quiero* and the other *ese suéter.* The back of the *Quiero* card should read *quiero* and the back of the *ese suéter* card should read *Lo.* At this point the students should flip their cards. The second student moves to the other side of the first, creating *Lo quiero.*
5. Repeat this process with variations, using sentences with *no* and a verb followed by an infinitive.
6. Delay the explanation of attaching the object pronoun to the infinitive. This will appear in *PASO A PASO B,* Chap. 11.
7. Remind students that they already know how to replace and combine a masculine and feminine subject with the masculine plural form.

Practice

Re-enter / Recycle

Ex. 2: calendar expressions and numbers 0–31 from *El primer paso,* adjective agreement from Chaps. 1 and 4, food from Chap. 4

Teaching Suggestions

Ex. 4: Review adjective agreement and *hace* + time expression. Show students how to arrive at the number of days (subtracting the date from April 26). Be aware that some math errors may occur. Point out that, like the direct object pronoun, *nueva* will change depending on the clothing item.

Have students first do this exercise without *hace* + time expression in order to focus on the use of the direct object pronoun.

Answers

1 la: chaqueta / lo: suéter / los: calcetines / las: camisas

2 ESTUDIANTE A

a. ¿Cuándo comes arroz?
b. . . . jamón?
c. . . . lechuga?
d. . . . sopa de tomate?
e. . . . queso?
f. . . . pan tostado?
g. . . . ensalada?
h. . . . pescado?
i. Questions will vary.

ESTUDIANTE B

Statements for *Estudiante B* will vary.

a. Lo como todos los días. / No lo como nunca. / b. Lo . . . /

1 Read the sentences on the left. Which noun on the right has been replaced by a direct object pronoun in each sentence?

Sí, **la** quiero.	camisas
No **lo** voy a comprar.	calcetines
María **los** tiene.	chaqueta
María y Juan **las** quieren comprar.	suéter

2 Ask your partner how often he or she eats certain foods.

A —*¿Cuándo comes pollo?*
B —*Lo como todos los días.*
o: *No lo como nunca.*

Estudiante A

a. b.

c.

d.

e.

f.

g.

h.

i.

Estudiante B

nunca
a veces
los (viernes)
en (el almuerzo)

Options

Strategies for Reaching All Students

Students Needing Extra Help

Ex. 2: Have students review the vocabulary for the foods pictured. If available, have them review their Organizers for Chap. 4 (food).

3 Discuss with your partner what color you prefer for these items of clothing.

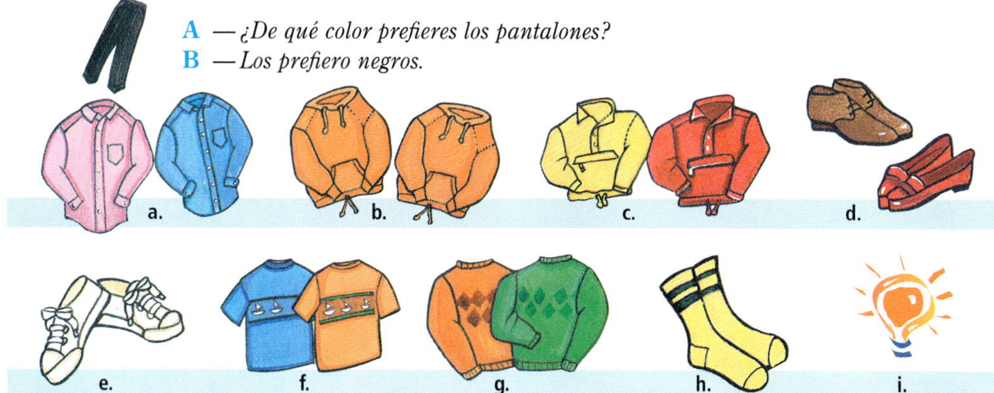

4 Today is April 26 and you recently did a lot of shopping for clothes. Use the calendar to answer your partner's questions.

A —*Tu chaqueta es nueva, ¿no?*
B —*Sí, la compré hace once días.*

c. La . . . / d. La . . . / e. Lo . . .
f. Lo . . . / g. La . . . / h. Lo . . .
i. Answers will vary.

3 ESTUDIANTE A

a. ¿De qué color prefieres las camisas?
b. . . . las sudaderas?
c. . . . las chaquetas?
d. . . . los zapatos?
e. . . . los tenis?
f. . . . las camisetas?
g. . . . los suéteres?
h. . . . los calcetines?
i. Questions will vary.

ESTUDIANTE B

a. Las prefiero . . . / b. Las . . .
c. Las . . . / d. Los . . . / e. Los . . .
f. Las . . . / g. Los . . . / h. Los . . .
i. Answers will vary.

4 Order of dialogues will vary.

A —Tu camisa es nueva, ¿no?
B —Sí, la compré hace veinte días.

A —Tus tenis son nuevos . . .
B —. . . los compré . . . dieciocho días.

A —Tu suéter y tu camiseta son nuevos . . .
B —. . . los compré . . . dos semanas (catorce días).

A —Tus jeans son nuevos . . .
B —. . . los compré . . . nueve días.

A —Tus calcetines son nuevos . . .
B —. . . los compré . . . tres días.

A —Tu sudadera es nueva . . .
B —. . . la compré . . . dos días.

Practice

Re-enter / Recycle

Ex. 5: school supplies, school subjects, and *necesito / necesitas* from Chap. 2

Ex. 6: school supplies and *necesito / necesitas* from Chap. 2

Teaching Suggestions

Ex. 5: Have students first practice using the direct object pronoun without *para mi clase de* ___. To preview, have students point to the object and name it *(esta carpeta de argollas)* before using the direct object pronoun.

Answers

5 Order of questions will vary.

ESTUDIANTE A

¿Necesitas estos bolígrafos?
. . . esta calculadora?
. . . estas carpetas?
. . . esta chaqueta?
. . . este cuaderno?
. . . este diccionario?
. . . estos lápices?
. . . esta regla?
. . . este suéter?
. . . este tenis?
. . . esta manzana?
. . . esta mochila?
. . . estos libros?

5 You're trying to help your partner clean out a messy locker. Ask whether he or she needs the objects pictured.

A —*¿Necesitas esta carpeta de argollas?*
B —*Sí, la necesito para mi clase de ciencias de la salud.*
o: *No, no la necesito.*

Options

Strategies for Reaching All Students

Spanish-Speaking Students

Exs. 5–6: Pair Spanish-speaking students.

Students Needing Extra Help

Ex. 5: Have students review the vocabulary for the items pictured. If they have their Chap. 2 Organizers, have them review them for school supplies.

Remind students that they will be using direct object pronouns in the answers.

Ex. 6: Remind students that the direct object pronoun comes before the first verb in *Estudiante B*'s question.

6 You're talking to a friend about some school supplies you need to buy. With a partner, take turns asking and answering questions about five items.

A —*Necesito comprar un diccionario.*
B —*¿Cuándo lo quieres comprar?*
A — . . .

ESTUDIANTE B
Answers will vary, but look for correct use of direct object pronouns.
Sí, los necesito para . . . (No, no los necesito.)
. . . la necesito . . .
. . . las necesito . . .
. . . la necesito . . .
. . . lo necesito . . .
. . . lo necesito . . .
. . . los necesito . . .
. . . la necesito . . .
. . . lo necesito . . .
. . . lo necesito . . .
. . . la necesito . . .
. . . la necesito . . .
. . . los necesito . . .

6 Order of dialogues will vary. Make sure students use correct indefinite articles and direct object pronouns. A sample dialogue is as follows:
A —Necesito comprar unos lápices.
B —¿Cuándo los quieres comprar?
A —Mañana.
B —¿Dónde los vas a comprar?

 **Practice Wkbk. 6-7, 6-8**

 **Audio Activity 6.4**

 **Pruebas 6-7, 6-8**

 **Comm. Act. BLMs 6-2, 6-3**

Apply

Pronunciation Tape 6-3

Todo junto A

Play

Todo junto B

Play

Using the Video

Video segment 3: See the Video Teacher's Guide.

Video Activity C

Re-enter / Recycle

Activities 1–2: numbers 0–31 from *El primer paso,* numbers 32–59 from Chap. 2, numbers 60–100 from Chap. 5

Activities 1–3: adjective agreement from Chaps. 1 and 4

Teaching Suggestions

Choose the most appropriate activities for your class. Change the order if necessary.

Here are some additional words students might request: *la manga (corta / larga):* (short / long) sleeve; *el algodón:* cotton; *la lana:*

Here's an opportunity for you to put together what you learned in this chapter with what you learned earlier.

1 ¡Vamos de compras!

With your partner, play the roles of a store clerk and a customer who wants to buy an item of clothing. First, fold a sheet of paper into three sections. Brainstorm the following with your partner:

- things you can buy in a department store
- things you might say to a salesperson
- things the salesperson might say to you

Write as many words or expressions as you can in each category. Using your brainstorming sheet as a reference, now play the roles of the salesperson and customer. Here are some of the things you might include in your conversation.

- Polite greetings
- Questions and answers about a purchase you want to make, such as the price and the colors they have it in
- Decision about whether or not you will buy the item and why or why not
- Polite close

2 ¿Qué vas a comprar?

Imagine that you and some friends are helping a mail-order company increase its sales to teenagers. Work with a group to prepare a catalogue of clothing items to be sold. You may use magazine or catalogue pictures or draw them yourselves.

Describe your merchandise to two other groups. Have each of these groups select the one item from your catalogue they think would be most popular.

Make a bulletin board display of the items selected from each group's catalogue. Be sure to write a caption for each item.

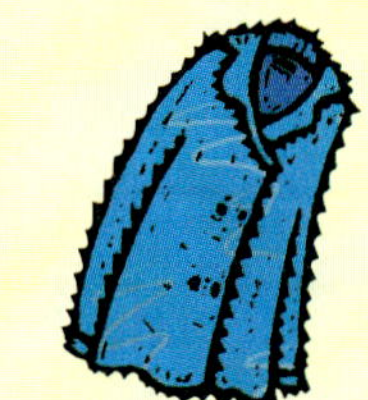

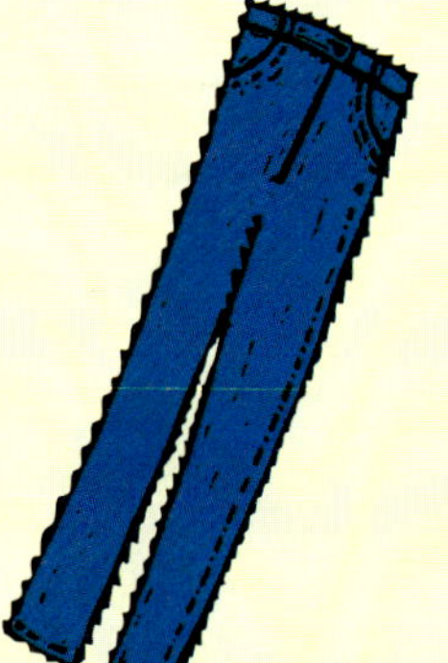

Options

Strategies for Reaching All Students

Students Needing Extra Help

Ahora lo sabes: Have students write this section so that they can chart their progress.

Enrichment

¡Vamos de compras!: As a homework assignment, have students write a dialogue in which the parent wants the son or daughter to buy certain kinds or colors of clothes. Ask volunteers to role play and act out the dialogues.

Cooperative Learning

Have students work in groups of three or four to role play fashion designers. Their assignment is to come up with the best-looking outfit design for today's teenager. Using pictures and text, have one student in each group be responsible for presenting wool; *a rayas:* striped; *a cuadros:* checked; *claro, -a:* light colored; *oscuro, -a:* dark colored; *la ropa interior:* underwear; *el cuero:* leather (presented in *PASO A PASO B,* Chap. 8).

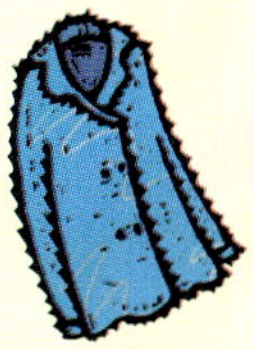

¡Vamos de compras!: Provide students with this model.
A—Perdón.
B—¿Qué desea, señor (señora / joven / señorita)?
A—Me gustaría ver ese suéter amarillo, por favor.
B—¿Este suéter?
A—Sí. ¿Cuánto cuesta?
B—Veinticinco dólares.
A—¿Lo tiene en verde también?
B—Sí, aquí lo tiene.
A—¡Qué bonito! Lo compro.

Answers: Ahora lo sabes

Answers will vary, but look for adjective agreement, adjective placement, and direct object pronouns.

- Elena tiene dos suéteres azules y una chaqueta roja. *(pp. 232–233, 242–243, 253)*
- ¿Quién es esa mujer? *(p. 255)*
- ¿La tiene en rojo? *(p. 261)*

Writing Activities

Comm. Act. BLMs 6-4, 6-5

Examen de habilidades 2

3 ¿Quién es?

Write your name on a card, then get together in small groups and put all the cards upside down in a pile. Choose one student in the group to be the moderator. He or she picks a card, but doesn't let anyone see it. Take turns asking *sí/no* questions in order to guess whose name is on the card. For example: *¿Es una muchacha? ¿Tiene pelo rubio corto? ¿Lleva un suéter rojo?* The first person who guesses correctly becomes the next moderator.

Ahora lo sabes

Using what you have learned so far, can you:

- **identify and describe articles of clothing?**
- **point out specific people and things?**
- **avoid repeating a noun by replacing it with *lo, la, los,* or *las?***

and explaining the new design to the class. Allow the class to vote for the best outfit. As an alternative, allow students to design outfits or school uniforms using newspaper, crepe paper, and markers. Award prizes for creativity and fashion.

Apply

Process Reading
For a description of process reading, see p. 60.

Teaching Suggestions
Mira la lectura: Since the grammar of this chapter includes adjective word order, students may ask about the adjective + noun order of *el mayor surtido.* Explain that this is an alternative word order used to avoid awkward sentences.

Tell students that "percent" is read as *por ciento.*

Answers
Antes de leer
Answers will vary, but students may mention: *números, la hora, la fecha, el nombre de la tienda de ropa.* Assist students with any unfamiliar vocabulary: *la ganga* (sale), *los precios* (prices), etc.

Mira la lectura
Answers will vary.

¡Vamos a leer!

Antes de leer

STRATEGIES ➤ **Using prior knowledge**
Making predictions

What are some things you might find in a clothing store ad? Working with a partner, make a list of three things in Spanish.

Mira la lectura

STRATEGY ➤ **Skimming**

Skim the ads on page 269 to get a general idea of what is for sale. Which store would you shop in?

STRATEGY ➤ **Scanning**

Scan the ads. Did all of them include the three things you listed in *Antes de leer?*

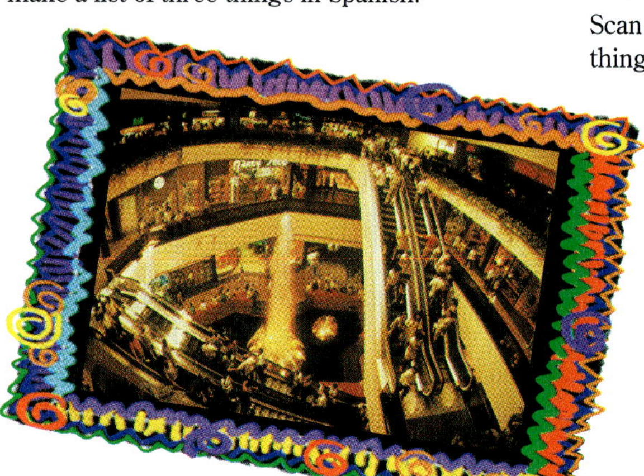

Plaza de las Américas en San Juan, Puerto Rico

Infórmate

STRATEGY ➤ **Using context to get meaning**

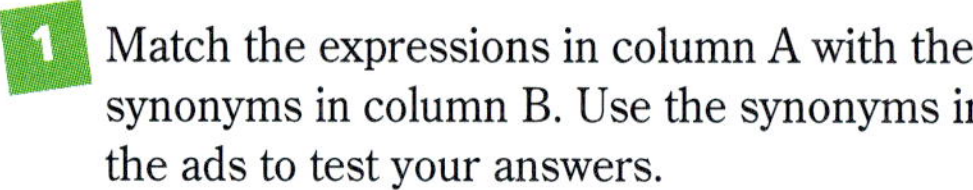

1. Match the expressions in column A with the synonyms in column B. Use the synonyms in the ads to test your answers.

A	B
el mayor surtido	costos
precios	historias imaginarias
leyendas	la selección más grande

2. Imagine that you are visiting New York. Use the information in the ads to choose two items that you might buy to take home with you. Which stores would you buy them in?

Aplicación

1. Read these advertising slogans in English. What similar phrases can you find in these Spanish-language ads?

   a. Like no other store in the world.
   b. Insider's Club saves you 10%.
   c. More than just a hamburger.
   d. Big savings.

2. Explain to a partner at least one reason you think ads in Spanish might be distributed in New York.

Options

Strategies for Reaching All Students

Students Needing Extra Help
Mira la lectura: Make sure students understand the nature of skimming. Have students work in pairs, where one student answers the questions and the other records the responses. Set a limited amount of time for this activity.

20%-70% de descuento

No hay otra tienda como Green's Basement. El centro de descuento más famoso del mundo en ropa para mujeres, jóvenes y niñas. Este mes el lugar ideal para comprar zapatos elegantes pero baratos.

GREEN'S BASEMENT
132 CANAL STREET

La selección más completa en ropa deportiva de New York University

J. Jones Co.
1320 University Place
(Cerca de NYU)

ABIERTO
lunes a viernes
9:30 a 10:00
domingo
12:00 a 6:00

En Nueva York, el mayor surtido de chaquetas de cuero. Más que chaquetas de cuero, son leyendas americanas.

- Chaquetas, pantalones y camisas para hombres, mujeres y niños
- Servicio y precios excelentes
- Descuentos especiales para pilotos y policías

10% de descuento con este anuncio

Cockpit

492 Lexington Avenue, entre las calles 32 y 33

¡La última moda para los jóvenes!

URBAN AVENGER

749 Quinta Avenida (*cerca de la calle 57*)
Tenemos ropa deportiva de todos los colores para jóvenes y adultos atrevidos. ¡Ya están aquí! ¡Los últimos estilos! Tus padres nunca compran su ropa aquí.

Infórmate

1 el mayor surtido, la selección más grande / precios, costos / leyendas, historias imaginarias

2 Answers will vary.

Aplicación

1 a. No hay otra tienda como Green's Basement.
b. 10% de descuento con este anuncio.
c. Más que chaquetas de cuero, son leyendas americanas.
d. 20%–70% de descuento

2 Answers will vary, but students may say that a large population of Spanish-speaking people live in New York.

Cultural Notes

(p. 268, photo)
One of the most convenient places to browse and buy merchandise in Puerto Rico is la Plaza de las Américas, the largest shopping mall in the Caribbean. This multi-storied structure contains about 200 shops, restaurants, and movie theaters. Other malls on the island include la Plaza Carolina, la Plaza del Carmen in Caguas, la Plaza del Caribe in Ponce, and the Mayagüez Mall.

Apply

Process Writing

In this chapter, the revise and edit steps will appear in an abbreviated form.

For information regarding writing portfolios, see p. 62.

Teaching Suggestions

Step 4: Have students illustrate their ads with drawings or magazine pictures.

Allow them to write their copy separate from the picture and have the class guess which description goes with which picture.

Answers: ¡Vamos a escribir!

Look for correct use of adjectives and verbs. Encourage students to use the full range of vocabulary.

Multicultural Perspectives

The fashion industry has been influenced by styles and designs typical of Spain and Latin America. (Two of the leading fashion designers in the world are from Latin America: Óscar de la Renta and Carolina Herrera.) *Gauchos* are the cowboys of the Pampas in Argentina. The word *gauchos* is also used to describe a type of women's baggy trousers that are often gathered at the ankles. Ask students if they know of any other types of clothing from various cultures.

¡Vamos a escribir!

Create an ad for an article of clothing that might appear in a young people's magazine or catalogue.

1 First, think about what might appeal to you and your friends. What article of clothing are you going to sell? What colors does it come in? Where can you buy it? How much does it cost? Jot down the answers to these questions in Spanish.

Invent a brand name for your clothing. Create a slogan for the brand or the store. Use the slogans from the ads in *¡Vamos a leer!* as a guide.

2 Make a rough copy of your ad, then show it to a partner. Ask for comments on what he or she likes as well as what might be changed. Think about the changes your partner suggests and any others you might want to make, and rewrite your ad.

3 Make a clean copy of your ad. Copy edit it using the following checklist:

- spelling
- capital letters
- punctuation
- position of adjectives
- correct use of direct object pronouns (*lo, la, los, las*)

4 Now you're ready to share your ad. You can file it in your writing portfolio, or the entire class can collect the ads into a catalogue called *Ropa de Primavera / Verano / Otoño / Invierno de (año)*.

Options

Strategies for Reaching All Students

Spanish-Speaking Students

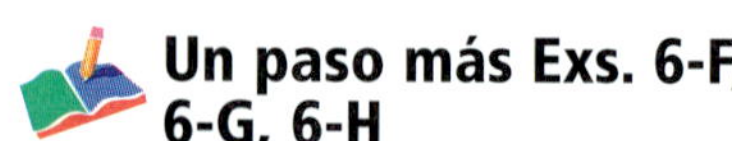
Un paso más Exs. 6-F, 6-G, 6-H

Students Needing Extra Help

Step 1: Use the Organizer.
Step 2: If you elect to have students do this activity in groups, try to get an art-gifted student or visual learner in each one.
Step 3: Use Organizers from other chapters.

Enrichment

As an extension of this activity have students bring in a picture from a magazine and write the advertising copy for the clothing shown.
Have groups of students collaborate with an art class on a poster showing what clothes

 **Writing Activities**

 **Mi portafolio**

 **Test Generator**

Resumen del capítulo 6

Use the vocabulary from this chapter to help you:

- **describe the color, fit, and price of clothes**
- **ask about and buy clothes**
- **tell where and when you bought clothes and how much you paid for them**

to identify articles of clothing
la blusa
el calcetín, *pl.* los calcetines
la camisa
la camiseta
la chaqueta
la falda
los jeans
los pantalones (cortos)
las pantimedias
la ropa
la sudadera
el suéter, *pl.* los suéteres
los tenis
el vestido
el zapato

to describe clothes
la ganga
barato, -a
caro, -a
corto, -a
nuevo, -a
¿Cómo te queda(n)?
Me queda(n) bien.
¡Qué + *adjective!*

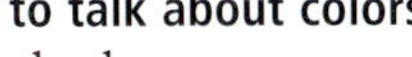

to talk about colors
el color
¿De qué color?
amarillo, -a
anaranjado, -a
azul, *pl.* azules
blanco, -a
gris, *pl.* grises
marrón, *pl.* marrones
morado, -a
negro, -a
rojo, -a
rosado, -a
verde

to talk about places to shop for clothing
el almacén, *pl.* los almacenes
la tienda de descuentos
la tienda de ropa
la zapatería

to talk about shopping
buscar
comprar:
(yo) compré
(tú) compraste
llevar
pagar:
(yo) pagué
(tú) pagaste
para mí/ti
por

to indicate a specific item or items
ese, -a; esos, -as
este, -a; estos, -as
lo, la; los, las
otro, -a

to discuss prices
ciento un(o), una . . .
¿Cuánto?
Cuesta(n)
el dólar

to assist customers in a store
¿Qué desea (Ud.)?

to address people
joven

to start a conversation
perdón

to tell when something happened
hace + *time expression*

to indicate location
por aquí

students will be wearing in the future. Encourage them to make up titles for their posters. Have students also label the clothes they display, indicating what they are and their color. Display the posters in class or the hallways.

Sección de consulta
Los verbos

Infinitive	Present		Preterite	

Regular Verbs
(You will learn the verb forms that are in italic type next year.)

Infinitive	Present		Preterite	
comprar	compro	compramos	compré	*compramos*
	compras	compráis	compraste	*comprasteis*
	compra	compran	*compró*	*compraron*
comer	como	comemos		
	comes	coméis		
	come	comen		
vivir	vivo	vivimos		
	vives	vivís		
	vive	viven		

Stem-Changing Verbs
(You will learn the verb forms that are in italic type next year.)

Infinitive	Present	
costar (o → ue)	cuesta	cuestan
empezar (e → ie)	*empiezo*	*empezamos*
	empiezas	*empezáis*
	empieza	*empiezan*
jugar (u → ue)	juego	*jugamos*
	juegas	*jugáis*
	juega	*juegan*
llover (o → ue)	llueve	
nevar (e → ie)	nieva	
poder (o → ue)	See *Irregular Verbs.*	
preferir (e → ie)	prefiero	*preferimos*
	prefieres	*preferís*
	prefiere	*prefieren*
querer (e → ie)	See *Irregular Verbs.*	

INFINITIVE	PRESENT		PRETERITE	

Verbs with Spelling Changes

(You will learn the verb forms that are in italic type next year.)

pagar	pago	pagamos	pagué	*pagamos*
	pagas	pagáis	pagaste	*pagasteis*
	paga	pagan	*pagó*	*pagaron*

Irregular Verbs

(You will learn the verb forms that are in italic type next year.)

estar	estoy	estamos
	estás	estáis
	está	están
ir	voy	vamos
	vas	vais
	va	van
poder	puedo	*podemos*
	puedes	*podéis*
	puede	*pueden*
querer	quiero	*queremos*
	quieres	*queréis*
	quiere	*quieren*
ser	soy	somos
	eres	sois
	es	son
tener	tengo	tenemos
	tienes	tenéis
	tiene	tienen

Infinitive	Present		Preterite
ver	veo	vemos	
	ves	veis	
	ve	ven	

Los números

0	cero	13	trece	26	veintiséis
1	uno	14	catorce	27	veintisiete
2	dos	15	quince	28	veintiocho
3	tres	16	dieciséis	29	veintinueve
4	cuatro	17	diecisiete	30	treinta
5	cinco	18	dieciocho	40	cuarenta
6	seis	19	diecinueve	50	cincuenta
7	siete	20	veinte	60	sesenta
8	ocho	21	veintiuno	70	setenta
9	nueve	22	veintidós	80	ochenta
10	diez	23	veintitrés	90	noventa
11	once	24	veinticuatro	100	cien
12	doce	25	veinticinco		

Los días de la semana y los meses del año

La hora

¿Qué hora es?

Es la una.

Son las dos.

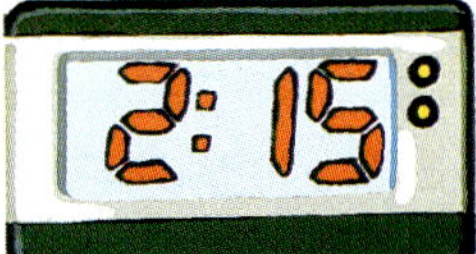

Son las dos y cuarto.

Son las dos y media.

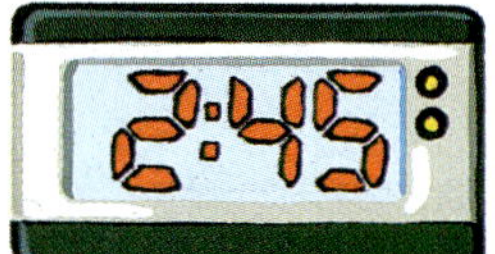

Son las dos y cuarenta y cinco.

Son las tres.

Los Colores

Palabras interrogativas

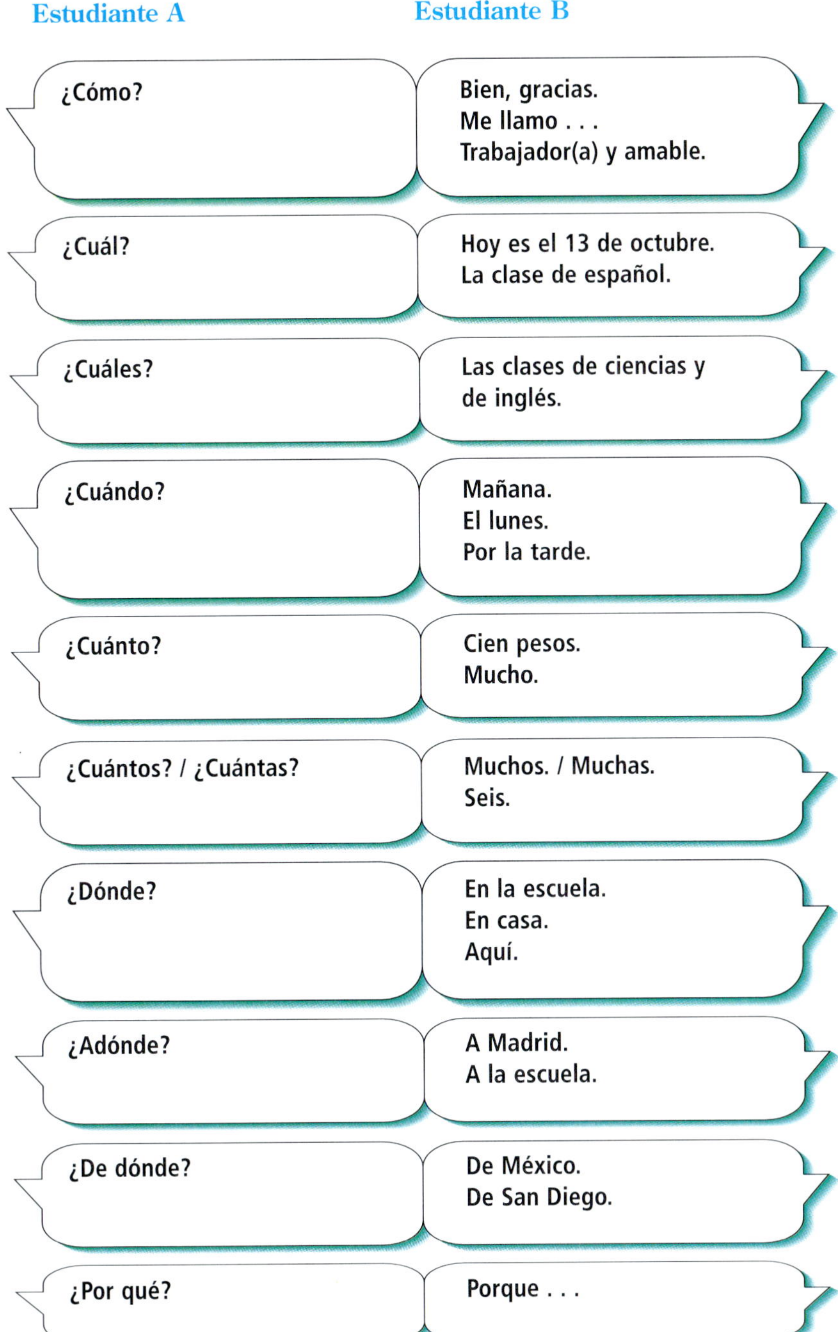

Estudiante A	Estudiante B
¿Cómo?	Bien, gracias. Me llamo . . . Trabajador(a) y amable.
¿Cuál?	Hoy es el 13 de octubre. La clase de español.
¿Cuáles?	Las clases de ciencias y de inglés.
¿Cuándo?	Mañana. El lunes. Por la tarde.
¿Cuánto?	Cien pesos. Mucho.
¿Cuántos? / ¿Cuántas?	Muchos. / Muchas. Seis.
¿Dónde?	En la escuela. En casa. Aquí.
¿Adónde?	A Madrid. A la escuela.
¿De dónde?	De México. De San Diego.
¿Por qué?	Porque . . .

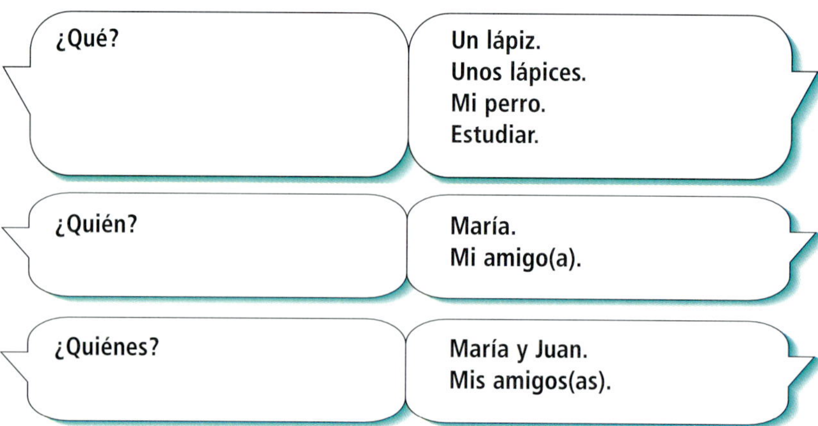
¿Qué?
Un lápiz.
Unos lápices.
Mi perro.
Estudiar.
¿Quién?
María.
Mi amigo(a).
¿Quiénes?
María y Juan.
Mis amigos(as).

VOCABULARIO ESPAÑOL-INGLÉS

The *Vocabulario español-inglés* contains all active vocabulary from the text.

A dash (—) represents the main entry word. For example, **en el —** after **el almuerzo** means **en el almuerzo.**

The number following each entry indicates the chapter in which the word or expression is presented. The letter *P* following an entry refers to *El primer paso*.

The following abbreviations are used: *adj.* (adjective), *dir. obj.* (direct object), *f.* (feminine), *fam.* (familiar), *inf.* (infinitive), *m.* (masculine), *pl.* (plural), *prep.* (preposition), *pron.* (pronoun), *sing.* (singular).

a to (1, 3); at (2)
 a la, al (a + el) to the (1, 3)
abril April (P)
el **abuelo, la abuela** grandfather, grandmother (5)
los **abuelos** grandparents (5)
adiós good-by (P)
¿adónde? (to) where? (3)
agosto August (P)
el **agua** *f.* water (4)
al *see* **a**
algo something (4)
allí there (2)
 — está there it is (2)
el **almacén,** *pl.* **los almacenes** department store (6)
el **almuerzo** lunch (2, 4)
 en el — for lunch (4)
alto, -a tall (5)
amable kind, nice (1)
amarillo, -a yellow (6)
el **amigo, la amiga** friend (1, 3)
anaranjado, -a orange *(color)* (6)
antipático, -a unfriendly, unpleasant (5)
el **año** year (P)
 ¿cuántos —s tienes? how old are you? (P)
 tener . . . —s to be . . . years old (P, 5)
 tengo . . . —s I'm . . . years old (P)
aprender to learn (2)
aquí here (2)
 — está here it is (2)
 por — around here (6)
la **argolla: la carpeta de —s** three-ring binder (2)
el **arroz** rice (4)
el **arte** art (2)
artístico, -a artistic (1)
asco: ¡qué —! yuk! that's disgusting! (4)
así, así so-so, fair (P)
atractivo, -a attractive (5)
atrevido, -a bold, daring (1)
ayudar to help (1)
azul, *pl.* **azules** blue (5, 6)

bajo, -a short *(height)* (5)
barato, -a cheap, inexpensive (6)
el **básquetbol** basketball (3)
beber to drink (4)
la **bebida** beverage, drink (4)
el **béisbol** baseball (3)
bien well (P)
el **bistec** steak (4)
blanco, -a white (6)
la **blusa** blouse (6)
el **bolígrafo** pen (P)
bonito, -a pretty (5)
bueno (buen), -a good (P, 4)
buscar to look for (6)
el **café** coffee (4)
el **calcetín,** *pl.* **los calcetines** sock (6)
la **calculadora** calculator (2)
callado, -a quiet (1)
la **camisa** shirt (6)
la **camiseta** T-shirt (6)
el **campo** country(side) (3)
canoso: pelo — gray hair (5)
cansado, -a tired (3)
cariñoso, -a affectionate, loving (5)
caro, -a expensive (6)
la **carpeta** pocket folder (2)
 la — de argollas three-ring binder (2)
la **casa: en —** at home (1)
castaño: pelo — brown (chestnut) hair (5)
catorce fourteen (P)
la **cebolla** onion (4)
la **cena** dinner (4)
 en la — for dinner (4)
el **centro comercial** mall (3)
el **cereal** cereal (4)
cero zero (P)
la **chaqueta** jacket (6)
cien one hundred (5)
las **ciencias** science (2)
 las — de la salud health (science) (2)
 las — sociales social studies (2)

ciento un(o), -a; ciento dos; etc. 101, 102, etc. (6)
cinco five (P)
cincuenta fifty (2)
el **cine** movie theater (1)
ir al — to go to the movies (1)
claro:
¡— que sí! of course! (3)
¡— que no! of course not! (3)
la **clase (de)** class (2)
después de las —s after school (3)
la sala de —s classroom (P)
cocinar to cook (1)
el **color** color (6)
¿de qué —? what color? (6)
comer to eat (4)
comercial *see* **centro**
la **comida** meal, food (4)
¿cómo? how? (P)
¿— eres? what are you like? (1)
¿— está (Ud.)? how are you? *formal* (P)
¿— estás? how are you? *fam.* (P)
¿— se dice . . . ? how do you say . . . ? (P)
¿— se escribe . . . ? how do you spell . . . ? (P)
¿— se llama(n)? what is his/her/their name? (5)
¿— te llamas? what's your name? (P)
el **compañero, la compañera** classmate (P)
comprar to buy (6)
compras: ir de — to go shopping (3)
con with (1, 3)
conmigo with me (3)
contigo with you (3)
corto, -a short (6)
los pantalones —s shorts (6)
costar *(o → ue)* to cost (6)
creer to think, to believe (4)
creo que no I don't think so (4)
creo que sí I think so (4)
el **cuaderno** spiral notebook (2)
¿cuál(es)? what? (P); which? which one(s)? (4)
¿cuándo? when (P)
¿cuánto? how much? (6)
¿cuántos, -as? how many? (P, 5)
¿— años tiene . . . ? how old is . . . ? (5)
¿— años tienes? how old are you? (P)
cuarenta forty (2)
cuarto, -a fourth (2)
y — *(time)* quarter after, quarter past (2)
cuatro four (P)
cuesta(n) it costs (they cost) (6)
el **cumpleaños** birthday (P)

de from, of (P); of, — 's, — s' (5)
— nada you're welcome (3)
¿— veras? really? (1)
deber ought to, should (4)
decir:
¿cómo se dice . . . ? how do you say . . . ? (P)
¡no me digas! really?, you don't say! (3)
¿qué quiere — . . . ? what does . . . mean? (P)
se dice . . . it is said . . . (P)
los **deportes** sports (1)
deportista athletic (1)
el **desayuno** breakfast (4)
en el — for breakfast (4)
el **descuento: la tienda de —s** discount store (6)
desear: ¿qué desea Ud.? may I help you? (6)
desordenado, -a messy (1)
después de after (3)
— las clases after school (3)
el **día** day (P)
buenos —s good morning (P)
¿qué — es hoy? what day is it? (P)
todos los —s every day (3)
dibujar to draw (1)
el **diccionario** dictionary (2)
dice:
¿cómo se — . . . ? how do you say . . . ? (P)
se — . . . it's said . . . (P)
diciembre December (P)
diecinueve nineteen (P)
dieciocho eighteen (P)
dieciséis sixteen (P)
diecisiete seventeen (P)
diez ten (P)
difícil difficult, hard (2)
digas: ¡no me —! really?, you don't say! (3)
la **diversión: el parque de diversiones** amusement park (3)
doce twelve (P)
el **dólar** dollar (6)
domingo Sunday (P)
el — on Sunday(3)
¿dónde? where? (3)
¿de — eres? where are you from? (P)
dos two (P)

la **educación física** physical education, gym class (2)
el the *m. sing.* (P, 2)
él he (2); him *after prep.* (3)
ella she (2); her *after prep.* (3)
ellos, ellas they (2); them *after prep.* (3)

empezar *(e → ie)* to begin, to start (2)
en in, at, on (P)
encantar to love (4)
le encanta(n) he/she loves (5)
me encanta(n) I love (4)
enero January (P)
enfermo, -a ill, sick (3)
la **ensalada** salad (4)
enseñar to teach (2)
eres you *fam.* are (P, 1)
es it is (P); he/she is (2)
escribir:
¿cómo se escribe . . . ? how do you spell . . . ? (P)
se escribe . . . it's spelled . . . (P)
escuchar to listen (to) (1)
la **escuela** school (1)
ese, -a; -os, -as that; those (6)
el **español** Spanish *(language)* (P, 2)
la **estación,** *pl.* **las estaciones** season (3)
estar to be (1, 3)
aquí/allí está here/there it is (2)
¿cómo estás/está Ud.? how are you? (P)
este, -a; -os, -as this; these (6)
el/la **estudiante** student (P)
estudiar to study (1)

fácil easy (2)
la **falda** skirt (6)
la **familia** family (3)
favor: por — please (P)
febrero February (P)
la **fecha** date (P)
feo, -a ugly (5)
la **fiesta** party (3)
el **fin** *(pl.* **los fines) de semana** weekend (3)
física: la educación —physical education, gym class (2)
fritas: las papas — French fries (4)
las **frutas** fruit (4)
el **fútbol** soccer (3)
el **— americano** football (3)

la **ganga** bargain (6)
el **gato** cat (5)
el **gemelo, la gemela** twin (5)
generalmente usually, generally (3)
generoso, -a generous (1)
¡genial! great! wonderful! (3)
el **gimnasio** gymnasium (3)
la **grabadora** tape recorder (2)
gracias thank you (P)
gracioso, -a funny (1)
grande big, large (5)
gris, *pl.* **grises** gray (5, 6)
guapo, -a handsome, good-looking (5)
los **guisantes** peas (4)
la **guitarra** guitar (1)
gustar to like (1)
le gusta(n) he/she likes (5)
me/te gusta I like, you like (1)
me gusta más I prefer (1)
(A mí) me gustaría I'd like . . . (3)
¿(A ti) te gustaría? would you like . . . ? (3)
gusto: mucho — pleased/nice to meet you (P)

hablar to talk (1)
hacer to do (1)
hace + *(time expression)* ago (6)
hambre: tener — to be hungry (4)
la **hamburguesa** hamburger (4)
hasta luego see you later (P)
hay there is, there are (P)
¿cuántos, -as . . . —? how many . . . are there? (P)
helado: el té — iced tea (4)
el **hermano, la hermana** brother, sister (5)
los **hermanos** brothers; brother(s) and sister(s) (5)
el **hijo, la hija** son, daughter (5)
los **hijos** sons; sons and daughters (5)
la **hoja de papel** sheet of paper (P)
¡hola! hi!, hello! (P)
el **hombre** man (5)
la **hora** period; time (2)
¿a qué —? at what time? (2)
¿qué — es? what time is it? (2)
el **horario** schedule (2)
horrible horrible (4)
hoy today (P)
— no not today (3)
el **huevo** egg (4)

igualmente likewise (P)
impaciente impatient (1)
el **inglés** English *(language)* (2)
inteligente intelligent (5)
el **invierno** winter (3)
ir to go (1, 3)
— a + *inf.* to be going to + *verb* (3)
— de compras to go shopping (3)
— de pesca to go fishing (3)

el **jamón** ham (4)

los jeans jeans (6)
joven young (5)
el/la joven young man, young lady (6)
las judías verdes green beans (4)
jueves Thursday (P)
el — on Thursday (3)
jugar *(u → ue)* to play (3)
el jugo juice (4)
— de naranja orange juice (4)
julio July (P)
junio June (P)

la the *f. sing.* (P, 2); it, *f. sing. dir. obj. pron.* (6)
el lápiz, *pl.* **los lápices** pencil (2)
las the *f. pl.* (2); them *f. pl. dir. obj. pron.* (6)
lástima: ¡qué —! that's too bad! what a shame! (3)
le:
— encanta(n) he/she loves (5)
— gusta(n) he/she likes (5)
la leche milk (4)
la lechuga lettuce (4)
leer to read (1)
el libro book (P)
la limonada lemonade (4)
llamar:
¿cómo se llama(n)? what is his / her / their name? (5)
¿cómo te llamas? what's your name? (P)
me llamo my name is (P)
se llama(n) his / her /their name is (5)
llevar to wear (6)
lo it *m. sing. dir. obj. pron.* (6)
— siento I'm sorry (2)
los the *m. pl.* (P, 4); them *m. pl. dir. obj. pron.* (6)
— + *day of week* on + day of week (3)
luego: hasta — see you later (P)
lunes Monday (P)
el — on Monday (3)

la madre mother (5)
malo, -a bad (4)
la manzana apple (4)
mañana tomorrow (P, 3)
la mañana morning (3)
por la — in the morning (3)
el marcador marker (2)
marrón, *pl.* **marrones** brown (5, 6)
martes Tuesday (P)
el — on Tuesday (3)
marzo March (P)
más more (4)
— o menos more or less (4)
me gusta — I prefer (1)
las matemáticas math(ematics) (2)
mayo May (P)
mayor older (5)
media: y — half-past (2)
menor *pl.*, **menores** younger (5)
menos less (4)
más o — more or less (4)
la merienda afternoon snack (4)
el mes month (P)
la mesa table (P)
mi, mis my (P, 3)
mí *after prep.* me (1, 3)
a — me gusta(n) I like *(emphatic)* (1, 3)
miércoles Wednesday (P)
el — on Wednesday (3)
la mochila backpack (2)
morado, -a purple (6)
el muchacho, la muchacha boy, girl (5)
mucho a lot (1)
mucho, -a a lot of, much (2)
— gusto pleased / nice to meet you (P)
la mujer woman (5)
la música music (1, 2)
muy very (P, 1)

nada:
de — you're welcome (3)
no me gusta — . . . I don't like . . . at all (1)
nadar to swim (1)
nadie nobody, no one (5)
la naranja orange (4)
necesitar to need (2)
negro, -a black (5, 6)
ni . . . ni neither . . . nor, not . . . or (1)
no no, not (P)
creo que — I don't think so (4)
la noche night, evening (P)
buenas — s good evening, good night (P)
por la — in the evening (3)
el nombre name (5)
nosotros, -as we (2); us *after prep.* (3)
noventa ninety (5)
noviembre November (P)
nueve nine (P)
nuevo, -a new (6)
el número number (P)
nunca never (4)

o or (P)
ochenta eighty (5)
ocho eight (P)

octavo, -a eighth (2)
octubre October (P)
ocupado, -a busy (3)
el ojo eye (5)
once eleven (P)
ordenado, -a neat, tidy (1)
el otoño fall, autumn (3)
otro, -a another, other (6)

paciente patient *adj.* (1)
el padre father (5)
los padres parents (5)
pagar to pay (6)
el pan bread (4)
  el — tostado toast (4)
los pantalones pants (6)
  los — cortos shorts (6)
las pantimedias pantyhose (6)
la papa potato (4)
  la — al horno baked potato (4)
  las —s fritas French fries (4)
el papel paper (P)
  la hoja de — sheet of paper (P)
para for (2)
el parque park (3)
  el — de diversiones amusement park (3)
el pasatiempo pastime, hobby (3)
patinar to skate (1)
pelirrojo, -a red-haired (5)
el pelo hair (5)
pequeño, -a small, little (5)
perdón excuse me (6)
perezoso, -a lazy (1)
pero but (1)
el perro dog (5)
la persona person (5)
pesca: ir de — to go fishing (3)
el pescado fish (4)
la piscina pool (3)
la pizarra chalkboard (P)
el plátano banana (4)
la playa beach (3)
la plaza town square, plaza (3)
poder *(o → ue)* can, to be able to (3)
el pollo chicken (4)
  la sopa de — chicken soup (4)
por for (6)
  — aquí around here (6)
  — favor please (P)
  — la mañana / la tarde / la noche in the morning / afternoon / evening (3)
  ¿— qué? why? (3)
  — teléfono on the phone (1)
porque because (3)
practicar to practice (1)
preferir *(e → ie)* to prefer (4)
la primavera spring (3)
primero (primer), -a first (P, 2)
el primo, la prima cousin (5)
el profesor, la profesora teacher (P)
prudente cautious (1)
puedo, puedes I can, you can (3)
pues well *(to indicate pause)* (1)
el pupitre student desk (P)

que that, who (5)
¿qué? what? (2)
  ¡— + *adj.!* how + *adj.!* (6)
  ¿— tal? how's it going? (P)
quedar to fit (6)
  me queda(n) bien it fits (they fit) me well (6)
querer *(e → ie)* to want (3)
  ¿qué quiere decir ...? what does ... mean? (P)
el queso cheese (4)
¿quién(es)? who? whom? (2, 5)
quiere: ¿qué — decir ...? what does ... mean? (P)
quiero, quieres I want, you want (3)
quince fifteen (P)
quinto, -a fifth (2)

el refresco soft drink (4)
la regla ruler (2)
rojo, -a red (6)
la ropa clothes (6)
rosado, -a pink (6)
rubio, -a blond(e) (5)

sábado Saturday (P)
  el — on Saturday (3)
sabroso, -a delicious, tasty (4)
la sala de clases classroom (P)
la salud health (4)
  las ciencias de la — health (science) (2)
el sandwich sandwich (4)
sed: tener — to be thirsty (4)
segundo, -a second (2)
seis six (P)
la semana week (P)
  el fin *(pl.* **los fines) de —** weekend (3)
el semestre semester (2)
señor (Sr.) Mr., sir (P)
señora (Sra.) Mrs., ma'am (P)
señorita (Srta.) Miss (P)
septiembre September (P)
séptimo, -a seventh (2)
ser to be (5)
serio, -a serious (1)
sesenta sixty (5)
setenta seventy (5)
sexto, -a sixth (2)

sí yes (P); do + *verb (emphatic)* (1)
siempre always (4)
siento: lo — I'm sorry (2)
siete seven (P)
simpático, -a nice, friendly (5)
sociable outgoing (1)
social: las ciencias —es social studies (2)
solo, -a alone (3)
sólo only (5)
son (they) are (4)
  — las it is . . . *(in telling time)* (2)
la **sopa** soup (4)
soy I am (P, 1)
su, sus his, her (5)
la **sudadera** sweatshirt (6)
el **suéter** sweater (6)

tacaño, -a stingy (1)
tal: ¿qué —? how's it going? (P)
también also, too (1)
  a mí — me too (1)
tampoco (not . . .) either (1)
la **tarde** afternoon (P)
  buenas —s good afternoon, good evening (P)
  por la — in the afternoon (3)
la **tarea** homework (2)
te you *fam. obj. pron.* (1)
el **té** tea (4)
  el — helado iced tea (4)
el **teléfono** telephone (1)
  hablar por — to talk on the phone (1)
  el número de — phone number (P)
la **tele(visión)** television (1)
tener to have (2, 5); *see also* **año, hambre, sed**
tengo *see* **año, tener**
el **tenis** tennis (3)
los **tenis** sneakers (6)
tercer, -a third (2)
terminar to finish, to end (2)
ti *after prep.* you (1)
  ¿a — te gusta(n)? do you like? *(emphatic)* (1)
la **tienda** store (6)
  la — de descuentos discount store (6)
  la — de ropa clothing store (6)
tienes *see* **año, tener**
el **tío, la tía** uncle, aunt (5)
  los tíos uncles; aunts and uncles (5)
tocar to play (1)
todos, -as all; everyone (5)
  — los días every day (3)
el **tomate** tomato (4)
  la sopa de — tomato soup (4)
tostado: el pan — toast (4)
trabajador, -a hard-working (1)
trece thirteen (P)
treinta thirty (P, 2)
tres three (P)
tu, tus your *fam.* (P, 2, 3)
tú you *fam.* (P, 2)

un, una a, an, one (P, 2)
  es la una it's one o'clock (2)
único, -a only (5)
uno one (P)
unos, -as a few, some (4)
usted (Ud.) you *formal sing.* (P, 2)
ustedes (Uds.) you *formal pl.* (2)
la **uva** grape (4)

veces: a — at times, sometimes (1)
veinte twenty (P)
veintiuno (veintiún) twenty-one (P)
ver to see, to watch (1)
  a — let's see (2)
el **verano** summer (3)
veras: ¿de — ? really? (1)
¿verdad? isn't that so?, right? (4)
verde green (5, 6)
las **verduras** vegetables (4)
  la sopa de — vegetable soup (4)
el **vestido** dress (6)
el **videojuego** video game (3)
viejo, -a old (5)
viernes Friday (P)
  el — on Friday (3)
el **vóleibol** volleyball (3)
vosotros, -as you *fam. pl.* (2)

y and (P, 1)
yo I (P, 2)

la **zanahoria** carrot (4)
la **zapatería** shoe store (6)
el **zapato** shoe (6)

ENGLISH-SPANISH VOCABULARY

The *English-Spanish Vocabulary* contains all active vocabulary from the text.

A dash (—) represents the main entry word. For example, **— school** following **after** means **after school.**

The number following each entry indicates the chapter in which the word or expression is presented. The letter *P* following an entry refers to *El primer paso*.

The following abbreviations are used: *adj.* (adjective), *dir. obj.* (direct object), *f.* (feminine), *fam.* (familiar), *inf.* (infinitive), *m.* (masculine), *pl.* (plural), *prep.* (preposition), *pron.* (pronoun), *sing.* (singular).

a, an un, una (2)
able: to be — poder *(o → ue)* (3)
affectionate cariñoso, -a (5)
after después (de) (3)
  — school después de las clases (3)
afternoon la tarde (P)
  — snack la merienda (4)
  good — buenas tardes (P)
  in the — por la tarde (3)
ago hace + *(time expression)* . . . (6)
all todos, -as (5)
alone solo, -a (3)
also también (1)
always siempre (4)
am soy (P, 1)
amusement park el parque de diversiones (3)
and y (P, 1)
another otro, -a (6)
apple la manzana (4)
April abril (P)
around here por aquí (6)
art el arte (2)
artistic artístico, -a (1)
at en (P); a (2)
athletic deportista (1)
attractive atractivo, -a (5)
August agosto (P)
aunt la tía (5)
  —s and uncles los tíos (5)
autumn el otoño (3)

backpack la mochila (2)
bad malo, -a (4)
  that's too — ¡qué lástima! (3)
banana el plátano (4)
bargain la ganga (6)
baseball el béisbol (3)
basketball el básquetbol (3)
to **be** estar (1, 3); ser (5)
  — from ser de (P)
  to — able poder *(o → ue)* (3)
beach la playa (3)
beans: green — las judías verdes (4)
because porque (3)
to **begin** empezar *(e → ie)* (2)
to **believe** creer (4)
better: I like . . . — me gusta(n) más (1)
beverage la bebida (4)
big grande (5)
binder (3-ring) la carpeta de argollas (2)
birthday el cumpleaños (P)
black negro, -a (5, 6)
blond(e) rubio, -a (5)
blouse la blusa (6)
blue azul, *pl.* azules (5, 6)
bold atrevido, -a (1)
book el libro (P)
boy el muchacho (5)
bread el pan (4)
breakfast el desayuno (4)
  for — en el desayuno (4)
brother el hermano (5)
  —(s) and sister(s) los hermanos (5)
brown marrón, *pl.* marrones (5, 6); *(hair)* castaño (5)
busy ocupado, -a (3)
but pero (1)
to **buy** comprar (6)

calculator la calculadora (2)
can poder *(o → ue)* (3)
  I/you — puedo, puedes (3)
carrot la zanahoria (4)
cat el gato (5)
cautious prudente (1)
cereal el cereal (4)
chalkboard la pizarra (P)
cheap barato, -a (6)
cheese el queso (4)
chestnut (-colored) castaño, -a (5)
chicken el pollo (4)
  — soup la sopa de pollo (4)
child el hijo, la hija (5)
  only — el hijo único, la hija única (5)
class la clase (de) (2)
classmate el compañero, la compañera (P)

classroom la sala de clases (P)
clothes la ropa (6)
clothing store la tienda de ropa (6)
coffee el café (4)
color el color (6)
  what —? ¿de qué color? (6)
to cook cocinar (1)
to cost costar *(o → ue)* (6)
  it —s (they —) cuesta(n) (6)
country(side) el campo (3)
course:
  of — ¡claro que sí! (3)
  of — not ¡claro que no! (3)
cousin el primo, la prima (5)

daring atrevido, -a (1)
date la fecha (P)
  what's today's —? ¿cuál es la fecha de hoy? (P)
daughter la hija (5)
day el día (P)
  every — todos los días (3)
December diciembre (P)
delicious sabroso, -a (4)
department store el almacén, *pl.* los almacenes (6)
desk *(student)* el pupitre (P)
dictionary el diccionario (2)
difficult difícil (2)
dinner la cena (4)
  for — en la cena (4)
discount store la tienda de descuentos (6)
disgusting: that's —! ¡qué asco! (4)
to do hacer (1)
dog el perro (5)
dollar el dólar (6)
to draw dibujar (1)
dress el vestido (6)
drink la bebida (4)
to drink beber (4)

easy fácil (2)
to eat comer (4)
egg el huevo (4)
eight ocho (P)
eighteen dieciocho (P)
eighth octavo, -a (2)
eighty ochenta (5)
either: not . . .— (no . . .) tampoco (1)
eleven once (P)
to end terminar (2)
English *(language)* el inglés (2)
evening la noche (P)
  good — buenas noches, buenas tardes (P)
  in the — por la noche, por la tarde (3)
every day todos los días (3)
everyone todos, -as (5)
excuse me perdón (6)
expensive caro, -a (6)
eye el ojo (5)

fair así, así (P)
fall el otoño (3)
family la familia (3)
father el padre (5)
February febrero (P)
few: a — unos, unas (4)
fifteen quince (P)
fifth quinto, -a (2)
fifty cincuenta (2)
to finish terminar (2)
first primero (primer), -a (P, 2)
fish el pescado (4)
fishing: to go — ir de pesca (3)
to fit quedar (6)
  it —s (they —) me well me queda(n) bien (6)
five cinco (P)
folder la carpeta (2)
food la comida (4)
football el fútbol americano (3)
for para (2, 6); por (6)
forty cuarenta (2)
four cuatro (P)
fourteen catorce (P)
fourth cuarto, -a (2)
French fries las papas fritas (4)
Friday viernes (P)
  —s los viernes (3)
  on — el viernes (3)
friend el amigo, la amiga (1, 3)
friendly simpático, -a (5)
from de (P)
fruit las frutas (4)
funny gracioso, -a (1)

generally generalmente (3)
generous generoso, -a (1)
girl la muchacha (5)
to go ir (3)
  how's it —ing? ¿qué tal? (P)
  to be —ing to + *verb* ir a + *inf.* (3)
  to — fishing ir de pesca (3)
  to — shopping ir de compras (3)
good bueno (buen), -a (P, 4)
  — afternoon buenas tardes (P)
  — evening buenas noches (P)
  — morning buenos días (P)
  — night buenas noches (P)
good-by adiós (P)
good-looking guapo, -a (5)
grandfather el abuelo (5)
grandmother la abuela (5)
grandparents los abuelos (5)
grape la uva (4)
gray gris, *pl.* grises (5, 6)
  — hair pelo canoso (5)
great! ¡genial! (3)

green verde (5, 6)
— **beans** las judías verdes (4)
guitar la guitarra (1)
gym *(class)* la clase de educación física (2)
gymnasium el gimnasio (3)

hair el pelo (5)
half: — **-past** y media (2)
ham el jamón (4)
hamburger la hamburguesa (4)
handsome guapo, -a (5)
hard difícil (2)
hard-working trabajador, -a (1)
to **have** tener (2, 5)
he él (2)
health la salud (4); (class) las ciencias de la salud (2)
hello! ¡hola! (P)
to **help** ayudar (1)
may I — you? ¿qué desea (Ud.)? (6)
her su, sus (5)
here aquí (2)
around — por aquí (6)
— **it is** aquí está (2)
hi! ¡hola! (P)
his su, sus (5)
hobby el pasatiempo (3)
home: at — en casa (1)
homework la tarea (2)
horrible horrible (4)
how + *adj.!* ¡qué + *adj.!* (6)
how? ¿cómo? (P)
— **are you?** ¿cómo está (Ud.)? *formal;* ¿cómo estás? *fam.* (P)
— **many?** ¿cuántos, -as? (P, 5)
— **much?** ¿cuánto? (6)
— **old are you?** ¿cuántos años tienes? (P)
—**'s it going?** ¿qué tal? (P)
hundred cien (5); ciento (6)
hungry: to be — tener hambre (4)

I yo (P, 2)
iced tea el té helado (4)
ill enfermo, -a (3)
impatient impaciente (1)
in en (P)
inexpensive barato, -a (6)
intelligent inteligente (5)
is es (P, 2)
it *dir. obj. pron.* lo (6)

jacket la chaqueta (6)
January enero (P)
jeans los jeans (6)
juice el jugo (4)
orange — el jugo de naranja (4)
July julio (P)
June junio (P)

kind amable (1)

lady: young — la joven (6)
large grande (5)
later: see you — hasta luego (P)
lazy perezoso, -a (1)
to **learn** aprender (2)
lemonade la limonada (4)
less menos (4)
more or — más o menos (4)
let's see a ver (2)
lettuce la lechuga (4)
to **like** gustar a (1, 5)
he / she —s le gusta(n) (5)
I / you — (a mí) me / (a ti) te gusta(n) (1)
I'd — (a mí) me gustaría (3)
would you —? ¿(a ti) te gustaría? (3)
likewise igualmente (P)
to **listen (to)** escuchar (1)
little pequeño, -a (5)
to **look for** buscar (6)
lot:
a — mucho (1)
a — of mucho, -a (2)
to **love** encantar (4)
he / she —s le encanta(n) (5)
I — me encanta(n) (4)
loving cariñoso, -a (5)
lunch el almuerzo (2, 4)
for — en el almuerzo (4)

ma'am señora (P)
mall el centro comercial (3)
man el hombre (5)
young — el joven, *pl.* los jóvenes (6)
many: how —? ¿cuántos, -as? (P)
March marzo (P)
marker el marcador (2)
math(ematics) las matemáticas (2)
may I help you? ¿qué desea (Ud.)? (6)
May mayo (P)
me *after prep.* mí (1)
meal la comida (4)
meet: pleased to — you mucho gusto (P)
messy desordenado, -a (1)
milk la leche (4)
Miss (la) señorita (Srta.) (P)
Monday lunes (P)
—**s** los lunes (3)

on — el lunes (3)
month el mes (P)
more más (4)
— or less más o menos (4)
morning la mañana (3)
good — buenos días (P)
in the — por la mañana (3)
mother la madre (5)
movies: to go to the — ir al cine (1)
movie theater el cine (1)
Mr. (el) señor (Sr.) (P)
Mrs. (la) señora (Sra.) (P)
much mucho, -a (2)
how —? ¿cuánto? (6)
music la música (1, 2)
my mi, mis (P, 3)

name el nombre (5)
his / her / their — is se llama(n) (5)
my — is me llamo (P)
what's your —? ¿cómo te llamas? (P)
neat ordenado, -a (1)
to **need** necesitar (2)
neither . . . nor ni . . . ni (1)
never nunca (4)
new nuevo, -a (6)
nice amable (1); simpático, -a (5)
— to meet you mucho gusto (P)
night noche (P)
at — por la noche (3)
good — buenas noches (P)
nine nueve (P)
nineteen diecinueve (P)
ninety noventa (5)
no no (P)
nobody, no one nadie (5)
nor: neither . . . — ni . . . ni (1)

not no (P)
— at all no . . . nada (1)
notebook el cuaderno (2)
November noviembre (P)
number el número (P)
phone — el número de teléfono (P)

o'clock son las dos, tres, etc. (2)
it's one — es la una (2)
October octubre (P)
of de (P, 5)
— course (not) ¡claro que sí (no)! (3)
old viejo -a (5)
how — are you? ¿cuántos años tienes? (P)
how — is . . . ? ¿cuántos años tiene . . . ? (5)
I'm . . . years — tengo . . . años (P)
older mayor (5)
on en (P)
one uno, -a (P, 2)
it's — o'clock es la una (2)
onion la cebolla (4)
only sólo (5)
— child el hijo único, la hija única (5)
or o (P)
not . . . — ni . . . ni (1)
orange la naranja (4)
— juice el jugo de naranja (4)
orange *(color)* anaranjado, -a (6)
other otro, -a (6)
ought to deber (4)
outgoing sociable (1)

pants los pantalones (6)
pantyhose las pantimedias (6)
paper el papel (P)
sheet of — la hoja de papel (P)
parents los padres (5)
park el parque (3)
amusement — el parque de diversiones (3)
party la fiesta (3)
past:
half- — y media (2)
quarter — y cuarto (2)
pastime el pasatiempo (3)
patient *adj.* paciente (1)
to **pay** pagar (6)
peas los guisantes (4)
pen el bolígrafo (P)
pencil el lápiz, *pl.* los lápices (2)
people: young — los jóvenes (6)
period la hora (2)
person la persona (5)
phone el teléfono (1)
on the — por teléfono (1)
— number el número de teléfono (P)
physical education la educación física (2)
pink rosado, -a (6)
to **play** *(musical instruments)* tocar (1); *(games)* jugar *(u → ue)* (3)
to — sports practicar deportes (1)
please por favor (P)
pleased to meet you mucho gusto (P)
pocket folder la carpeta (2)
pool la piscina (3)
potato la papa (4)
baked — la papa al horno (4)
French-fried —s las papas fritas (4)
to **practice** practicar (1)
to **prefer** preferir *(e → ie)* (4)
I — me gusta más (1); prefiero (4)
pretty bonito, -a (5)

purple morado, -a (6)

quarter past y cuarto (2)
quiet callado, -a (1)

to **read** leer (1)
really? ¿de veras? (1); ¡no me digas! (3)
red rojo, -a (6)
— **-haired** pelirrojo, -a (5)
rice el arroz (4)
right? ¿verdad? (4)
ruler la regla (2)

said *see* **say**
salad la ensalada (4)
sandwich el sandwich (4)
Saturday sábado (P)
on — el sábado (3)
—s los sábados (3)
to **say:**
how do you — . . . ? ¿cómo se dice . . . ? (P)
it is said . . . se dice . . . (P)
you don't — ! ¡no me digas! (3)
schedule el horario (2)
school la escuela (1)
after — después de las clases (3)
science las ciencias (2)
season la estación, *pl.* las estaciones (3)
second segundo, -a (2)
to **see** ver (1)
let's — a ver (2)
— you later hasta luego (P)
semester el semestre (2)
September septiembre (P)
serious serio, -a (1)
seven siete (P)
seventeen diecisiete (P)
seventh séptimo, -a (2)
seventy setenta (5)
shame: what a —! ¡qué lástima! (3)
she ella (2)
sheet of paper la hoja de papel (P)
shirt la camisa (6)
shoe el zapato (6)
— store la zapatería (6)
shop la tienda (6)
shopping:
— center el centro comercial (3)
to go — ir de compras (3)
short *(height)* bajo, -a (5); *(length)* corto, -a (6)
shorts los pantalones cortos (6)
should deber + *inf.* (4)
sick enfermo, -a (3)
sir señor (6)
sister la hermana (5)
six seis (P)
sixteen dieciséis (P)
sixth sexto, -a (2)
sixty sesenta (5)
to **skate** patinar (1)
skirt la falda (6)
small pequeño, -a (5)
smart inteligente (5)
snack: afternoon — la merienda (4)
sneakers los tenis (6)
so: isn't that —? ¿verdad? (4)
soccer el fútbol (3)
sock el calcetín, *pl.* los calcetines (6)
social studies las ciencias sociales (2)
soft drink el refresco (4)
some unos, unas (4)
something algo (4)
sometimes a veces (1)
son el hijo (5)
—s and daughters los hijos (5)
sorry: I'm — lo siento (2)
so-so así, así (P)
soup la sopa (4)
Spanish *(language)* el español (2)
spell:
how do you — . . . ? ¿Cómo se escribe . . . ? (P)
it's spelled se escribe (P)
spiral notebook el cuaderno (2)
sports los deportes (1)
spring la primavera (3)
to **start** empezar *(e → ie)* (2)
steak el bistec (4)
stingy tacaño, -a (1)
store la tienda (6)
clothing — la tienda de ropa (6)
department — el almacén, *pl.* los almacenes (6)
discount — la tienda de descuentos (6)
student el / la estudiante (P)
to **study** estudiar (1)
summer el verano (3)
Sunday domingo (P)
on — el domingo (3)
—s los domingos (3)
sweater el suéter (6)
sweatshirt la sudadera (6)
to **swim** nadar (1)
swimming pool la piscina (3)

table la mesa (P)
to **talk** hablar (1)
to — on the phone hablar por teléfono (1)
tall alto, -a (5)
tape recorder la grabadora (2)
tasty sabroso, -a (4)

tea el té (4)
iced — el té helado (4)
to **teach** enseñar (2)
teacher el profesor, la profesora (P)
telephone el teléfono (1)
on the — por teléfono (1)
television la tele(visión) (1)
to watch — ver la tele(visión) (1)
ten diez (P)
tennis el tenis (3)
thank you gracias (P)
that que (5); *adj.* ese, esa (6)
isn't — so? ¿verdad?(4)
—'s too bad! ¡qué lástima! (3)
the el, la, los, las (P, 2)
theater *(movie)* el cine (1)
them *after prep.* ellos, ellas (3); los, las *dir. obj. pron.* (6)
there allí (2)
— is / are hay (P)
— it is allí está (2)
these *adj.* estos, estas (6)
they ellos, ellas (2)
to **think** creer (4)
I don't — so creo que no (4)
I — so creo que sí (4)
third tercer, -a (2)
thirsty: to be — tener sed (4)
thirteen trece (P)
thirty treinta (P)
this *adj.* este, esta (6)
those *adj.* esos, esas (6)
three tres (P)
— -ring binder la carpeta de argollas (2)
Thursday jueves (P)
on — el jueves (3)
—s los jueves (3)
tidy ordenado, -a (1)
time la hora (2)
at —s a veces (1)
at what —? ¿a qué hora? (2)
what — is it? ¿qué hora es? (2)
tired cansado, -a (3)
to a (3)
— the a la, al (1, 3)
toast el pan tostado (4)
today hoy (P)
not — hoy no (3)
what's the date —? ¿cuál es la fecha de hoy? (P)
tomato el tomate (4)
— soup la sopa de tomate (4)
tomorrow mañana (P, 3)
too también (1)
me — a mí también (1)
T-shirt la camiseta (6)
Tuesday martes (P)
on — el martes (3)
—s los martes (3)
twelve doce (P)
twenty veinte (P)
twin el gemelo, la gemela (5)
two dos (P)

ugly feo, -a (5)
uncle el tío (5)
unfriendly antipático, -a (5)
unpleasant antipático, -a (5)
us *after prep.* nosotros, -as (3)
usually generalmente (3)

vegetables las verduras (4)
— soup la sopa de verduras (4)
very muy (P, 1)
video game el videojuego (3)
volleyball el vóleibol (3)

to **want** querer *(e → ie)* (3)
I / you — quiero, quieres (3)
to **watch** ver (1)
water el agua (4)
we nosotros, -as (2)
to **wear** llevar (6)
Wednesday miércoles (P)
on — el miércoles (3)
—s los miércoles (3)
week la semana (P)
weekend el fin *(pl.* los fines) de semana (3)
welcome: you're — de nada (3)
well bien (P); *(to indicate pause)* pues (1)
what? ¿cuál? (P); ¿qué? (2)
—'s your name? ¿cómo te llamas? (P)
when? ¿cuándo? (P)
where? ¿dónde? (3)
from —? ¿de dónde? (P)
(to) —? ¿adónde? (3)
which?, which one(s)? ¿cuál(es)? (4)
white blanco, -a (6)
who que (5)
who? whom? ¿quién(es)? (2, 5)
why? ¿por qué? (3)
winter el invierno (3)
with con (1, 3)
— me conmigo (3)
— you contigo (3)
woman la mujer (5)
wonderful! ¡genial! (3)
would *see* **like**

year el año (P)
I'm . . . —s old tengo . . . años (P)
to be . . . —s old tener . . . años (P, 5)
yellow amarillo, -a (6)

yes sí (P)
you *fam.* tú; *formal* usted (Ud.) (P, 2); *pl.* ustedes (Uds.); *pl. fam.* vosotros, -as (2); *fam. after prep.* ti (1)

young joven (5)
— lady la joven (6)
— man el joven (6)
— people los jóvenes (6)
younger menor (5)

your tu (P, 2); tus (3)
what's — name? ¿cómo te llamas? (P)
yuk! ¡qué asco! (4)

zero cero (P)

Índice

In almost all cases, structures are first presented in the *Vocabulario para conversar,* where they are practiced lexically in conversational contexts. They are explained later, usually in the *Gramática en contexto* section of that chapter. Light-face numbers refer to pages where structures are initially presented or, after explanation, where student reminders occur. **Bold-face numbers** refer to pages where structures are explained or otherwise highlighted.

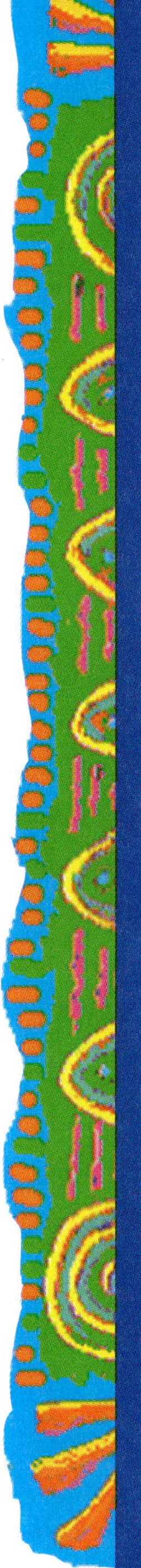

ACKNOWLEDGMENTS

Illustrations Rod Vass: pp. **VI, 7, 10, 13, 15–16, 18, 21, 23, 87–89, 91, 96, 103;** Min Jae Hong: pp. **VII, XII, 44–45, 248–249;** Pat Lenihan Barbee: pp. **VIII;** Elizabeth Wolf: pp. **X, 150–151, 153, 158–159, 161,162–163, 167, 169–170, 176–177, 180, 185;** Rob Porozinski: pp. **X, 165;** Lori Osiecki: pp. **XIII, 266–267;** Neverne Covington: pp. **11, 46, 125;** Peg Magovern: pp. **30–33, 35, 38–42, 50, 56–57, 63;** Arthur Friedman: p. **42;** Andy Myer: p. **54;** James Mellett: pp. **68–71, 73, 76–79, 97, 103;** Joe VanDerBos: pp. **84–85;** Rob Porazinski: p. **98;** Pat Lenihan-Barbee: p. **99;** Tom Bachtell: pp. **108–111, 113, 116–121, 128–129, 135, 137, 143;** Dan Clyne: p. **134;** Steven Mach: pp. **138–139, 206–207;** Jean Cassels: pp. **140–141, 154;** Joseph Scrofani: pp. **148–149, 156–157, 185;** Tuko Fujisake: p. **160;** Susan Blubaugh: p. **173;** Patti Green: p. **180;** Karen Pritchett: pp. **190–191, 193, 197, 200–202, 205, 206–207, 212, 214, 227;** Deborah Melmon: pp. **232–237, 239, 242–246, 253–256, 262–263, 271;** Fran Lee: p. **260;** Steve Musgrave: p. **263;** Betsy Everitt: pp. **264–265,** Mike Hagel: p. **269.**
Unless acknowledged otherwise, all photos are the property of ScottForesman & Company.

Photographs **Front Cover:** Sherlyn Bjorkgren/DDB Stock Photo; **Back Cover:** Joe Viesti; **II:** Joe Viesti; **IV:** (t)Courtesy Michelle Ryan; (b)Courtesy Rosi Marshall; **VI:** Chip and Rosa María de la Cueva Peterson; **VI–V:** Chip and Rosa María de la Cueva Peterson; **V:** Frerck/Odyssey/Chicago; **VIII:** Ulrike Welsch; **IX** (t)©Tony Arruza; (c)Frerck/ Odyssey/Chicago; (b)Ulrike Welsch; **XIII:** Peter Menzel/Stock Boston; **XVI–1:** Miriam Lefkowitz/Envision; **2:** ©Peter Menzel; **3:** Beryl Goldberg, Photographer; **5:** Sherlyn Bjorkgren/DDB Stock Photo; **6:** (tl)Bob Daemmrich/The Image Works; (tr)Chip and Rosa María de la Cueva Peterson; (c)Richard Hutchings/PhotoEdit; (b)Bob Daemmrich/Stock Boston; **8:** ©Ken Laffal; **19:** David Ryan/DDB Stock Photo; **25:** (t)David Phillips; (c)Chip and Rosa María de la Cueva Peterson; (b)Beryl Goldberg, Photographer; **26–27:** Beryl Goldberg, Photographer; **28:** Chip and Rosa María de la Cueva Peterson; **29:** (t)Chip and Rosa María de la Cueva Peterson; (b)Beryl Goldberg, Photographer; **36:** ©Diane Joy Schmidt; **37:** (t)Beryl Goldberg, Photographer; (b)Chip and Rosa María de la Cueva Peterson; **42:** The Kobal Collection; **44:** (t)Frerck/Odyssey/Chicago; (l)David R. Frazier PhotoLibrary; (c)Nancy d'Antonio; (b)David R. Frazier PhotoLibrary; **45:** Frerck/Odyssey/Chicago; **46:** Giraudon/Art Resource, New York; **51:** Illustration by John Borgman/©Creative Therapy Associates, Inc.; **53:** Chip and Rosa María de la Cueva Peterson; (inset)Bob Daemmrich/The Image Works; **55:** Owen Franken/Stock Boston; **61:** Frerck/Odyssey/Chicago; **64–65:** Bob Daemmrich Photography; **66:** ©Peter Menzel; **67:** (t)Ulrike Welsch; (b)Bob Daemmrich Photography; **73:** Cameramann International, Ltd.; **75:** Ulrike Welsch; **77:** ©Peter Menzel; **80:** David R. Frazier PhotoLibrary; **81:** Ulrike Welsch; **93:** Rob Crandall/The Image Works; (inset)Ulrike Welsch; **97:** Ulrike Welsch; **104–105:** Ulrike Welsch; **106:** Frerck/Odyssey/Chicago; **107:** (t)©Tony Arruza; (b)Ulrike Welsch; **111:** (l)Owen Franken; (r)Ulrike Welsch; **114:** Ulrike Welsch; **115:** (t)Tom Gibson/Envision; (b)D. Donne Bryant; **120:** Chip and Rosa María de la Cueva Peterson; **126:** Tim Gibson/Envision; **128:** Frerck/Odyssey/Chicago; **132:** Frerck/Odyssey/Chicago; **133:** Frerck/Odyssey/Chicago; **136:** Stuart Cohen/Comstock; **140:** Courtesy Pacific Trading Cards, Inc.; **142:** Ulrike Welsch; **144–145:** Comstock; **146:** John Neubauer/PhotoEdit; **147:** (t)John Neubauer/PhotoEdit; **150** Courtesy Royal Festival Hall, Hayward Gallery of the South Bank Centre. Private Collection; **155** (t)Chip and Rosa María de la Cueva Peterson; (b)Ulrike Welsch; **159** Scala/Art Resource, New York; **161** Thomas Hoepker/Magnum Photos; **171** Ulrike Welsch; **172** Steve Vidler/Leo de Wys, Inc.; **173** Tony Freeman/PhotoEdit; **174** ©Loren McIntyre; **175** (t)Tony Freeman/PhotoEdit; (b)CLEO/PhotoEdit; **177** ©Robert Fried; **186–187** ©Robert Fried; **188** Suzanne Murphy/Tony Stone Images; **189** (t)Joe Viesti; (b)Miriam Lefkowitz/Envision; **197:** Frerck/Odyssey/Chicago; **205:** Bob Daemmrich/Stock Boston; **208:** (t)Scala/Art Resource, New York; (b)Courtesy Carmen Lomas Garza/Photo by Wolfgang Dietz; **210:** Tony Freeman/PhotoEdit; **211:** Beryl Goldberg, Photographer; **215:** Bob Daemmrich/Stock Boston; **216:** Suzanne Murphy Larronde; **217:** (t)Tony Alfaro/DDB Stock Photo; (b)Ulrike Welsch; **218:** Courtesy *Furia Musical;* **219:** ©Rice Wagner; **221:** ©Jack Parsons; **228–229:** Suzanne Murphy Larronde; **230:** Frerck/Odyssey/Chicago; **231:** (t)Chip and Rosa María de la Cueva Peterson; (b)Joe Viesti; **237:** Frerck/Odyssey/Chicago; **240:** (t)Mark Antman/The Image Works; (b)Chip and Rosa María de la Cueva Peterson; **241:** David R. Frazier PhotoLibrary; **255:** Frerck/Odyssey/Chicago; **258:** Joe Cavanaugh/DDB Stock Photos; **259:** (t)Peter Menzel/Stock Boston; (bl)Bob Daemmrich Photography; (bc)Stacy Pick/Stock Boston; (br)Don Pitcher/Stock Boston; **268:** Courtesy Puerto Rican Tourism Company.